Popular Stories and Promised Lands

STUDIES IN RHETORIC AND COMMUNICATION
Series Editors:
E. Culpepper Clark
Raymie E. McKerrow
David Zarefsky

Roger C. Aden

Popular Stories
and Promised Lands
Fan Cultures and Symbolic Pilgrimages

The University of Alabama Press   Tuscaloosa and London

Copyright © 1999
The University of Alabama Press
Tuscaloosa, Alabama 35487-0380
All rights reserved
Manufactured in the United States of America

∞

The paper on which this book is printed meets the minimum requirements of
American National Standard for Information Science–Permanence of Paper for
Printed Library Materials, ANSI Z39.48-1984.

Library of Congress Cataloging-in-Publication Data

Aden, Roger C. (Roger Craig), 1962–
    Popular stories and promised lands : fan cultures and symbolic
pilgrimages / Roger C. Aden.
    p. cm. — (Studies in rhetoric and communication)
    Includes bibliographical references (p.) and index.
    ISBN 0-8173-0938-1 (paper meets minimum requirements)
    1. Popular culture—United States—History—20th century. 2. Mass
media—Social aspects—United States. 3. Narration (Rhetoric)—Social
aspects—United States. 4. Narration (Rhetoric)—Psychological
aspects—United States. 5. Fans (Persons)—United States—Psychology.
6. Imaginary places in mass media. 7. Escape (Psychology)—United
States. I. Title. II. Series.
    E169.12 .A224 1999
    306'.0973—ddc21
                                                98-19755

British Library Cataloguing-in-Publication Data available

Contents

Acknowledgments

The potpourri of ideas in this book have been inspired by a number of people whose work is not listed in the reference pages. These individuals helped me develop and refine my ideas in a process that has occurred throughout my life. Thanks initially to all those people who call themselves 'Huskers, most especially my immediate family, including my mother Harriett, my father Roger, my brother Chuck, and my grandmother Varla. Neither they nor I knew at the time, but my formative years—as a fan of Nebraska football, as a reader of the Three Investigators series, and as a devotee of James Bond and John Wayne films—did indeed help me form the central ideas in this book.

The expression of those ideas was assisted by my education at the University of Nebraska, where Professors Jack Kay and James Klumpp taught me how to write as a rhetorical critic and where my colleague Matthew Sobnosky inspired me to think more deeply and critically.

More recently a number of colleagues, fans, and students contributed to my work by talking to me, editing me, encouraging me, and motivating me. Thanks first to all the approximately 175 fans who shared their experiences, feelings, and insights (and to Roberta Davilla, who transcribed the interviews from the Field of Dreams site). I am especially grateful to those of you who read drafts of my chapters then offered perceptive observations that helped me refine my ideas. Thanks are also due to the faculty and graduate students of

Ohio University who read various drafts and/or led me to investigate ideas that were new to me. I want to thank all of you—fans and/or academics—who offered me inspired ideas along the way: Christina Beck, Alyssa Fernandez, Mary K. Hall, Anita James, Mark May, Donna Simmons, Tim Simpson, John Smith, Robert Westerfelhaus, and Andy Wood. I am also indebted to the anonymous reviewers of this book. Their kind words and gentle prodding were incredibly helpful. In addition I want to thank Christina Beck, Rita Rahoi, and Christina Reynolds. They contributed their ideas in early versions of chapters six and seven as coauthors. If you find concepts in those chapters puzzling, it's no doubt because of the changes I made in developing the coauthored articles into substantially different book chapters.

I also want to thank the fans whose interest in particular popular stories led me to become more of a fan. My friend Jon Johnston introduced me to *Dilbert,* my former student Arnie Niekamp introduced me to *The X-Files,* my dad introduced me to *Sports Illustrated,* and my friends Tim Borchers, Susanne Williams, and Melanie Mason introduced me to the Field of Dreams site.

The support to complete this book was provided by my school director, Sue DeWine, who encouraged my efforts to secure internal funding from Ohio University's College of Communication and the university's Office of Research and Sponsored Programs. Curtis Clark of The University of Alabama Press was also quite supportive of my efforts, especially when I decided to change about 75 percent of what I had written in the first draft.

Finally, I want to thank Christie. She has served as an inspiring role model, unwavering supporter, and avid reader. More important, she makes me better.

Popular Stories and Promised Lands

Introduction

I'm a Big Fan

Popular Stories, Habitus, and Places That Matter

At the risk of sounding like the big guy in the recliner who did pro-mos for CBS broadcasts of NFL football, let me begin by saying, "I'm a big fan!" I watch TV, see movies, read fiction, check out the comics, and subscribe to magazines. Sometimes I like what I see and read; other times I don't. When I find something I like—such as the one summer I checked out every Alfred Hitchcock movie owned by the local library—I join the millions of other people in this country who consider themselves fans of particular stories located in what we call popular culture. This book is about why we are fans and what we get out of being fans. I believe that what we get is a lot more than most people might think. To illustrate why, let me start by explaining why I'm a big fan of *Movieline* magazine.

One of the magazine's monthly features asks celebrities to name their favorite scene in their favorite movie video. Their answers run the gamut from *Casablanca*'s Humphrey Bogart telling Claude Rains he came to the city for the waters to Richard Widmark's shoving a wheelchair-bound woman down a flight of stairs in *Kiss of Death*. I, too, turn to older movies for many of my favorite scenes: Steve McQueen desperately searching for a way through the Swiss-German border fence on his motorcycle in *The Great Escape*, Paul Newman and Robert Redford frozen in the final frame of *Butch Cassidy and the Sundance Kid*, and Gary Cooper disgustedly throwing his tin star into the dirt at the end of *High Noon*. But the scene I recall most vividly is Jimmy Stewart staring into the river from the Bedford Falls bridge on Christmas Eve in *It's a Wonderful Life*. Stewart's conundrum is similar to one faced by many of us at some point in our lives: we feel out of place and peripheral to the events occurring around us, yet in many ways—financially, emotionally, spiritually, physically— we feel bound to that place at the same time. All his life Stewart's character, George Bailey, thought his place was somewhere outside of Bedford Falls, and his failure to leave town permeated his soul, creating a nagging sense of unease. Only when a guardian angel named Clarence visits does George Bailey recognize that his place has been in Bedford Falls all along.

Unfortunately, I doubt that many of us have a guardian angel named Clarence to help us search for ways to develop a sense of comfort with this paradox. I say "unfortunately" because today answers to the age-old question of "where is my place?" seem more difficult than ever to generate, for the United States is in the midst of a cultural transition that has disrupted our traditional senses of place—and that has a lot to do with being a fan of popular stories. But I'm getting ahead of myself. This cultural transition is mostly economic and technological, but its changes are sending rippling aftershocks throughout other parts of our lives, leaving us to wonder just where we are in the "grand scheme of things." Author Alvin Toffler predicted this transition, and its attendant unease, over twenty-five years ago in his bestseller, *Future Shock*. According to Toffler (1970), future shock consists of "the shattering stress and disorientation that we induce in individuals by subjecting them to too much change in too short a time" (p. 2). Quoting psychiatrist James S. Tyhurst, Toffler's explanation of the psychological effects of geographic mobility provides a fairly accurate mirror of our sense of unease: " 'Characteristic of this are increasing anxiety and depression . . . and some degree of hostility and suspicion. The sense of difference and helplessness becomes increasingly intense and the period is characterized by marked discomfort and turmoil' " (p. 78). So despite what appears to be economic growth over the past two decades, we feel worse about where we are—or to be more accurate, we're not really sure where we are— making the symptoms of future shock seem readily apparent. Notes Schulte (1996) in a summary of a Knight-Ridder poll, "To varying degrees, people in virtually every age group and at nearly every income level express a nagging uneasiness about the future. . . . Pollsters and economists call it 'free floating anxiety,' a pervasive angst among those who think that the rules have changed" (p. 4B).

"The rules" make reference to a particular set of assumptions about life in America, namely that if we work hard, we'll experience success and fulfillment. This sentiment reflects a normative narrative unique to the United States that we call "the American dream." This story, like many other stories, packs a rhetorical wallop not only because it reflects individual aspirations but also because it is imbricated in our cultural conditions (contemporary and historical). The dream is "American" because it envelopes the histories of immigration and assimilation, economic hardship and success, and constraint and opportunity particular to the United States. As economist Robert Samuelson (1995) points out, such is the power of this story that many of us have come to expect its happy ending in our own lives, just as early American citizens believed in the preordained greatness of the land and the nation's people. The sites of these anticipated happy endings are what I call "promised lands"; they are the places where dreams of progress come true.

Embedded in the previous paragraph are three concepts that drive this book. First, the "rules" refer to an unwritten set of norms, behaviors, expectations that a culture deems commonsensical. Bourdieu calls the cultural manifestation of these rules our "habitus" because they construct—in a cultural sense—the space in which we live. Second, we rely on stories fueled by imagination to make sense of, and to transcend, the seemingly invisible boundaries of the habitus. Lyotard labels stories that embody a culture's most valued ideas "grand narratives"; in most western cultures, the grand narratives reflect a desire for progress, a linear movement from the present to a promising future. Third, then, this yearning to move from one location to a better location suggests we have a need to find places that matter. The places that matter the most, those that represent what we define as the best of all possible worlds, are promised lands, the culminations of grand narratives. I discuss these concepts throughout the book, but as a means of orientation let me offer an introductory description of each. In so doing I hope to sketch their interconnectedness within the context of this book.

According to Bourdieu, *habitus* is our collective, cultural sense of place that is forged through the reproduction of history.[1] In other words, our sense of where we are, culturally speaking, depends largely on where we've been. Our daily practices of living not only reflect those historical beliefs and values; they also tend to reaffirm them at an unconscious level. Habitus, as Bourdieu (1972/1977) explains, then becomes "history turned into nature" (p. 78), and it reproduces history in the process. "In short, the habitus, the product of history, produces individual and collective practices, and hence history, in accordance with the schemes engendered by history" (Bourdieu, 1972/1977, p. 82). Thus what we do and say and how we do and say it become tools that perpetuate habitus. "Through commonplace daily practices, dress codes, use of language, comportment and patterns of consumption," Knox (1993, p. 26) writes, we ensure the continuation of historical habitus.

The perpetuation of habitus through history is fueled in part by the repetition of the *stories* that Lyotard calls grand narratives. These stories offer a stirring vision of the future, a sense of purpose to be accomplished by the collective culture. Typically these represent "an Idea" such as freedom, progress, or socialism. "Unlike myths," Lyotard (1988/1993) writes, grand narratives "look for legitimacy, not in an original founding act, but in a future to be accomplished, that is, an Idea to be realized" (p. 18). In western cultures, I believe, many grand narratives are supported by the Idea of "progress"; for example, freedom was used by civil rights advocates and socialism by European labor reformers to agitate for improvements in the status quo. Their rhetoric reflected an image of moving forward, of making things better in the future.

At the end of such movements are *places* I call *promised lands.* "Place," writes Lippard (1997), "for me is the locus of desire" (p. 4). Places that matter the most, for individuals and communities of people, are promised lands. By "promised lands," I mean the symbolic visions shared by a culture that provide a destination, unique to the culture, where the members of the culture expect to find ultimate fulfillment. Typically the promised land is envisioned as the geographic contextualization of the grand narrative's Idea, the place in which individuals would find themselves once the Idea is realized. In the United States our ostensible duty as citizens of the nation has been to strive to escape the present condition so that collectively we might reach the promised land represented by the current manifestation of the American dream. For example, as chapter one explains in more detail, the history of the United States has featured two dominant cultural visions of promised lands: the United States as a sacred garden and the secular paradise we believed technological progress would deliver.

The relationship between grand narratives and habitus is generally considered to be pessimistic and constraining, one in which the reliance on grand narratives perpetuates what a culture considers "common sense" or "the rules." Those people who do not adhere to grand narratives or who engage in cultural practices that fly in the face of "common sense" are typically depicted or imagined as odd or unusual. If I had written this book in longhand or used a typewriter, to offer a low-key example, I might be considered eccentric by my peers and/or students because I would have disdained the technological apparatus of progress. Consequently, when we envision promised lands at the end of grand narratives we ensure continuation of the habitus.

Adherence to the grand narratives that are told and retold means "the rules" remain relatively unchanged.

Thus habitus relies on the stories of grand narratives to perpetuate visions of places that matter. Naturalized through our everyday living—we see and read stories of progress in any number of places every day—habitus is endowed with the hue of neutral commonsense. The "rules" are not questioned; imagination is seemingly limited to what the grand narrative's boundaries contain as possibilities. Summarizes Bottomley (1992): "Habitus is the process whereby those who occupy similar positions in social and historical space tend to possess a certain sense of place, including categories of perception and appreciation that provide a commonsense understanding of the world, and especially of what is 'natural' or even imaginable" (p. 122). But Bottomley's definition of habitus—one that is similar to many other definitions of habitus—is a deterministic one; it allows little hope for change and little possibility for seeing through the rules of the habitus and the boundaries of grand narratives.

Although this interpretation of Bourdieu is plausible—he (1980/1990) does emphasize that habitus is limiting, "mak[ing] possible the free production of all the thoughts, perceptions and actions inherent in the particular conditions of production—*and only those*" (p. 55; emphasis added)—he also points to the possibility of a more optimistic interpretation just a few pages later. He notes that "only in *imaginary experience* (in the folk tale, for example), which neutralizes the sense of social realities, does the social world take the form of a universe of possibles equally possible for any possible subject" (p. 64; emphasis added). Thus Bourdieu admits that imaginative stories allow opportunities to transcend habitus, making possible the envisioning of—and symbolic escape to—alternative social worlds. Unlike Bottomley's interpretation of a habitus that limits what is "even imaginable," this image of habitus suggests stories *other than grand narratives* may be used as alternatives to such narratives. Through these stories our imaginations can envision new places that matter.

Such a belief lies at the heart of writers on imagination and storytelling. They propose that our imaginations can be used to shed the material world of the habitus, to tell stories that run counter to the constraints of grand narratives, and to envision places that can serve as alternative promised lands accessible to those who have had their access limited to habitus-inspired versions of places that matter. "On a practical level," writes Goodall (1996), "what we imagine ourselves to be—alone or in the company of others—defines the boundaries of what we believe is possible" (p. 22).

Perhaps the best way to talk about imagination in relation to the stories we tell is to clarify how I'm defining it. To begin I borrow from Bachen and Illouz (1996): "We define imagination not as make-believe play in the behavioral sense—as it is usually the case in social psychology—but as the set of symbols and meanings we use when trying to communicate to ourselves or others a *possible,* yet non-existent, situation" (p. 280; emphasis in original). Although I find much to admire in this concise definition, and will rely on it to inform much of my writing, I do want to quibble with one element: in attempting to distinguish their conceptualization of imagination from social psychology, Bachen and Illouz take much of the "play" out of imagination. That is, although imagination *is* about "the set of symbols and meanings we use," it is *also* about make-believe as an alternative set of symbols and meanings. We enter the imaginary worlds of popular stories, I believe, to engage in *purposeful play.* Kendall Walton's (1990) work, *Mimesis as Make-Believe,* inspires much of my thinking on this issue.[2]

Walton argues that what he calls "representational works of art," such as fictional novels, function as props in adult games of make-believe, much "as dolls and teddy bears serve as props in children's games" (p. 11). Playing make-believe with these props is thus a form of escapism. But escapism, I want to emphasize, is not necessarily a disavowal of interest in one's material situation. Instead, escapism through imagination is purposeful; it allows us to move from an unsatisfactory material place to a fulfilling place of the imagination, a promised land of our own creation. As Walton explains, even children's games are purposeful play: "It is generally recognized, I believe, that such games—and imaginative activities generally—do indeed, as their prevalence suggests, have a profound role in our efforts to cope with our environment. . . . Most imaginings are in one way or another dependent on or aimed at or anchored in the real world" (pp. 12, 21). Escapism then can be envisioned as purposeful play in which we symbolically move from the material world to an imaginative world that is in many ways *a response to* the material. Although I will tackle the issue of "purpose" in more detail throughout the book, I do want to emphasize at this point that our "selves" *do* move from the material to the imaginative.

Snow and Anderson (1987), for example, found homeless persons to engage in three forms of "identity talk": distancing between themselves and others, embracement of their roles, and *storytelling as a means of symbolically escaping their material circumstances.* Telling stories, and reading or viewing stories, is important work as we make sense of our selves. English professor and storyteller N. Scott Momaday (1997), for example, argues that storytelling "is a very old and sacred business, and it is very good. At that moment when we are drawn into the element of language, we are as intensely alive as we can be; we create and we are created" (p. 169). Similarly, Walton reminds us that when we become involved with stories, we find ourselves both observing and participating in the imaginary—yet real—world created through language. "We don't just observe fictional worlds from without," he writes. "We live in them. . . . True, these worlds are merely fictional, and we are well aware they are. But *from inside* they seem actual . . . [which] gives us a sense of intimacy with characters and their other contents" (p. 273).

Walton's observations are directed mainly at "respected" stories, but Nelson (1989) points out that couch potatoes engage in similar symbolic journeys. She talked with a number of people who watched television and asked them to describe their experiences as viewers. Their responses, summarized in Nelson's first-person voice, provide empirical support for the theoretical musings of Walton, Momaday, and others: "While lying on the couch, I do not really live in what my body touches—the couch that I lie on, the body that I live, and the people around me are not at all the 'nearest' phenomena. I have temporarily forgotten them. . . . My physiological body is forgotten and left unattended while I watch television, which becomes my immediate environment. Only after the event is over do I 'return' and consciously attend to my body and its situation" (p. 396). Our "escapes" through popular stories, then, are in many respects nearly literal, not merely symbolic. They are movements to places that matter.

Not surprisingly, my take on using popular stories for escapism runs counter to that of scholars and commentators who describe these stories as *mere* escapist "trash" that numbs our minds and diverts our attention from making substantive changes in our social, economic, and political structures. To dismiss these "diversions" into popular culture as shallow escapism is to overlook the rich messages about our anxieties and needs that such escapism fulfills. As popular culture scholar John Fiske (1987) explains, "Such an easy dismissal ignores the fact that escapism or fantasy necessarily involves both an escape from or evasion of something and an escape to a preferred alternative: dismissing escapism as 'mere fantasy' avoids the vital questions of *what* is escaped from, *why* escape is necessary, and *what* is escaped to" (p. 217). As symbolic visions of fulfillment, promised lands envisioned through popular stories are at once responses to the habitus, alternatives to grand narratives, and sites of opposition to both the habitus and grand narrative. They are a means of *coping* with the mundane material living conditions found in a culture as well as images that represent a *hoping* for an idealized future.[3]

Using popular stories for escapism, I believe, represents the beginnings of evolutionary changes in our habitus. Rather than adhering to grand narratives that, as chapter one points out, have lost much of their luster, we turn to popular stories to seek alternative visions of places that matter. To be sure, popular stories may harbor the lingering residue of grand narratives, but they offer their fans much more than that; they offer us an opportunity to use our imaginations to see new promised lands nearly every day. The narratives may not be "grand" in the sense of far-reaching, but they are "grand" in the sense that they encourage us to envision alternative places that matter, places that give us purpose and direction. These promised lands are accessible to us through the stories that circulate (and recirculate) in popular culture forms such as television, film, printed fiction, comics, and magazines. We use these forms of communication to escape temporarily into imaginary, or symbolic, places where in our minds everything makes sense and we feel somehow centered.

The "we" to whom I refer are those of us who repeatedly engage in the "out of body" experiences described by Nelson's television viewers. Just as the repetition of grand narratives helps perpetuate the historicity of the habitus, the repetition of popular stories offers us a means of perpetuating our alternative visions. This book then is about those of us who are fans of particular popular stories. In the realm of fandom we can openly acknowledge our commitment to reading a series of popular stories, or revisit the same popular story, again and again (much like the man pictured on the front page of an area newspaper who was the first in line to see the reopening of *Star Wars*, despite having seen the movie eighty times previously by his count [Hoover, 1997]). My discussions of fans rely on definitions of "devoted" and "avid" television fans provided by Reeves, Rodgers, and Epstein (1996):

Devoted viewers will make arrangements to watch every episode of their favorite show. For the devoted viewer, a favorite show is a "special event" that disrupts the flow of television and inspires more intense levels of identification and attention than typical television fare. . . . Avid fans will not only take special pains to watch every episode of the show but, today, will tape the episodes so that they can review them or even archive them. The show is not only a special event but also a major source of self-definition, *a kind of quasi-religious experience.* (p. 26; emphasis added)

As my highlighting of the last phrase in this excerpt suggests, I believe the kind of escape popular stories promote is a ritualistic journey of the mind to spiritually powerful places where a vantage point that is anything but mundane affords us a reassuring view of an imagined promised land. This book illustrates how repeated reading of four kinds of popular stories—comic strips, weekly magazines, episodic television programs, and movies—can prompt escapist journeys to our own promised lands.

This romantic description of personal promised lands should not be read as a dialectic counterpart to the habitus-filled promised lands of grand narratives. After all, we live *in* a habitus. If we temporarily travel away from it through the imaginative play of reading stories, we must return to it at the story's conclusion. Moreover, our memories and experiences are colored by our habitus, meaning that our "transcendence" is never really a complete escape; habitus travels with us to some degree. As subsequent chapters make clear, I envision fans' adventures with popular stories as *simultaneously* constraining and enabling experiences. They are constraining in the sense that because popular stories are infused with elements of grand narratives, they tend to reproduce the habitus. To be popular, stories must be familiar, and familiarity means acknowledging the workings of traditional "rules." But popular stories are enabling in the sense that they also encourage us to use our imaginations to transcend the habitus. To be popular, stories must be different, and a break from the "rules" offers an opportunity to see how the rules limit us.

My approach thus differs from many scholars of popular culture who envision the intersection of constraining and enabling as an either/or dilemma. For example, Taylor (1993a) projects a relationship between imagination and habitus in popular film, but he emphasizes the workings of the habitus as he outlines the possible results of visiting a symbolic community: "In constructing an imaginary site where events are introduced, complicated, and resolved, film refers not to a 'real' world but to ideological visions of physical and social space. These visions organize film narratives so that certain structures of political, economic, and sexual relationships are promoted as 'natural' and 'inevitable,' are challenged, *or* are simply reproduced" (p. 376; emphasis added). My approach emphasizes the enabling aspects of being a fan, for my primary interest is in understanding how we enact a personal sense of power while negotiating the rules of the habitus, but I do focus briefly on how fans are constrained by their interactions with popular stories. The rationale for my emphasis on "purposeful play to escape from the habitus" should become more clear as you make your way through chapters two and three. For now, a preview of coming attractions.

Symbolic Pilgrimage

I have chosen the label *symbolic pilgrimage* to describe the type of purposeful play I envision. Rather than embarking upon a "real life" journey to a holy shrine, symbolic pilgrimages feature individuals ritualistically revisiting powerful places that are symbolically envisioned through the interaction of story and individual imagination. That we make such moves individually does not mean that imagining through stories is not a social experience, however, for we are imagining within the context of habitus and recognize that others share some of our experiences and perceptions. "Analysis, interpretation, and speculation, *building a community through shared texts* and playfully appropriating them for their own ends—these are the defining features of fandom," notes Clerc (1996, p. 51; emphasis added).

Being a fan is being a member of a purposeful play community in which individual interpretations remain unique yet overlap with others' interpretations. Knopp's (1997) reflections on living in a material place can be read as reflective of this symbolic experience of imagining individually and socially at once: "Inhabitants know that the outer boundaries of their home region are determined by the point at which their stories run out. This means that each dweller in the land possesses an individual and changing set of boundaries. Thus an accurate representation of a region requires a set of maps, one from each dweller in the land, one map superimposed upon another and another" (p. 26). Knopp's mapping project is impractical yet laudable; imaginings need to be understood both as individual and social manifestations of symbolic places. Accordingly, I intersperse my interpretations and understandings (or imaginings) of the stories discussed in this book with the imaginings of other fans of the stories. In addition, I asked a number of those fans to re-read my interweaving of our stories. Their initial stories, and their reactions to my interpretations, helped me understand and explain how we engage in what I call symbolic pilgrimages, those purposeful, playful, repeated journeys in which we imagine ourselves leaving the material world of habitus to enter the symbolic worlds of promised lands.

These journeys, I argue, become purposeful when they are responses to those unavoidable (and unresolvable) tensions we encounter in our everyday lives, those moments when our habitus jumps up and bites us. For Radway's (1984) romance readers, for example, the pressure of conforming to the expectations of being the model housewife made journeying to the symbolic places of the novels a rejuvenating experience, an almost spiritual process of purification that temporarily washed away the stress of needing to be all things to all people while simultaneously providing the symbolic resources with which to cope with the habitus upon one's return from the pilgrimage: "Romance reading and writing might be seen therefore as a collectively elaborated female ritual through which women explore the consequences of their common social condition as the append-ages of men and attempt to imagine a more perfect state where all the needs they so intensely feel and accept as given would be adequately addressed" (p. 212). Reading the romances, as Radway also notes, surely did not directly change the material conditions in which the women found themselves. But, I would argue, their escapes just as surely generated a sense of identity, power, and community that could be used to steel the women against those conditions they saw as irreversible. In this way the women *indirectly* altered their habitus, making the material environment less onerous in the process.

In this respect symbolic pilgrimages, as I detail in chapter three, do not differ greatly in function and process from literal pilgrimages. The primary distinction is that symbolic pilgrimages occur in the metaphorical terrain of culture rather than in its material manifestation. Thus a symbolic pilgrimage, like a literal pilgrimage, "serves not so much to maintain society's status quo [or habitus] as to recollect, and even to presage, an alternative mode of social being" (Turner & Turner, 1978, p. 39).

Conclusion/Preview

I will return to the concept of enjoying popular stories as symbolic pilgrimages to promised lands in more detail in the third chapter. The first two chapters of the book, meanwhile, are intended to strengthen the foundation for understanding this concept. Chapter one outlines a brief cultural history of dominant visions of promised lands in the United States, ultimately pointing out that we have become quite aware that those visions form our habitus and that they are insufficient for guiding our everyday lives. The last part of chapter one outlines some initial responses, both popular and scholarly, to this increased awareness of habitus then suggests how we may benefit from synthesizing those responses. Chapter two "returns" to the idea of places that matter, looking at how geographers, symbolic interactionists, cultural studies scholars, and feminist theorists have addressed the issue. The chapter concludes with a suggestion for intertwining the "best" of the thinking on places that matter to produce an image of our encounters with popular stories and promised lands as dynamic, purposeful escape and quest experiences. Chapter three develops the assumptions presented in this introduction, borrows from the ideas presented in chapter two, and explains how we respond to the problems of habitus presented in chapter one. Specifically, chapter three articulates the concept of symbolic pilgrimage.

Chapters four through seven offer illustrations of symbolic pilgrimages in four different kinds of popular media. Chapter four tackles the comic strip *Dilbert*. Chapter five examines the creepy Fox television series *The X-Files*. Chapter six explores the weekly magazine *Sports Illustrated*. Chapter seven analyzes the appeal of the film *Field of Dreams*. Each of these chapters was written through a similar process. First, I identified a popular story that I personally revisited as a devoted or avid fan. Second, relying on textual analysis and introspection, I developed an image of the place to which the stories seemed to invite readers (or myself, at the very least). Third, I looked to see what other fans of the story had to say about their escapist experiences, attempting to knit their ideas into my narrative without losing a sense of their voices. The ideas that emerge from these four analyses are brought to bear on the concepts presented in the first three chapters in a conclusion that I hope prompts additional conversation about the role popular stories play in our desire to find promised lands.

As I work through these chapters, I attempt to interweave a number of different theoretical concepts. To readers familiar with the concepts I apologize in advance for the short shrift I give some of them. Although I believe my depictions of ideas are faithful to their proponents' understandings, my primary goal in this book is to examine interactions among ideas and to explore a new possibility—the symbolic pilgrimage—for envisioning their relationships. As a result some complex concepts are presented in fairly basic terms. I encourage readers interested in learning more about such concepts to explore the References section for starting points.

As a means of orienting you to what follows, here's a brief overview of the key concepts introduced in the following chapters. We'll look at how fans of popular stories use their imagination to: (1) engage in resistance to—and critique of—the habitus, (2) travel through cultural space to find places that matter, (3) develop senses of individual and community identity, (4) negotiate the decreased relevance of historical promised lands located in grand narratives, (5) work with the cultural logics of modernism, romanticism, and postmodernism, and (6) understand different ways of knowing and believing. But, most important, we'll examine how rhetoric provides the symbolic resources to pull these disparate functions together.

Notes

1. Readers familiar with cultural criticism may ask at this point, "Why use 'habitus' as a central term when it is but one of the many images scholars have employed to describe the constraining features of cultures?" Two rea-

sons. First, I find it less deterministic than other, institutionally based images (such as Foucault's [1977/1995] panopticon, Weber's [1958] iron cage, or Marx's [1867/1906] superstructure). Habitus is less rigid and accounts for the possibility of evolutionary change. Second, because this book emphasizes issues of "place," I am attracted to the place connotation of the term "habitus." Bourdieu's image suggests that we literally live *in* a habitus, a notion that works well with my development of symbolic pilgrimage as a movement away from the place in which we materially reside. This connotation makes me more comfortable using "habitus" than other images that also account for evolutionary change in a less deterministic manner (such as Baudrillard's [1973/1988] codes or Gramsci's [1971] hegemony). That said, I do turn to alternative images of cultural constraint throughout the book as a means of clarifying particular issues that develop (for example, the panopticon assumes a central role in my discussion of *The X-Files* in chapter five, the iron cage is mentioned in chapter four, and Baudrillard's codes undergird my discussions of consumerism in chapters one and seven).

2. I owe Mark May a huge "thanks" for recommending the Walton book to me.

3. My approach does share with uses and gratifications theory an assumption that audiences of popular stories don't just passively absorb the stories but instead use them to serve particular functions and/or fulfill specific needs (see Rubin, 1993, for a brief overview of the theory). I depart from this research tradition, however, by emphasizing the interrelationship of the texts/stories and audience members.

Part 1

Theoretical Development

1

The Search for Promised Lands

Dominant Visions of Sacred Places
in U.S. Culture

Americans are antsy people. We like to be going somewhere, doing something. For us action equals purpose. We're also a paradoxical people. We often can't wait to get home, to settle in and relax after we've been out "doing something." Comfort is the reward for purposeful action. We like to be at home as much as we like to get away from home. Explains Relph (1976), "Our experience of place, and especially of home, is a dialectical one—balancing a need to stay with a desire to escape" (p. 42).

I like to travel, to get out and do something, as much as the next person—but I can't wait to get back home either. Part of my "antsiness" may well stem from growing up in a Nebraska panhandle town of 14,000 people called Scottsbluff that was the biggest town to be found within 100 miles in any direction. Part of it may stem from a jigsaw puzzle of the United States my mother handed down to me when I was a child—so many places, so little time. When my family did hit the highway—to visit relatives across the state in Hastings or Omaha, to go sightseeing in the Black Hills of South Dakota or the Rocky Mountains of Colorado—my brother Chuck and I would imaginarily traverse that jigsaw puzzle map by playing the license plate game. On longer trips we would sometimes "collect" over half of the 50 states; I still remember our excitement when we eyed our first plate from Canada. I recall that I was amazed at the sheer amount of movement around me. I still am. Where are all these people going? What are they doing? When are we going to get home?

A very general answer to these questions, one that forms the foundation of this book, is found in a recurring sight on the road: the Mayflower moving van. I don't know much about the company—I even used a different mover when I came to my present home in Athens, Ohio—but Mayflower has always been a favorite company of mine, rhetorically speaking. Tapping the collective memory of the European founding of the nation, the Mayflowers of today reflect the cultural impulse toward moving to a new, better place. "The vast, and for the first time, democratic migration in space," Carey (1975) writes of these early forays from Europe to America, "was above all an attempt to trade an old world for a new, and represented the belief that movement in space could in itself be a redemptive act. It is a belief Americans have never quite escaped" (p. 4). The original Mayflower journeyed to the New World that was defined as a promised land, "a sacred garden; it was a garden because America was the land that God created and challenged with a special purpose; America was sacred because the New World was the meeting place of God and human beings" (Ostwalt, 1990, p. 26). The original Mayflower is represented as a progressive journey of the Spirit. The contemporary Mayflowers, on the other hand, represent the spiritual fulfillment that comes from Progress. They reflect the "triumph of technology," the ability to use machines to make our lives better, to move forward, to progress, for "it is technology that has come to provide the meaning of the term 'Progress'" (Hopper, 1991, p. 33).

Both trips, then, are at once secular and spiritual, for we believe spiritual fulfillment comes from progress and vice versa. Both trips also reflect a search for promised lands, places that offer sacred images of the result of our progress, as well as a concomitant rhetorical quest to define these lands as new homes. Images of past promised lands linger in our cultural history as part of our habitus; as destinations, they are the culmination of grand narratives that have helped define us and limit us, that suggest to us how—and where—we should move in cultural space. In the United States, then, two grand narratives of progress/spirit seem to have dominated: (1) a founding story that featured the "settling" of the nation as the establishment of a sacred garden paradise where God's work was done and (2) a story of maturation that featured the "development" of the nation as the establishment of a secular utopia where the work of machines provided plentiful goods. The first narrative called upon self-sacrifice for community development, whereas the second narrative called upon machines to provide for self-development.

Today most cultural observers suggest the maturation story's promised land of a secular utopia is no longer relevant, that instead we have developed the self to such an extent that we now lack community or even a sense of where the self is located. The reasons for this rupture are explored later in this chapter, but for now I want to point out that the breech provides us with an opportunity to learn from our pasts. Without a clear grand narrative driving us forward, we can now recognize, first, how these past promised lands *function* as part of our habitus, how their boundaries have excluded and included certain people, places, and ideas. As Edgerton (1996) reminds us, every place has borders: "The concept of the other is a crucial one for understanding the construction of a sense of place. Creation of a notion of what constitutes them and us, the meaning derived from difference, of who, therefore, is other and the subsequent exclusion of the other (even within one's self) are often critical elements of a sense of place" (p. 134). For many of us and our ancestors, then, the two visions of promised lands that have dominated U.S. culture were neither accessible nor desirable.

The second opportunity we have is to reflect upon possibilities for grand narratives that do not necessarily involve a linear, forward movement but instead may espouse moving back, or cycling through, time and the cultural terrain. Our promised lands may not necessarily lie at the end of a progressive journey. For example, Lears (1998) argues in support of learning through nostalgia: "Why grant legitimacy to one form of sentimentality [progress] and not the other?" (p. 59). In other words, as we explore the history of the dominant promised lands of U.S. culture, we should do so with an understanding of how these images have perpetuated a habitus that constrains us. Although many historians and cultural observers lament the apparent loss of a single, shared vision of U.S. culture (e.g., Schlesinger, 1992), in reality we are simply becoming increasingly cognizant of the fact that such dominant visions were just that: dominant, not universal.

Thus as you read the descriptions of dominant promised lands in this chapter, I encourage you to remember two points: (1) as part of the habitus, these promised lands are rhetorical visions of naturalized history and thus, for many people, still powerful visions today (they are home); (2) as part of the habitus, these promised lands are rhetorical reminders of the limitations that have historically been placed upon them by the "commonsense" structures reproduced over time (they are a reason to leave home). In both cases, and individuals may simultaneously experience both sentiments, an awareness of habitus points to imperfections in our cultural conditions and, in turn, calls forth rhetorical responses (see Payne, 1989).

My use of inclusive personal pronouns suggests "we" are all generally affected by the legacy of these promised lands, and we all rely on rhetoric to come to terms with that legacy but in different ways. For some of us the images of dominant promised lands are still appealing, giving rise to a nostalgic desire to move backward. For some of us the wish to hold on to our traditions—whether they have contributed to the maintenance of a habitus or to its evolution—leads us to engage in cyclical movements that seek a sense of harmony in light of cultural changes. For some of us the opportunity to envision promised lands that oppose those dominant places provides an incentive to think of progress in a number of different, not necessarily linear, directions. Some of us may engage in all of these movements. No matter who we are, however, we are using rhetoric to reconcile the passage of time (history) and the changing of space (the cultural terrain) with our own desire to find places that matter. I encourage you, as a reader, to interpret my ideas in a manner that suits your particular experiences.

To learn where and how we might travel in time/space, we need to know how time and space have changed. Thus we begin our theoretical journey with a review of dominant promised lands in U.S. history/culture.

America as a Sacred Promised Land

A predominant belief in the first one hundred or so years of American culture was that of the nation as an earth-bound Eden; the land was seen as "a potential utopia" (Segal, 1994, p. 4). To European settlers the land was an unspoiled garden, ripe with the potential to provide material and spiritual comfort for all who entered its gates; "the garden of America was sacred space in two different ways. It represented a sacred and paradisiacal natural world; however, it also symbolized a sacred social world where people could aspire to live without sin and in total harmony with one another" (Ostwalt, 1990, p. 25). Not surprisingly, these two different but interrelated images of the American garden bloomed from two different but interrelated forms of rhetoric: the fire-and-brimstone sermons of early Puritan preachers and the political persuasion of early patriots. As Ritter and Andrews (1978) note, "The experience of the early Puritans served as proof that Americans were under God's special protection . . . [whereas] not surprisingly, [political] speakers applied the notion that God guided American destiny to the immediate Revolutionary situation" (pp. 17, 18).

In particular, claim Ritter and Andrews (1978), this melding of Puritanism and patriotism produced for the settlers three recurring rhetorical themes that "set the new land apart. . . . They came to believe that America had been chosen by God as the land promised to

His people, that it was destined to become a great republican empire, and that it was endowed with the unique and sacred trust of providing the home for liberty" (p. 28). The successful revolution reinforced the rhetorical power of these images, leading early citizens to define their triumph "not as an accident of European power politics, but as a sign of God's favor" (Ritter & Andrews, 1978, p. 28). The reification of this belief led to the ensconcement of a rhetorical style favored by American politicians in and beyond the Revolution that was characterized by "a religification of the founding of the government and a glorification of its original basis" (Bormann, 1985, p. 239). Although Bormann cites Lincoln as the apogee of what he calls the romantic pragmatist style, Smith (1950) argues convincingly that the image of America as Eden persisted throughout the settling of the westernmost regions of the nation following the Civil War. In fact, Ritter and Andrews (1978) argue the founders' rhetoric "has had a significant influence on our rhetoric ever since" (p. 28). .

Perhaps one of the reasons for the endurance of this rhetorical promised land is its similarity with the creation story of the Judeo-Christian tradition. Just as Adam and Eve were new people in a new world with a fresh opportunity, "America is a fresh place, a new beginning, an opportunity. . . . Americans are a *new* people, formed out of a migration of people seeking freedom in a *new world*" (Robertson, 1980, pp. 29, 26; emphasis in original). The land itself contributed to this image, for the terrain represented to the Europeans "a virgin continent. . . . Access to undefiled, bountiful, sublime Nature is what accounts for the virtue and special fortune of Americans. It enables them to design a community in the image of a garden" (Marx, 1964, pp. 3, 228). Both the Puritans' preachings and the patriots' persuasion strengthened the creation metaphor, for both emphasized in their own ways the special purpose Providence had unfolded in front of them: to carve a sacred community out of the wild natural paradise. This image of a promised land, then, also fueled western expansion well after the Civil War (and, to some extent, still does so today as the western states experience an influx of new residents). As Robertson (1980) summarizes, "The American sense of uniqueness has come also from the belief that the mission of its people was to create a nation where a nation did not exist. . . . So Americans were crusaders, bringing civilization and freedom to the wilderness" (p. 26).

This image of America, with its emphasis on the sacred nature of the nation and its citizens as spiritually motivated crusaders, meshes with the philosophical school of thought called romanticism (as Bormann, 1985, points out). According to Gergen (1991), romanticism "is a perspective that lays central stress on unseen, even sacred forces that dwell deep within the person, forces that give life and relationships their significance" (p. 19). Those sacred forces residing in the individual, Gergen says, are not exclusively religious but include characteristics such as "passion, soul, creativity, and moral fiber" (p. 6). In other words, the romantic self is spiritually aware and committed to doing good works for the community. Romanticism encourages community progress through the self-sacrifice of spiritually committed believers. In late-1970s popular culture the characters of Jake and Elwood Blues—the Blues Brothers created by Dan Akroyd and John Belushi—were ironic manifestations of the romantic self. Claiming that they were "on a mission from God" to save an orphanage, the Blues Brothers used their passion for blues music as an expression of their souls. Although their moral fiber was at best questionable (lying, stealing, and numerous moving violations constituted but a few of their transgressions), their spirit was ostensibly pure.

Technology as a Secular Promised Land

As the Blues Brothers' eponymous movie suggested, however, romanticism became something of an anachronism in an American culture that seemed to be less spiritually inclined and more rooted in the sub/urban experience fostered by the growth of industry. The romantic image of the garden is still a powerful one, to be sure, but as the nation matured its dominance gave way to an image of a promised land in which the machine dismantled much of the garden symbol's power (Marx, 1964). Taking romanticism's place as a dominant philosophical vision was modernism, a school of thought that finds its roots in the parallel developments of the Enlightenment and the Industrial Revolution. The modernist self, explains Gergen (1991), is a product of Enlightenment philosophy in that individuals were depicted as possessing the capacity for transcendent reason or objectivity. "The modernist depended on reason and observation; moral values and sentiments had no rational justification, they were relativistic and 'unreasonable emotions'" (Gergen, 1991, p. 208). When paired with the Industrial Revolution's emphasis on technology and efficient production, Enlightenment thinking produced a culture in which rationality was key. Modernism can perhaps best be summarized by the managerial style of the fast-food industry, a style Ritzer (1996) has labeled "McDonaldization." This rational approach, Ritzer claims, has permeated our society well beyond the golden arches and its cousins. Its characteristics—efficiency, calculability, predictability, and control (Ritzer, 1996, pp. 9–11)—are found throughout contemporary society as well.

The appeal of modernism, at its inception and to some extent still today, was helped by the romantics' Puritan-influenced expectation of impeccable moral conduct. As Bormann (1985) outlines, "The rhetoricians of the tradition of romantic pragmatism . . . had dramatized the righteous life style and the commendable behaviors of the community in such clear terms and set such goals of perfection that it made their achievement, despite the zealous efforts of many, impossible to attain. . . . Charged with guilt, they were susceptible to other visions" (p. 237). Modernism finally provided just such an alternative vision in the late 1800s.[1] Modernist thought imagines individuals as rational beings who can step outside of themselves, assess the situation, and develop an appropriate response; in short, they can control their actions rather than be ruled by passion and spirit. This ability to control oneself, coupled with the development of technology that expanded the abilities of the self, led to a secularization of the notion of America as promised land—and made the attainment of this promised land seem more likely. As Segal (1994) notes of this period, "Human beings, not God, would be primarily responsible for transforming America from a potential to an actual utopia" (p. 6).

The promised land invoked by modernism, then, was a secular technological utopia, the inevitable result of progress through machines. Corn (1986b), in fact, labels "the vision of the future as a technological paradise . . . a central theme in American culture" (p. 8). Stoked by the modernist law of the excluded middle that defined ideas as one thing *or* another, the promised land of technological paradise virtually eradicated the notion of spirituality as manifested in romanticism. First, the moral code of self-denial preached by the Puritans, and rhetorically reflected in other forms, was incompatible with an industrial society's need to consume the products it manufactured (Lears, 1983). As Daniel Bell (1973) explains, "Mass production and mass consumption . . . destroyed the Protestant ethic by zealously promoting a hedonistic way of life" (p. 477). Second, the rational individual was defined as an autonomous unit rather than as part of a spiritual community, divorcing the self from the garden community. Self-fulfillment emerged through the earning of "status badges of material possessions and by the promotion of pleasure" (Bell, 1973, p. 477). Consumption allowed individuals to "deny the social basis of their identity" while they were being beguiled by "consumerism's promise that one can become anything one wishes" (Coontz, 1992, p. 177). As Goodall (1996) summarizes, "The Enlightenment project also largely erased Spirit from any dialogue between Self and Other, and in so doing obscured the mythic and ritualistic foundations of sustainable communities" (p. 1). Third, technological paradise was accorded the status of the sacred, co-opting romantic visions of the garden. Whereas religion was re-defined as "an evil to be overcome if new possibilities of life were to be secured for this world" (Hopper, 1991, p. 53), "technology became the new secular God" (Rifkin, 1995, p. 44) and experts in its use "invested with the charisma of priestliness" (Postman, 1992, p. 90). In other words the spirit was yanked from its roots in the garden and awkwardly transplanted into the technological machine. Accordingly, fourth, the image of the garden was replaced by the image of the machine. Explains Mills (1982), the Industrial Revolution spawned a new attitude toward nature, that of a controlling machine. Meanwhile, Enlightenment thinkers Isaac Newton and René Descartes had preached respectively that "our universe is a machine" and that "our bodies and minds are machines as well" (Fox, 1994, p. 4).

Blending the ideals of the Enlightenment and the Industrial Revolution, modernist believers in the technological utopia envisioned themselves as rational machines working to reach an earthly paradise that could be pragmatically and efficiently attained (Segal, 1985). The development of the microchip and the increasing computerization of American society make this image of the promised land still seem compelling today. Contemporary observers note this emphasis on technology's invisible power in a number of different arenas. Cellular phones allow us to be in contact with others no matter where we are. "Modern machines," notes Haraway (1991), "are everywhere and they are invisible. Modern machinery is an irreverent upstart god, mocking the Father's ubiquity and spirituality" (p. 153). Domestic appliances, Sack (1992) observes, "are advertised as a means of making the home less a place of repose than a place of factorylike efficiency" (p. 151). Even farmers, who work the land for a living, Peterson (1991) points out, speak of the earth as a metaphoric machine. Not surprisingly, then, we sometimes think of ourselves as machines that can make our lives better. Bellah, Madsen, Sullivan, Swidler, and Tipton (1985), for example, detail the pervasive presence of what they call the "therapeutic ethos," an emphasis on individual autonomy and self-improvement. At the intersection of these machinistic movements is the promised land of progress. As Judis (1994) claims, "In the twentieth century, the promise of America—once religious salvation—became an ever rising standard of living" (p. 26).

To summarize, whereas the promised land of the garden reflects the romantic ideal of belonging to an enveloping community (a sense of place is provided by being ensconced within its borders), the promised land of technological utopia reflects the modernist ideal of a centered self (a sense of place is provided by one's ability to master her/his surroundings). Romantics sought to forge community out of the wilderness. As that land, and the nation, was developed through industry and technology, the power of the community was subordinated by the power of the individual consumer.

Certainly the emphasis on individual consumerism is alive and well today (as the following section illustrates). Yet the lurking paradox of this promised land of technological utopia—"the technological future has resonated in American culture precisely because the actual technological changes of the last century have been accompanied by so much privation, conflict, and dislocation" (Corn, 1986a, p. 228)—has been gradually oozing to the cultural surface. The promised land's connection to the habitus is more apparent than ever. The chief problem, argues economist Robert J. Samuelson (1995), is that "we blurred the distinction between progress and perfection. . . . Our most expansive hopes were unrealistic. We transformed the American Dream into the American Fantasy" (p. xiii). Samuelson's (1995) controversial diagnosis—which, as I outline in the next section, overlooks some very real economic factors that indicate we have neither perfection nor progress—certainly does not explain all of our disillusion. In fact modernism is also due a large chunk of the blame. Its emphasis on single causes and steady, linear progression—what we can call temporal reasoning—means we have no "rational" explanation for our apparent failure to reach technological utopia (technology was *the* cause of the desired effect of progress), *and* we seemingly have no other means of attaining an alternative promised land because the either/or reasoning privileged in modernism necessitates our having one vision *or* another (thus the apparent cultural erasure of romanticism). As a result we feel "confused and dispirited" about our economic condition (Strobel, 1993, p. xi), the same sorts of "feelings of unreality" (Lears, 1983, p. 6) and "estrangement and dislocation" (Ostwalt, 1990, p. 25) other scholars identify as occurring during the transition from romanticism to modernism. Unfortunately, the transference of the spiritual from the individual to the machine that transpired during the previous transition has seemingly left us with little rhetorical recourse. Or as Daniel Bell (1973) prophesied over 20 years ago, "The system is completely mundane, for any transcendent ethic has vanished" (p. 477).

Where Are We? Problems with the Promised Lands

The disappearance of a "transcendent ethic" stems mainly, I believe, from concerns regarding the transition in the United States from the industrial to the postindustrial age, with all the cultural aftershocks (such as doubt in dominant grand narratives) that follow such a seismic shift. Oddly enough, the postindustrial features an even greater reliance on technology than the industrial age, to the point that its debilitating aspects become more visible while its machines grow more mysterious (they lack many of the moving parts of the industrial machines). Although I am no doubt oversimplifying distinctions between the two systems, what follows is a brief comparison. In the industrial age U.S. citizens produced many of the world's goods with the assistance of moving-parts machines. This age was fairly labor intensive, with a credo that increasing production increases the standard of living; in addition many products were consumed within the same market/nation in which they were made. That production process, Hage and Powers (1992) note, was typically restricted to a particular time and place (i.e., the second shift at the plant). The postindustrial age, on the other hand, features a reliance on technologically advanced machines that reduce the need for labor, shifting a substantial amount of unskilled work to the service sector of the economy, while more jobs require skilled labor (Hage & Powers, 1992).[2] Unskilled workers who do not find work in the service industry thus find full-time jobs more difficult to obtain. Yet the proliferating technology must pay for itself through increased consumption. Accordingly, explains Barber (1995), production has shifted from *meeting* consumer demands for products we "need" to *creating* demand for services we desire, making the latter appear to be the former. McDonald's, for example, transforms the service of providing fast food to a product we must have: we "need" a Big Mac because "we deserve a break today."

The defining feature of the postindustrial economy, then, is *created demand*. In industrial society demands were met through the production, primarily within the nation's borders, of necessary goods (e.g., shoes) that were in demand. In postindustrial society necessary goods such as shoes are produced in such numbers that they proliferate beyond the point of need. Yet each pair of shoes we purchase is "needed." For example, I possess shoes for tennis and shoes for basketball, although both games are played on hardcourts. Either pair would suffice for both sports, but my desire for different pairs of shoes was translated into a need for both pairs. This change in our economic system generates a concomitant change in our cultural system, for our economic role shifts from being primarily producers to being chiefly consumers now that production is increasingly global rather than local or national.

Two effects of this role change are apparent. First, consumerism offers us a new form of individuality, a new sense of self. In a postindustrial economy, we define ourselves and others more by what we consume than what we produce. "When we consume objects," writes

Ritzer (1997), "we are consuming signs, and in the process are defining ourselves" (p. 80). This shift is most clearly observed in advertisements that decreasingly emphasize the qualities of the product or service and increasingly emphasize the type of person we would be by consuming the product or service. For example, sport utility vehicles are in many respects quite impractical products for anyone who does not live in a remote, rural setting. As Harrop (1997) notes, "Commercials show the monsters scaling mountains, but few climb anything steeper than a parking-garage ramp" (p. 3B). Moreover, she continues, they are gas guzzlers, and they do more damage in accidents than other vehicles. Yet these SUVs or 'utes (consumption is enhanced through catchy acronyms or nicknames) are tremendously popular among people who live in the suburbs, for their owners—the commercials suggest—can see themselves as rugged, independent iconoclasts, in short, as individuals. Accordingly, suggests Coontz (1992), "Consumer society has increasingly broken down our sense that we depend on others" (p. 176).

As a result, and second, consumerism changes our sense of community by subordinating it to individualism and by suggesting that being different from others is the basis for a looser kind of community. Sport utility vehicle owners, for instance, may be inclined to see themselves as belonging to a symbolic community of rugged individualists that differs markedly from the homogeneity of their suburban enclave. As White (1992) points out in her analysis of the Home Shopping Club, consumerism fosters a need to make distinctions, to value what is different. Consequently, Turow (1997) argues, we have been—and continue to be—segmented by advertisers into "image tribes" that encourage the recognition of differences. These image tribes encourage consumption by suggesting that we can be more special and unique, that we can be part of the "in crowd" that differs from the rest, through our purchases. In creating image tribes postindustrial corporations and advertisers "signaled that people should find their own kind in media communities designed for them" (Turow, 1997, p. 198). Consumption, in other words, is a process of communication in which we enact the individualistic self and envision the unique, but secondary, community through difference.

Although postindustrialism's consumerist philosophy seems to offer us the potential for power, a means of defining ourselves that *seemingly* does not rely on the judgments of others, it offers a less-than-ideal path to individual and communal fulfillment. As Ritzer (1997) points out:

Fast-food restaurants offer people foods that tend to be high in cholesterol, sugar, salt, and so on that are harmful to their health.

Credit cards induce people to spend more than they should and beyond their available means, buying things they do not need and may not even want.

Shopping malls entice people into buying things they may not need.

TV shopping networks and cybermalls permit people to shop 24 hours a day, seven days a week, thereby increasing the likelihood that they will spend more than they should.

Catalogues allow people to purchase products from anywhere in the world, and they may be induced into buying unnecessary products. (p. 223)

Such means of consumption, Ritzer (1997) summarizes, provide us with power while simultaneously constraining us. They "enable people to do things they could not do before, but they also constrain them financially, psychologically, and materially to buy more than they need; to spend more than they should" (p. 223). Bell (1973) goes so far as to say that consumerism is little more than cultural hedonism, a reckless form of play that indulges our selves. Such indulgences encourage an immediate gratification that can never be fulfilled. Consumption must be continuous; to remain a unique self who is part of a distinct community, we must continue to consume. "If we acknowledge that a need is not a need for a particular object as much as it is a 'need' for difference (the desire for social meaning), only then will we understand that satisfaction can never be fulfilled" (Baudrillard, 1970/1988, p. 45).

The result of this constant quest for the new, exciting, and different is a culture increasingly lacking depth and memory, what Baudrillard and other scholars have labeled the postmodern culture. (Postmodernism, as we will see later in this chapter, also refers to a particular means of responding to this cultural shift.) The postmodern society, Jameson (1984) argues, features superficiality and depthlessness, the waning of emotion or affect, and a loss of historicity. In short, "meaning" doesn't mean as much as it used to; past promised lands may have seemed profound, important, and traditional, but now they have been sapped of much of their historical importance. Although in many ways such a development is troubling, suggesting that "meaning is momentary," in other ways a postmodern culture affords us an opportunity to transcend the habitus, the perpetuation of history in the cultural terrain. When history is devalued, alternatives are easier to develop.

On the one hand, then, the emergence of a postindustrial economy and postmodern culture marks the decreased relevance of either historical promised land featured in the dominant discourse of U.S. culture. As Lyotard (1988/1993) argues, the emergence of postmodernism parallels the death of grand narratives and hence the apparent discarding of the idealized conclusions of those narratives: promised lands. Although modernism and romanticism are implicitly embedded in postindustrialism's focus on consumerism—being satisfied with what we have, halting or slowing our consumption, will leave us behind (we won't progress) and feeling empty (we'll lack spirit)—progress and spirit are not achieved primarily through the attainment of the historical promised lands of the romantic garden or the modernist technological utopia but through the consumption of goods and services. Postindustrialism points out, first, that the ability of our Selves to achieve Progress is suspect and, second, that Community and Spirit have been muffled. These developments, though discussed separately, are most certainly interrelated.

On the other hand, these developments also offer an opportunity to develop alternative visions of promised lands that may be positioned outside the historical habitus, a notion to which I turn following a discussion of the diminished importance of the promised lands of technological utopia and the sacred garden. In speaking of the diminishment of these historical forces, and in distinguishing postindustrialism and postmodernism as "breaks" in an historical chronology, I leave myself open to Best and Kellner's (1991) charge that "both postindustrial and postmodern social theory . . . greatly exaggerate the alleged break or rupture in history" (p. 277). My distinction here, as with my line-drawing throughout the book, is simply for purposes of clarity As I indicate later in this chapter, contemporary culture is infused with *multiple* ideas and memories that intersect and interact, creating a cacophony of rhetorical fragments that is much more complicated than any single distinction or dialectic could hope to grasp.

"Are We There Yet?" Progress and Self-fulfillment

The belief that with more technology comes more progress has been sorely tested in our move to the postindustrial age. Although many economic measures suggest we are doing better financially and that we are making real progress toward higher standards of living (see Samuelson, 1995, for example), a quite compelling case can be made to support the claim that we are growing worse financially and thus spiritually and socially. This evidence suggests that "the rules" of the habitus, the guiding principles of dominant grand narratives, have been broken. Their fragmenting diminishes the allure of dominant visions of past promised lands. As Mishel (1995) argues, "Some analysts feel that our productivity growth is so strong and the promise of computerization so great that we are on the verge of a new, golden economic age. There's only one problem with this celebration:

The living standards of the middle class have remained in continuous decline despite the robust aggregate performance" (p. 60).

The decline in living standards, in fact, leads many economists to suggest that we are experiencing just the opposite of progress. Katherine Newman (1988, 1993) contends that for many of us the phrase "downward mobility" accurately describes our economic situation. We are not centered selves but falling selves. University of Nebraska economist Wallace Peterson (1994) goes so far as to suggest that we have been suffering through what he calls a "silent" economic depression. According to Peterson, "Four-fifths of American families have experienced falling or stagnant *real* incomes" since 1973 (p. 30). What makes this statistic even more troubling is evidence demonstrating that as a whole U.S. citizens are working longer hours than ever before, adding nearly a month's worth of work to our lives during the calendar year (Schor, 1992). And it is not just the broad middle class suffering from this conundrum. "Millions of workers in the bottom one half to three quarters of America's labor force are . . . doing worse than they once did, or than their parents did, and working harder than ever while falling behind the better-off," according to Dentzer (1991, p. 39). If a person does not possess the skills needed in an increasingly technological economy, the prospects for improvement are dim. As Rifkin (1995) pessimistically observes, we have developed an apparently permanent underclass that is "unskilled and unneeded, the commodity value of their labor . . . rendered virtually useless by the automated technologies that have come to displace them in the new high-tech global economy" (p. 80). Not surprisingly, given these figures and observations, "Incomes steadily fell among the bottom 80 percent of families from 1989 through 1993" (Mishel, 1995, p. 61). Despite some improvement since 1993, from 1990 to 1997 real median hourly wages dropped 45 cents an hour (Belton, 1997). Summarizes Bell (1996), "Every generation of Americans had expected that they would build a better life for their children than they themselves had. This may no longer be the case. . . . It is, instead, the fear of the end of 'the American dream'" (p. 318).

As these economic indicators point to our feeling out of touch with the American dream, the type of work we do moves us further away from a feeling of being at the center of a journey toward Progress, for the postindustrial era is changing just what we mean by "work." As Shoshana Zuboff (1988) reports from her studies of organizational change, many of us now complete our jobs *through* machines, distancing us from the process of labor as technological devices mediate our efforts. Moreover, the abstract nature of "doing" the work on a computer screen further removes the body from the process of bodily labor. Clerks do not file as much; mill workers do not touch the machinery as much. "In diminishing the role of the worker's body in the labor process, industrial technology has also tended to diminish the importance of the worker" (Zuboff, 1988, p. 22). My father, to his increasing frustration, went through just such a process in his work at the local newspaper. Beginning as a linotype operator, he used a machine to set the type for the page plates that would be run through the press. He used a machine, but he had his hands on the machine and manipulated its parts. When the paper moved to offset printing, though, he became a paste-up artist, printing images from a computer, then sticking them on a sheet that would be photographed and turned into a plate to be run through the press. A few years ago he made another transition, doing the paste-up work entirely on a computer screen; his hands touched only the keyboard.

In other areas of the economy, we see a proliferation of service jobs—what my students derisively call "McJobs"—that distance the individual from the labor process in another way. Rather than producing a tangible something of value, service workers function as consumption assistants. Service work directly reminds us that our economic role is peripheral; service work exists to satisfy the demands of others we see. Rather than generating durable products, we increasingly serve people. The diminished cache of these jobs is reflected not only in their nickname but also in the fact that they do not provide either the spiritual element of seeing the results of one's work or the wages necessary to achieve economic progress.[3] In addition, these jobs pose a threat to what Kaus (1992) calls social equality, for in our minds, jobs that require us to serve other people send the implicit message that the person being served is somehow worthy of more respect than the server. Conclude Krymkowski and Krauze (1992), "Unless the meaning of *success* is modified, substantial changes in the availability of nonmanual positions would have to occur in order to provide Americans with the opportunities to which they have become accustomed" (p. 155). This statement reflects just how much of a difference postindustrialism and postmodernism make in our efforts to feel centered. Not only are we distanced from the process of labor and from our fellow human beings, we are distanced from the American dream.

The billboards alongside the modernist road to Progress advertise "the expectation that by dint of personal effort—hard work, education, saving, and playing by the 'rules of the game'—one's economic well-being will steadily improve" (Peterson, 1994, p. 20). However, hard work in today's transitional economy does not guarantee that we are behind the wheel, motoring down the road to Progress. Instead we are like the bus passengers in the movie *Speed*; some crazed lunatic (who must be played by Dennis Hopper) we can't see is in control of a bus with no clear destination, and we can't get off because it's moving too fast. Although admitting the traditional rules of work did not always guarantee success for those who followed them, Coontz (1992) points out that "the past two decades have stripped away the illusion of fairness, as well as much hope of winning by the old rules, without leading to construction of any new rules. . . . Consequently, people feel embattled, if not embittered, and, above all, very much alone" (p. 277). The journey down Progress Road afflicts us with what truckers call "white line fever"; as we grow disoriented from staring at the rapidly passing lines on the road, time elapses, but the signs indicate we're getting further away from our destination. The reciprocal connection between time and space in modernism—if time elapses, space is covered—is seemingly severed. We know time has passed, but we do not feel as if we have moved forward; we are not where we're supposed to be.

Jost (1993) reports that the number of Americans who felt their personal economic condition was getting worse rather than better reached its highest point in 20 years in 1992; nearly one-third (32 percent) of the persons surveyed believed their situation was getting worse. The kids riding in the backseat of the car can't be very excited about their future, either. While they clamor to know "are we there yet," half of the adults polled by *The New York Times* in early 1996, "thought it unlikely that today's youth would attain a higher standard of living than they have" (Uchitelle & Kleinfield, 1996)—a dispiriting notion to say the least.

"Who Cares?" The Decline of Spirit and Community

The disillusioned response of the adults in the front seat speaks to the void left by modernism's silencing of the romantic spirit. "The loss of Spirit is painfully apparent," Goodall (1996) says, now that we are "driven by the modernist language and logic of machine and systems metaphors" (p. 30). Because we have been living within this machine metaphor, pinning our hopes of progress on the pumping of its pistons, "the desacralization of work lies at the heart of our alienation" (Fox, 1994, p. 12). Although the rules of the habitus imply that work is fulfilling and a means of connecting ourselves with a community of others, a good deal of economic and cultural evidence suggests we have lost attachments to spirit and community.

The dominant visions of romanticism and modernism have imbued the work experience with different images of spiritual fulfillment, but throughout American history work has been envisioned as

a part-time basis or as contractors or freelancers" (p. 190). Not surprisingly, then, the total employment figure decrease among the nation's 500 largest companies nearly mirrors the total employment figure increase among business service subcontractors (Bernstein, 1995). Working temporary and/or multiple jobs distances individuals from the work community, too. Rather than belonging to the one "tribe"—even for a period of a few years—temp workers visit, but do not dwell, in multiple work environments in a year, perhaps a month, sometimes even in a day.

DISTANCING THE SELF FROM THE SOCIAL COMMUNITY. The promised land of technological paradise has not only failed to deliver on its vision of economic plenitude, it contributes to our growing sense of displacement as members of a social community. Traditionally, Meyrowitz (1985) reminds us, the United States has been a nation where physical places reflected social meanings. That is, a physical place such as a building or neighborhood was home to specific activities not found in other physical places. For instance, Philipsen (1976) explains how porches, streets, and corners each constituted a discrete site for specific kinds of interactions within an urban neighborhood. Then, most neighborhoods featured hangouts where individuals could relax and mingle with friends who were not necessarily co-workers. Oldenburg (1989) labels such hangouts "third places" in that they are neither home or work, the two primary places in our lives. Now, technology works to reduce our physical connections to others.

As Boorstin (1978) points out, "Technology aims to insulate and immunize us" from our surroundings (p. 11), which can "encourage further privatism and isolation" (Robins, 1993, p. 313). We can be entertained, shop, visit with friends, and do our jobs without ever leaving the house. Sherry Turkle (1996) calls this phenomenon "social atomization," noting that "we seem to be in the process of retreating further into our homes, shopping for merchandise in catalogues or on television channels or for companionship in personal ads" (p. 52). Robert Putnam (1996) argues, "TV watching comes at the expense of nearly every social activity outside the home, especially social gatherings and informal conversations" (p. 47), but he could just as well be talking about home technology in general. Statistically speaking, he says, "each hour spent viewing television is associated with less social trust and less group membership" (p. 47). In other words we stay at home, and we lose a feeling of involvement with others. Since 1965, Putnam reports, the amount of time devoted to socializing in America has declined by about 25 percent, and the time spent with clubs and organizations is down about 50 percent. He blames both primarily on the fact that television makes us homebodies. Even the act of watching television is disconnecting, say some scholars. "We experience a presence, but at a distance. We are involved, yet we are uninvolved. We are affected, yet we are unaffected" (Gozzi & Haynes, 1992, p. 221).

Yet at the same time that our physical interactions with others have decreased, "the technological achievements of the past century have produced a radical shift in our exposure to each other" as we find ourselves technologically connected to a tremendous number of people and places (Gergen, 1991, p. xi). "Instead of communities of place, characterized by interaction and the activities of the street and immediate vicinity, involvement has shifted to unrestricted relationships facilitated through media connection" (Gumpert & Drucker, 1992, p. 195). As a result we find ourselves without a discrete sense of place, socially speaking. Explains Meyrowitz (1985), "electronic media destroy the specialness of place and time. . . . Through such media, what is happening almost everywhere can be happening where we are. Yet when we are everywhere, we are also no place in particular" (p. 125). A number of cultural observers make a point similar to Meyrowitz's, including Gergen (1991), who suggests the self has become so saturated with information and mediated relationships that we no longer have a clear sense of who we are as individuals, let alone to what social community we belong.

Even home, the place where we would likely feel most secure, is undergoing dramatic changes, and not just because of the increased use of technology in our houses and apartments. In the past 20 years the number of households with two wage-earners increased 41 percent as women entered the workforce in growing numbers (Lawlor, 1994, p. B1). This means that for many Americans of parenting age (roughly over 20 years old), home life is different from that in which they grew up (let me emphasize *different*, for the increasing number of women in the workforce is most certainly a net benefit for the nation). Meanwhile, parents will raise their children in more homes than they themselves grew up in as geographic mobility among families increases with career advancement by women (Markham, 1987). Economic changes have also disrupted interactions within the home. Many companies have moved to 24-hour work schedules in the last 20 years (Melbin, 1984). Now, one of every five full-time workers labors during a nontraditional shift, altering the definition of home for families and leaving many unmarried individuals feeling isolated when they go home while much of the rest of the world is at work ("Living," 1993). In some cases, though, people's home life is different because they do not have a family in their home. Because growing numbers of individuals choose to postpone marriage (Goldscheider &

Waite, 1991)—many for career reasons—the percentage of unmarried adults has jumped from 28 percent to 48 percent between 1974 and 1994 (Putnam, 1996). Economic changes, too, have made it more difficult for individuals to buy their own home. The percentage of one's income needed to pay off a mortgage has doubled in the last 30 to 40 years, and 90 percent of renters can't generate the funds needed for a downpayment on a home (Peterson, 1994). Not surprisingly, then, "according to Harvard's Joint Center for Housing Studies, the rate of home ownership among those ages 30–34 fell to 50 percent in 1992 from 61 percent in 1980" (Jost, 1993, p. 640).

The change in family structure, the search for quality jobs, the attempt to become upwardly mobile, the decrease in ties to a particular physical location, and the technological ability to travel more frequently are also reflected in our being a more geographically mobile nation than we were in the first part of this century (even though the aging of baby boomers has slowed the nation's overall geographic mobility rate in recent years, since people move less as they age, leading to debate over whether the nation as a whole is any more geographically mobile than it was 50 years ago; see Putnam, 1996). As Jackson (1995) proclaims, "Ours is a century of uprootedness. All over the world, fewer and fewer people live out their lives in the place where they were born" (p. 1).

In the United States, in particular, the percentage of people who live in the state of their birth "has steadily dropped" since World War II (Gober, 1993, p. 5). "On a given date," notes Glick (1993), "nearly one-fifth of the [sic] Americans are living at a different address from the one where they resided 12 months earlier. This means that over 40 million persons of all ages move within one year's time. In addition, almost one-half of the U.S. population changes residences within a five-year period" (pp. 31–32). During 1995–96, for example, over 1.2 million people moved to the southern states from a different region of the country, whereas another 1.1 million people moved from the South to another region (U.S. Bureau of the Census, 1997, p. 32). Geographic relocation is so rampant in some parts of the country that it has spawned its own industry, especially in California, where consultants offer advice for people wishing to relocate to another state (Ellicott, 1993). All of this moving around suggests we're still searching for that promised land.

Unfortunately, the areas to which most of the movement is occurring—the suburbs—are planned in such a way that new community ties are difficult to form. First, business and residential development occur simultaneously rather than in stages that allow for easier planning. As Hiss (1990) explains, suburban areas now "may be seen as immediately suitable sites for three kinds of development that used to arrive in stages: weekend homes, residential neighborhoods, and office districts. In this latest development era, 'urban and suburban sprawl' is no longer descriptive, because the sprawl has been transformed into urban and suburban gobbling up and tearing at the ground" (p. 130). As a result the suburbs' "most distinctive feature is that they have no center" (Eberle, 1994, p. 3). Second, suburban neighborhoods are constructed in patterns that decrease interaction among neighbors—mainly because suburbs provide homes for people who work elsewhere. As landscape architect Keith Myers explains, " 'Instead of a neighborhood designed for people, you've got a subdivision designed for the car,' " (quoted in Blundo, 1994, p. J1). Organizing neighborhoods by cul-de-sac at once disorients people and isolates them into nooks and crannies; traffic is vehicular rather than pedestrian because there is no place to visit within walking distance; houses are built with back decks rather than front porches, further distancing neighbors from one another (Myers in Blundo, 1994). Third, suburbs are distanced from downtown by "quite imposing physical barriers, notably urban expressway links, [that] separate the core from adjoining neighborhoods" (Bennett, 1990, p. 36). Fourth, suburbs in different parts of the country, as well as those in the same metropolitan area, seem to share a formulaic abstractness in their design. Housing developments rely on similar blueprints, malls feature the same kinds of stores, the same fast-food places dot commercial strips. Concludes Kunstler (1996) in his historical overview of America's suburban development, "Suburbia fails in large part because it is so abstract. It's an idea of a place rather than a place. The way you can tell is because so many places in this country seem like no place in particular" (p. 17). Finally, zoning laws in many areas discourage building that might forge a sense of communal connection. For example, Kunstler (1993) reports in an earlier work that zoning laws have been written with suburbs in mind, meaning that individuals who want to build and/or remodel in older areas of town have to conform to standards that would disrupt the character of the neighborhood.

Consumption is such an overwhelming influence on the development of a sense of community that Ritzer (1997) sees the mall as a place that invades all previously distinct places found in a community: "It could be argued that more and more places are taking on the characteristics of a shopping mall. We have already discussed how amusement parks are growing more and more like malls. Then there are college student unions, airport and train terminals, and the like, which are increasingly like shopping malls. With the arrival of TV home-shopping networks, our living rooms and dens have become outposts of the malls. Soon our studies and offices will be extensions of the cybermalls" (p. 236). To Ritzer's list I would add the college or university, a place where students "shop" for classes during the drop/add periods at the start of the term, where administrators brag about retention rates (satisfied customers) and enrollment increases (new customers), and where instructors are informally rated on a "cool/not cool" binary by students who increasingly expect to be entertained while they are served/taught. One must wonder, though in the form of hyperbole, whether Ritzer's (1996) claim about the McDonaldization of society means college gates will be increasingly envisioned as academic golden arches that proudly proclaim how many have been served. Summarizes Ritzer (1997), "There used to be many areas where one could escape from, be free of, shopping. Those areas are being drastically reduced as more and more of them become malls, or at least extensions of them" (p. 236).

The "malling" of America reflects the extent to which consumerism has permeated our postmodern culture. Consumerism, I want to emphasize, has the ability to produce pleasure, to give us a sense of power through revised definitions of the individual self and the special community. At the same time, those definitions point to the diminishment of historical promised lands and the separation of self and community. At a cultural level, we are at once feeling better and feeling worse about where we find ourselves. We want to move, but we feel at home.

An Opportunity to Envision Alternatives to the Habitus

Clearly postindustrialism appears to preclude the attainment of promised lands based on either modernist technological progress or romantic spiritual fulfillment. Its vision of technology is one in which the individual is marginal rather than central to its operation, and its shattering of "commonsense" assumptions about work and social community make a revalorization of community incompatible with existing social conditions. Moreover, the former dampens the romantic spirit of work, while the latter impedes the development of self. The ubiquity of Wal-Mart, which recently passed General Motors to become the largest corporate employer in the world (Jones, 1997), exemplifies these interconnected processes. Its commercials often feature "regular folks" talking about their fulfilling work in order to present us with a reassuring image of a neighborhood store. A partially retired senior citizen will greet you as you enter the store, not unlike my memories of entering the candy store across the street from Lincoln Heights Elementary to be greeted by the owners, my partially retired next-door neighbors. Yet Wal-Mart's presence in a community more often than not represents the demise of community and spirit represented by my neighbors' candy store. Wal-Mart's greeters may have a great deal of experience in what used to be well-paid, production-oriented jobs; now, they work for little more than minimum wage saying "hi" to hundreds of people a day. The remainder of Wal-Mart's employees are almost entirely part-time workers, some of them temporary. They are not unionized, nor do they routinely work together on projects in the store. And, finally, when Wal-Mart comes to town, small towns experience a dramatic drop-off in business along Main Street; the distinctive character of a place is partially erased as Wal-Mart homogenizes the retail industry across the nation. Of course, my modernist inclinations—as a person who uses his dollars efficiently—occasionally lead me to a Wal-Mart or one of its brethren, despite my misgivings about what the chain represents.

And therein lies the dilemma we face in an emerging postindustrial society/postmodern culture: we both enjoy the benefits of the changing economy and abhor many of its cultural outcomes. We still want to believe in the technological paradise that has attempted to usurp the spiritual aura of the garden as promised land, but the machine has been unable to keep its promise of rekindling our spirits—no matter what its advantages. No wonder Houston (1978) writes of "the placelessness of man's [sic] own spirit in a world where the human scale and human values are being subordinated to the dictates of technocracy" (p. 224). The habitus of postindustrialism appears to limit the attainment of either modernist or romantic ideals, yet we simultaneously seem to enjoy the power of being consumers.

The dilemma is clear. The road to the promised land of Progress through the sacred garden is closed, the new highway of technological advancement is under construction, and the detour through postindustrialism in some ways moves us further away from our destination. We've been on the road for so long we don't know how to find our way home. The road signs are confusing, the maps are outdated, and there's no one to turn to for directions. In short, "no one is quite sure of the ground on which they stand, which direction they are facing, or where they are going" (Keith & Pile, 1993, p. 3).

AND THEREIN LIES AN OPPORTUNITY. As I have noted throughout the chapter, the two visions of promised lands with which I've been working have been "dominant" visions. That is, they have been presented as images shared by all members of the nation, an assumption that is patently false. For example, my observations about the consumerism found in higher education are not likely shared by all instructors and certainly not by all students or parents. The decreased relevance of these dominant promised lands, then, is an opportunity to remember that for many "immigrants" who did not travel to this country voluntarily, the image of a sacred promised land holds little sway and that many individuals have had limited access to the technological wonders designed to ensure progress. For those of us who have subscribed to dominant visions of promised lands, their decreased relevance is no doubt disturbing, but the lack of a *single, universal* alternative promised land presents all of us with the opportunity to develop and appreciate *multiple* visions of promised lands—for each promised land is a vision of how to create a good and just society. That goal is one we all share. Understanding one another's grand narratives and visions of promised lands helps us reach that goal. Accordingly, I ask the reader to remember the rhetorical definition offered earlier in this book, one in which the inclusive pronouns of "we" and "us" refer to those fans of popular stories who imaginatively and purposefully play with rhetoric to envision promised lands that are alternatives not just to historical habitus but to its manifestation in the consumer culture marked by the emergence of postindustrialism and postmodernism. Although the promised lands I discuss tend to reflect my interests and values, I believe we all can, and do, envision promised lands that are responsive to our own material situations. "We" all share the desire to construct a culture replete with places that matter.

Rhetorical Responses to the Promised Land "Problem"

In essence we are experiencing a cultural crisis of direction. Our history seems inhospitable to the present, the structures of our habitus are more visible, and no shared promised land shimmers on the horizon. "How do we tell what happened in the past if we do not have the familiar framework of the logic of problem solving, the theology of damnation and redemption, the economics of progress, or the politics of revolution to guide us?" asks Nichols (1994, p. 2). Nichols's question is rhetorical in more than one way, for into the cultural void left by the questioning of the garden and the machine steps rhetoric. In simple terms the exigence of disappearing dominant promised lands calls forth rhetorical responses. Rather than unconsciously accepting the negative effects of our dispersal into image tribes, as Turow (1997) implies we do, I believe we seek antidotes to this dispersal. That is, instead of simply settling for connections with others narrowly like us, we also require a sense of connection with others unlike us. Our image tribes fulfill us at the same time that they remind us of what we're missing. Our rhetorical responses range from the modernist re-centering of one's self in the past through nostalgia,

to the romantic seeking of community security through spirituality, to the postmodern playing with fragments of discourse through
seemingly random symbolic movements. I discuss each of these three
separately in the next few pages but then argue in this and subsequent chapters for their convergence in the purposeful play that I call
symbolic pilgrimage. Such play recognizes the multiple centers we
call home. As Lippard (1997) observes, "We are living today on a
threshhold between a history of alienated displacement from and
longing for home and the possibility of a multicentered society that
understands the reciprocal relationship between the two" (p. 20). I
believe symbolic pilgrimages, as chapter three explains in detail,
help us reach such an understanding. But first, on to an understanding of our responses to an increasingly visible habitus, one that lacks
a dominant promised land.

Modernism's Nostalgia

First is a collection of modernist narratives in which we can find a
stable, historical place through nostalgia; the glorified past provides
the site of promised lands. Central to nostalgic rhetoric is a belief that
"it is hard not to live in the past if that is where so much of your
happiness resides" (Bragg, 1996, p. A17). Moreover, nostalgia may
provide an alternative vision of linear movement, a moving backward
rather than forward. "Renewed respect for nostalgia," writes Lears
(1998), "could provide a powerful antidote to linear notions of progress—by underwriting the conviction than once, at least in some
ways, life was more humane and satisfying than it is today" (p. 62).
Nostalgia is often described as an evasion of the present, a disavowal
of responsibility to work within one's current material predicament.
But, Lears (1998) continues, "the sense that something of value might
have passed from the scene could reveal a more genuinely historical
frame of mind than the assumption that change is always irreversible
and generally beneficient" (p. 66).
    Although nostalgia is present in some form in most any era, its
more pronounced presence in American culture probably began in
the 1970s—the time that most economists suggest the move to a
postindustrial economy gathered momentum—with the revisiting
of 1950s styles and stories. *American Graffiti* and *Grease* wowed big
screen audiences, *Happy Days* pulled in the crowds through living
rooms, and The Stray Cats fueled a resurgence of interest in rocka-
billy music. Since then, we have been taken on a number of nostalgic trips roughly parallel to the 20-year gap that marked the 1970s/
1950s phenomenon. Today it's the return of the Brady's (with a link

to *Gilligan's Island* at the end of *A Very Brady Sequel*), reruns of *American Bandstand* shows from the 1970s on VH-1, a soundtrack full of Abba in the film *Muriel's Wedding,* and the return of clogs and bell-bottoms. But nostalgia can be manifested in other ways, too. Hayes-Bautista and Rodriguez (1994) report young Hispanics in the Los Angeles area—especially recent immigrants—have formed clubs and hold parties where technobanda (a form of music that combines Mexico's traditional military band sound with synthesizers and other electronic sounds) is played. Alienated Generation Xers are tuning in to *Sesame Street* again (Hulbert, 1994), architects are returning to regional and historical styles of construction (Adler, 1995; Ley, 1989), and hobbyists participate in massive Civil War reenactments such as the bloody battle of Antietam ("12,000 . . . ," 1997).

Nostalgia is a rhetorical response that provides a modernist sense of certainty and stability, a comforting notion in a time of confusion about cultural goals. When we don't quite know where we are or where we're going, we can return to a favorable past—or recall one if our immediate histories are painful—to regain our bearings. In fact, notes Davis (1979), "the nostalgic evocation of some past state of affairs always occurs in the context of present fears, discontents, anxieties, or uncertainties" (p. 34). In the midst of all this uncertainty, returning to a time and place we "know" reaffirms a sense of who we are by reminding us of who we were. "Buffeted by change, we retain traces of our past to be sure of our enduring identity" (Lowenthal, 1975, p. 9). We transcend time and cultural space by going back to the past while living in the present.

Romanticism's Spirituality

A second rhetorical response is a collection of romantic narratives in which we find a stable, communal place through spirit; the sacred garden community of others is the site of promised lands. These narratives are often cyclical in nature, promising a return to a natural, sacred home as one travels through life. Christian narratives espouse cycles of purification and redemption, with heaven as a coming home of sorts. Narratives of indigenous peoples, now increasingly prominent in "mainstream" culture, often rely on seasonal cycles or a return to the earth as part of a life's journey. Environmentalists promote the recycling of synthetic materials and the rejuvenation of nature as means of continually replenishing the earth. To some extent this rhetorical response is also nostalgic—just as nostalgia is somewhat romantic—in that it culls gardenic images from the past to make sense of the present.

Evidence of our desire for these cyclical journeys is scattered throughout popular and scholarly literature. Commentator Bill Moyers (1996) opines that "people yearn for spiritual certainty and collective self-confidence," so they are "turning—or returning—to the Bible as a guide through the chaos" (p. 4). Pollster George Gallup Jr. has also noticed a spiritual renaissance in his analysis of 45 years of Gallup polls on the subject, pinpointing "'a slow but unmistakable shift from materialism to spirituality'" (quoted in Donahue, 1996a, p. 1A). This shift is reflected in a *TV Guide* poll in which "61 percent of the respondents said that they'd like to see more references to God, churchgoing, and other religious observances in prime time [television], and why 68 percent were particularly eager to see more prime-time spirituality" (Kaufman, 1997, p. 34).

Popular magazines have reported on surges in searches for the sacred for several years now. As *Newsweek* put it in a 1994 cover story, millions of Americans have made a spiritual turn in order "to understand their place in the cosmos" ("In Search," 1994, p. 53). Meanwhile, sightings of the Virgin Mary have been reported throughout the United States in recent years. One sighting, at a farm home in Conyers, Ga., has drawn tens of thousands of people from every state and a number of European countries since 1990 (Dvorchak, 1994). This need to find a spiritual path to establish connections with one another, Miles (1997) offers, is reflected in "the extraordinary success of all kinds of religious literature in recent years" (p. 26). In particular, McManus (1995) points out, an increasing emphasis on spirituality accounts for the recent boom in the popularity of angels. Woodward (1993) notes that millions of books about angels have been sold, and Gibbs (1993) reports on a survey in which 69 percent of the respondents believed in the existence of angels. Whereas Clarence from *It's a Wonderful Life* may have been an anachronism not too long ago, he has now been joined by recent popular incarnations of angels, such as the CBS hit *Touched by an Angel* or, more irreverently, John Travolta's *Michael*.

Prompted by the recognition that "the need for such satisfaction of the spirit remains a common quest for most people" (Gumpert & Fish, 1990, pp. 1–2), a number of rhetorical scholars have advocated the romantic return of the spirit as well. Goodall (1996) suggests rejuvenating the spirit can help generate the sense of community that modernism's emphasis on individual fulfillment neglected. He argues that spirit can be "the holistic force for connecting ourselves to Others, for connecting our interests to better interests of community, for connecting our communities' interests to the best interests of the Earth" (p. 212). In addition, Smith (1993) claims that "we cannot deepen our theory nor advance our understanding of the art of rhetoric without investigating the spiritual dimension" (p. 268), and McPhail (1996) asserts that connecting Zen and rhetoric generates a force of coherence that is spiritual, or what he calls "an attitude that recognizes first and foremost our common humanity, and privileges affirmation and peaceful interaction" (p. 193). And Rushing (1993) claims spirit can transcend the opposing forces of modernism and postmodernism, bringing us together in the process. Before exploring these connections in more detail, however, we need a brief introduction to postmodernism.

Postmodernism's Play

The third rhetorical response is a collection of postmodern narratives in which we find a multiplicity of changing places through play; the convergence of different discourses offers numerous, open promised lands that we may visit. Thus whereas both the modernist and romantic responses to postindustrialism offer fairly static representations of promised lands, a postmodern response suggests an image of purposefully nonlinear movement, of active play within circulating fragments of discourse. Postmodernism is at once a critical approach and a descriptor of contemporary cultural conditions (as noted earlier in this chapter)—though it is also defined in a number of other ways, depending on the context in which it is used (Rose, 1991)—that suggests we are bombarded with such an onslaught of signs, meanings, and messages that the modernist self is unable to rise above the chaos to make sense of them. In Gergen's (1991) phrase, our selves are so totally "saturated" with communication we simply cannot transcend our context as the rational, modernist self would seek to do; our self is de-centered. In its most elementary definition, as I have noted, postmodernism is generally considered to be the cultural manifestations of postindustrialism (Rose, 1991); the barrage of messages and meanings is, to a large extent, made possible by the widespread electronic media technology of postindustrialism and its emphasis on consumption.

Postmodernists argue that we do not possess a single identity; we do not exist in a single cultural space that is located only as a point along the historical timeline of progress. Instead we inhabit multiple spaces and rely on multiple identities *at one time*, shifting among those spaces and identities as our social interactions change; our community affiliations are multiple and changing. Rather than living among modernist "either/or's," postmodernists say, we wallow in a plethora of "both/and's" that grow more complex the more we encounter them. (Hence my distinctions between historical modernist and romantic promised lands, as I explain in note 1 in this chapter, are forced distinctions.) Beck (1997) provides an excellent summary of the transition from modernist to postmodernist thinking in these words: "the purity of absolutism has shifted to the shadows of ambiguity" (p. 39). The Bradys, for example, are not merely a fictional family from the 1970s represented in the 1990s. They are both a 1970s phenomenon and a 1990s cultural icon. Or, as Greg and Marcia disturbingly discovered in a subplot of the second Brady movie, they are not simply siblings brought together by the marriage of their respective father and mother, they are *both* siblings not related by blood *and* sexual beings. In other words rhetoric recirculates, recombines, and can be reconstituted.

"Once we are aware of the ironies of self-reflection," Gergen (1991) wonders, "how are we to regard them? What response can we make? Those working within the postmodern idiom have a common rejoinder—essentially an invitation to play" (p. 137). McGee (1990), in fact, suggests individuals should take advantage of the morass of floating fragments of rhetoric to "make" their own texts or collages using messages they receive, experiences they possess, stories they have encountered, and so forth. "This condition of a multiplicity of choices was a problem for the modern self, producing anxiety and crisis," Kellner (1995)—a critic of much postmodern thought—points out, but "for the postmodern self . . . anxiety allegedly disappears for immersion in euphoric fragments of experience and frequent change of image and identity" (p. 247). Postmodernism, then, redefines the decentered self as happily mobile rather than depressingly distanced, connected with many communities rather than separated from one.

In short, postmodernists acknowledge the illusory nature of a single promised land or grand narrative, recognize different points of view, and incorporate disparate ideas into what modernists say is an incommensurate combination. In the spirit of postmodernism such a process is *both* playful *and* critical, as the power to borrow and redefine removes any aura of "common sense" from a particular idea (see Belsey, 1980). Postmodernism recognizes that the habitus has naturalized history, simplified its effects, and excluded other possibilities that, though they may not be "common," still make sense. McKerrow's (1989) delineation of "critical rhetoric" is an exemplar of postmodernist rhetorical theory; critique should be constant, he says, because all beliefs are susceptible to reification and because all forms of consensus inevitably exclude some ideas and individuals. Thus postmodernism permits white, suburban teenage boys to enjoy gangsta rap as both ironic playfulness (annoying their Frankie Valli– and Four Seasons–lovin' parents) and critical commentary (the homogeneity of their suburban lifestyles)—which is *not* to say that all or even most of these listeners take such a point of view in their listening. As postmodernism suggests, any number of interpretations of such music may be circulating.

These three rhetorical responses are often defined, as I have suggested for clarity's sake in the preceding pages, as incommensurate. Romanticism's avowal of spiritual community is allegedly incompatible with modernism's privileging of the rational, transcendent individual, and postmodernism's suggestion that belief in the stable essences found in modernism and romanticism is out of touch with the sensibilities of critical play. Yet this "either/or" logic connects the beliefs through modernist thinking, just one of the points where all three philosophies intersect. For example, romanticism and postmodernism—both responses to modernism in their own ways—share an interest in seeking Other voices (Berry, 1992; Kroeber, 1988); the former defines Other in metaphysical terms, the latter in cultural terms. In addition, modernists and romantics believe in universals; modernists seek comprehensive answers, and romantics believe all individuals have, in their souls, something in common (Cranston, 1994). Williams (1973) argues, furthermore, that one traditional vision that emerges in longing for the past is the pastoral, garden image. The modern and romantic schools of thought also intersect in economic terms. Peckham (1995), for example, claims the deification of industry and progress by Enlightenment-inspired modernists was in many ways a secularization of the Judeo-Christian tradition, and Weber (1958) offers a profound exploration of the connections between spirit and rationality in the workplace. Weber suggests that we have reframed our idea of a "calling," divorcing it from its religious foundations and imposing it on a sense of career. All of these approaches, however, share the common goal of creating a good and just society.

New, alternative promised lands, then, can embody more than one of the discourses found in dominant visions of promised lands. In fact, in his interpretation of Old Pasadena, Dickinson (1997) provides an insightful analysis of the ways in which nostalgia embodies all three of these discourses. Within that nostalgic area, he writes, "different nostalgic strategies, then, provide a message of both personal and collective memories . . . [and] they also recognize a fragmentation of contemporary life. There is no one past, no one nostalgia" (p. 15). Unfortunately, few scholars seem inclined to work with all three of these seemingly oppositional viewpoints, relying on the unstated either/or logic of modernism rather than exploring possibilities for the both/and use of multiple discourses. Ironically, some postmodernist voices are among the most vociferous in drawing conceptual boundaries, implying that if something is not postmodern it must be modern or romantic (Berg, 1993). As Griffin (1993) points out, "Many philosophers seem to think that the term 'postmodern' definitely includes certain beliefs, attitudes, and stances, and definitely excludes others" (p. 32). The problem, Griffin claims, is that many postmodernist scholars rely too heavily on the deconstructive foundations of Jacques Derrida's work. Derrida encourages, and practices, playing with language, just as he espouses the infinite mobility of meanings and refuses to privilege particular positions. Postmodernists following Derrida's lead, then, tend to emphasize the first word in the phrase "critical play," excluding the possibility that in a space of free-flowing ideas modernism and romanticism can partake in the play. Postmodernism, in this definition, is better labeled "anti-modernism," according to Soja (1996, p. 4).

Gergen (1991), for one, believes such dogmatism is misdirected: "Postmodernism opens the way to the full expression of all discourses, to a free play of discourses. . . . In this respect, neither the romantic nor the modern traditions need be lost from the culture" (p. 247). Ritzer (1996), for instance, believes McDonaldization strongly reflects modernist beliefs, yet he notes how other scholars have found aspects of McDonald's to be quite postmodern. Both interpretations are possible, he says. Gergen and Ritzer have company in their case for a more open playground of language, one that acknowledges but does not back down from the bully of deconstruction. For example, Griffin (1993) and colleagues propose an approach they label "constructive postmodernism," which adheres to the belief that multiple viewpoints should be recognized yet searches for affirmations rather than engaging in a constant critique of language. Combining postmodern and romantic inclinations, Griffin (1990) uses the phrase "postmodern spirituality" and describes the process of meaning-making in terms strikingly similar to McGee's (1990) "fragments" explanation. Borrowing Whitehead's notion of "prehension" as a mystical form of perception, Griffin (1990) writes, "Each event is a unification of many prehensions, and each prehension is the taking in of causal influences from previous events" (p. 7).

In his book *Thirdspace: Journeys to Los Angeles and Other Real-and-Imagined Places* (1996), Soja offers a thorough explanation and illustration of how multiple discourses can collide and overlap. He explains that we can temporarily determine how and where we are by exploring the intersections among time, sociality, *and* space rather than treating each of the three as a distinct means of orientation. "We are first and always historical-social-spatial beings," he writes, "actively participating individually and collectively in the construction/production—the 'becoming'—of histories, geographies, societies"

(p. 73). This process of being and becoming clearly reflects postmodern thinking, yet Soja intentionally complicates postmodernism by suggesting that we think about real and imagined spaces as existing simultaneously, playing off one another, in what he calls a thirdspace, a space "that not only permits but encourages a creative combination of postmodernist and modernist perspectives, even when a specific form of postmodernism is being highlighted" (p. 5).

I too will suggest a rhetorical response that makes room for alternative discourses within a postmodern framework. In particular, I believe we need to examine the interactions among modernism, romanticism, and postmodernism. We need to understand that a good and just society may be envisioned not just through forward-moving grand narratives but through those stories that may encourage other types of movement, not necessarily linear, to reach promised lands. Such an investigation becomes especially important given the modernist tendency to dichotomize self and community, the romantic tendency to find value in static images of self and community, and the postmodern tendency to de-center both self and community. That we seek a centered self who is also ensconced within a special community, yet endowed with the ability to travel to and from that community (in a variety of ways), is a notion that permeates the remainder of this book. Our awareness of habitus suggests a reasoning, centered self; our desire to escape that habitus through imagination suggests a moving self; and our movement toward alternative promised lands that transcend habitus suggests a quest for community. In short, I believe each of us *must* subscribe to some form of grand narrative in order to function within a culture that, paradoxically, seems to discount grand narratives. Each of us requires a sense of telos, or purpose, and we typically find such telos in the stories that help us to envision promised lands.

The distinction between my espousal of grand narratives and Lyotard's dismissal of them lies in scope; the grand narratives I envision are those told through a series of popular stories. The repetition of these stories allows them to take the form of smaller "grand narratives" that are accessed by particular audiences of avid and devoted adherents, or fans. The promised lands that lie at the end of these stories are thus not universal but are specific to contextualized communities and are individually accessible through imaginative journeys. These smaller grand narratives do not necessarily produce Turow's (1997) image tribes, for as I explain later—indirectly in the following chapters, directly in the conclusion—such stories may also help us to see how we are alike.

As the next two chapters demonstrate, I believe the image of "symbolic pilgrimage" helps to explain how we imagine numerous promised lands (postmodernism) while, as transcendent individuals, we are grounded in a particular place (modernism) yet embark on spirit-filled journeys to sacred places to seek communion with others (romanticism). Such an image suggests, to the contrary of Bell's (1973) description of consumerism as cultural hedonism, that the imaginative play of fans who repeatedly re-read popular stories is purposeful and its residues powerful; it is both romantic and modern, as well as postmodern. And it can take many forms. As play theorist Johan Huizinga (1938/1970) observed many decades ago: "A play-community generally tends to become permanent even after the game is over. Of course, not every game of marbles or every bridge-party leads to the founding of a club. But the feeling of being 'apart together' in an exceptional situation, of sharing something important, of mutually withdrawing from the rest of the world and rejecting the usual norms, retains its magic beyond the duration of the individual game" (p. 31). Before explaining the idea of symbolic pilgrimage as purposeful play in more detail, however, I need to provide a theoretical foundation for its development. In so doing I visit a number of lines of scholarly conversation about what it means to have a sense of place and how we encounter the cultural terrain as we find these places. As the following chapter illustrates, I find much value in these conversations, but each of them tends to emphasize only one or two elements of the self-community-movement triumvirate.

Notes

1. Modernism most certainly had been a feature of American society prior to the late 1800s. As Marx (1964) points out, early Americans placed modernist aims within the romantic context. Jefferson, in particular, believed the nation's agrarian foundation would co-opt the forces of the new industrial machines. Writes Marx, "In this sentimental guise the pastoral ideal remained of service long after the machine's appearance in the landscape" (p. 226). That the romantic ideal has not disappeared has allowed it to resurface periodically as a reaction to the forces of modernism; even in the 1700s some romantic thinkers envisioned their approach as a response to modernism (Cranston, 1994). In other words both schools developed in the 1700s and have coexisted since that time; their dominant periods in American history, however, are the basis of my somewhat forced attempts to put them in timeline form.

2. Because many service jobs rely on manufactured goods, however, there is a good deal of overlap in the kinds of work that occur in industrial and postindustrial economies (see Cohen & Zysman, 1987, for an argument that the postindustrial age is merely an evolution of the industrial). Ritzer (1996, 1997), in fact, argues that many of the jobs some analysts associate with the

postindustrial (e.g., low-paying, low-status work in fast-food establishments) are industrial, assembly-line jobs moved to a different context. Ritzer relies on Bell's (1973) definition of a postindustrial society, one that skews toward an emphasis on only professional occupations. I argue that a postindustrial economy is marked by an emphasis on service work *of all kinds,* for such work encourages consumption more so than production, a distinction that I believe resides at the heart of the difference between industrial and postindustrial economies (see Barber, 1995). Furthermore, consumption is increasingly valued in a postindustrial society in which "desires" are depicted as "needs."

3. Industrial jobs, of course, are not known for their ability to generate economic progress (except perhaps at the height of unionization), but they allow workers a means of coping with the mind-numbing, repetitive nature of their tasks by permitting them to see a tangible product result from their efforts. Industrial workers may have "owed their soul to the company store" (Tennessee Ernie Ford via Tim Simpson), but they engaged in work where they were aware of their souls, whereas postindustrial workers encounter sanitized, soulless jobs. Neither work environment, I hasten to add, is anywhere near ideal.

2

The Foundations of Symbolic Pilgrimage
Theoretical Conversations About Places That Matter

When in 1989 I began thinking about the idea of places that matter, I was starting from scratch. My education and experience at that point were geared toward traditional rhetorical criticism. Thus when I first wrote about place as a rhetorical construction (with Christina L. Reynolds in an earlier version of chapter six), my attention was drawn to metaphor. Increasingly I became aware that the places I continued to write about were not so much metaphorical as they were imaginatively real; they were places I—and others—traveled to when we engaged popular stories as fans. That they were visual symbols of the mind co-constructed with other fans and/or story creators did not make them any less powerful than material symbols I perceived in other ways; both types of symbols resonate for me. As a result I began to read in geography to see how scholars in that field talked about place. That route took me in a number of different directions, as have the suggestions and writings of colleagues. The results of my meanderings are presented in this chapter and in the next. Here I engage in analysis, providing distinctions (some of them forced) among scholarly writings on place. Then in chapter three I engage in synthesis, culling from the material here to illustrate how the idea of symbolic pilgrimage accounts for the interaction of centered selves, quests for community, and symbolic movement.

Let me begin with a caveat: labels are dangerously deceptive; what follows is my recounting of conversational strands, and in placing some ideas and people in one strand, I do not mean to suggest they do not or cannot also participate in another strand (in fact, many do participate in more than one strand). Because this exchange of conversations preceded my arrival at the theoretical cocktail party, I want first to provide an overview of what we may have missed. Four general stories are being told at this point: (1) geographers speak of a sense of place generated by cultural and/or material conditions; (2) symbolic interactionists speak of situated accomplishments and interpretive communities; (3) cultural studies scholars speak of discursive movement within a metaphorical cultural terrain; and (4) feminist theorists speak of the situated knowledges of standpoint epistemologies. My reaction to these stories is interspersed throughout their telling, summarized briefly at the end of the discussion in this chapter then elaborated upon in the following chapter.

Geographers and a Sense of Place

Two strands of geography, humanistic and cultural, are especially interested in how we interact with the places around us. In this, the first of several forced distinctions to come in this chapter, I should note that many geographers do both humanistic and cultural geography, some collapse the distinctions between two to separate themselves from physical geographers, and some would call themselves cultural studies scholars (see Agnew, Livingstone, & Rogers, 1996, for a collection of humanistic and cultural geographers' writings on the subject of place). Nevertheless, I will talk about the two strands distinctly for purposes of clarification. Humanistic geography, as its moniker implies, emphasizes the role of the mobile self in negotiating a sense of place within the cultural and physical terrain. Cultural geography focuses on the role played by the physical terrain in our development of a sense of community or culture; the self is part of this equation but primarily as it makes its connections with a community or culture. Because geographers generally emphasize stable senses of place, the visions of promised lands articulated by romantic and modernist philosophies underlie much of their writing.

Humanistic Geography

Humanistic geographers approach the idea of places that matter from the perspective of the individual. Combining psychological, sociological, and geographical insights, these scholars attempt to explain how we, as individuals, develop a personal sense of our place as we meander through and among the physical lands surrounding us. At the heart of this approach to place is the idea that we are engaged in a constant process of centering ourselves in relation to the people and places that fall into and out of orbit around us, a sense-making scheme Ryden (1993) compares to a Ptolemaic universe. Tuan (1974) concurs with this modernist conception of the self, noting that "human beings, individually or in groups, tend to perceive the world with 'self' as the center" (p. 30). Our Ptolemaic impulse to see ourselves at the center of our world is based on the functioning of our senses. In very literal terms Paul Rodaway (1994) explains in *Sensuous Geographies* how we "make sense" of the world: "We are the centre of our world, always experiencing the environment firstly from within this 'circumambient space' or immediate geography. As one moves, one's left and right, back and front, and so on also move. This immediate geography is extended by the body's sense, the intimate sense of touch and smell and the distant sense of sight and hearing" (p. 32). In particular we rely on our sense of sight. As we see people and places, Tuan (1977) points out, we experience "the effect of putting a distance between self and object. What we see is always 'out there'" (p. 146). We envision ourselves in a constant "here," defining everything else in terms of its relation to our center. In short, humanistic geographers see us as "insiders" who define other places and people as "outside" our realm.

When we position ourselves in a particular spot, we have a perspective on the events and people that surround us, what Berger (1972) calls a way of seeing the world. These places "constitute a vital source of both individual and cultural identity and security, a point of departure from which we orient ourselves in the world" (Relph, 1976, p. 43). Change the place and the perspective changes. We see things differently, causing us to see ourselves differently. When I visit my parents in the house I lived in from ages 6 to 18, I view myself as a son. When I am in front of the classroom, I am a teacher. When I'm playing in a pickup basketball game, I'm an athlete (well, at least I like to think I'm an athlete!). I may not be consciously aware that I am defining myself in these ways, but my senses are working to orient me to these conditions. Anne Buttimer (1980) calls this "an essentially creative process authored by people themselves. The meanings of place to those who live in them have more to do with everyday living and doing rather than thinking" (p. 171).

When we go about our everyday living and doing, humanistic geographers claim, we are working as everyday cartographers in that we are using our senses to construct cognitive maps of all that is outside, inside, and around us (Golledge & Stimson, 1997). Although he did not use the phrase, urban planning scholar Kevin Lynch was one of the first to explain how cognitive maps work. According to Lynch (1960), we generate mental images of our environment that are based on "immediate sensation and . . . the memory of past experience, and [they are] used to interpret information and to guide action" (p. 4). In popularizing the phrase "cognitive maps" Downs and Stea (1977) describe these mental constructs as "a person's organized representation of some part of the spatial environment . . . [that] vary according to a person's perspective on the world" (pp. 6, 20). These organized representations generated from our particular perspectives perform the basic function of allowing us to operate in our physical surroundings. More than that, however, "they can also be maps of the imaginary environments represented in literature, folk tales, legends, song, paintings, or film" (Golledge & Stimson, 1997, p. 234). Cognitive maps, then, provide us with "not just spatial information but also attributive values and meanings" (Golledge & Stimson, 1997, p. 235). In assigning a position to something within a material or symbolic landscape, we also categorize and/or rank it in relation to concepts/places we value and/or dislike.

Recent evidence suggests cognitive maps are fundamental to our lives because they are the products of our genetic makeup. Cognitive scientists at MIT report that mice have a specific gene that controls their ability to make mental maps of the places that surround them (Manning, 1996). Humans, geographers argue, are thus able to store these mental maps even after we have left the particular physical environment. Accordingly, our individual cognitive maps serve as guides to important and meaningful places that transcend different time periods or material circumstances. For instance, a bowling alley where I spent most of my Saturday mornings as a youngster, Crown Lanes, is still an important part of my cognitive map even though I haven't visited the building in years (it now houses a furniture store). Even now, on those infrequent occasions when I enter a bowling alley, I evaluate it based on my memorized map of Crown Lanes. Downs and Stea (1977) would find my reaction utterly predictable, for they suggest that "a sense of place provides a sense of security, which blends together past and future" (p. 160).

This blending of past and future is one of the ways we attempt to convince ourselves that in a fragmented culture at least one part of our selves remains steady and unchanging. Our pasts provide a foundation for acting in an uncertain present that transforms into an unpredictable future. The mental maps we use to navigate through physical and cultural terrain help us to determine who we are. The point of view represented in their images, as I point out in the upcoming standpoint epistemology section, is *our* point of view, part of our identity as an individual and member of groups. As Downs and Stea (1977) observe, "In some very fundamental but inexpressible way, our own self-identity is inextricably bound up with knowledge of the spatial environment. . . . [T]here can be no personal biography of 'what' things happened 'when' *without* a sense of the place in which they happened" (p. 27; emphasis in original).

Place, then, is intimately connected to our sense of identity, according to humanistic geographers. Explains Relph (1976), "To have roots in a place is to have a secure point from which to look out on the world, a firm grasp of one's own position in the order of things, and a significant *spiritual* and psychological attachment to somewhere in particular" (p. 38; emphasis added). Relph's words, echoed in other forms by most human geographers, illuminate the romantic underpinnings of human geography. A "sense of place" is an unseen yet powerful force that provides the foundation for our identity. As Buttimer (1980) summarizes, "It appears that people's sense of both personal and cultural identity is intimately bound up with place identity. Loss of home or 'losing one's place' may often trigger an identity crisis" (p. 167). In fact, notes Godkin (1980), psychiatrists acknowledge the significant role place performs "in the development of self-identity" (p. 74).

Despite its modernist emphasis on the centered self, humanistic geography is in many ways a fairly contemporary response to the modernist influences that permeated the social sciences in the years following World War II, especially in the 1960s. Reacting to the predominance of positivist approaches to geography in that time, Rose (1993) explains, humanistic geographers instead "focused on the emotional response of people to places: Places for them were locations which, through being experienced by ordinary people, became full of human significance" (p. 41). In this respect, then, humanistic geography also relies on romantic notions of communal connection between people and places. Together these elements suggest that humanistic geography's devotion to developing theoretical explanations for "a sense of place"—which bloomed in the late 1970s and early 1980s—is also a preliminary response to the cultural confusion fired by the first salvos of the postindustrial age. Finding secure, stable places became a primarily modernist, but somewhat romantic, means of sheltering oneself from the storm of shifting cultural conditions. As Tuan (1977) suggests, "Place is permanent and hence reassuring to man [sic], who sees frailty in himself and chance and flux everywhere" (p. 154). For humanistic geographers a sense of place provides stability for a self that strives to be centered.

Traditional cultural geographers, typically associated with the American Berkeley School of Geography (see Sauer, 1925), strike a slightly different pose. They focus on a "sense of place" as well, and they are interested in how place influences identity, but they locate meaning more in the material landscape than in the individual and are more concerned with how physical places promote a sense of sociality. Places influence our identities, they say, because places are stable, fixed landmarks that conjure collective memories and meanings. As we interact with others in these places or acknowledge our shared interpretation of the meaning of these places, we generate communal bonds with others who may inhabit the same place. For instance, in a hypothetical discussion about the perennial patron Norm in the television sitcom *Cheers*, humanistic geographers would say Cheers is on Norm's cognitive map and he sees himself surrounded by familiar faces and places there (Cheers is outside Norm), whereas cultural geographers would say Norm's identity is bolstered by the sense of community he experiences while in Cheers (Norm is inside Cheers). The cultural geography perspective is best summarized by Hiss (1990), who says, "In short, the places where we spend our time affect the people we are and can become" (p. xi). Our selves are thus enveloped in our communities.

This effect that places have on our identity can work in at least three ways. First, a physical place typically has clear boundaries, making it a particular "here" for those of us who are inside it and a particular "there" for those of us outside it. "Borders and boundaries carry a certain mystery and fascination," notes Ryden (1993). "They imply a transition between realms of experience, states of being; they draw an ineffable line between life as lived in one place and life as lived in another" (p. 1). Let's take living in a metropolitan area as an example. The core of the metropolitan area is the city, which usually means the cutting edge of culture, the place where trends begin. "In black popular culture, the city is hip. It's the locale of cool. In order to be 'with it,' you must be in the city, or at minimum, urban culture must be transplanted, simulated, or replicated outside of the city wherever possible" (Jeffries, 1992, p. 159). In neighborhoods just outside of the city core, though, you're likely to find a different kind of place: refurbished, gentrified homes in what are called "transitional" neighborhoods. In this part of the metropolitan area we are likely to find young professionals hoping to capture a sense of nostalgia by living in and/or renovating older homes. These individuals enjoy the sense of authenticity activated by residing in historical areas. For example, the neighborhood called German Village in a city near where I live is separated from downtown (the city) only by an interstate highway yet is one of the more expensive parts of the city in which to live, mostly because of its stately old homes. As Mills (1993) explains in general terms, young professionals who live in refurbished, gentrified parts of cities see their urban residences as part of their cosmopolitan identity. For other individuals, though, the city or its transitional neighborhoods may mean crime, noise, and pollution. Thus those with the financial means to leave the city are prone to romanticize the idea of the suburbs or rural living. Gold and Gold (1990), for example, show how promotional material for a British suburban development cast the area as a peaceful haven from the city. Each of these three parts of a metropolitan area suggests a different sense of place because of the borders that are associated with them. In this respect place becomes "a way of seeing the world, a codification of social order. . . . Places encapsulate and communicate identity" (Mills, 1993, p. 150).

Second, the character of a place may promote a particular kind of sociality. The convenience store on the way to school, the neighborhood park, the coffee shop downtown, and the break room at work all encourage us to see ourselves in a particular way, for these places encourage a particular kind of interaction between ourselves and our environment. As two communication scholars explain, "Place functions as a medium of communication. The nature of sociability is shaped by how and where interaction occurs" (Gumpert & Drucker, 1995, p. 8). If we visit places frequently, they can become part of our social pattern, such as when Norm turns Cheers into his own living room. "The nature and quality of a place can sink deep into you," writes Ryden (1993), "influencing and conditioning the way you think, see, and feel, working far down into your very bones by simple virtue of residence and time" (pp. 289–290).

Third, landscapes may activate collective memories, allowing us to feel connected to a social group even when we are alone. I remember being profoundly influenced as a youngster by growing up in the shadow of one of the Oregon Trail's most visible landmarks, Scotts Bluff National Monument, in the Nebraska panhandle. I recall walking with my parents and brother along the wheel ruts carved into the sandstone by the prairie schooners and thinking that somehow the character of the pioneers was embedded in the rock too. And as I walked in their footsteps I felt that I was growing up with some of their fortitude. In this respect landscape serves to connect us to our ancestors as well as to our peers. As Duncan and Ley (1993) point out, "Landscapes consolidate shared meanings; they act as community builders" (p. 17). Years later my memories of the landscape of Scotts

Bluff returned to me as I drove through northwestern New Mexico and read about how the Navajo believe the jagged basalt formation named Shiprock represents the giant bird that brought their ancestors from the north. That connection between place and identity was also reaffirmed for me when I visited Australia and learned of the Aborigines' belief that their landscape was formed by Ancestral Beings in the time before recorded history, which they call Dreamtime (Stock, 1993). The landscapes we are surrounded by, then, may be imbued with sociocultural significance, allowing us to feel connected to others when we are in a particular place.

The primary point made by both humanistic and cultural geographers is worth remembering: our sense of place will influence how we see ourselves and others. In this respect place functions ontologically, as a means of understanding ourselves as beings. Nothstine's (1988) explanation encompasses both forms of geography. He writes, " 'Place,' 'topos,' can suggest not simply location of objects separate and independent from the self, but rather the situation of the self within a world of things and possibilities . . . a particular point of view, a perspective, from which one regards one's world" (p. 155). That Nothstine is a rhetorical scholar not writing about geography emphasizes the relevance geographers' ideas possess for our study of meaning and culture. Both materially and symbolically we want to feel centered, but we do not want to feel alone; we want to be in the middle of a comfortable place where we have company that accepts and reinforces our identity.

Neither geographical approach, however, accounts for the cultural changes that help to generate our desire for a "sense of place." Despite its romantic tendencies, for instance, the humanistic approach focuses on the individual spirit much more so than the communal spirit. Its implication that the individual is an autonomous being capable of comprehending—even transcending—her/his particular environment to discover its essence is decidedly modernist as well (see Rose, 1993, for other indictments of humanistic geography). Traditional cultural geography, on the other hand, does take account of the social aspect of places but seems to suggest these places—and, more important, their meanings—are unchanging. In this respect traditional cultural geographers also neglect part of the cultural context that gives the place its meanings. Studies examining the particular character of a particular place, Massey (1994) claims, assume "a view of place as bounded, as in various ways a site of authenticity, as singular, fixed and unproblematic in its identity" (p. 5).

In romanticizing the function places serve in our attempts to forge individual and community identities, both forms of geography bypass the postmodern possibility that the same collection of rhetorical symbols may be constituted in different forms. For example, the rock formation near my hometown known as Scotts Bluff may be a land-mark on the Oregon Trail to me, but to the descendents of the Sioux living in the area that landmark is the place where Crazy Horse had his vision for unifying the Sioux people—a sense of place never re-layed to me in the 18 years I lived in the area. Finally, humanistic and cultural geographers generally envision a unidirectional flow of influence—the belief that places affect how we see ourselves and others—rather than a reciprocal system in which our identities may influence how we see what lies around us. (These critiques are also noted by Anderson and Gale [1992] as they outline more contempo-rary forms of cultural geography, which I discuss under the cultural studies section in this chapter).

If we are to understand how we envision promised lands, then, we must move from the material to the symbolic or discursive. Human-istic geographers, spurred by Wright's (1947) call to pay attention to "the informal geography contained in non-scientific works" (p. 10), made such a feint in their work with depictions of place in litera-ture (e.g., Pocock, 1981; Porteous, 1990), but most efforts along these lines—including those by communication scholars (e.g., Loukides & Fuller, 1990)—treat place as the scene or setting of the action rather than as an abstract location that may be created through the interac-tion of text, context, and reader. This more fully developed sense of symbolic place/space as "imaginary" places that transcend material conditions is found in the writings of symbolic interactionists, cul-tural studies scholars, and feminist theorists. First, we'll turn to sym-bolic interactionism.

Symbolic Interactionists and the Creation of Situated Accomplishment and Interpretive Communities

Symbolic interactionism relies on the ideas of George Herbert Mead (1934), who proposed that the self is composed of two parts: a creative, expressive "I" and a reflective, analytic "me." The "me" serves as a filter of sorts for the "I" in that the "me" takes into ac-count the perspectives of others as the self is formed. Thus our selves are constructed through interactions with others. Meanings, too, are formed in the process of symbolically interacting with others. Symbolic interactionists, then, see senses of place as co-constructed through communication. Two senses of place, in particular, are high-lighted by symbolic interactionists. First, we co-construct a sense of place in face-to-face communication to engage in a process called "situated accomplishment." Second, we co-construct a sense of place through mediated communication to develop interpretive communities. Both senses of place result from the self and community interacting; thus symbolic interactionism reflects modernist and romantic thinking.

Situated Accomplishment

First, communication between and among individuals is described by many symbolic interactionists as situated accomplishment. Stewart and Philipsen (1984) explain that this phrase means "communication is a process which is situated and situating, is contextualized by and constitutive of society" (p. 178). Stewart and Philipsen (1984) explain that communication as situated accomplishment occurs in two senses: "In the first, it is assumed that speakers and hearers draw deeply from their shared experiences to produce and hear speech, in ways that are finely sensitive to situational context. . . . The second sense . . . [is] on speaking as a process wherein participants constitute a social reality in and through their systematic and artful but creative exploitation of shared resources for spoken life" (p. 212). Another way of conceptualizing this excerpt, and of contextualizing it in our discussion of place, is that physical place influences the communication that occurs within its borders and that the individuals communicating create a shared understanding of their social place.

Situating one's self, then, is a process of identity formation that relies upon our interaction with others as well as manifestations of communities. For instance, Philipsen's (1992) fieldwork in a blue-collar, ethnic neighborhood of Chicago he called Teamsterville revealed "a concern with place [in] every conversation" (p. 4). Not only did a physical place (such as corner tavern, street corner, front porch) influence the communication patterns of its inhabitants, but participants in the conversation wanted to know where others were from, to the degree that "it seemed that every reference to a person included a reference to that person's ethnicity. . . . In addition, where persons stand in relation to each other according to a social code of power and position—a person's place in the social hierarchy—was mentioned directly or indirectly in virtually every conversation in which I participated" (p. 4). In southern California, however, Philipsen (1992) discovered almost the opposite orientation to social place. There conversational participants attempted to generate a discursive convergence so that each person would be in the same social place yet acknowledged as a unique individual. These individuals, explains Philipsen, "believed strongly that one's place in the family, defined by a role such as 'father,' should not be a basis for interrupting or curtailing the speech of others, because each person's contribution is believed to be uniquely valuable" (pp. 5–6). In both instances individuals used communication in an attempt to define themselves as well as their social place in a community, yet the means by which they did so differed dramatically. The practices of the southern Californians, notes Philipsen (1992), "would puzzle and offend a proper Teamsterviller" (p. 6) and vice versa no doubt.

This process of situated accomplishment, like the notion of a sense of place discussed by geographers, involves both modernist and romantic ideals. Initially the modernist element appears in the belief that individuals are uniquely positioned in one place *or* another and that we communicate to improve our selves or to progress. Explain Katriel and Philipsen (1990), we each "inhabit a 'personal space' which can be penetrated through the act of 'communication'; each person is unique and this is a resource to be exploited for one's growth and development; lack-of-growth-through-'communication' equals stagnation, even the loss of identity" (p. 83). In addition Katriel and Philipsen (1990) observe that formal requests for talk function as communication rituals that blend romantic and modernist ideals by defining the self as a sacred object. That is, reaffirming the self through situated accomplishment centers us yet also connects us with others: "Just as prayer takes as its theme man's [*sic*] separation from God, and solves it through ritual acts of obeisance to a deity, so the 'communication' ritual takes as its theme the reality of human separation and solves it through acts of obeisance to the co-construction of selves in and through 'communication'" (Katriel & Philipsen, 1990, p. 91). The promised land sought through situated accomplishment, then, is a location where the sacred self improves through connection with others—a blend of romanticism and modernism.

Interpretive Communities

Because the improving, developing being engages in communion with groups as well as with other individuals, symbolic interactionists have developed a second type of place: the interpretive community. An interpretive community "is characterized by commonalities of purpose and practice in media use, and its members share certain common meanings and ideologies that structure the community's interaction with and reception of media texts" (Carragee, 1990, p. 86). Interpretive communities serve as romantic, discursive sites for identity reinforcement, then; our sacred selves congregate with similar selves to form a community of believers. For example, in a light-hearted interpretive community, individuals who find the popular Latin line dance "the Macarena" (which, oddly enough, was repeatedly performed at a recent Oktoberfest celebration I attended) more perplexing than compelling visit the Web site called "The Macarena Files," where they can discuss how to keep the dance "from destroying civilization as we know it" (Isackson, 1996, p. 11A).

Even individuals reading a book or watching television alone can participate in interpretive communities, I believe, as long as they engage in communication about the story with like-minded others after the fact *or* even imagine themselves to be connected to other fans of the story. Individual viewers of David Letterman's late night talk show, for example, "may not see themselves as experiencing it in isolation," claim Schaefer and Avery (1993, p. 262), because "nearly nine out of 10 (88.9%) of the survey respondents claimed that they regularly discussed the program with family, friends, and coworkers" (pp. 269–270). Thus interpretive communities result from situated accomplishment, not just the properties of the mediated text. In fact Scholes (1985) argues that Fish's (1980) groundbreaking description of interpretive communities posits "that meanings are produced by neither text nor reader but by interpretive communities" (p. 153).

Symbolic interactionist work in media research points to the lure of finding common ground with other individuals in interpretive communities, places where we metaphorically travel to find other fans like ourselves. In addition this research suggests we ritualistically engage in processes of situated accomplishment and interpretive community creation as part of a cyclical desire to build and affirm identity. Unfortunately, a number of weaknesses plague this approach to understanding media stories. Most important, symbolic interactionists' interest in audience members has led most of them to ignore the qualities of stories (e.g., characters, scenes, recurring themes) that can generate symbolic places. As Carragee (1990) notes, "It is ironic that approaches stressing meaning as a product of the interaction between media texts and audience interpretations have provided only limited analyses of those texts" (p. 88). Also little empirical or theoretical attention has been devoted to explaining how individuals who uniquely interpret stories packed with many possible meanings can congregate in interpretive communities, nor is there much discussion about whether we can see our selves in an interpretive community without talking with others. Finally, interpretive communities are not located in particular places in symbolic interactionist analyses; the existence of a community is posited, but its qualities are not explained and terrain rarely envisioned. We may know that fans of *ER* talk about, imagine, and/or negotiate shared interpretations of the television drama, but we do not necessarily gain a rich, thick description of how the members of this community "see" their swatch of cultural landscape. Interpretive communities lack the concrete "sense of place" humanistic geographers say we require to make sense of the terrain around us.

The romantic and modernist qualities found in the work of geographers and symbolic interactionists have generated skepticism and disdain among a group of scholars generally working within the realm of the postmodern. According to these scholars, who inhabit an area called cultural studies, we should be less concerned about defining the alleged stable essence of places—material or symbolic—and more interested in examining how powerful movements may be enacted in various ways in and around those places as a means of creating sites, or spaces, that are open to interpretation. In fact the notion of place is defined as an "evil" of sorts by cultural studies scholars, as we will see in the next section.

Cultural Studies and Moving Through the Spacious Cultural Terrain

Working with a root metaphor of culture as terrain, cultural studies scholars use various metaphors of movement to describe our interactions with the cultural spaces around us. Inspired by postmodernism these scholars are concerned with examining how our symbolic movements are constrained by habitus and how we can resist those constraints to move more freely through the cultural terrain, redefining locations within that terrain in the process. Relying on de Certeau's (1984) distinction between spaces and places—the latter are built within the habitus to confine us, so we must create the former to move symbolically—cultural studies scholars consider the phrase "sense of place" anathema. Instead cultural studies scholars encourage visions of vaguely defined spaces in which movement is relatively unfettered. To reach these spaces cultural studies scholars say we first need to develop map reading skills so that we may avoid powerful forces that may push us off the road. Two general strains of research, then, are found in cultural studies: (1) a mapping project designed to demystify the habitus and (2) a resistance project designed to establish free spaces within the cultural terrain.

Cultural studies mappers believe the temporal nature of the (modernist) promised land narrative of progress disguises inequitable power relations in cultures; the temporal nature of progress, primarily concerned with where we're going, leaves little room for understanding the present spatial relations of power that have been historically reproduced in the habitus. Moreover, they see traditional cultural geography as suggesting that culture is immutable rather than "a process in which people are actively engaged" (Anderson & Gale, 1992, p. 3). Accordingly, they argue for a geographic metaphor that can expose the simultaneous, related, ever-changing nature of cultural practices within the habitus. As Soja (1989) explains, "The discipline imprinted in a sequentially unfolding narrative predisposes the reader to think historically, making it difficult to see the text as a map, a geography of simultaneous relations and meanings that are tied together by a spatial rather than a temporal logic" (p. 1). In short, claims Jackson (1989), "culture is spatially constituted" (p. 3).

Space becomes the preferred term in cultural studies for a number of reasons in addition to its intended function as a counterpoint to the temporal orientation of modernism. In particular de Certeau's (1984) articulation of power being used to establish *circumscribed places* has generated enthusiasm. According to de Certeau, those individuals and institutions with the most power employ what he calls "strategies" to define boundaries for those with less power. A strategy, he says, "postulates a *place* that can be delimited as its *own* and serve as the base from which relations with an *exteriority* composed of targets or threats (customers or competitors, enemies, the country surrounding the city, objectives and objects of research, etc.) can be managed. As in management, every 'strategic' rationalization seeks first of all to distinguish its 'own' place, that is, the place of its own power and will, from an 'environment' " (p. 36; emphasis in original). Places, then, attempt to limit what is acceptable, defining what is proper and reasonable within the habitus. As Harvey (1990) argues, "The assignment of place within a socio-spatial structure indicates distinctive roles, capacities for action, and access to power within the social order" (p. 419). Another motive for privileging space over place emerges from an antinostalgia position. Massey (1994) identifies this motive as drawing "upon the associations of 'a sense of place' with memory, stasis and nostalgia. 'Place' in this formulation was necessarily an essentialist concept which held within it the temptation of relapsing into past traditions" (p. 119) or, in other words, of reaffirming the habitus through the perpetuation of history. Many feminist theorists, too, are wary of the notion of place given the historically powerful images of "women's places" that have been used to confine rather than empower. As Rose (1993) points out, "If the only sense of place offered to women is one based on their role as mother, housewife and shopper, many feminists want nothing to do with it" (pp. 55–56).

Instead space becomes the province of the promised lands, the terrain in which de Certeau (1984) says we carve out our own lands within—and despite—the defining boundaries of the place around us. Calling for guerilla-like interpretive *tactics* such as "poaching" (or redefining) meanings, de Certeau envisions spaces as ambiguous and, as a result, difficult to define by the strategic forces of place. Of this version of promised lands, bell hooks (1990) writes: "Spaces can be real and imagined. Spaces can tell stories and unfold histories. Spaces can be interrupted, appropriated, and transformed through artistic and literary practice" (p. 152). In short, spaces are the creations of people responding to the constraining places established by institutional and historical mechanisms.

To utilize tactics most effectively, cultural studies scholars argue, we need to understand how power is manifested. Borrowing from Jameson's (1984) redefinition of cognitive mapping as "a pedagogical political culture which seeks to endow the individual subject with some new heightened sense of its place in the global system" (p. 92), cultural studies scholars have taken up the cartography of discourse to initiate "the project of mapping the spaces of power" (Grossberg, 1993, p. 7). The primary (though decreasingly popular) image they have generated is that of the cultural terrain as a center with margins. Put simply, the center is composed of those people and ideas that perpetuate cultural practices in which the already powerful dominate the less powerful. Residing in the margin are those people and ideas that espouse practices threatening the center. Generally speaking, the center and margin are described in demographic terms; the center is white, male, heterosexual, and Christian, whereas the margin is everything else. As the voices from the margin agitate for recognition and acceptance, the center moves to assimilate or accommodate their ideas in order to continue its hegemonic power over the culture. The center is a place that attempts to control spaces on the margins of the cultural landscape. For example, Nakayama and Krizek (1995) begin mapping the rhetorical construct of "whiteness," they say, in order to "seek an understanding of the ways that this rhetorical construction makes itself visible and invisible. . . . We see this conceptual move as one that is counterhegemonic, as it challenges the normalizing position of the center, whiteness" (pp. 293, 294).

Counterhegemonic moves, such as the one suggested by Nakayama and Krizek, generally tend to espouse a weakening of the center and a corresponding strengthening of the margins through tactics that redefine the margins as ambiguous spaces where power is manifested. As Shields (1993) elaborates, "Margins, then, while a position of exclusion, can also be a position of power and critique. They expose the relativity of the entrenched, universalising values of the centre" (p. 277). Such a move allows individuals in the margins to operate tactically. For example, hooks (1990) proclaims, "I am located in the margin. I make a definite distinction between that marginality which is imposed by oppressive structures and that marginality one chooses as site of resistance—as location of radical openness and possibility" (p. 153).

The statements in the preceding paragraph also illustrate one of the pitfalls of the mapping project: a tendency to map in the binary terms of center and margin. As Smith and Katz (1993) observe, "Social location, inherently fluid, is inadvertently mapped as absolute" (p. 77). The essentializing of attributes found in identity politics—and dismissed by many cultural studies scholars as oversimplified and static—can simply be translated to a fixed location on the cultural map. "This account implies that geographical terms of reference do the work done by essences in other formulations. It turns a politics of identity into a politics of location," claims Bondi (1993, p. 98). Such a move really accomplishes very little. Although many scholars heed Spivak's (1990) call to uncloak power through "strategic essentializing" (a self-reflexive essentializing), they, too, perpetuate identity politics. Two problems, in particular, erupt from this demographically based approach to cultural criticism. First, politics in a democratic society is coalitional; if residence in different locations on the cultural map precludes understanding of other locations, coalitions will not develop. Second, the master narrative of "majority rules"—which perpetuates marginalization—is enacted *within* the marginal location as differences within the identity are ignored (e.g., Log Cabin Republicans can't be "real" gays if they espouse conservative political beliefs).

In response to the rigid topography of the center-margin map, a number of cultural studies scholars have proposed more dynamic views of the cultural terrain. These views imagine the cultural terrain or space as unbounded, with shifting boundaries and mobile individuals who resist the disempowering forces in their lives through evasion. As Flores (1996) explains, "Creating space means rejecting the dichotomy of either at the margins or in the center" (p. 153). This freedom of movement, garnered through tactical redefinitions of established meanings and texts, allows for continued emancipatory interpretations.

Resisting to Emancipate

Although the mapping project can expose the conventionality of the commonsensical as a construction of the habitus, individuals still must develop a sense of agency or individual power in order to construct discursive spaces from within the places that constitute a habitus. Fiske (1989) says this process "is characterized by the creativity of the weak in using the resources provided by a disempowering system while refusing finally to submit to that power" (p. 47). According to cultural studies scholars, our ability to craft these symbolic promised lands depends upon the notion of cultural mobility; that is, although we may not possess the power to change directly the material conditions that lead to our feeling relatively powerless, we have the capability to travel to different cultural sites, making our own meanings—and creating our own spaces—as we go. Continues Fiske (1989), "The readings we make of a text as we momentarily 'dwell' within it are ours and ours alone" (Fiske, 1989, p. 33).

For example, Fiske (1986) illustrates how we could interpret a scene from the television series *Hart to Hart* in which Mrs. Hart refers to a ship's "window" that reminds her "of a laundromat." Mr. Hart informs her that the technically correct term is *porthole*. This scene can be read as an instance of the feminine "inability to understand or use technical language" or as a feminist effort "to distance her from one traditional connotation of portholes—their romance" (pp. 398, 402). Similarly Bennett and Woollacott (1987) point out that although James Bond books and films can easily be labeled "sexist, racist and reactionary," they provide audiences with the possibility of interpreting additional meanings: "Unless one subscribes to the view that the reading, cinema-going and television publics simply enjoy sexist, racist and reactionary texts, such approaches fail to explain why the Bond forms [books and films] have proved so popular, appealing to readers and viewers of both sexes from across the entire range of social classes, and at different periods of times" (p. 4). Our potential to interpret "against the grain," cultural studies scholars say, emanates from our ability to *move* through the fragments of circulating symbols that permeate our culture. As McGee (1990) argues, stories "provide readers/audiences with dense, truncated fragments which cue *them* to produce a finished discourse in their minds. In short, *text construction is now something done more by the consumers than by the producers of discourse"* (p. 288). Depending upon the scholar, our role as mobile constructors of texts (or, in cultural studies terms, as "subjects who possess agency") is metaphorically described as walkers, travelers, migrants, or nomads.

De Certeau (1984), for instance, uses the images of walking, traveling, and poaching in describing readers of popular culture as nomads: "Readers are travellers; they move across lands belonging to someone else, like nomads poaching their way across fields they did not write, despoiling the wealth of Egypt to enjoy it themselves" (p. 174). Among the scholars who have borrowed from de Certeau, Jenkins's (1988) work analyzing how fans of *Star Trek* act as "textual poachers" is one of the most intriguing. According to Jenkins, fans write their own fiction using the characters of the series but for their own ends. He writes, "For these fans, *Star Trek* is not simply something that can be reread; it is something that can and must be rewritten in order to make it more responsive to their needs, in order to make it a better producer of personal meanings and pleasures" (p. 87). For example, female fans frustrated by the token role played by female characters on the program, rewrote stories to develop a Spock–Nurse Chapel marriage.

Other movement metaphors arise from a number of different scholarly camps. Individuals interested in comparative cultural studies, including those who do postcolonial theorizing, emphasize the value of being between cultures, a site they call the diaspora. There individuals who find themselves living in a culture that is not their "original" culture negotiate the complications associated with a sense of place that is home but not home. Understanding these complications provides us with possibilities for developing agency or a sense of power within space. As Radhakrishnan (1996) explains, "My point is that the diaspora has created rich possibilities of understanding different histories. And these histories have taught us that identities, selves, traditions, and natures do change with travel (and there is nothing decadent or deplorable about mutability) and that we can achieve such changes in identity intentionally" (p. 210). Chambers (1990) makes a similar point. As a Briton living in Italy, he writes, he discovered how to see and understand his own, and another, culture; his travel afforded emancipation from his previously restricted point of view.

The specific image of travel is preferred by Clifford (1992), who proposes "a comparative cultural studies approach" that examines the reciprocal processes of traveling and dwelling; "this is not nomadology," he claims (p. 108). Clifford admits he is less than comfortable with his metaphor given that " 'travel' has an inextinguishable taint of location by class, gender, race, and a certain literariness" (p. 110), a point that Gregory (1994) makes as well in his critique of the image. Chambers (1994), in later work, also finds the travel metaphor too confining and suggests "migrancy" as an alternative. "For to travel," he says, "implies movement between fixed positions, a site of departure, a point of arrival, the knowledge of an itinerary. . . . Migrancy, on the contrary, involves a movement in which neither the points of departure nor those of arrival are immutable or certain" (p. 5). Falling somewhere between these two options is Braidotti's (1994) feminist-inspired resuscitation of Clifford's dismissed nomad (first proposed, to my knowledge, by Deleuze & Guattari, 1986). Ironically, she echoes his emphasis on the need for dwelling while traveling, yet she finds the constant travel in the image of nomadism appealing as well. The result is a nomad that is not a migrant or an exile or a traveler but a character who "has relinquished all idea, desire, or nostalgia for fixity" (p. 22), while acknowledging that "being a nomad, living in transition, does not mean that one cannot or is unwilling to create those necessarily stable and reassuring bases for identity that allow one to function in a community" (p. 33).

Braidotti's nomadism illustrates one of the weaknesses of the cultural studies approach: promoting the postmodern ideal of constant movement, it has difficulty accounting for the need to function from a particular position (e.g., the centered self of modernism). Lurking under the surface of this conundrum is a creature we visited briefly in the previous chapter: the postmodern shadow of modernism. No matter how fluid cultural studies scholars envision space and/or movement within it, they simply cannot avoid the dualism of "here" and "there" that is inherent in *any* geographical metaphor. Even if a person is temporarily located in a space, and even if s/he possesses multiple identities, s/he is at a particular cultural/physical place ("here") that is not some other place ("there"); even if determining where here and there are located is increasingly difficult, as Meyrowitz (1985) claims, we require—and thus create—points of view to serve as "here."

Modernism also rears its ugly (to postmodernists) head in the cartographic impulse to map that saturates much cultural studies work. "Maps are representations which employ a rhetoric of accuracy," note Pile and Rose (1992); "they are an attempt to bring a rational order to an unknown topography. To draw a map implies a knowing perspective, whether from the 'sky' or from the 'street'" (p. 132). Maps attempt to represent fixed, verifiable knowledge (e.g., we know the North Platte River flows between my hometown of Scottsbluff and the neighboring town of Gering; we can observe the river's course and chart it on a map), yet cultural studies work emphasizes multiple, shifting points of view that seem incommensurate with a mapping metaphor. Finally, the motivation for mapping emerges from the modernist grand narrative of progress; if we understand how power is reflected in cultural spaces and places, we can improve our society. Theorizing that cultural studies scholars may interpret as promoting ideas that inhibit progress is decried as backward. Massey (1994), for example, points out that postmodernists are generally hostile to nostalgia because it leads to "the comfort of Being instead of forging ahead with the (assumed progressive) project of Becoming" (p. 119). Similarly Harvey (1990) decries work valorizing a "sense of place" because it emphasizes "being" and has been (and can be) used to justify regressive beliefs.

Space is problematic in another sense as well, for the mappers are the individuals drawing our attention to these locations on the cultural map, thereby reinforcing a modernist "master-narrative of power over space" (Gregory, 1994, p. 128). That means "the spaces in which struggle may or should occur are being defined for the oppressed rather than by them," write Pile and Rose (1992, p. 133). Many feminist scholars are rightfully disturbed by this element of the space-mapping project. Jardine (1985) and Price-Chalita (1994), for example, claim postmodernism's desire to map space reflects patriarchy's concern with knowing the Other. "Knowing the Other through observation and spatial cataloguing (for example, by mapping)," writes Price-Chalita (1994), "is essential for controlling and dominating the Other" (p. 249). Women, in particular, are the targets of this mapping because women have been traditionally associated with space and men with time (e.g., Mother Nature, Father Time; see Pile, 1994). Under modernism patriarchal efforts were directed toward mastering time, whereas women were left to drift in space. But as women established locations for themselves in the cultural landscape and were able to "see" their oppression from their new perspectives, patriarchal forces responded with a postmodern interest in understanding space. "In other words," claims Price-Chalita (1994), "women and the space they occupy are getting out of control, and in order to control one must know" (p. 249). She concludes that "postmodern and feminist theorists do indeed seem to be appropriating the spatial to different ends" (p. 251).[1]

Not surprisingly, then, feminist theorists have led the move to imagining a more locatable, modernist form of cultural terrain. Understandably upset with the way "postmodernism assimilates feminist contributions" (Bondi & Domosh, 1992, p. 205), many feminist scholars take issue with the relativist assumptions that underlie most of the movement metaphors found in the image of cultural space. For example, if migrants and exiles and nomads never settle, they should find it difficult to "make sense" (in humanistic geography terms) of the cultural terrain. As Haraway (1988) argues, relativism functions as a totalization in that "both deny the stakes in location, embodiment, and partial perspective; both make it impossible to see well" (p. 584). Recognizing the necessity of being located in a particular "here," many feminist theorists promote the theory of standpoint epistemology, a theory that in many ways returns to humanistic geography's explanation of unique "ways of seeing" the world.

Feminist Theorists and Situated Knowledges/ Standpoint Epistemologies

The image of cultural wanderings leaves many feminist scholars uneasy. On the one hand, although their work has made a substantial contribution to cultural studies' efforts to shatter the myth of meanings as universal and "commonsensical," one of the primary results of that work is the removal of privilege from any position, including that of female voices. In this respect the postmodern turn leaves feminists back where they started: voiceless and positionless. As the following paragraphs make clear, many feminist theorists are uncomfortable with the notion that an essential feminist voice exists, yet they find little solace in postmodernism's option of no voice embodying the slightest essentialist twang. Theoretically, then, a number of feminist scholars have found a haven in the sense of place afforded by standpoint epistemology, the belief that rhetorical voices are plural yet situated in a particular location that gives the voice character. In short, standpoint epistemology attempts to center the self by locating it within a community.

Standpoint epistemologists work in the gaps between cultural studies and geography. Calhoun (1995) summarizes its basic tenets: "On the one hand the idea of standpoint is rooted in the notion of concrete, experiencing subjects. On the other hand, the idea of standpoint employs a categorical logic to analyze positions in social structure [habitus]" (p. 171). Like humanistic geographers, then, standpoint theorists suggest our different experiences provide us with a different sense of being centered. According to Wood (1992), standpoint theory suggests "individuals interpret their own experiences and imbue them with meaning" (p. 13). Like cultural geographers, standpoint theorists also acknowledge that one's experiences are tied to one's cultural or community position. Explains Wood, "Some [perspectives] are more partial than others since different locations within social hierarchies affect what is likely to be seen" (p. 13). And like cultural studies scholars, standpoint theorists argue that the habitus is the product of a naturalized history that limits possible viewpoints. Standpoint theory, explains Calhoun (1995), can "reveal aspects of social organization that tended to remain hidden by the reproduction of the standpoint of men as though it were gender-free and universal" (p. 167). Perhaps the tie that all geographers and cultural studies scholars share with standpoint theorists can be located in the body. For feminist theorists the body is one of the central reasons why women have different vantage points or visions; historically (and still today) possessing a woman's body meant the individual had limited or no access to parts of the cultural terrain. Cultural studies makes note of these "no trespassing" signs—Braidotti (1994), in fact, calls nomadism "the intense desire to go on trespassing, transgressing" (p. 36)—and humanistic geography observes that "geographical experience is fundamentally mediated by the body, [that] it begins and ends with the body" (Rodaway, 1994, p. 31).

As these three perspectives indicate, "vision" serves as a key metaphor for knowing because it acknowledges that different bodies have different forms of mobility within the habitus. The perspective propagated by habitus is thus not universal but partial, as are the viewpoints that provide alternative visions. Accordingly, standpoint theorists generally do not privilege a particular point of view (e.g., feminist). Instead they argue for understanding all points of view as partial. "A number of feminist theorists," Calhoun (1995) affirms, "have turned to the notion that better observation and reasoning will come not from invoking a fixed subject position but rather from recognizing the contradictions in many—perhaps all—subject positions" (p. 181).

Standpoint epistemology's discussion of cultural place reflects a meshing of the narratives of modernism and postmodernism. According to standpoint feminists, multiple points of view exist (postmodernism), yet each of these vantage points afford a somewhat transcendent or objective view of the cultural terrain (modernism). We are located in a particular "here," the awareness of which allows us to understand its limitations; we acknowledge that different views are possible in the numerous "theres" that exist all around us. Explains Haraway (1988), "Feminist objectivity means quite simply *situated knowledges*" (p. 581; emphasis in original). Being situated, moreover, provides us with the confidence to engage the forces of power that dominate the cultural terrain. As Price-Chalita (1994) emphasizes, "A standpoint implies a positionality, a ground upon which to stand, and a site for resistance" (p. 240).

This language of resistance, you might recall, evokes the images discussed under cultural studies; it also differs from cultural studies in its implication that one is "stuck" in one's standpoint, unable to move, while simultaneously claiming some sort of privileged, transcendent perspective that Denzin (1997) calls an ocular epistemology (knowing through seeing). Feminist theorists and cultural studies scholars can thus be allies or antagonists; some individuals even define themselves as both. In fact cultural studies scholars have used an implicit standpoint epistemology in many of their demographically oriented studies. Hall (1989), for instance, speaks of "the astonishing return to the political agenda of all those points of attachment which give the individual some sense of 'place' and position in the world, whether these be in relation to particular communities, localities, territories, languages, religions or cultures" (p. 133).

These points of attachment, however, can suggest static images of the cultural terrain. If one's marginalized demographic status, for instance, is unchanging, the map must forever be envisioned as a center-margins dichotomy. In response some feminist theorists/ cultural studies scholars have combined the theories of movement and standpoint epistemology to propose a more dynamic culture in which the formation of alliances is possible. Flores's (1996) examination of Chicana literature, for example, leads her to conclude, "Chicana feminists proclaim their identity and create for themselves not only a space but a home in which they can overcome feelings of isolation and alienation" (p. 145). Yet from this position or standpoint, she says, purposeful cultural journeys are possible, even desirable. Using the metaphor of building bridges across cultural gaps, Flores argues that "such a process allows for the construction of boundaries that establish the Chicana feminist homeland as distinct but are flexible enough to allow for interaction with other homelands" (p. 146).

Flores's language hints at the interconnections among romanticism, modernism, and postmodernism that are possible in our theorizing about popular culture. Chicana feminists are located in a particular home or here, yet they are not content to engage the cultural terrain from only this vantage point. Instead they also travel across bridges to learn to see from different vistas; they seek the wisdom of other communities, the experiences of other selves. This playful traveling is also purposeful and reflects Gergen's (1991) advice that postmodernism benefits from an interaction with romanticism: "To play is admirable, but play that is simply deconstructive doesn't recognize the possible interconnections among us all" (p. 194).

Rather than envisioning these standpoints as positions of empowerment, however, some cultural studies scholars speak of them as merely functional, perhaps even illusory, havens of security. Grossberg (1993), for one, notes "people can stop and *place* themselves" during their travels (p. 14; emphasis in original). "Such places," he claims, "are temporary points of belonging and identification, of investment and empowerment. Such places create temporary addresses or homes" (p. 14). Yet he also invokes the spectre of the modernist machine when he describes these homes as the product of "a territorializing machine [that] attempts to map the sorts of places people can occupy and how they can occupy them. It maps how much room people have to move, and where and how they can move" (p. 15). This language is of course reminiscent of de Certeau's description of powerful institutional forces constructing places of containment that constrain our ability to move to other standpoints or to create new spaces in the cultural terrain.

Standpoint epistemology, then, is a theory that can be used for a number of different purposes: to establish an unchanging position, to chart paths to other communities, and/or to claim locations are generated for, not by, individuals. In the remainder of this chapter, and throughout the next, I argue for a version of standpoint epistemology that most closely resembles the second purpose. The first and third versions, in my mind, allow very little room for movement or hope, both of which—I think—provide an incentive to travel symbolically away from one's "established" or circumscribed place, to use de Certeau's language. These versions of standpoint epistemology instead suggest cultural studies' goal of demystification is unattainable (maps are constantly being redrawn to create places that usurp spaces), and when that happens, says Krippendorff (1995), the second stage of emancipation in cultural studies' logic becomes impossible; if the forces constraining action are not definable, always changing their identity, the struggle to demystify and emancipate seems pointless. A more productive response, claims Krippendorff (1995), is "not to fix blame but to construct a lever by which one can bootstrap oneself out of the feeling of entrapment, to assume a position from which one can see possibilities for contestation, to shape the relationship one finds burdensome" (p. 123).

That said, I would like to propose an alternative metaphor of discursively created cultural terrain. Rather than envisioning this territory as a collection of ambiguous spaces colonized by powerful and constraining places, I suggest a metaphor of cultural terrain as a collection of known, changing places that we redefine in a struggle with those people and forces who attempt to limit our definitional choices through a reliance on the rules of the habitus. This metaphor emphasizes understanding how individuals and groups work with rhetoric to create places of security and power for themselves, despite others' use of rhetoric to constrain those options. The concern is less with how texts and structures of power invisibly work to maintain power relations and more on how individuals and groups *use* these texts to establish their own positions of power. In other words, the aim of scholars using this metaphor would be to understand how we center ourselves in a "here" to gain a sense of discursive and cultural power. We need places that matter, not ambiguous spaces, as a base for these rhetorical operations.

Such a move does not admit to the impossibility of changing power relations. Rather it marks a change of strategy, a revalorization of the less powerful. As Krippendorff (1995) argues, "History tells us that domination may also be eroded by withdrawing the kind of loyalties, obedience and admiration on which such authorities depend by either invoking higher authorities . . . or conceptually side stepping the resources along which obedience was commanded" (p. 125). In many ways I am suggesting something similar to de Certeau's (1984) vision of rhetorical guerilla warfare. Rather than operating on the fringes of the cultural landscape, making and breaking camps of spaces, we tunnel underneath, through, and around the heart of the habitus to establish secure, comfortable places that remain open for future visits. This tunneling, as Krippendorff suggests, does indeed "erode" the cultural landscape.

Purposeful Movement, A Sense of Place, Openness to New Perspectives

In the following chapter I develop in more detail an image of the cultural terrain that borrows a pinch of this and a dash of that from the four conversational strands outlined in this chapter. In essence I engage in a de Certeau–influenced practice of *theoretical poaching* in which I assemble the ingredients/ideas of other authors to concoct a newer dish that may not exactly reflect what the master chefs had in mind but that is nonetheless (I hope) an appetizing vision. Before presenting this creation in the next chapter, however, let me offer a summary/preview of what ingredients I believe are necessary for individuals who wish to cook up some theory about how we use popular stories to travel to promised lands and back again.

First, we need to account for multiple viewpoints. Cultural studies says we bring unique interpretations to texts and argues for the acknowledgment of marginalized voices, and standpoint epistemology claims our vision is limited by our perspective. Together these approaches suggest multiple stories are being told from a variety of points of view. No universal grand narrative is possible; but developing understandings of multiple, situated grand narratives is feasible, and is the postmodern foundation of this recipe.

Second, we need to explain how/why we seek connections with

others. Cultural geography finds this sense of community in physical landmarks, symbolic interactionism in interpretive communities. To some extent standpoint epistemology and cultural studies observe this necessity in their formulations of group perspectives. Although their approaches are too demographics bound for my tastes, Haraway's (1991) corrective of "affinities" is an appealing place to start. With affinities, she says, connections are forged "not by blood but by choice" (p. 155); I interpret her idea to mean that our beliefs rather than our demographic characteristics lead us to communal connections (others may disagree with my interpretation, while agreeing with the need to shift from a demographics orientation; see Larner, 1995, for example). As Haraway argues in an earlier (1988) work, "Subjugation is not grounds for an ontology" (p. 586). Community generates spirit and suggests we are located in a particular "here," making it resonate with the romantic and modernist narratives.

Third, we need to envision individual power, or what cultural studies scholars call agency. Humanistic geographers accord us the ability to center our selves through our sense-making abilities, and cultural studies scholars give us the capacity to make unique meanings from mass-produced texts. To a lesser extent cultural studies and standpoint epistemology ascribe to us the power to resist. Certainly the habitus constrains our freedom, but without a sense of agency or movement we are unable to act within these conditions. Even symbolic power has the potential to transform the material. This belief resides of course in both the modernist narrative (the transcendent individual able to progress) and the romantic narrative (the individual imbued with the communal power of spirit).

Fourth, we need to show how we can move meaningfully. Our awareness of multiple viewpoints comes from the individual power to move to different communities. Humanistic geographers say we reconfigure the world around us as we move. Cultural geographers claim we recognize the communal power of physical landscapes as we move. Symbolic interactionists argue we belong to multiple interpretive communities. Cultural studies scholars provide us with the symbolic ability to move through cultural space. When we move we exercise the spirit, seek to progress, and recognize the partiality of our experiences through critical play. When we move we enact all three narratives.

Our symbolic travels, then, will allow us to sample the experiences of others, fill ourselves with a sense of community, and taste the freedom of symbolic movement. The cooking metaphor is of course intentional. Just as enjoying different dishes represents a journey from the here and now to someplace new and exciting, consuming popular culture offers us the opportunity to whip up our own fulfilling promised lands. Moreover, during these journeys we can experience the stories of romanticism, modernism, and postmodernism—frequently during the same story. From the cook's postmodern playfulness and cannibalistic revenge in *The Cook, The Thief, His Wife, and Her Lover*, to the chef's modern nostalgia as his daughters moved away from home in *Eat, Drink, Man, Woman*, to the romantic equating of food and love in *Like Water for Chocolate* popular stories provide an appetizing array of promised lands. How we get from here to there is the subject of the next chapter.

Note

1. Some feminist theorists, however, appreciate postmodern theory for its challenging of an objective or neutral point of view. See Ritzer (1997, pp. 187–193) for a brief overview—and several citations of original works—of the relationship between feminist theory and postmodernism.

3

Symbolic Pilgrimages

Experiencing Popular Stories as Purposeful, Imaginary-Yet-Real Journeys

As the preceding pages have demonstrated, I believe a theory for understanding how fans read popular stories must account for the interconnections among modernism, romanticism, and postmodernism. In particular I believe we require a theory that sees fan encounters with popular stories as a communicative experience in which we are centered selves able to move symbolically, in a variety of ways, to communities that provide an alternative to historical habitus. Whether we have recognized the constraints of habitus since our early years, have recently become aware of its limiting qualities, or implicitly understand its manifestations only on rare occasions, we yearn to travel from the comforts and constraints of our home/habitus to reach someplace special: a promised land. Lacking a clear sense of a *single* promised land in a culture where material conditions have all but erased traditional dominant visions of past promised lands, or having been omitted from the rhetorical process of constructing these traditional promised lands, we create our own symbolic promised lands as a means of making sense out of the disorientations—material and otherwise—we routinely experience (this definition of promised lands does not eliminate the possibility of individuals crafting personal promised lands that rely heavily upon modernist and/or romantic ideals). Our personal promised lands can be multiple and playful as postmodernists encourage, yet they will also encourage a spiritual sense of communion with others and offer a transcendent perspective of the cultural terrain.

Symbolic pilgrimages acknowledge the inevitability of a postmodern consumer-oriented culture and use its tools to chisel at its foundation. That is, rather than repeating the actions of the Luddites (who, when faced with the new emphasis on machines during the advent of the Industrial Revolution, destroyed the machines), we also make our machines work *for* us. Instead of simply focusing on the technological and spiritual shortcomings of our interactions with machines, we also take advantage of the proliferation of popular stories generated by the very development of our technological machines. In so doing we are not avoiding addressing the changes in our material conditions, as some scholars would argue (a point I address more fully later in this chapter), but we are extracting rhetorical resources from our symbolic pilgrimages to help us address those conditions. In short, we are miners of meanings.

Our excavations are paradoxical. We use our power as consumers to engage in symbolic sojourns that transcend a consumerist culture. In using the technology of postindustrialism to access the stories, we can contribute to the sense of displacement discussed in chapter one. Yet in repeatedly immersing ourselves in those stories, we also counter the debilitating effects of the technology and its manifestations in a postmodern culture. This countering process works in two ways, both of which undergird the idea of symbolic pilgrimages. First, as Brummett and Duncan (1992) argue in their updating of Marshall McLuhan's ideas, we can consider "media as extensions of the self," not simply technology that distances us from our surroundings (p. 247). Such an image is similar to Haraway's (1991) suggestion (within the context of feminist theory) that we can find power—not just constraints—in our interactions with technology by envisioning ourselves as cyborgs, humans who have integrated ourselves with technology. Media become extensions of our imaginations. Second, the popular stories we revisit, as Lipsitz (1990) points out, become part of our collective cultural memory. We need not have a material connection to someone to share memories and a feeling of community with that individual if we can go to the library to read the same books, open the daily newspaper to read the same syndicated comic strips, go to the video store to rent the same movies, and turn on the television to watch the same sitcom. As postindustrialism facilitates the sharing of these stories through technology, the shared stories serve an orienting function, allowing our selves to feel centered within an imagined community (Beardslee, 1990). As Eberle (1994) argues, "Narrative allows us to reimagine our lives, not merely rethink them. In the story we also refeel how it is to be human and we reawaken the long dormant experience of being alive and connected" (p. 110). Imagining alternatives, as Goodall (1996) argues, is the first step toward enacting those alternatives.

Building on this general foundation, I hope to show how the specific image of symbolic pilgrimages permits us to be epistemologically mobile agents. We experience the perspectives of others (postmodern), yet we remain ontologically centered, transcendent selves who exist in a particular "here" rather than a particular "there" at a point in time (modern), and we bathe in the spiritual communitas, sharing our identities with like-minded souls (romantic). I'll return to this triple-feature later in the chapter (consider it "a preview of coming attractions"). For now, let me begin to explain how something as mundane and profane as watching television or reading a book can attain the sacred shape of a pilgrimage.

Pilgrimage, Communitas, and The Liminal/Liminoid

Anthropologist Victor Turner has written volumes (one with his spouse Edith) about the sacred notions of ritual and pilgrimage. Pilgrimages, in short, are ritual journeys that separate us from our homes, immerse us in a liminal experience as we visit a sacred place called a shrine, and reaggregate us at home with a new perspective. Before discussing the ritualistic nature of pilgrimage, however, I turn to two of its central concepts: the liminal/liminoid and communitas.

The Liminal/Liminoid

Liminality, according to Turner, is both a state and a process in which a ritual transition occurs. In rites of passage liminality refers to the indescribable time when the individual has left the past but has not yet arrived at his/her destination. This passage of time also marks a spatial change, for completing a rite of passage typically allows the participant to claim a new place in the cultural terrain. Liminality is the time of the journey encompassed by the leaving, arrival, and return—exclusive of the moment of separation upon leaving and the moment of reaggregation upon return; departure and return mark not only points of time outside of the liminal but points in cultural space where one's place or position is settled. Liminality is "a movement between fixed points [that] is essentially ambiguous, unsettled, and unsettling" (Turner, 1974, p. 274); it is a "no-place and no-time that resists classification" (Turner & Turner, 1978, p. 250) and is found not just in rites of passage but in "all phases of decisive cultural change" (Turner & Turner, 1978, p. 2).

The phrase "all phases of decisive cultural change" suggests that liminality may be both enjoyable and terrible. For example, as chapter one details, our awkward transition to a postindustrial economy, and the social ramifications of such a move, may reflect nationwide liminality. On the other hand, when we engage popular stories, we may find ourselves moving from the mundane to the sacred, and we may enjoy tremendously that individual liminality. Thus "liminality may be . . . the milieu of creative interhuman or transhuman satisfactions and achievements . . . [or] it may be anomie, alienation, angst, the fatal 'alpha' sisters of many modern myths" (Turner, 1983, p. 149).

Because the idea of liminality developed from the study of mandatory tribal rituals, Turner posits that the term is insufficient to capture the variety of experiences encountered in more technical worlds. Accordingly, he introduces the term *liminoid* ("resembling liminality") to describe the increasingly optional ritual experiences found in industrial and postindustrial societies. Liminal experiences, he says, "are centrally integrated into the total social process," whereas liminoid experiences "develop apart from the central economic and political processes, along the margins, in the interfaces and interstices of central and servicing institutions—they are plural, fragmentary, and experimental in character" (Turner, 1983, p. 158). To envision the distinction between the two experiences, we can recast the examples used in the previous paragraph. The postindustrial transition is "mandatory" and "centrally integrated" into the culture, making it a liminal experience. Immersing one's self in a popular story is an optional move (although it is made possible by the technology of a postindustrial economy), making it a liminoid experience. To contextualize these differences within my general argument, we find our socioeconomic liminal experience to be unsettling and thus turn to the liminoid as a means of finding alternatives to the anomie. Or as Turner (1983) summarizes, "One *works at* the liminal, one *plays with* the liminoid" (p. 159; emphasis in original).

Communitas

Assuaging the ambiguity experienced in liminality through liminoid play produces communitas, a special sense of togetherness that exists outside the habitus. According to Turner (1983), communitas resists habitus (he uses the phrase "social structure") by providing a contrast or alternative to it. Communitas, he (1983) says, may be said to exist more in contrast than in active opposition to social structure, as an alternative and more "liberated" way of being socially human, a way of both being detached from social structure (and hence potentially of periodically evaluating its performance) and also of a "distanced" or "marginal" person's being more attached to other disengaged persons (and hence, sometimes of evaluating a social structure's historical performance in common with them). *Here we may have a loving union of the structurally damned pronouncing judgment on normative structure and providing alternative models for structure.* (p. 154; emphasis added)

Four characteristics of communitas illustrate its potential to provide alternative models. First, communitas *releases* us from habitus. "Structures, like most species, get specialized; communitas . . . remains open and unspecialized, a spring of pure possibility as well as the immediate realization of release from day-to-day structural necessities and obligatoriness" (Turner, 1974, p. 202). Second, communitas *transcends* habitus because it, in Bourdieu's (1980/1990) terms cited in the introduction, "neutralizes the sense of social realities" (p. 64). Explains Turner (1974), "Communitas is almost always thought of or portrayed by actors as a timeless condition, an eternal now, as 'a moment in and out of time,' or as a state to which the structural view of time is not applicable" (p. 238). Third, communitas provides a perspective from which to *critique* the habitus. As we are released from the habitus and rise above it, we are able to see how its notions of "common sense" have been naturalized through history. Thus "from the point of view of those who control and maintain the social structure, all manifestations of communitas, sacred or profane, are potentially subversive" (Turner & Turner, 1978, p. 32). Finally, communitas *generates respect* for additional alternative perspectives. Because pilgrimages offer "an alternative mode of social being, a world where communitas, rather than a bureaucratic social structure, is preeminent . . . a respect may grow for the pilgrimages of others" (Turner & Turner, 1978, p. 39).

Yet communitas also possesses the potential to harden into habitus. In such cases "the experience of communitas becomes the memory of communitas, with the result that communitas itself in striving to replicate itself historically develops a social structure" (Turner, 1983, p. 150). As we saw in chapter one, dominant visions of promised lands in the United States provided at one time a sense of communitas for some citizens, yet many of us now consider these images part and parcel of our habitus. Thus a new kind of communitas is sought. This is where we are today: the communitas held out to us in the form of dominant visions of promised lands is seen by many as unattainable, even for those who purchased the visions.

Communitas gains the power to critique—and risks petrifying into habitus—through repetition. Thus individuals who seek communitas frequently engage in rituals to harness its symbolic energy. The importance of ritual lies in the notion that "if communitas can be developed within a ritual pattern it can be carried over into secular life for a while and help to mitigate or assuage some of the abrasiveness of social conflicts rooted in conflicts of material interest or discrepancies in the ordering of social relations" (Turner, 1974, p. 56). Unlike many modernist definitions of ritual that treat it as *simply* reinforcing established patterns of behavior and beliefs, then, Turner envisions the ritual associated with pilgrimage also as a possible challenge to those established patterns. Pilgrimage is undertaken as a purposeful escape from an unsatisfactory habitus, and it provides like-minded individuals with an opportunity to experience the communitas they find lacking.

Pilgrimages work through both the individual and the collective to achieve their power. Simply commencing a pilgrimage activates the affective bonds experienced in communitas, Turner claims, because pilgrims begin the journey of their own volition and meet individuals who have made similar choices along the road. Here Turner relies on the work of Mihaly Csikszentmihalyi, who discovered that individuals engaged in intense play found themselves in what he calls "a flow experience": "Flow denotes the wholistic sensation present when we act with total involvement. . . . We experience it as a unified flowing from one moment to the next, in which we feel in control of our actions, and in which there is little distinction between self and environment; between stimulus and response; or between past, present, and future" (Csikszentmihalyi, 1975, p. 43). Csikszentmihalyi argues that rules are required to generate the focus mandated by a flow experience, yet Turner (1983) claims "communitas has something of a 'flow' quality, but it may arise, and often does arise, spontaneously and unanticipated—it does not need rules to trigger it off" (p. 162). The primary difference between flow and communitas, explains Turner (1983), is that individuals experience "flow," but communitas requires a group experience. Perhaps the best way to envision the pilgrimage process, then, is as a journey that resembles a flow experience and that generates an increasingly stronger sense of communitas as the pilgrim encounters other pilgrims and/or gets closer to the shrine. "The decision to go on pilgrimage takes place within the individual but brings him [sic] into fellowship with like-minded souls, both on the way and at the shrine. The social dimension is generated by the individual's choice, multiplied many times" (Turner & Turner, 1978, p. 31).

As Turner (1974) emphasizes, the *combination* of the individual's journey and the sacred destination work to generate communitas: "Shrines exerted a magnetic effect on a whole communications system, charging up with sacredness many of its geographical features and attributes and fostering the construction of sacred and secular edifices to service the needs of the human stream passing along its arterial routes. Pilgrimage centers, in fact, generate a 'field' " (pp. 225–226). For instance, for many fans of the University of Nebraska's (my alma mater) football team, a home game takes on the dimension of a ritual pilgrimage. After rising the morning of the game, a Husker fan will don some combination of red apparel that would not otherwise make it out the door of a thrift store, let alone a middle-class closet. The morning stops on the way to the early afternoon game follow a predictable pattern, depending on one's route to the shrine. For people like myself the route includes a stop at the Sidetrack bar to sing along with Joyce and Paul as they belt out television themes, oldies, and—every 30 minutes or so—the Husker fight song; then it's on to a particular tailgate party and/or a stop at a Runza stand (a curious, but delicious, sandwich of beef, spices, and cabbage packed in an enclosed oblong bun). This morning route will bring the fan into contact with other "pilgrims" embarking on similar journeys, all of whom are winding their way to the shrine: Memorial Stadium, the unofficial third largest city in Nebraska, where they—now 76,000 strong—will worship the red-and-white clad practitioners of the state's secular religion. Together they celebrate the state's superiority over more populous "sophisticated" rivals, a time of communitas in which the "hick" fans transcend the social structure that has so named them to bask in their superiority as people who worked the ground (Nebraska's offense loves to run the ball) and withstood ferocious elements (a stout defense is such a hallmark of the team that its top defenders are called "blackshirts" for the honorary jerseys they wear in practice) to turn the great American desert into a core part of America's breadbasket. That this celebration has been sold out every time since 1962 clearly marks it as a ritualistic pilgrimage. The communitas these fans experience infuses the pilgrimage with a powerful romantic undercurrent as its participants experience "sharing, participation, association, fellowship, and the possession of a common faith," according to Carey's (1975, p. 6) definition of ritual communication.

In the anthropological vision of Turner, then, pilgrims follow different routes to an alternative, sacred place where they might develop a sense of communitas that responds to the status quo of their habitus. Their journey to and arrival at the shrines of their choosing bring them into contact with members who share their frustrations and beliefs. In the process of making this journey pilgrims also develop a healthy respect for others who make their own pilgrimages. Certainly this depiction of pilgrimage contains elements of the romantic, modern, and postmodern. The sacred, spiritual nature of communitas suggests an enhanced knowledge of one's (and others') self. The existence of specific shrines in specific places, in conjunction with the belief in the development of transcendental perspective, smacks of modernism. Yet the implicit critique of dominant beliefs, the awareness gained of others' perspectives, and the simultaneous existence in the material and imaginative worlds of communitas intersect to provide the pilgrimage with a postmodern flavor.

Symbolic Pilgrimages: The Process

To make Turner's description of pilgrimage resonate with our experience as fans of popular stories, we need to envision encounters with these stories as lived symbolic experiences. Before I proceed with a definition of symbolic pilgrimages, however, I want to note that I am by no means the first to suggest pilgrimage as a means of describing cultural experience. Neumann (1993), for instance, illustrates how an alternative group travel experience through the southwestern United States on a bus nicknamed "The Ark" reflects Turner's ideas: "The trip on The Ark had been much like a pilgrimage through the American Southwest. We had made our way to a series of sites (like the religious shrines of more traditional pilgrimages) that provided a source of personal renewal and reflection. Perhaps more significant, though, was how the journey encouraged a liminality that moved us toward communitas" (p. 229). Neumann's description of this cultural experience is similar to what I believe we experience when we ritualistically reencounter popular stories, but the alternative travel experiences I discuss involve journeys of the *mind* that *intersect* with materiality. Thus my use conception of pilgrimage is more closely aligned with Vande Berg (1995), who defines the ritual revisitation on television of John F. Kennedy's assassination as "living room pilgrimages" that serve "the same individual and societal functions for television's heterogeneous living room pilgrims as corporeal pilgrimages do" (p. 48).

Vande Berg's living room pilgrimages are clearly an inspiration for my work. In the course of this book I hope to extend and elaborate this concept by identifying how *all* forms of popular stories can encourage symbolic pilgrimages among their devoted and avid fans. As Janice Radway (1984) points out in her analysis of the denigrated genre of romance novels, even stories considered to be lurking about near the bottom of the good-taste "food chain" can provide readers with a very powerful, meaningful symbolic experience—one that carries over, so to speak, into material, lived experiences. Radway's particular critical take on popular stories, however, leads her to suggest that because "these women [i.e., readers of romance novels] never get together to share either the experience of imaginative opposition, or, perhaps more important, the discontent that gave rise to their need for romance in the first place" (p. 212), their symbolic escapes are largely irrelevant to changing their lived experiences. This emphasis on direct material change seems to undergird Clifford's (1992) rejection of "pilgrimage" as his key image (in favor of "travel"); as he explains, "Its 'sacred' meanings tend to predominate" (p. 110). Although Clifford attempts to avoid what he no doubt perceives as the stigma of romanticism with his disdain of the sacred, I want to embrace the spiritual dimension of pilgrimage in my discussion of how our encounters with popular culture are at once romantic, modern, and postmodern.

In so doing I will emphasize how *indirect* changes in our material conditions may occur through our symbolic pilgrimages. At the foundation of this claim, which I explore in further detail in the pages that follow, is Carey's (1975) definition of communication as "a symbolic process whereby reality [as we have come to know it] is produced, maintained, repaired and transformed" (p. 10). This definition assumes that communication, in whatever form it takes, *makes a difference.* Our sense of "reality"—the intersection of material and symbolic terrains—cannot help but be changed as we participate in the symbolic process of communication, for that process is continually producing, maintaining, repairing, and transforming the collision of symbols and material conditions that constitute our habitus. Even when communication "maintains," it also produces change in its users, since maintenance involves at the least the rhetorical reinforcement of the habitus in the face of symbolic challenges (a change in degree if not in kind), as well as the negotiation of those challenging discourses.

With Carey's definition of communication as context, let me provide a brief summary/preview of how I envision the imaginary-yet-real journey I have labeled a symbolic pilgrimage. Like literal pilgrimages, symbolic pilgrimages involve separation from home, liminoid experience, and reaggregation at home. And like literal pilgrimages, symbolic pilgrimages engender communitas, which allows fans to release, transcend, and critique the habitus while simultaneously gaining respect for the pilgrimages of others. Accordingly, I define symbolic pilgrimages by explaining how: (1) separating from one's "home" to enter a liminoid flow is a release from the habitus; (2) symbolically visiting a sacred place permits a transcendence of the habitus; (3) returning home a changed person generates respect for the pilgrimages of others; and (4) ritualistically repeating the journey encourages critique of the habitus through coping and hoping.

Releasing: Leaving Home to Enter the Liminoid Flow

To begin, a symbolic pilgrimage features an individual leaving "home" as s/he commences a journey to a sacred place—the separation stage. Our "homes" in this case are symbolic rather than literal. As Silverstone (1994) explains, "Home is a construct. It is a place not a space. . . . It is where we belong. Yet such a sense of belonging is not confined to a house or garden" (p. 26). This vision of *home* represents a "fluid and expansive sense of the word—people's physical, political, and spiritual homes—and the homes where they do the work that sustains them and their communities" (Thompson & Tyagi, 1996, p. xiv). Leaving home involves an imaginative leaving of the body and one's perceived place in the culture—much like Nelson's (1989) television viewers left their bodies on the couch—for "the body is also the material 'home' of subjectivity" or identity (Taylor, 1993b, p. 279).

Although some scholars may use *home* as a term to designate a place where we belong (see Silverstone above), home can also refer to our current positioning in terms of time (history) and space (the cultural terrain). That location may not necessarily be where we feel we belong. In such cases symbolic pilgrimages may be undertaken to escape from the inhospitable home and to seek a place of comfort. The Navajo (or Dine), for example, engage in prayer rituals that could be called performative symbolic pilgrimages to reestablish a traditional sense of home in the wake of some sort of personal or cultural disruption (see Gill, 1987). Some humanistic geographers believe all of us suffer from such disruptions. They borrow from existential ontology to claim we are inherently "alienated or estranged—at a distance from—the world" (Samuels, 1978, p. 33). As a result we constantly try to find roots, to center ourselves. "Most succinctly defined," Samuels (1978) writes, "the geography of alienation is a history of the search for roots; i.e., for places that bind and with which one can relate" (p. 34). Leaving home, then, is paradoxically a search for a home.

When we leave home, we use the technology of mass-mediated stories as our vehicles and our imaginations as our fuel. In this respect we're not much different from contemporary literal pilgrims, for as Edith Turner (1987) observes, the "modern pilgrimage is frankly technological: pilgrims travel by automobile and airplane, and pilgrimage centers publish newspapers and pamphlets" (p. 330). Our use of technology to access popular stories reflects the paradox with which I opened chapter one: we want to leave home and find home at the same time. Such apparent "irrationality" is entirely human, for as Soja (1989) explains, "To be human is not only to create distances but to attempt to cross them, to transform primal distance through intentionality, emotion, involvement, attachment" (p. 133).

Leaving "home" through the imagination allows us to enter the liminoid, the space where we search for places of attachment. That is, as a reader/viewer of the popular story, I am physically located in a material environment, but my mind has entered the realm of the story as I see it; I am in both the material environment and the story, yet I am fully committed to neither. I am instead in the liminoid in-between, a place of my own creation. In one sense I am immersed in the story. Radway (1984), for example, found that for her romance readers the act of reading "as an activity, so engages their attention that it enables them to deny their physical presence in an environment associated with responsibilities that are acutely felt and occasionally experienced as too onerous to bear" (p. 93). Yet as Chesebro (1989) explains, I am in a place distinct from the story because "the story occurs in a context-free environment; that is, the environment of the reader is unrelated to the context of the story" (p. 14). The act of reading or viewing the popular story, then, serves to put us in "a place apart" from the mundane material world of the habitus and the fictional world of the story. In other words, the fan's place, writes de Certeau (1984), "is not *here* or *there*, one or the other, but neither the one nor the other, simultaneously inside and outside, dissolving both by mixing them together" (p. 174; emphasis in original). For example, Harrington and Bielby's (1995) discussions with devoted soap opera fans reveal that the fans "*construct their own narratives* by blending their own histories, memorable moments in the story lines, personal friendships, celebrity encounters, inside information . . . and other peak experiences with significant events in their real lives" (p. 177; emphasis added).

As we orient ourselves to the settings, become familiar with the characters, and vicariously experience the action in popular stories, we immerse ourselves in a flow experience that provides "a sense of discovery, a creative feeling of transporting the person into a new reality" (Csikszentmihalyi, 1990, p. 74). We rip through the last pages of a compelling book of fiction because we identify with the struggles of the characters. We grip the armrest in the movie theater as we imaginatively walk with a character through a deserted alley, jumping as s/he does when the obligatory cat sends the equally obligatory trash can clattering. Yet we instinctively "know" we're not in the world of the story. Instead we become enmeshed in another world in between, caught up in the individual flow experience—"a sense of clarity and enjoyment that stands out from the blurred background of everyday routine" (Csikszentmihalyi, 1987, p. 362)—that Turner ascribes to pilgrimages.

But as Turner points out, pilgrimages involve more than an individual flow experience. They require movement to a sacred place where a sense of communitas is experienced. In other words, the individual fan's experience cannot be a symbolic pilgrimage unless s/he symbolically visits a sacred place in the company of others. Our in-between world promises a transcendence of, not merely a release from, our habitus.

Transcending: Communing at Sacred Places With Other Fans

To visit sacred places we first need to create them. To see ourselves as part of a special community we need to know *where* the community is located. Not surprisingly, then, I rely on the work of humanistic geographers to explain how we create sacred places for our selves. I next turn to the ideas of symbolic interactionists to illustrate how we develop a sense of community in such places. Unlike consumerism's subordination of community to individualism, then, symbolic pilgrimages center the self—while keeping it unique— within the community. I illustrate these points with my own experiences as a fan of James Lee Burke's series of novels featuring Cajun detective Dave Robicheaux.

CREATING SACRED PLACES. As I hope to demonstrate more fully in chapters four through seven, the sacred places generated through our encounters with popular stories are more than the settings established by the authors of those stories. To be sure, the setting is important to the development of a sacred place—as Johnstone (1990) observes, "A story gains rhetorical authority from belonging to a place" (p. 125)—but the story itself is simply one of the textual fragments (and is itself composed of textual fragments) pasted on to the collage of the place. Additional fragments are brought to bear through the contexts in which the story is told and our personal scrapbooks of experiences. "Each reader, like each author," Ley and Duncan (1993) point out, "brings a past biography and present intentions to a text, so that the meaning of a place or landscape may well be unstable, a multiple reality for the diverse groups who produce readings of it" (p. 329). The result of this collision among traditional forms of text, reader, and context is what Peter McCormick (1987) calls "real fictions" or "virtual worlds." Such worlds are the imaginative property of the individual fan, although—as I demonstrate shortly—others can share in the space/place that surrounds the individual's chunk of territory.

For example, in my meanderings through the stories of James Lee Burke I encountered the vivid textual fragments he provides. I symbolically experienced life in swanky (garden district), skanky (French quarter) New Orleans, rural New Iberia, and the swampy lands of Acadia and learned what it was like to live as a once-divorced, once-widowed, recovering alcoholic with a quick temper, who suffers from disturbing nightmares in his sleep and a nostalgia for the past in the daylight. No doubt Burke's work reflects most fictional authors' attempts at mimesis, the desire to create "authentic" images of characters and places. Yet try as he might to create a particular place, his readers bring their own texts and contexts to the interpretive process and create fairly similar yet unique places.

To frame this process another way, and to reverse de Certeau's definition, I propose that Burke created a space for interpretation in which I, as reader, constructed a particular place of my own. Renowned humanistic geographer Yi-Fu Tuan's (1977) observations about material terrain illustrates this inversion of de Certeau's notion of the symbolic realm: "What begins as undifferentiated space becomes place as we get to know it better and endow it with value" (p. 6). My first visit to Burke's space (through the novel *The Neon Rain*) was exploratory, so much so that I could not call it a pilgrimage. Yet as I grew involved in the novel, I began to feel comfortable. The particular "shrine" or place I was building out of Burke's space (and revisited/rebuilt as I tore through the series of novels in one summer) was fashioned from his prose as well as bits of my own experience. To recall McGee's (1990) thoughts noted in the preceding chapter, stories are created by their readers more so than by their authors because of the reader's ability to harvest fragments from other stories and experiences in each communicative encounter.

Thus I read *The Neon Rain* in light of other texts I had encountered about detectives (e.g., the "no weakness" machoism of Lucas Davenport, the central figure of John Sandford's *Prey* series of novels) and about the seedy side of New Orleans and bayou Louisiana (e.g., the films *The Big Easy* and *Belizare the Cajun*). Other factors include my love of zydeco music and my three visits to New Orleans as a conference attendee who managed to engage in some tourism on the side.

This collision of various kinds of texts led to my interpretation, my particular construction of a place based on, but distinct from, the settings in the novel. I defined that place differently, of course, as I read more Robicheaux novels, saw the film based on one of the novels, *Heaven's Prisoners*, and talked with a friend who recommended the series to me in the first place. This sacred place, or shrine, to which I symbolically journeyed is the intersection of setting, characters, actions, and previous texts that led me—through my imagination—to "see" and "experience" a place of my own creation, or in McCormick's (1987) terms, a "virtual world."

McGee's explanation of how we employ fragments of text to generate our own interpretations of stories resonates with postmodernism, romanticism, and modernism. For instance, his redefinition of text as the production of an individual reader is reminiscent of deconstructionist claims that the author is symbolically "dead," his/her intended meanings being replaced by audience members' unique understandings of the story. At the same time, however, Beardslee (1990) argues that the fragments we cull from our past endow the meaning-making process with spiritual as well as postmodern possibilities as we sense the invisible interconnections that bind us with others and their experiences. He writes, "But the elements of the past are not mere unrelated fragments, despite their miscellaneous character. They offer us tracts of meaning, directional, transformative possibilities as we relate our own stories to them" (p. 172). Yet from the modernist point of view the depiction of an individual as an active compiler, synthesizer, and creator of texts certainly suggests the modernist image of a transcendent, rational self able to comprehend and make sense of her/his surroundings through empirical observation and analysis.

In this respect we are ontologically centering beings, as humanistic geographers suggest, but in a way that is not simply modern but also postmodern and romantic. Rather than our senses reaching out and pulling information in to our center, our imaginations enter the text, tugging at its parts while gleaning other related textual fragments from our memory to engage in a different kind of "sense-making" project. As Dickinson (1997) points out, this means of making sense is nothing less than a reconceptualization of the classical rhetorical canon of invention. "The shift from the invention of linguistic arguments to the invention of selves," he writes, "shifts the rhetorical 'subject' from an abstract argument to the inventor him or herself" (p. 21). In this version of an individualized Ptolemaic universe we are establishing a center for ourselves, a position from which to make sense of the textual fragments orbiting around us while we are reinventing our selves. This center, which shifts and changes with each addition and/or subtraction of textual fragments, serves as our point of perspective, our standpoint for coming to know the world and our selves. In the terms of cognitive mapping, these centers will "vary according to a person's perspective on the world" (Downs & Stea, 1977, p. 20). We also may have more than one center within our selves because we have more than one identity. For example, Eliade and Sullivan (1987), writing an overview of the concept of "the center" in religious theories, speak of "the tendency to find the center of the universe in multiple locations" (p. 169).

To be centered individually, however, is incomplete; we must be centered *in relation to* "some thing" to find meaningful attachments; to translate our individual flow experience into a feeling of communitas requires interaction with others. Borrowing from symbolic interactionists, I argue that symbolic pilgrimages create a sense of community through our interactions—sometimes imagined, sometimes real—with other fans of the story. These communities surround the personal promised land of the individual fan yet sufficiently share in its characteristics to be a site of sharing. This site is at once a concrete place shared with others and a vaguely defined space outside of one's own sphere; it is part of the individual fan's cognitive map. The communities in which fans locate themselves also generate a symbolic feeling of communitas.

CREATING COMMUNITIES. While our understandings and uses of popular stories are necessarily personal, they also necessarily overlap with interpretations produced by other readers. As Haraway (1988) explains, our particular points of view connect us to others: "Situated knowledges are about communities, not about isolated individuals. The only way to find a larger vision is to be somewhere in particular" (p. 590). Thus our journeys as fans of popular stories represent not just postmodern playfulness but also the purposeful movement designed to seek locations of commonality; in other words, they attempt to discover a particular "here" (modernism) for the purpose of enjoying the spiritual benefits of communitas (romanticism).

Because the locations of commonality we generate through our interactions with stories are generally shared by others, they can be thought of as symbolic communities. In fact Cohen (1985) argues that community is largely a symbolic construct in that "culture—the community as experienced by its members—does not consist in social structure or in 'the doing' of social behavior. It inheres, rather, in 'the thinking' about it. It is in this sense that we speak of the community as a symbolic, rather than a structural, construct" (p. 98). The notion of symbolic community is increasingly important, for as the first chapter points out, our connections to traditional communities have been weakened by the onset of postindustrialism. In symbolic communities, Gergen (1991) says, "physical immediacy and geographic closeness disappear as criteria of community" (p. 214). Symbolic communities, then, are more open to interpretation than structural communities. As Anderson (1991) explains, "Communities . . . are imagined. Communities are to be distinguished, not by their falsity/genuineness, but by the style in which they are imagined" (p. 6). They need not be defined as static places but can instead be envisioned as possessing much of the same dynamism cultural studies scholars ascribe to "spaces," for not every fan will envision the boundaries of the community as inscribed in the same locations. Massey (1994), in a particularly compelling explanation of the dynamic possibilities of "place," notes "the identities of places are inevitably unfixed. They are unfixed in part precisely because the social relations out of which they are constructed are themselves by their very nature dynamic and changing" (p. 169). Symbolic communities are thus both spaces and places.

These symbolic communities are a particular form of interpretive community, and they have come under assault by critics for the lack of explanation of *how* they come to be (e.g., Carragee, 1990; Sholes, 1985). I argue that we can form such communities through real and imagined communicative interactions with others. We can imagine ourselves in the company of like-minded readers, as members of Oprah Winfrey's book club do (Donahue, 1996b), or we can talk to them at work the next day, as Schaefer and Avery (1993) found viewers of David Letterman's nightly talk show do. We can rhetorically participate in symbolic communities by reading and writing letters to the editor of magazines. For example, a *Movieline* magazine devotee reflects the irreverent attitude of the magazine—and its readers who also participate via letter—by arguing articles on young movie stars Leonardo DiCaprio and Alicia Silverstone were overly glowing: "Give me the *real* Hollywood people who have talent and sex appeal, not young piss-ass kids who suck!" (Crawford, 1995, p. 6; emphasis in original). We can form fan clubs, which are proliferating in cyberspace, and communicate directly with other members of the community—whether it be by participating in MUDs (multiuser dungeons) that create alternative realities and characters for internet users (e.g., Dibbell, 1996) or by rewriting story lines from popular narratives a la Jenkins's *Star Trek* poachers discussed in chapter two. As an example of the latter, fans frustrated by the on-again, off-again romance in the early episodes of the main characters in television's *Lois and Clark: The New Adventures of Superman* took advantage of computer-mediated communication to share their stories of the two characters' love with other fans. In fact an entire Web site is devoted to the warehousing of Lois and Clark stories and poems—a catalog of 681 that was visited over 100,000 times between May 1996 and October 1997 (Lois and Clark, 1997).

Most of the means of generating interpretive communities mentioned in the preceding paragraph rely on manifest communication between and among fans. Such communication allows fans to mark themselves as unique individuals expressing their individuality yet as participants in an inclusive community where individualistic expression is appreciated and understood by other members of the community. Even without such direct communication, I believe, fans' encounters with popular stories may enhance both individual identity and communal connection. For instance, when reading about Dave Robicheaux, I can feel connected with my friend Todd, who recommended James Lee Burke's Robicheaux books to me, despite living nearly 1000 miles away from him. That's because Todd shares some experiences with me (mainly from our days as undergraduates at the University of Nebraska in the early 1980s) and has read some of the same non-Burke books that I have. At the same time, however, I know we're reading Robicheaux slightly differently. We have each read a number of books the other has not, and we have had quite different experiences in the decade or so that has elapsed since we lived in the same city. Consequently, even though we encounter the same words on the pages of the Burke books, we bring different textual fragments to bear on the interpretation of those words. Within the interpretive space of the books, we craft similar but not identical places. Social psychologist John Shotter (1986) explains this crafting is possible because we share forms of individuality with others, leading us to position ourselves metaphorically in a manner that allows us to "share a sense of how [we] are all situated and how [we] are each placed in relation to one another" (p. 210). That other fans make similar trips through these popular spaces offers us the comfort of belonging to a community, even if we do not communicate in person with them; we know they are out/in there. Despite my differences with Todd, then, we can share a general understanding of each other's place regarding the Robicheaux novels as well as a sense of belonging to a community of readers who find Robicheaux's battles with his internal and external demons terribly compelling.

By engaging in situated accomplishment and forming symbolic communities, we are in a sense spiritually fulfilled as well (as Katriel and Philipsen [1990] indicate). This spiritual fulfillment emerges not only through the interconnections developed through our real and imagined interactions with other fans but also through our construction of these symbolic communities in a transcendent plane that exists *above* the material moorings of our habitus. Because the boundaries of the symbolic communities we visit are laid out by us—through our imaginations and our rhetorical efforts—their boundaries can exist "in the minds of their beholders" (Cohen, 1985, p. 12). And as we saw in the introduction, using our imaginations is a form of grown-up play. This is because "a symbolic system is like a game in that it provides a separate reality, a world of its own where one can perform actions that are permitted to occur in that world, but that would not make much sense anywhere else" (Csikszentmihalyi, 1990, p. 118). Such play, Huizinga (1938/1970) reminds us, encourages the transcendence of the habitus and the development of communitas in a sacred place: "We said at the beginning that play was anterior to culture; in a certain sense it is also superior to it or at least detached from it. In play we may move below the level of the serious, as the child does; but we can also move above it—in the realm of the beautiful and the sacred" (p. 38). And there is something sacred in creating a place, whether through playful imagination or, as Eliade (1957/1959) discusses, through physical labor. He believes that the establishment, organization, and habitation of places is an act of "creation" that is "equivalent to consecrating" the land (p. 34). Moreover, the symbolic can also transcend the material in terms of scale. Our symbolic worlds can suggest larger chunks of cultural terrain than the material world, encouraging us to see ourselves in someplace above and/or beyond the habitus-infested material world. Tuan (1993), for instance, reports that the Oglala Sioux consider a pipe with four ribbons to connote the same symbolic terrain as the course of the sun, opening their symbolic world to a landscape that stretches far beyond the horizon. In creating this symbolic world, the Oglala also structure the actual world, symbolized by the four ribbons. Using imaginative play to provide this sacred order generates what Huizinga (1938/1970) calls "a temporary, a limited perfection" (p. 29).

By transcending and experiencing the sacred in symbolic communities, groups of fans function more as members of a congregation than the relatively antiseptic phrase "interpretive community" suggests. Of course, not all symbolic or interpretive communities necessarily experience communitas as Turner's anthropological studies define it; our connections with other fans may take many forms, several of them indirect, compared to the personal contact Turner's pilgrims experience. I *am* proposing, though, that when fans routinely revisit the symbolic communities they find in popular stories and through real/imagined interactions with others, some nourishment of the spirit occurs through what Griffin (1990) calls "sacred interconnections." For example, Camille Bacon-Smith's (1992) study of hundreds of women who poached and wrote fan fiction related to the *Star Trek* series illustrates "the *joy* of creating a new kind of community that fulfills women's needs to reach out and be heard" (p. 6; emphasis in original). Energized by the sense of clarity and enjoyment we discover when we engage our favorite popular stories, we learn as fans different ways of seeing through our symbolic journeys. These new perspectives generate a new respect for the pilgrimages of others, just as Turner and Turner (1978) predicted with respect to literal pilgrimages.

Respecting: Returning Home a Changed Person

According to Turner (1973), pilgrimages involve "returning, ideally 'changed,' to a Familiar Place" (p. 213). In symbolic pilgrimages, I argue, we return changed because of our experiences, but the familiarity of "home" is altered. Our journeys alter our standpoints. This section explores how we change; the next section examines how our homes change.

When we engage in symbolic pilgrimages, we meet other people in other locales along the way. As Harrington and Bielby (1995) point out in relation to perhaps the most denigrated television genre, "Soap operas offer viewers the chance to stand on the boundaries between multiple worlds and see real life as connected to, and informed by, a variety of perspectives" (p. 180). Becoming aware of these other perspectives, Cohen (1985) claims, generates respect for other people, their communities, and their cultures: "People become aware of their culture when they stand at its boundaries: when they encounter other cultures, or when they become aware of other ways of doing things, or merely of contradictions to their own culture. The norm is the boundary: its reversal, a symbolic means of recognizing and stating it. Such awareness is a necessary precondition for the valuing of culture and community" (p. 69). Not all symbolic pilgrimages, of course, involve crossing borders, but fans of popular stories generally are attracted to something different from their everyday experiences. My fascination with detective novels, for example, has allowed me to experience the complex cultures represented in Dave Robicheaux's life. Moreover, in reading the novels of Tony Hillerman I have symbolically interacted with Navajo tribal police officers Jim Chee and Joe Leaphorn, just as I have been able to see through the eyes of post–World War II Los Angeles private detective Easy Rawlins by reading Walter Mosely's work.

My participation in these symbolic pilgrimages places me inside the experiences of others symbolically but outside of their experiences materially. My journey thus blurs the boundaries between inside and outside that prompt scholars such as Olsson (1981) to claim, "Insiders experience and outsiders understand; whereas experience is confined to one logical type at the time, understanding is in the act of crossing categorical boundaries" (p. 126). As an insider involved in the story, I vicariously experienced the perspective of Navajo and African American detectives; as an outsider crossing categorical boundaries, I increased my understanding. Accordingly, my position as a symbolic pilgrim within the cultural terrain is postmodern, both inside and outside, not wholly either. Actually, I may see a third way as well, if I engage in reflection or introspection upon my return home. If I do I can become aware of what Buttimer (1980) calls my "taken-for-granted ideas and practices within one's personal world and [learn] to reach beyond them toward a more reasonable and mutually respectful dialogue" with others (p. 172). The dialogue, in turn, reminds me of the spiritual element of this postmodern/ modern process; in Griffin's (1990) terms, my awareness of "the reality of spiritual energy is affirmed . . . [as it exists] within and between all nodes in the cosmic web of interconnections" (p. 2). As the simultaneous undercurrents of postmodernism, modernism, and romanticism flow through symbolic pilgrimages, Turner and Turner's (1978) prediction of the results of physical pilgrimages is affirmed. Respect for the pilgrimages of others grows.

Seeing from other points of view, and appreciating the possibility of additional perspectives, suggests that those fans who consume popular stories in this fashion are epistemologically mobile. De Certeau (1984) explains how we experience this sense of mobility: "A different world (the reader's) slips into the author's place. This mutation makes the text habitable, like a rented apartment. It transforms another person's property into a space borrowed for a moment by a transient" (p. xxi). From each pilgrimage, or "apartment renting," comes wisdom and perspective. As Donna Haraway (1988) urges, "All these pictures of the world should not be allegories of infinite mobility and interchangeability but of elaborate specificity and difference and the loving care people might take to learn how to see faithfully from another's point of view" (p. 583). For instance, the wave of "trading places" movies in the 1980s and 1990s (e.g., *Trading Places*, *Big*, and *Carbon Copy*) demonstrates how a number of characters develop a new sensitivity to other points of view by being in a different body. In material life, however, experiencing the perspective of another body is difficult (save for dramatic weight loss, cosmetic surgery, sex change operations, and so forth), but repeatedly reading our favorite popular stories allows us to experience a symbolic change of body by assuming the point of view of the narrator, camera, protagonist, and so forth. For example, listeners of Garrison

Keillor's radio monologues, Foss and Foss (1994) suggest, "experience [a feminist epistemology] as enacted or embodied. . . . They come to know through or from within a feminist perspective—they are able to try it on and to discover how it works and feels in their lives" (p. 424). That epistemology certainly will not "fit" everyone who tries it on, but we can appreciate how it may look good on someone else.

Paradoxically, then, as we return home from the imaginary-yet-real worlds of popular culture stories, we realize the distance we have traveled and the boundaries we have crossed have likely changed our perceptions. We are engaged in a dynamic series of movements through the cultural terrain. Or as Samuels (1978) points out in the context of humanistic geography, "Human history is a geography of movement, of uprootedness, of collapsing or changing reference points" (p. 34). Our epistemological mobility enhances our knowledge of additional texts, encouraging us to pull more texts and points of view into our sense-making orbits. Such unlimited mobility suggests a playful postmodern traveler, wandering about the cultural terrain, making new meanings as s/he sojourns. Yet we are not simply travelers, migrants, or nomads. We generally return home from these elliptical, purposeful journeys renewed, invigorated, more aware of our "inner" selves as well as the spiritual nature of others. By seeing through the eyes of others, we learn to see differently ourselves. "As we move through culture, culture moves through us" (Neumann, 1996, p. 183). Thus upon our return home we find our centers have shifted. We are no longer in the same place because it does not look the same; our vision has changed with experience. With each symbolic pilgrimage, each ritual journey, the process is repeated. As Soja (1996) urges in his discussion of epistemology, "We must always be moving on to new possibilities and places" (p. 82).

Consequently, existential ontologists argue, our search for roots reminds us of our lack of roots. "The paradox or dilemma of human existence," Samuels (1978) claims, "is that [the] search for roots always reveals lack of rootedness" (p. 34). This Sisyphean journeying highlights the romantic, modern, and postmodern elements of a symbolic pilgrimage. Our journeys to other places teach us about ourselves. "As we sense our inner diversity we come to know our limitations. We understand that we do not and cannot know things completely, not the outside world and not ourselves" (Turkle, 1995, p. 261). They also remind us of how we are always located in a particular "here" rather than "there" as we create personal cognitive maps of our sojourns. "There is the need to face up to—rather than simply deny—people's need for attachment of some sort, whether through place or anything else" (Massey, 1994, p. 151). Yet the knowledge we gain reminds us of the constantly changing nature of our home or center, for "to be estranged from 'place' is to be at the same time conscious of the placing character of 'place' " (Kluback & Wilde, 1958, p. 25). Symbolic pilgrimages are thus paradoxically enlightening *and* disorienting, perpetuating our need to engage in such imaginary-yet-real excursions into the symbolic domain of popular stories.

Critiquing: Ritualistically Repeating the Journey to Cope and Hope

Symbolic pilgrimages are generative rituals. When we complete one, we are likely to desire another. Their cyclical nature derives from two characteristics. First, our individual and collective memories prompt a desire to "recapture" both the experience of home and the promised land we visited. Because our travels ensure that neither place remains "the same" as we remember it, we want to travel again. Second, the lure of the antistructure we encountered in the promised land beckons us again and again. Our return home reminds us that the achievement of creating a more material version of a promised land is always in process, never complete. Both of these characteristics point to the interrelated nature of coping, hoping, and reflection as parts of critiquing—an amalgam best illustrated by Ono and Sloop's (1995) concept of vernacular discourse.

According to Ono and Sloop, "local" communities and/or cultures (their examples are of material, demographically based communities and cultures) that feel excluded from the mainstream respond by using rhetoric to craft alternatives to dominant images and rules. In so doing they "create a unique form that implicitly and often explicitly challenges mainstream discourse, while at the same time affirming and creating the community and culture that produce vernacular discourse" (Ono & Sloop, 1995, pp. 23–24). The challenging of mainstream discourse, I believe, may be interpreted as a process of *coping* with, or extricating oneself from, the rules of the habitus. The affirming process, on the other hand, is one of *hoping*; it offers an alternative to the habitus. Together these rhetorical moves produce a critique of the habitus; they offer us critical equipment for living within a culture. But borrowing from McKerrow's (1989) notion of critical rhetoric, Ono and Sloop argue that such critique is insufficient if it does not also include self-critique or *reflection*, a recognition that— and I am imposing my language on their ideas here—each vernacular discourse also helps to perpetuate the rules of the habitus. Every community is "in a state of persistent transition," they argue (p. 26), so we should always examine how the community's vision of a promised land is inherently a work in progress.

Ideally then the ritual of symbolic pilgrimages generates three types of critique: (1) a therapeutic coping with the rules of the habitus; (2) a hoping for an alternative promised land; and (3) a self-reflective critique of the imagined promised land. Engaging in this three-pronged process will not only encourage more symbolic pilgrimages, it should make subsequent journeys more fulfilling. To unpack this brief description I first explain how the concept of memory perpetuates the ritual of symbolic pilgrimage. I then turn to an explanation of how our imagined promised lands offer opportunities for coping and hoping. I conclude this section with a brief description of how coping, hoping, and memory should encourage us to engage in self-reflective critique.

MEMORY AND THE RITUAL PROCESS. Home is a confusing phenomenon, as I indicated at the beginning of the first chapter. We seek to leave it, yet paradoxically we yearn for it as we find ourselves between places or in other places. Consequently, our symbolic pilgrimages leave us longing for a return to a comforting standpoint even as we enjoy the view from other places. As Silverstone (1994) points out, these complex feelings reflect our struggle with the discourses of modernism, postmodernism, and romanticism. Longing for home, he says, is a romantic yearning, whereas "the struggle between place and placelessness is a struggle, perhaps, between modernity and postmodernity" (p. 27). Denzin (1993) echoes this sentiment: "The postmodern journeying self . . . must, however, be willing to listen to that tiny voice that harkens back, always to the world left behind, for that world left behind is the one where the self . . . is always anchored. And so, romantics all, we have to journey away from home to discover who we really are" (p. 75). But, paradoxically, our symbolic pilgrimages both help us to discover and to change our perceptions of "who we really are." We are, as existential ontologists point out, always looking for places of attachment because "the identities of places are inevitably unfixed. They are unfixed in part precisely because the social relations out of which they are constructed are themselves by their very nature dynamic and changing" (Massey, 1994, p. 169). Home, as a place, changes. We are fulfilled by the journeys that prompt our reenvisioning of home, yet we are left longing for the security of an unchanging home. So, we commence another symbolic pilgrimage.

The paradox of home within symbolic pilgrimages can be better understood with a discussion of *memory*, both individual and collective. As Clifford (1992) explains, memory provides us with a sense of dwelling while we travel. As we move through time and space, we bring our memories with us; our histories, our experiences, our social relationships all serve as baggage that simultaneously encumbers us and provides us with resources. In memory a place or community is seemingly fixed, a point from which we draw a sense of identity; it is embedded in our individual cognitive maps, those representations of "environments that are either known to exist or are imagined but not necessarily present" (Golledge & Stimson, 1997, p. 234). Accordingly, write Morley and Robins (1993), "identity, it seems, is also a question of memory, and memories of 'home' in particular" (p. 10). Although those memories of home are typically personal, communities, too, rely upon memory as a source of identity, for they serve as "homes" as well. As Cohen (1985) explains, "Individuals refer to their cognitive maps to orient themselves in interaction, [and] the same is true also of collectivities" (p. 101). In fact, argue Middleton and Edwards (1990), "collective remembering is essential to the identity and integrity of a community" (p. 10).

The memories of individuals and communities, of course, cannot be so easily distinguished; they have a reciprocal relationship. The fictional detective Dave Robicheaux, for instance, feels uncertain about his individual identity in part because he sees his community changing and feels powerless to do anything about it. Our individual identities are thus enmeshed in the feeling of belonging to a part of a community that itself has memories as a collective. Johnstone (1990) elaborates:

Like the shared knowledge of geography that enables people to create a sense of belonging by jointly evoking cognitive maps in conversation, shared knowledge of a community's stories is part of what creates a sense of community in a group. Collective knowledge of a place evokes the collective memory that defines a group. Individuals' relationships to groups are mediated through shared memories, memories organized around places and the stories that belong to places. (p. 121)

These memories, as I indicated in chapter one, can prompt modernist forays into nostalgia. Knowing our homes have changed, we can tell stories about the good ol' days. We can also—especially if we don't have many memories of good ol' days—revisit the symbolic communities we have created. As constructions of rhetorical fragments that we have built, they seem impervious to change, a fact of which Robicheaux is well aware in *The Neon Rain*: "I reflected upon the ambiguous importance of the past in our lives. In order to free ourselves from it, I thought, we treat it as a decaying memory. At the same time, it's the only measure of identity we have. There is no mystery to the self; we are what we do and where we have been. So we have to resurrect the past constantly, erect monuments to it, and keep it alive in order to remember who we are" (Burke, 1987, p. 155). This reliance on memory is at once reassuring and suffocating. It provides us with a sense of identity, a means of orienting ourselves. But it also is generally unresponsive to historical and cultural changes; memories are fixed, but time and space are dynamic. When home seems to constantly change, we often seek to "go home again" through the repetition of past stories, experiences, etc. In short, we engage in *ritual.*

Rituals in the realm of popular culture can include everything from the religious viewing of a particular television program (or a block of programs, such as NBC's "Must See TV" on Thursday nights) to the routine reading of a daily comic strip or the revisiting of an anthologized character's exploits in a series of fictional books. "The ritual act," Huizinga (1938/1970) explains, "has all the formal and essential characteristics of play . . . , particularly so far as it transports the participants to another world" (p. 37). It's not surprising, then, that Geertz (1972) concludes in his famous study of the Balinese ritual game of cockfighting that "the cockfight, set aside from [everyday] life as 'only a game' [is] reconnected to it as 'more than a game'" (p. 28). Geertz's claim that such structured play is culturally meaningful suggests a more radical purpose for rituals than most scholars of popular culture assert. For instance, Kellner (1982)— like most scholars of myth and ritual—claims television rituals "traditionally integrate individuals into the social order and celebrate dominant social values" (p. 133). The playful yet ordered ritual of the symbolic pilgrimage, however, can also apparently serve as Turner's antistructure in that it leads us to romantic-tinged "other" worlds rather than simply reifying the habitus. When we feel extricated from the habitus, and we recognize our role in creating the symbolic community, we gain a sense of power that encourages us to be critical actors.

Rituals, to be sure, can reaffirm the status quo, but they may also be used to provide alternatives to the status quo. For example, Riggs (1996) explores the ritual watching of the television series *Murder, She Wrote* by elderly female viewers and concludes that "ritual forms of communication may serve as a means of continual validation of the self in a stage of life when one's identity may be in doubt" (p. 311). In particular, asserts Riggs, elderly viewers may feel as if they are engaged in a stressful role reversal in which their children are beginning to become their caretakers in a society that frequently equates aging with incapacity. The ritual of watching Jessica Fletcher, Riggs reports, provides elderly women with a sense of order and stability (a modernist process of ontologically centering the self) and simultaneously encourages them to resist being labeled as feeble (a postmodern resistance to "common sense" definitions) and to generate connections with other women (a romantic generation of community). One of Riggs's viewers explains this double-edged process as she accounts for her motivations for watching the program: " 'Not to solve mysteries, no,' Bernadette told me [Riggs]. 'But maybe to do more things on my own. Maybe she just reassures me that I can make my own day-to-day decisions, that I don't need to ask my children' " (p. 314).

Bernadette's ritual experiences with the popular stories of *Murder, She Wrote* provide her with reaffirmation of her identity as a capable, contributing citizen in a culture where she feels increasingly less valued. Her experiences are no doubt shared by fans of other popular stories. We read the novels of a particular author, we go to see particular kinds of movies, we watch our favorite television programs at the same time every week (sometimes in a group of other ritual-seekers). We seek the comfort and familiarity of the remembered communitas, the memory that affirms our identities. As Campbell (1987) points out in his elaboration of the metaphorical ground of the venerable television program *60 Minutes:* "What *60 Minutes* ultimately offers its large audience through the detective, analyst, and tourist metaphors is the comfort, concreteness, and familiarity of a middle ground, a center to go back to (or start from) each week. The power of its formula and metaphor is to . . . secure a sense of place, a *middle ground,* where we map out meanings and discover once again *who we are*" (p. 347; emphasis in original). As Campbell suggests, the texts of popular stories offer invitations to ritual journeying; the *60 Minutes* fans he describes find meaning, identity, and symbolic community when they revisit the program each week. Although their interpretation of that place may evolve with each journey, the memory of its appeal harkens fans of the programs from their standpoint homes.

When we rely so heavily on our individual and collective memories, we are implicitly living by modernist principles. We think of places as fixed, certain, unchanging—of possessing a stable essence. From this certainty the shrine and pilgrimage derive much of their symbolic power. In this respect the romanticism of communitas depends upon modernist definitions of place—the belief that the community remains unchanged and stable. Yet, paradoxically, spiritual fulfillment is also gained through the interconnections that come from epistemological mobility, which changes the meanings of our places. This postmodern both/and situation allows communitas to exist in the "in between," in no place in particular yet in a knowable place for those within its boundaries. These places then serve as antistructures that are "potentially subversive" (Turner & Turner, 1978, p. 32). Symbolic pilgrimages function—to reframe a phrase of Kenneth Burke's (1965)—as *critical* "equipment for living."

COPING AND HOPING THROUGH CRITICAL EQUIPMENT FOR LIVING. "Equipment for living," which Burke (1941) discusses in terms of literature and which Brummett (1991) extends to include stories transmitted via electronic media, suggests we use the stories we consume to *cope* with our habitus and to *hope* for an alternative. The cope/hope pair, first mentioned in the Introduction, points to the primary functions of symbolic pilgrimages. First, they provide therapeutic rhetoric in a time of unsettling liminality, a way of adjusting to— not avoiding—historical and cultural changes. Second, they provide a means to critique the habitus, a way of envisioning alternatives to historical arrangements and the current cultural terrain.

"The idea that rhetoric has therapeutic benefits is not new," writes Payne (1989). "Indeed, the idea is as old as rhetorical study itself" (p. 151). Not surprisingly, then, a number of scholars have addressed the therapeutic nature of popular stories in particular (e.g., Gumpert & Fish, 1990), including Bruno Bettelheim's (1977) famous work on fairy tales, which he says are therapeutic "because the patient finds his [*sic*] *own* solutions, through contemplating what the story seems to imply about him and his inner conflict at this moment in his life" (p. 25; emphasis in original). Although I have tried throughout this chapter to explain how the individual and the community are intertwined in the therapeutic experience of symbolic pilgrimage, I should note that some scholars are less than enthusiastic about the "therapeutic ethos" because in their view it distances the individual from the community (e.g., Bellah et al., 1985). For example, just as Radway says the possibilities of the symbolic influencing the material are limited when romance readers *merely* imagine themselves in communities (rather than forming such material communities), Peck (1995) argues that "therapeutic discourse translates the political into the psychological—problems are personal (or familial) and have no origin or target outside one's own psychic processes" (pp. 75–76).

Omitting the reflexive relationship between the imaginary and the real in these discussions, however, reflects the either/or thinking that unfortunately permeates some critical approaches. A theory of symbolic pilgrimage recognizes the reflexive relationship between the real and the imaginary, "a space of extraordinary openness, a place of critical exchange where the geographical imagination can be expanded to encompass a multiplicity of perspectives that have heretofore been considered . . . to be incompatible, uncombinable" (Soja, 1996, p. 5). Thus the therapeutic ethos in symbolic pilgrimages goes beyond individual improvement. As Payne (1989) argues, rhetoric can heal schisms between the self and society, the past and the future, and the spiritual and the material. We use rhetoric, he says, to cope with the failure that is bound to emerge when (and here he relies on Kenneth Burke's [1969b] work on identification) our repeated identifications produce continued divisions. "Loss and the fact of failure are consolingly interpreted in ways that make the consequences less painful, easier to accommodate, or even valuable according to some alternate set of priorities" (Payne, 1989, p. 152). When priorities are reenvisioned, we become critical actors rhetorically responding to our material conditions. We can affirm new concepts of self, see new possibilities for group identity, and/or explore alternative connections with others. Through symbolic pilgrimages, in particular, we can gain these understandings through symbolic forms and put them into practice in material circumstances to alter our habitus.

In this respect symbolic pilgrimages adhere to what McPhail (1996) identifies as one of the basic assumptions of a philosophy of rhetorical coherence: the "recognition of the potential for symbolic action to shape and transform social action" (p. 86). Symbolic extrication and connection, in other words, are therapeutic and serve material purposes. For example, Steiner (1988) illustrates how readers of *Ms.* magazine contribute extreme examples of sexism in a way that is simultaneously therapeutic, affirming, and distancing: "Reclaiming and sharing insulting texts may have other purposes besides therapy. Most centrally, the activity gives shape and meaning to group experiences, symbolically marking the group's normative boundaries and reconfirming its convictions and commitments. The group must demarcate its world view from that of the dominant culture. The newly produced texts both violate the dominant code and, by extension, the value system it sustains. They also produce and nourish alternative codes and values" (p. 11). These symbolic places or real fictions, then, *do* influence the habitus, leaving us with a reciprocal process reflective of epistemological mobility; that is, the material encourages us to engage in symbolic pilgrimages that in turn alter how we interact with the material upon our return. The home we left is not the same home to which we return. Consequently, I believe symbolic pilgrimages are the theoretical medicine Goodall (1996) urges us to imbibe: "What we need is a transformative vision for communication capable of allowing ourselves to accept that how we act on the world we know *creates* the world as we know it" (p. 224). Symbolic pilgrimages thus provide *hope* through critique.

Popular stories allow us to locate ourselves in a particular place within cultural space *but* in a way that helps us make sense of the space; the place provides a vista from which we assess our position within the culture. Brereton's (1987) words point to this dual function of sacred places: "A life without purpose or meaning is often expressed in spatial metaphors; it is to be 'lost,' 'disoriented,' and 'without direction.' Because they are defined spaces, sacred places are natural maps that provide direction to life and a shape to the world" (p. 53). And as Lutwack (1984) elaborates in his discussion of the role of place in literature, that direction often has to do with an alternative to the present because "all places . . . cater to some human desire or craving beyond present reality" (p. 32).

Lutwack's "beyond present reality" phrase reminds us how communitas involves our movement *to* a specific symbolic place as well as an escape *from* an unpleasant habitus. A definition of escapism that mentions only movement to a fantasy place would be an incomplete explanation of this process; the symbolic journey must be specifically explained within a social and historical milieu. Explain Seiter, Borchers, Kreutzer, and Warth (1989), "There is nothing inherently progressive about pleasure. . . . Therefore we have to remind ourselves that the relationship between pleasure and politics has to be historicized, contextualized, and specified" (p. 5). Thus symbolic pilgrimages consist of an extrication from our habitus and a connection to appealing symbolic surroundings, a journey from social structure to antistructure in which the structures are culturally contextualized; coping and hoping occur simultaneously. "Finding the way home, then, entails finding the way out—out of the master's house," argues feminist scholar Ruth Frankenberg (1996, p. 3). For instance, Debra Grodin's (1991) interviews with women who read self-help books reveal that the women were purposefully seeking a means of enhancing autonomy as well as contact with others who shared their beliefs. "Their sense of self," Grodin writes, "pivots upon a desire for autonomy and a desire for connection to a world beyond the self" (p. 416). In other words, "As pronounced as women's interests in *connecting* to others to establish identity and independence were their accounts of *extrication*—disconnection from the noxious influence of others" (Grodin, 1991, p. 416; emphasis in original). As Grodin points out, these symbolic movements occur within the social and historical culture of patriarchy, an environment where women find difficulty in achieving autonomy. Even something as mundane as visiting Disneyland or going to the mall can serve the symbolic purposes of extrication and connection. Explains Warren (1993), "By frequenting or generally paying attention to these landscapes [of leisure], people find the resources to make sense of their lives" (p. 183). Experiences in malls and amusement parks can be orderly, purposeful, and seemingly full of positive choices. Encountered in these terms, landscapes of leisure can be interpreted not just as monuments to consumerism but also as places where we go to discover a sense of control, freedom, and abundance—qualities we may well believe we lack in the work place.

The reality we create in our symbolic journeys helps define for us what is possible as a response to our habitus. This is because imagination is not subject to social constraints, despite our use of our imaginations as responses to those constraints; thus, our symbolic communities, our shrines of communitas, are constructed by our own rules. As we transcend the social structure and create the antistructure we have helped to imagine, we give ourselves the opportunity to be critical actors. As Clarke (1976) explains in his analysis of British skinheads: "The 'recreation of the community' [was] indeed a 'magical' or 'imaginary' one, in that it was created without the material and organisational basis of that [material] community and consequently was less subject to the informal mechanisms of social control characteristic of such [material] communities" (p. 102). Writing about marginalized groups in general, Sawicki (1994) adds, "Narratives of oppressed groups are important insofar as they empower these groups by giving them a voice in the struggle over interpretations without claiming to be epistemically privileged or incontestable" (p. 306).

The symbolic pilgrimages we make to imagined-yet-real communities give us hope upon our return to the material, for our perceived home will appear to have changed, granting us new perspective. Or as Goodall (1996) explains:

We imagine, *therefore*, we may know. . . . We may even go to the place of our imagining, exploring its boundaries and planting the national flags of some imagined certainty on its surfaces, only to return home again to that inevitably in-between place where we first proposed what we since have done, and know it now as just that: an *imagined* place where we have been to, the work of metaphors and stories that further propose a further imagining, that call us to consider again the relationship of imagined patterns, parallel worlds, and the divine possibility of interconnections of those worlds to our lived experiences. (p. 175; emphasis in original)

These places are not wholly real or necessarily possible, McCormick (1987) says in his discussion of "virtual worlds," but they exist symbolically for us (and therefore seem "real") and help us to function within the constraints of the habitus. A virtual world, he claims, "works central and at times liberating effects on the persons who are its interpreters. Such effects are centered on cognitive and affective processes but most importantly on the mechanisms, contours, and ranges of human praxis" (p. 269).

McCormick's last sentence emphasizes the extent to which our symbolic experiences and our material experiences reciprocally influence one another; it's simply another way of envisioning how the personal is the political or how the individual coping is inseparable from the community hoping. Our symbolic pilgrimage experience changes us, which changes our habitus slowly but surely. Our habitus ensures our continued need to escape to appealing symbolic environments that are imagined yet somehow real. This process certainly does not encourage radical change, which is frustrating for those who wish to right wrongs immediately (and many of us can see injustices that demand more pressing attention), yet change does occur.

The key to change is a playful attitude that encourages irreverence toward the accepted, the normative. Kenneth Burke's comic frame suggests just such an attitude. Taking a charitable stance toward the perceived follies of ourselves and others, Burke claims, leads people to see alternative possibilities; assuming a judgmental stance, on the other hand, results in resistance and denial. Burke's light-hearted "corrective" encourages us to imagine "people not as *vicious*, but as *mistaken*," (Burke, 1937, p. 41; emphasis in original). This playful attitude is congruous with postmodernism, although because Burke's writing predates this school of thought, he also casts the approach in modernist terms. "The comic frame," he concludes, "should enable people *to be observers of themselves, while acting*. Its ultimate would not be *passiveness*, but *maximum consciousness*. One would 'transcend' himself [*sic*] by noting his [*sic*] own foibles" (p. 171; emphasis in original).

Critically acting while irreverently playing is also possible through the use of irony. Irony, as Hutcheon (1994) explains, can assume many forms and be interpreted in a multitude of ways, but its hallmark is what she calls its "edge." Relying on an audience member's ability to interpret the unstated as meaning something other than what was stated (often the opposite, in fact), irony works "by playing the new off against the old" (Rorty, 1989, p. 73). In this type of irreverent play irony offers an indirect but pointed evaluation. As a result, "An ironist hopes that by the time she has finished using old words in new senses, not to mention introducing brand-new words, people will no longer ask questions phrased in the old words" (Rorty, 1989, p. 78).

Illustrating irony's irreverence, Daughton (1996) suggests it can function in modernist as well as postmodernist terms. She points out how the film *Groundhog Day* ironically takes its male protagonist through a feminine quest. This irreverent lesson teaches the protagonist to adopt a transcendent perspective that provides "an acceptance of oneself as a whole and wholly participatory *and* responsible member of a loving community" (p. 140; emphasis in original). As a playful postmodernist who ritualistically relives the same day, the protagonist comes to develop himself, find connections with others, and develop his spirit. He simultaneously reaches the modernist promised land of (individual) progress, the romantic promised land of spiritual fulfillment, and the postmodernist promised land of playful connections with others.

Movies often have happy endings, a sense of closure, a belief that all the problems have been solved. But each happy ending is not just an end, for a new story begins and/or continues. Accordingly, borrowing from Ono and Sloop (1995), we need to recognize that the process of developing promised lands is ongoing. We need to engage in self-critique or *reflection*.

Ideally, then, symbolic pilgrimages offer three possible ways of seeing the cultural terrain when most cultural observers tend to think of "seeing" in only one or two dimensions. Denzin (1997), for instance, equates seeing with a disembodied point of view, the province of detached observers such as scientists or tourists. Neumann (1996) believes we can see in two ways: either as introspective autobiographers looking in or as dispassionate describers of other worlds. Lippard (1997) offers a twofold method of seeing as well, but she suggests we see places from the inside and landscape from the outside. Synthesizing the observations of these three scholars, I propose that symbolic pilgrims simultaneously see the cultural terrain from the outside (as travelers passing through) and sacred places from the inside (they symbolically live in these places), but they also may look inside themselves upon their return home as they reflect on their experiences, both material and symbolic.

Engaging each of these points of view can help us to better understand ourselves, others, and our cultures. We can understand how others live by traveling to a new story, but this option is available to all consumers of popular culture. Symbolic pilgrims can enhance this understanding by journeying again and again to a place they define and create and by looking out from inside this sacred place. All symbolic pilgrims can gain this understanding. Once they exit this promised land and return home, they not only may see the insides of their homes in a different light, but they may look at themselves anew by reflecting on their travels.

As we will see throughout the following pages, different fans within the same symbolic communities employ different levels of reflection upon their return home. Those who engage in more reflection, I argue, benefit more from their symbolic pilgrimages; they are aware of the borders they have crossed, and this awareness generates in them a stronger appreciation for others' perspectives and a healthier sense of their fluctuating "place" within cultural space. As Larner (1995) urges, we have a challenge "to recognise the situatedness of [our] own knowledge, and to engage ethically with the knowledges of others. . . . This process is one that will require openness, respect and the ability to live with apparent contradictions" (p. 187). The key to gaining from such a process is to appreciate how others see from their situations. Explains Ahponen (1996), "Taking the stranger's position into consideration, it is possible to problematize how to encounter the world as a world of differences" (p. 177). In so doing we are better able to envision alternatives to the habitus, to *hope* for changes. Fans who ponder less, or not at all, gain the benefit of *coping* but are less able to see possibilities for the future, for they are more interested in what I believe is the futile creation of a static, unchanging sense of place in the midst of increasingly chaotic cultural change. In an attempt to "practice what I preach," I conclude each of the following chapters with a reflexive critique of the promised lands I, and other fans, have envisioned. These critiques, although initially difficult to write, reaffirmed for me the value of reflection. I am still a fan of each of the four popular stories examined, but my affective investment in the promised lands described is tempered by an appreciation for what the boundaries of those, and all, promised lands exclude.

Summary and What Lies Ahead

Symbolic pilgrimages are paradoxical journeys. The vehicles for these travels are mass-mediated stories that are delivered to us through technological devices that at once disorient us and fulfill us. Symbolic pilgrimages arise out of a yearning for attachments, yet we continue to seek attachments because we undertake such journeys. We appreciate the perspectives we gain through symbolic pilgrimages, but we miss the security of home that our sojourns disrupt. Clearly, symbolic pilgrimages should prompt fans to do some reflective thinking. The amount of introspection in which fans engage, I believe, is related to the value they attain from the imaginative journeys I call symbolic pilgrimages. Accordingly, what I have described in the preceding pages is an *ideal* vision of a symbolic pilgrimage. Not all fans engage in the reflective thinking about home (even implicitly), nor do fans who think reflexively necessarily do so in all their symbolic pilgrimages. Avid or devoted fans—to use Reeves et al.'s (1996) definition from the introduction—may be so involved that they do not engage in reflection, *or* deep involvement may prompt reflection; the possibilities are as varied as the processes of imaginative invention that fans employ.

In the following chapters I borrow from my own experiences as a fan of popular stories, rely on my abilities as a critic of rhetoric to dig into the textual and discursive elements of the stories, and talk to other fans (in focus groups and via e-mail) about their encounters with my favorite stories. After completing drafts of the chapters, I also asked some of the fans—as well as colleagues who share my interest in audiences, popular culture, and/or pilgrimage—to provide me with ideas for revision. The combination of insights provided by personal narrative, scholarly analysis, everyday experts, and self-reflection provides, I hope, an intriguing and engaging discussion of how symbolic pilgrimages allow us to release, transcend, and critique the habitus, while leaving us simultaneously fulfilled and unsatisfied. I'll let you judge for yourself, of course, as you read about the comic strip *Dilbert* in chapter four; Fox Television's *The X-Files* in chapter five; the nation's most popular sports weekly magazine, *Sports Illustrated,* in chapter six; and a movie whose vision has inspired real-life pilgrims, *Field of Dreams,* in chapter seven.

Each of these four chapters presents a localized habitus in which the self is de-centered, separated from a community, and seemingly immobile. In chapter four, Dilbert and his colleagues are dehumanized by management discourse, then separated from one another and the larger work environment through cubicles that restrict their movement. In chapter five FBI special agents Fox Mulder and Dana Scully are led by others who surveil and constrain them, while their work isolates them from their FBI colleagues and limits their social lives. In chapter six sports fans are reminded that sport can either reinforce or resist the postindustrial, technological machine's tendency to equate humans with mechanical parts, isolate them from others, and insert them into a fixed position. In chapter seven the Kinsellas are stuck on a farmstead, out of touch with the rural lifestyle of the community and unsure of their direction. Yet in each case my imagination—and the imaginations of other fans—works in concert with the story to envision an alternative to the localized habitus. After articulating those alternatives, I reflect on how the communitas presented in these sacred places also possesses the possibility of petrifying into habitus. In other words, each promised land can limit and constrain some of us just as dominant visions of promised lands have. Following these illustrations, I offer a conclusion designed to synthesize my observations from those chapters with the theoretical and contextual information I have provided to this point.

Part 2

Illustrations

4

Exiled in Cubeville, Striving for Nerdvana

Dilbert as a Critique of Phony Meritocracy

DILBERT: I have become one with my computer. It is a feeling of ecstasy . . . the perfect blend of logic and emotion. I have reached . . .
DOGBERT: "Nerdvana."

—*Dilbert* (Adams, 1995a; ellipses in original)

I was visiting an old college friend and his family in Minneapolis a few years back when I had my first encounter with the comic strip *Dilbert*. My friend, a computer systems consultant, encouraged me to check out the strip when the morning paper arrived. I don't recall the details of that first strip, but I remember that I was amused enough to ask for "its story" from my friend. He, being sympathetic to life in Dilbert's techno-jungle, was only too happy to oblige. I felt a little like a newcomer to a television soap, learning the nuances of the characters and their predilections for trouble. I learned that the oblong Dilbert is the socially obtuse, but fairly technologically proficient, engineer; his pet, Dogbert, hatches various plans to take over the world; his colleagues, Wally and Alice, are perennially bitter at the unfair treatment they receive in their unnamed, cubicle-filled workplace; his boss, who has no name, is both socially and technologically inept. Their interactions in the work world—with Dogbert frequently cashing in as an amoral consultant—provide the grist for the stories featured in the daily *Dilbert*s.

Unfortunately, when I returned home from my visit, I also returned to a daily newspaper that did not carry *Dilbert*. Not too long after that, however, the retirement of *The Far Side*'s Gary Larson, *Outland/Bloom County*'s Berke Breathed, and *Calvin and Hobbes*'s Bill Watterson opened up holes for quirky humor in newspapers around the country. My daily paper picked up *Dilbert* to fill one of those holes, and it apparently had plenty of company. In 1993 the comic appeared in fewer than 150 newspapers and was in danger of being dismissed by its distributor, but its distribution doubled in 1995. By 1997 *Dilbert* was featured in over 1600 newspapers in 39 countries (Stall, 1997) and was being read by roughly 60 million people (Van Biema, 1996), making it the fastest-growing comic strip in the country (Astor, 1996). In addition, more than one million Dilbert books have been sold (Leonhardt, 1996), his Web site is visited an astounding average of 1.5 million times a day (Levy, 1996), and an irreverent management handbook featuring the wisdom of Dilbert has gone to press 22 times with nearly one million copies in print as of September 1996 (Maryles, 1996). With this response it's no wonder that *Dilbert*'s creator, Scott Adams, receives about 300 e-mail messages a day from fans of his lumpen progeny (Hamilton, 1996) and that over 200,000 people have subscribed to his electronic newsletter (Adams, 1997b).

Clearly Dilbert's world is being visited not just by a number of new readers but by faithful fans who can't seem to get enough of the dumpy engineer. A number of fans, in fact, told me that reading *Dilbert* is a ritual part of their lives. Steven told me by e-mail that he reads the Dilbert daily calendar "the first chance I get in the day (usually at midnight or 1 am, as I am usually still up. I can't read them before midnight, though, as that would be sacrilege)."[1] (Steven has more willpower than I; sometimes I'll peek ahead several weeks on my Dilbert daily calendar.) Wayne reads the strip "usually the 1st thing I do once I logon each day when I'm at school," whereas Ian saves it as the "last in the bunch so that I can enjoy the best comic in the paper last." For Gretchen, reading the *Dilbert* daily calendar "is the first thing I do when I sit down at my desk." These and other fans of the comic strip repeat this ritual not just each day, but several times a day. Leland reads *Dilbert* "in as many ways and as often as I can. I have four different 1997 Dilbert calendars at my desk (monthly, weekly, daily and date book), I have all of the different Dilbert books (comic collections and novels) and I also always check the Dilbert strips on the Unitedmedia site." Sid gets his daily *Dilbert* fix "in the paper and on a day-by-day calendar," and Steven reads "the new dilbert strips on the web or in the weekly campus newspaper . . . whichever I get to first. Most of the time I read the strips in both, so I get a double dose. Plus I have the dilbert daily calendar" (ellipsis in original).

These repeat visits—through daily reading of the comic strip, browsing of the Web page, and/or purchase of Adams's books—to the promised land *Dilbert* represents suggest these and other fans find something of value in their ritual reading experiences. That "something of value" unfolds in more detail as this chapter progresses, but for now and at the very least we can note that the strip provides fans with a means of finding connections with others. As Ian explains, "I usually use Dilbert and his friends/coworkers in conversation . . . it's really no secret on how much of a fan I am" (ellipsis in original). Gretchen agrees, noting, "I keep my favorite strips for use in classes. I also share the 'best ones' with colleagues for whom the strip may be particularly appropriate on any given day."

Dilbert's experiences in and observations of a workplace so dysfunctional that it should have its own 12-step program appear to resonate with individuals who encounter their own share of workplace foibles as well as with students who suspect what the work world will be like. Adams, in fact, relies on reports of workplace inanities from his e-mail correspondents to provide the context for the humor in *Dilbert*—and he *has* turned those experiences into something of a 12-step program with the publication of *The Dilbert Principle* and *Dogbert's Top Secret Management Handbook* (a first printing of 500,000 copies relaying the wisdom of Dilbert's Machiavellian pet). The former features chapter titles such as "Great Lies of Management," "Pretending to Work," and "How to Get Your Way" yet, ironically, has become required reading for the managers it belittles. Jeffrey A. Sonnenfeld, director of the CEO College at Emory University, tells *Business Week* that *The Dilbert Principle* " 'is being talked about more than any single management book right now' " (quoted in Leonhardt, 1996, p. 46).

Dilbert's playful irreverence toward the assumed wisdom of managers reflects its postmodern critique of modernist management practices, although paradoxically, its nostalgic undertone for the days when managers were seemingly selected for their competence indicates a belief in *a* right way of managing. Meanwhile, Dilbert's implicit bond with his fans who share in this understanding of how "things oughtta be" suggests a romantic belief in the existence of a community of people who know how to make business work if they only were to receive the opportunity; this sense of community is most certainly enhanced by Adams's willingness to receive their e-mail messages and include them in his growing newsletter distribution. That newsletter recipients are invited by Adams to be part of Dogbert's "New Ruling Class" (DNRC) when Dogbert finally succeeds in his quest to conquer the world reaffirms not only their romantic connections but also the modernist belief in either/or logic (DNRC members or nonmembers) and the critique of material conditions.

Thus fans of *Dilbert* such as myself engage in our personal symbolic pilgrimages through the ritual re-reading of the comic strip. This re-reading constitutes the symbolic journey from home and back again that endows fans with a powerful sense of escape; experiencing *Dilbert* is a symbolic critique of the material conditions from which the escape occurs. Communitas is generated through sharing the meanings of the comic strip with coworkers and friends, participation in the DNRC, and the realization that others you don't know share similar experiences. Epistemological mobility is practiced through the inversion of power relations exemplified in *Dilbert*, but because some fans journey differently (as noted earlier in this chapter) we're aware of our ontological centering at the same time.

The preceding preview may read more like a summary of the thoughts in this chapter, and to some extent it is. I'm hoping that by knowing where my analytical journey ends, you'll take time to enjoy the scenery along the way. As a tour guide, I want to illustrate how *Dilbert* generates visions of symbolic promised lands for its readers, as well as how it engages the discourses of romanticism, modernism, and postmodernism during the symbolic pilgrimages to those lands. To prepare for this trip I examined the collection of Dilbert books that reprinted previously distributed strips, sought the opinions of people who indicated an interest in *Dilbert* on their World Wide Web home pages, and visited with colleagues at work who identified themselves as fans of the engineer and his potato-shaped dog. Illustrations from these sources are interwoven throughout the chapter. The next section establishes a context for these excerpts.

Social Equality and Meritocracy

In chapter one I discussed the connection between work and spirit, mentioning Kaus's (1992) idea of social equality, the axiom that we are social equals—no matter how unequal our financial situations—because we believe we work equally hard and make equally important contributions to the nation's economy. In an industrial economy, that belief is relatively easy to sustain. Blue-collar workers know their tedious jobs require a great deal of physical labor and that their products are vital to the economic health of their community and country. Thus, even though those jobs are in many ways demeaning, the people who perform them can take pride in what they produce as well as in the kinship fostered by lifetime employment in one company and/or union membership (see Morrow, 1993; Sloan, 1996). In his documentary *Roger & Me*, for example, Michael Moore points out how displaced GM workers in Flint, Mich., were distressed by their firings because they had identified with the company and were proud of their assembly-line work. One scene in the film, in fact, shows workers cheering their final product as it rolls off the line, even though—as another worker tells the camera—they shouldn't be so happy because they just lost their jobs.

In a postindustrial economy, however, the concept of social equality is more difficult to perpetuate. To begin, the need for physical labor continues to be reduced as services encroach upon blue-collar industries' territory. In addition, high-paying jobs depend increasingly on the possession of particular skills that can be attained only through training and/or education rather than union membership (Kaus, 1992). As a result the decline in union membership and the globalization of production sites means individuals in lower-skill jobs cannot bargain from a position of strength in wage negotiations. This development leads to downward pressure on wages in low-skill jobs and in some cases the elimination of those jobs, as *Roger & Me* poignantly illustrates (Judis, 1994). The confluence of these forces generates an economic structure in which income distribution depends increasingly on one's intellect. As Kaus (1992) explains, the shift in pay scales creates a culture in which one's position in the income hierarchy can be more easily connected to a social hierarchy: "It's one thing to have an unequal distribution of income. It's another thing to have the same distribution of income rigorously based on schooling and skills. In the latter situation, those with more money will be able to claim not just that they have more money, but that they have something else, *knowledge,* that makes them more valuable" (p. 37; emphasis added). This tendency to link income and social position threatens our traditional sense of social equality, Kaus claims, and at the same time introduces another form of egalitarianism: meritocracy. In a meritocracy our pay is linked to our contributions to society; the idea of "all work is equal" shifts to "the more you contribute, the more you receive." For instance, the physician who saves lives apparently contributes substantially more to society than does the road-crew worker who holds the "Slow" sign; thus, we are willing to pay the physician substantially more money than the road worker.

To be sure, the meritocratic impulse is always present in capitalist economies, but it—and its tendency toward class distinctions—has been "officially" muted by our cultural emphasis on social equality. In recent years, however, Kaus argues that the widening division between pay scales is being progressively translated into social judgments; that is, physicians today are increasingly more socially valued than road crew workers. Such a scenario can easily breed smugness and resentment, respectively, and "that's likely to be bad for social equality" (Kaus, 1992, p. 41). Strangely enough, then, "the more arbitrary and random the economy's judgments, the more they are perceived as the result of luck or qualities widely recognized as otherwise valueless or trivial, the less likely it is that individuals will ascribe larger significance to economic success or failure, and the less likely it is that money inequality will translate into social inequality" (Kaus, 1992, p. 48). In other words, we implicitly *count on* haphazard decision making in our places of employment and unpredictability in our national economic conditions. If we feel like *economic* failures in a meritocratic society, we have no rational explanation but to consider ourselves *social* "losers" because "the bottom, after all, is where some people will end up" in a true meritocracy (Kaus, 1992, p. 47).

As I illustrated in chapter one, however, many of us count our pennies and reach the logical conclusion that we are not improving financially, nor do we see signs indicating we will be able to do so in the near future. Consequently, "seven years into an expansion that is being billed as an economic miracle, U.S. workers feel insecure and stressed out" (Belton, 1997, p. 1B). This realization, acknowledged within the context of a postindustrial economy, encourages us to use a modernist logic that produces an either/or dilemma: either we are becoming social "losers" who are unable to climb the proverbial ladder of success or economic decisions make no sense. Not surprisingly, we tend to lean toward the latter as an answer.

The evidence of our leanings is plentiful. Downsizing, for example, is depicted by corporate America as a rational response to an increasingly competitive global economy. Ritzer (1996) would likely categorize such rhetoric under the rubric of "McDonaldization." This model of decision making attempts to ensure the best possible *logical* outcome, one that makes workers and managers more productive and consumers happier. Downsizing rhetoric typically suggests that some workers must be "let go" to make the business operate more soundly, thus enhancing the security of the remaining workers, offering the consumers more choices, and providing managers a more responsive structure with which to work. For example, the chair of the board at Sears justified cutting 50,000 jobs by invoking the security of the remaining employees, and the chair of the board at Tenneco, Inc., said his downsizing made the company more competitive (Uchitelle & Kleinfield, 1996). Couched in these rational economic terms, downsizing makes "perfect sense."

Yet as Ritzer (1996) explains, "Rational systems inevitably spawn irrational consequences" (p. 13). The modernist-influenced rational model, then, harbors a postmodern paradox: the rational is also irrational. *The New York Times* reached just such a conclusion in its 1996 series on downsizing. "The conundrum," write *Times* reporters

Louis Uchitelle and N. R. Kleinfield, "is that what companies do to make themselves secure is precisely what makes their workers feel insecure" (p. 26). Readers of the series confirmed their insecurity in a barrage of messages sent to the newspaper. Here are some of the many responses printed two weeks after the series commenced: "No longer yuppies, now we work and work and yet are barely solvent"; "[My] two jobs pay approximately 10 percent of what my one job used to pay"; "If I lose my job again it will destroy me"; "[H]aving an education is no guarantee that one won't be left behind"; "He told me he was protecting the company" (quoted in Lohr, 1996, p. 5). Perhaps the most appropriate response—for my purposes, at least—was offered by Encitas, Calif., resident Tom Scott, who remarked, "Five years ago, I thought [W. Edwards] Deming could be the voice of the corporate world. Now I know it is really Dilbert" (quoted in Lohr, 1996, p. 5).

For those workers who remain on the job, uncertainty lurks along the road to progress, too. One reader of *The New York Times* explains that "downsizing makes life very stressful for the ones who hang on to their jobs a little longer, as well. Mostly, we are living in fear that we are next" (quoted in Lohr, 1996, p. 5). Not surprisingly, 70 percent of workers polled in a July 1997 Princeton Survey Research Associates survey said job security has decreased in the past two to three decades (Belton, 1997). This land of uncertainty, located on the road to Progress, can be called "Cubeville" in honor of the November 17, 1996, *Dilbert*, that opens with the boss thinking, "The powerful leader enters Cubeville to inspire the wretched underlings." The theme of this particular strip is a familiar one for *Dilbert* readers: the worker is depicted as isolated, degraded, powerless, and confined within the cubicle. Metaphorically speaking, s/he is stuck in an unpleasant, uncertain place in which no options are visible on the horizon. Such a sentiment certainly resonates with displaced workers as well as with those who have not been displaced yet still fear the dark vision of the future looming outside their cubicles. Dilbert thus has company—not just the displaced but the 35 million people who, office furniture maker Steelcase, Inc., says, work in partitioned environments (see Wolf, 1997).

Many of these people are no doubt fans of *Dilbert*. For them, reading the daily *Dilbert*s may well provide ritualistic experiences similar to those reported by the fans I quoted a few pages back. As I move forward, I first explain how the comic strip symbolically represents the dehumanizing community of Cubeville. There Adams's depiction of the workplace habitus of "irrational progress" is enacted as workers are treated like animals and inmates. Next I suggest how fans of *Dilbert* engage in an imaginative release from the habitus to construct the symbolic, liminoid community of Nerdvana, a transcendent sacred place where "respect" provides the foundation for a critique of the rules of the habitus. There the unstated rules of the habitus are redefined so that the powerless become powerful and antisocial activities are envisioned as playful. Nerdvana becomes a place to cope and hope. Finally I conclude with an examination of how the communitas of Nerdvana may well perpetuate the habitus of meritocracy rather than generate a nostalgic antistructure of social equality.

Cubeville as Office Tenements

In a rational model power and control are exercised to achieve the modernist promised land of Progress. In this vision threats to progress must be confined and transgressions of the established order controlled if the society is to reach its goal. Progress is rationally measured through efficiency, productivity, and the bottom line. Companies do not "stand pat"; they continue to seek improvements, giving rise to an entire cottage industry of management strategies. Managers implementing these strategies attempt to control the work environment and, thus, the workers in order to achieve progress. Much of this control, though, relies on rhetoric that defines power relationships in a way that engenders control. That is, the modernist land of Progress has petrified into habitus, and that unstated set of rules means "managers know best." For example, the authors of a recent study on how managers should communicate information to workers following downsizing conclude, "The results of this investigation indicate that some of the effects of RIF's [reductions in force] can be predicted and controlled and that practitioners can successfully manage survivor reactions without compromising organizational goals" (Johnson, Bernhagen, Miller, & Allen, 1996, p. 162). This type of controlling rhetoric can be found throughout the social scene. Dwight Conquergood's (1992) account of life in a Chicago tenement building called Big Red illustrates how rhetoric presaged the moving of the tenants by depicting urban decay as transgression requiring control. "The domination and displacement of the residents of Big Red," Conquergood writes, "were underwritten by a rhetoric of redevelopment. Before the Big Red residents were physically vacated, they were discursively displaced" (p. 134).

A similar rhetorical venture is reflected in the stories of *Dilbert*. Cubeville is a collection of office tenements in which incompetent authority is pervasive and unending. In this respect Cubeville is akin to an urban housing project, a vestige of the decaying modernist machines of industrialism and big-city politics. As Conquergood (1992) points out, Big Red's physical deterioration was exacerbated by political and socioeconomic neglect. Its residents, like those in Cubeville, had little hope of progress, lacked faith in those in power, and simply tried to survive in an irrational place influenced by rationalist principles run amok. Feeling de-centered as individuals and distanced from the center of the physical community in which they resided, the residents of Big Red and Cubeville had packed their bags for a symbolic journey in which their individual selves could congregate in a community at the center of the world. As e-mail fan Matt puts it, "Dilbert . . . is trapped in a world so similar to that in which I am trapped. You know, surrounded by idiotic rules, red tape, and clueless people." Matt's language suggests that not only is he aware of being "trapped" by the forces of habitus but that he has also begun the process of re-centering himself, or creating a place for himself within the undifferentiated space of the habitus, by noting that he is "surrounded" by the habitus.

Matt's words also indicate that although the reassuring foundation of social equality in Big Red and Cubeville has been weakened through the emphasis on meritocracy, the tenement inhabitants *know* they are not "losers" in the new regime. The meritocracy, as Kaus (1992) would say, is "phony," but its structure is sturdy; the liminal work environment—moving from social equality to meritocracy—is hardening into habitus. Thus the residents are increasingly left with only a belief in irrationality to explain their apparent inability to move to places of progress, such as higher positions, offices with real walls, and houses in the 'burbs. Residents' recognition of this habitus is outlined through an examination of Cubeville's strategies of depicting people as animals and inmates. Residents' responses are outlined in the next major section's description of the imagined life of Nerdvana.

Residents as Animals

In Cubeville, like Big Red, residents are confined in tenement structures. Confinement is reaffirmed through reminders of the dangers of transgression. These reminders come in two forms in Cubeville. First, the workers are defined as animals that require human supervision. Exiled to a box, treated like a rat that must navigate the maze of bureaucracy for a reward, Dilbert monotonously and helplessly searches for meaning in his work. In fact, Dilbert realizes, "I feel like I'm an animal in some warped behavioral study," as he reaches for a pellet from the dispenser installed on his cubicle wall (Adams, 1996a, p. 218). As several of the strips suggest, Dilbert and his colleagues feel so dehumanized living in the Cubeville project that they *do* see themselves as animals. In one strip, for instance, a conversation between Dilbert and a visiting monkey (it's a long story!) reveals the not-so-subtle connection between the worker and an animal. As the monkey explains, "Eventually, humans will be kept in cages as pets." Indignant, Dilbert responds, "Impossible! We humans will never allow ourselves to be treated like that! Now get out of my cubicle!" (Adams, 1996a, p. 90). In another strip cubicles are depicted as the equivalent of stalls in a stable. A promoted worker tells Dilbert and his friend Wally that he will "still have a little cubicle like yours. The only difference being that I'll keep a pony there. That way it's close to my office" (Adams, 1996a, p. 11).

These strips suggest the residents of Cubeville are treated *as if* they were animals, but other strips depict the workers *as* animals. For instance, Adams offers a not-so-subtle comparison between cubicle workers and prairie dogs, picturing the cubicles as holes from which the workers peek to see what's happening in the outside world (Adams, 1995a, p. 194). Prairie dogs, of course, are famous for what humans see as transgressions that violently destroy humans' efforts to control nature, leading to the confining inventions of organized prairie dog kills and a giant vacuum that sucks the dogs out of their holes. In both cases the rodent dogs are subjugated by humans in an attempt to restrict the dogs' wasteful rampages. Similarly, Dilbert is treated like a *Wild Kingdom* creature as his boss offers him an "employee locator device" that will enable "sensors in the building . . . to track you at all times." The device, which looks suspiciously like an animal collar, is described by Dilbert as "the final humiliation," a lament that is answered by his boss: "Once you got used to working in cubicles, like gerbils, we knew anything was possible" (Adams, 1996a, p. 76).

Temporary workers are treated even more harshly, literally tossed into the dumpster by the boss after they have been used. When Dilbert wonders, "The dumpster seems a bit inappropriate," the boss rationally replies, "They're way too big to flush" (Adams, 1996e, p. 121). The "animals" of Cubeville, then, are not simply the cared-for zoo and/or laboratory animals—they are as disposable as the goldfish that invariably float to the top of the aquarium. Cubevillians don't even "make great pets" (my apologies to the band Porno for Pyros for borrowing the lyrics to one of their songs); they are unloved, and therefore abused, pets—subject to what e-mail fan Wayne, in a perhaps inadvertent intertextual reference to David Letterman, calls "stupid management tricks." Dilbert, for example, is told by the boss that he's "being temporarily transferred to the field sales organization. Normally we use these assignments to round somebody out for management. But in this case I'm just yanking your chain" (Adams, 1996e, p. 7). Kept at the end of a short leash, Cubevillians are held in an organizational form of house arrest. Rather than wearing simple pet collars, they wear "belts-o-authority" around their heads. "From time to time," the boss intones, "I'll use my 'belt-o-authority' to send you painful electric shocks." Searching for perhaps a rational, behavioral modification foundation for his superior's actions, Dilbert asks, "When our performance is bad?" "That's one theory, sure," replies the boss (Adams, 1996e, p. 16).

Residents as Inmates

In this respect the Cubeville tenements are prison like, perhaps Weber's (1958) iron cage at its ultimate, with "the boss man" serving as warden. In a three-strip series the boss even decides to lease empty cubicles to the state to ease prison overcrowding, a move consultant Dogbert explains will actually require an *upgrade* in the condition of the cubicles, "a little paint, new carpet and we're there" (4/24/95).[2] The prisoners are "just like employees" minus one small mistake, Dogbert explains, although the inmates' "health plan is better," he admits (4/25/95). Just as prisons are overcrowded and housing projects stuffed, so the company's cubicles possess insufficient space, leading the boss/warden to go from single cubicles to shared cubicles to, finally, velcro strips (Adams, 1995a, p. 22). Cramming Cubevillians into confined spaces reinforces the perception that they are not respected by the boss, a notion he affirms with the implementation of monitors that "adjust the cubicle size according to your value" (4/8/95).

Literally boxed in, the Cubeville residents are robbed of their dignity and treated like inmates, the second strategy of confinement. Like inmates, the Cubevillians are stripped of their rights, denied a voice in their environment, and thoroughly degraded. Their work in the office tenement is metaphorically similar to the work done by chain gangs on the side of the road or on prison farms. As the boss taunts the workers in one strip, "I just realized I can double your workload and there's nothing you can do about it. You're lucky to have jobs in today's economy! You'll gladly sacrifice your personal lives for no extra pay!" (Adams, 1996a, p. 20). He continues this motivational technique in another strip by reminding Dilbert that "as long as all the other companies are downsizing too, you have no leverage. I can get away with anything!" He then reinforces his observation by jabbing the engineer in the back with a pencil (Adams, 1996a, p. 117). The workers in Cubeville are dehumanized by such treatment; they are rhetorically named as replaceable parts and not even valuable ones at that. Explains the boss, "Money is our most valuable asset. Employees are ninth," just behind carbon paper (Adams, 1996e, p. 40).

To ensure Dilbert and his colleagues understand their status, the boss routinely "makes examples" out of others. For instance, relying on the advice of consultant Dogbert, the boss employs inhumane methods of firing workers. In one strip he announces, "Throughout the day I'll be sneaking up on people and stamping 'cancelled' on their backs" (Adams, 1995a, p. 170). In another strip he uses a Dogbert invention called the "can-o-matic." "Disguised as a restroom stall," Dogbert explains, "the can-o-matic randomly fires people by slapping a pink slip on their backs and catapulting them out of the building." The boss is a bit disappointed in this option, not because of its violence but because he "won't get to see the expressions on their faces" (Adams, 1995a, p. 170).

Clearly this boss/warden is no benevolent Brubaker. In fact, the sadistic, spiteful behaviors of the nameless boss are reminiscent of the vengeful actions of Clint Eastwood's man with no name in *High Plains Drifter.* The two also share not-so-subtle connections with the land down under (and we're not talking Australia here). Eastwood's character forces the local townsfolk to paint their entire community red, for instance, and "the boss man" in *Dilbert* has horns of hair that have grown over the years. Both characters deem their underlings unworthy of respect because of previous transgressions and their inability to act like civilized human beings. In this respect individuals at the lower levels of a social hierarchy find their bodies appropriated for organizational interests, treated as disposable inhuman parts to keep the bureaucratic machine moving. The organization, as Taylor (1993b) notes, works to produce images of workers' bodies that negate the subjectivity or humanness of those individuals.

These images of workers as animals, inmates, and/or sinners "kept down" imply the workers, respectively, are being cared for, kept out of trouble, and/or punished by individuals who are able to control their primitive impulses. Such a system suggests a rational model taken to the extreme, a mode of thinking found in colonizing rhetoric as well as in religious rhetoric. These two rhetorics, founded on Enlightenment thinking that suggests we are able to (and should) transcend our circumstances in order to progress, have been employed in conjunction throughout western history (see Said, 1978, for an examination of a particular instance of such rhetoric in "the Orient"); they are ingrained in our habitus. Native Americans, for instance, were once depicted as unintelligent wild heathens. In this belief system the inferior must be overseen by the superior; the managers/

colonizers/missionaries must civilize and tame the savage beasts known as workers/natives/unsaved souls. Social equality is abolished in this system because, in this case, the Cubeville residents are treated as inhuman and thus unworthy of equal status, just as African American slaves were defined as animals undeserving of "full human" status (leading to their designation in the Constitution as three-fifths of a person when populations were counted to determine representation in the House). In its place is a phony meritocratic system in which the most worthy individuals are supposed to have risen to the top of the hierarchy. The rationality espoused by meritocracy suggests these individuals should make decisions for the less rational persons. Yet as *Dilbert* points out, the least rational individuals are those making the decisions. Coming to terms with this realization and then critically responding to it are made possible through symbolic pilgrimages to the imagined community of Nerdvana.

Nerdvana as the 'Hood

In both rhetorical forms of redefinition found in Cubeville—workers as animals and/or inmates—the discursive strategies are similar to those used to define the dangerous residents of urban areas. They are either animals who have no respect for human decency or thugs who have no respect for human life. "Respect" recurs in the previous sentence for good reason; it is of central importance to those individuals who redefine themselves in response to rhetorical efforts to confine and control. Lacking respect from others, they see such respect as integral to the harmony of an alternative community. As Conquergood (1994) explains in his discussion of Chicago gang culture: "One of the cardinal sins of life in the hood [is] disrespect. In a mainstream world where residents of the inner city have been marginalized socioeconomically and stripped of human dignity, the reciprocal courtesies of street politesse help restore respect, repair the loss of face, and redress the daily humiliations of poverty and prejudice" (pp. 42–43). Similarly, Adams explains of Dilbert, "'He's doing what he can to keep his dignity intact'" (quoted in J. Adams, 1996, p. 5). Rhetorically respecting another person as an equal, whether it is in the gang in the hood or the gang at the water cooler, defines that person as a partner in the community and provides her/him with a means of opposing the structural conditions that "keep one down." Symbolic pilgrimages function in this context to generate respect from others who engage in similar pilgrimages.

To maintain their dignity people in both groups require reassurance that they are among social equals. In one *Dilbert* strip, Wally appears to have made the analogy between the work world and urban gang life literal as he carries his binders in a shopping cart, expresses himself through graffiti, and indicates he is "thinking of joining a gang" (Adams, 1996a, p. 212). In Cubeville respect is lacking at both ends of the spectrum of power. As Adams explains in an interview: "Now, there are workers, average workers, who are often much more knowledgeable about their areas than their leaders. So the whole respect thing has gone to zero. . . . Those who don't have power yet . . . deserve it, because they have the intelligence and the ability, but, because of the corporate structure, they don't have the respect" (quoted in Brown, 1995, p. 18). Responding to such material conditions requires an alternative point of view, a new way of envisioning the cultural terrain. Communitas, as Turner (1974) points out, provides such a view because it "remains open and unspecialized, a spring of pure possibility" (p. 202). There, as the Turners (1978) note, respect for the pilgrimages of others may grow.

In the hood one response to habitus is to join a formal community or gang, such as the Latin Kings (see Conquergood, 1994). In Dilbert's world respect is enhanced through joining the informal community of Dogbert's New Ruling Class (DNRC). In both cases members engage in behaviors that enact promised lands where the de-centered can acquire respect and power. The Latin Kings name offices that members can hold, such as "Incas, Coronas, Caciques, and Crown Councils" (Conquergood, 1994, p. 33). DNRC members select their own names, such as "Cardinal of Limbo, Lord High Everything Else, and Minister of Things That Go 'Plonk' When You Hit Them With a Stick" (Adams, 1994b, pp. 3–4).[3] The symbolic borders of these promised lands are enacted through nonverbal communication codes accessible only to those members of the community or those who respect the community. The Latin Kings engage in nonverbal forms of communication called "representing" that includes "throwing up hand signs" (Conquergood, 1994, p. 40). DNRC members "make a fist, simulating Dogbert's roundish body, extend the pinky finger, simulating Dogbert's tail, [and] wag [their] pinky three times" (Adams, 1995f, p. 3). The movement from one world to the other relies on technological communication devices that allow their users to be more than one place at once. Meyrowitz (1985) indicates that such devices increase cultural fragmentation, but they also may provide the means of accessing transcendent places that respond to our increased awareness of cultural fragmentation. For example, gangs like the Latin Kings are "very responsive to certain communication technologies," such as pagers (Conquergood, 1994, pp. 48–49), and DNRC members scattered around the globe rely on communication technologies such as e-mail (where DNRC membership is represented by an emoticon O- that resembles a view of Dogbert from above) and the internet, where United Media keeps a Web site called The Dilbert Zone that attracts 1.5 million hits each day (Levy, 1996). As I noted at the beginning of the previous chapter, communication technologies are paradoxical; they contribute to our fragmentation yet allow us to extend ourselves into imaginative worlds of our creation in response to that fragmentation.

These communication practices can thus be defined as distancing tactics, means of distinguishing between oneself and unpleasant others. In symbolic pilgrimage terms they represent the separation or release from one's home into a liminoid flow. The distancing of the self from the habitus is the first step in the round-trip journey that marks the pilgrimage. As the journey continues, the distancing tactics assist in the creation of a symbolic promised land in which individuals are re-centered. "Such distancing behavior and talk," Snow and Anderson (1987) found in their interviews of homeless people in Austin, Tex., "represent attempts to salvage a measure of self-worth. In the process, of course, the homeless are asserting more favorable personal identities," much as the Latin Kings and DNRC members do (p. 1353). By exchanging their demeaning urban roles for the more romantic communal roles of gang participation, individuals in both groups engage in role distancing in particular, "an active and self-conscious attempt to foster the impression of a lack of commitment or attachment to a particular role in order to deny the virtual self implied" by the cultural norms of the habitus (Snow & Anderson, 1987, p. 1350). The communication practices of the Latin Kings and the DNRC, then, both deny the dehumanized roles assigned to them by the habitus and serve as empowering images that generate enhanced self-worth. In short, the gangs' communication is a form of vernacular discourse (discussed in chapter three), simultaneously resisting demeaning images and building affirming images (Ono & Sloop, 1995). As Turner (1974) predicts, they build a form of communitas that transcends the habitus.

To do so both groups create symbolic communities through gangs. Gangs are among the many community-building activities that Conquergood says help urban residents cope with oppressive material conditions. Big Red residents, for example, would serve meals to neighbors and watch others' children throughout the day, creating a feeling of kinship even among those individuals who came from different ethnic backgrounds. In a neighborhood where living standards were abysmal, Conquergood (1992) explains, exchanging respect and helping one another cope "enable people to experience dignity and joy in structures like Big Red, refashioning them into 'dwelling-places'" that transcended the material conditions of the neighborhood (p. 127).

Dilbert's promised land involves a translation of the confining tenements of Cubeville to a place in which technological proficiency and wisdom are integrated in a new rationalist utopia called Nerdvana (borrowed from a 1991 *Dilbert* strip in which the engineer experiences "a feeling of ecstasy" in having "become one with my computer," a state Dogbert labels "Nerdvana"; see Adams, 1995a, p. 65). Nerdvana becomes a sacred place through temporal transcendence, blending the past promised land of technological utopia with a future reenvisioning of the workplace environment. Nerdvana is a place in between the past and future but not of the present; it exists above and beyond the habitus. In this respect the Cubevillians' approach to coping with material conditions is similar to the image I outlined early in chapter three: resistance through technological extension, a.k.a. cyborgs (Haraway, 1991). Their superior knowledge of technology allows them to envision a "true" meritocracy in which individuals with cognitive skills and the ability to reason are exalted over those who prosper through the auspices of the "phony" meritocracy. This symbolic place of escape and resistance is the "dwelling-place" or promised land for persons who have little power to change their material conditions, so they *cope* with those conditions by envisioning their lived work environment as a place where rationality rules and the irrational decisions of incompetent managers are resisted. The phony meritocracy of Cubeville is laid bare by shifting the standpoint of readers from the corner office to the tenement-like cubicle. Epistemological mobility accompanies this movement from one standpoint to the next, allowing the characters/readers to see how, in the ideal meritocracy of Nerdvana, the competent are allowed to display their abilities and to succeed.

Ritualistically reading (and re-reading) *Dilbert* allows fans to escape the material conditions of Cubeville temporarily and to *hope* for a material change through critique. By moving from the material to the symbolic they experience—and in some cases enact (more on this later)—the modern, romantic haven of Nerdvana. In this promised land power relations are reversed and the work world operates in ideal, pure meritocratic terms. Imagining the possibility of this sacred place, then ritualistically and symbolically journeying to it, allows fans of *Dilbert* to envision alternatives to their material conditions. The journey itself may not immediately change those conditions, but making their pernicious character visible can promote gradual change. As Brown (1997) points out, "What Adams has done is to take virtually every HR [human resources] issue of the past 20 years and catapult it to the top of many management agendas. . . . 'Dilbert' is about human rights, human purpose and human potential" (p. 3).

In short, Dilbert, like the urban gangs Conquergood describes, uses symbolic resources to resist his habitus. When fans of *Dilbert* ritualistically read about the engineer's exploits, they are equipped with a similar rhetorical arsenal. They possess, in Scott's (1985) words, "weapons of the weak" that are used to reframe power relationships. Scott, writing about peasant resistance in Malaysia, explains how this process of symbolic redefinition works:

> Above all, the symbolic resistance of the poor rejects the categories the rich attempt to impose upon them. They know that the large farmers increasingly see them as lazy, unreliable, dishonest, and grasping. They know that, behind their backs, they are blamed as the authors of their own victimization and that, in daily social encounters, they are increasingly treated with little consideration or, worse, ignored. Much of what they have to say among themselves is a decisive rejection of the attempt to relegate them to a permanently inferior economic and ritual status and a decisive assertion of their citizenship rights in this small community. (p. 236)

Although Scott is discussing a context seemingly far removed from corporate America, the following pages illustrate how we may easily substitute the words "cubicle dwellers" for "poor" and "managers" for "rich/large farmers"—just as Scott's quotation could appear in Conquergood's writing by replacing "large farmers" with any number of nouns (e.g., suburban residents, middle/upper class, politicians, slumlords, etc.).

Coping Through Recognition

Nerdvana's modernist sense of place, imbued with the romantic feeling of connections and community found in all utopias, begins with a postmodern move that reveals the paradoxical irrationality in the rational. Nerdvanians realize the incompetent are promoted into positions from which they oversee the competent. They understand how the illusory image of meritocracy is dangled in front of them. In its place, they know, is a nonsensical conglomeration of guesses masquerading as decisions. Fan Sarah, for instance, uses e-mail to describe *Dilbert* as "a comic strip that accurately illustrates the absurdity of corporate managerial decision-making." Her assessment is reinforced by a number of *Dilbert* strips, including one where the executives of Dilbert's company meet to discuss the need "to fire employees until we're stronger than the competition." When one exec asks, "How will the work get done with no employees?" the other responds, "I'd better form a task force to study that" (Adams, 1996a, p. 176). Such leadership becomes self-perpetuating because the irrational executives make promotion decisions. For example, Dilbert's colleague Tim, who has been going without sleep or food to meet a deadline, becomes an unintelligible gelatinous mass spouting gobbledygook. "As a result," the boss intones, "your work has been muddle-brained and incomprehensible. You leave me no choice, Tim." The irrational choice, Wally later explains to Dilbert, is that "Tim got promoted to division manager" (Adams, 1995a, p. 199).

Meanwhile, the rational, competent workers in Cubeville are denied the opportunity to succeed. In an early *Dilbert* the boss tells the engineer that he's taking a vacation and needs "competent leadership while I'm gone." While Dilbert silently exclaims, "At last he's giving me an assignment with responsibility," the boss continues, "That's why I got this talking sock monkey. Pull the string twice a day and do what he says" (Adams, 1994c, p. 24). Such decisions seem to suggest Cubeville's managers are sufficiently rational to recognize their irrationality on occasion, a notion reinforced when Dilbert and his competent colleague Alice are denied a promotion. As the boss explains, they possess "technical knowledge that is too valuable to lose. . . . [Thus] the only logical choice is to promote Al because he has no valuable knowledge" (Adams, 1996a, p. 187). In lieu of promotions, Nerdvanians receive false promises of social equality. As the boss explains, management is "flattening the organization to eliminate levels and put everybody in a wide salary band." In this system, he explains, "instead of not getting a promotion you'll only not get a raise." When Wally pursues the logic behind the move by asking, "So, what job title do we use?" the boss adds to the irrationality of the decision by answering, "You'll all be named Beverly" (1996a, p. 53). Meanwhile, the managers are promoted in Cubeville simply because they look the part. For instance, Dilbert is introduced to the company's "newest fast-track manager" named Ben. "Ben has no real experience," explains the boss, "but he's very tall, so we know he'll go far." Adds Ben, "I also have executive style hair," an inanity that the boss amplifies: "We think it will turn silver" (Adams, 1995a, p. 209).

Those with the competence to perform the work in Cubeville are deemed too valuable to promote, and those lacking competence are irrationally shuffled into management. Their decisions perpetuate the cycle of irrationality and ultimately create a dispirited work environment. In such an environment the "true" criminals are the managers. "Managerial disdain is bad enough, Adams seems to be saying; insincere and dishonest disdain is criminal!" claims one *Dilbert* observer (Brown, 1997, p. 3).

Hoping Through Redefinition

Once this definition of the rational as irrational is accepted, other paradoxical rhetorical moves may follow as a means of both critiquing the habitus and providing hope for an alternative arrangement. In a kind of *1984*ism the switching of binary opposites promulgated by the rational/irrational redefinition reveals the arbitrary nature of language in the habitus (i.e., "rational" and positions of authority are not inherently related); the commonsensical is unveiled as historically and socially constructed. Such a revelation encourages *additional* redefinitions of antithetical terms. The first rhetorical move reverses the power dynamic. The second rhetorical move redefines the antisocial as playful. Together they reflect the notion that "naming is always an exercise of power" (Gunkel & Gunkel, 1997, p. 133).

REVERSING THE POWER DYNAMIC. Those who do not have power in Cubeville, namely Dilbert and his colleagues, possess the power in Nerdvana. Conquergood's (1992) tale of Big Red is helpful here. In Big Red the tenement residents banded together to dig to, then open, a city water line that had been closed during a heat wave because the absentee landlord had not paid his bills (Conquergood, 1992). Similarly, rather than dwelling with the incommensurability between the system as envisioned and the system in practice, *Dilbert's* denizens redefine Cubeville as a promised land in which they create and adhere to their own rules, since the rules allegedly in force are irrational. Nerdvana's reliance on meritocracy means some of the people are labeled as "losers," for it is a rational system in which a bottom must exist. Meanwhile, in Cubeville the losers are the technologically oriented workers who are exiled from success by an irrational cadre of managers, marketers, and sales representatives whose decisions dictate the lives of the tenement dwellers. Nerdvana reverses this dynamic, casting the illegitimate authorities as losers who are unable to understand technology, not cognitively complex, and prone to spouting inane buzzwords as cover for their ignorance.

To begin, technological proficiency allows Nerdvanians to circumvent attempts to control them with power, just as the Big Red residents circumvented the city's misguided attempts to control water usage with their blue-collar skills. Dilbert, for instance, silently inventories the capabilities of his computer, "35 inch monitor, 20 megs of RAM, 1.2 gigabytes of hard disk space" as he realizes he doesn't require human interaction to succeed, causing him to break into a joyous refrain of "People . . . who don't need people . . . are the ha-a-a-ppiest people" (Adams, 1996a, p. 72; ellipses in original). Technological proficiency is also used to reverse power, not just to circumvent its controlling grasp. A coworker named Irv, for instance, appears to do little real work for Dilbert's company. When pressed by Dilbert to account for his situation, Irv explains, "I wrote the code for our accounting system back in the mid-eighties. It's a million lines of undocumented spaghetti logic." An awed Dilbert exclaims, "It's the holy grail of technology!!" (Adams, 1996a, p. 120). Wally uses his e-mail system to take a six-month "in-cube sabbatical," sending old e-mail messages while he refuses to work on current projects (2/15/95).

Those who do not possess technological proficiency are at the mercy of Dilbert's gang of techno-guerillas. When a marketing employee, operating from the standpoint of Cubeville, taunts Dilbert, "Ha ha! Now that the engineers must charge their time to marketing, we *own* you!" the engineer reverses the power relationship from his Nerdvanian perspective: "I'll just reprogram your computer through the LAN so its radiation will alter your DNA." Responds the marketer, "Is that possible??!" (7/3/95; emphasis in original). The new power dynamic is reinforced when a marketing employee temporarily trades jobs with Dilbert. The marketer looks at Wally's computer—"a fifty MIP Sparc work-station," Wally tells him—and wonders, "What kind of microwave oven is this?" while fretting that "it's going to take *forever* to warm my croissant" (Adams, 1995a, p. 149; emphasis in original). Even the boss is unable to understand the little glowing machines. After seeking Dilbert's help to upgrade his computer, the engineer points out, "The computer in your office is a cardboard prop that came with your desk." Apparently not understanding even what technology looks like, the boss continues, "So, I need a new motherboard, right?" (Adams, 1996a, p. 101).

Technological knowledge becomes a weapon of sorts for the Nerdvanian water cooler gang. They use their wisdom and expertise to disarm the fools behind the curtain who disguise their incompetence with illegitimate power. Mocking refrains of "If I Only Had a Brain" echo through the landscape in Nerdvana, as Cubeville's voluntary expatriates reveal the "strawman" arguments offered by their alleged superiors. The ignorance of management in general is exposed when the boss seeks to quash a "rumor" that management is "not planning to relocate the company to the South Pole where easily trainable native Eskimos will replace" the workers (4/5/95). Dilbert's response, "That's good because there aren't any Eskimos at the South Pole," causes the startled boss to blurt, "Excuse me, I have to make a phone call" (4/5/95). Earlier that week the boss asked Dilbert and Wally for help with his laptop computer. Dilbert remarks, "Remember you have to hold it upside down and shake it to reboot," after which Wally wonders if the boss will "ever realize we gave him an 'etch-a-sketch' " (4/3/95). Dilbert's boss is so obtuse, the comic strip implies, that his concern for using empowering language causes him to overlook a direct insult. Reading Dilbert's report, in which the engineer claims "the project is delayed 'due to the ongoing bungling of a clueless, pointy-hair individual,' " the boss suggests, "Instead of saying 'due to,' it would read better as 'facilitated by' " (5/24/94). In another strip Wally and Dilbert gang up on the boss, telling him that he can dry his rain-soaked clothes by putting them in the microwave for 60 minutes. Wally confides to Dilbert after their prank, "You know, ever since the downsizing began, I've felt much less company loyalty" (6/1/97).

That the boss and other executives in Cubeville are incompetent is further demonstrated in a story line tracking Dogbert's rapid ascent of the corporate ladder. Explaining his phenomenal success to the company president, the dog notes, "It was easy to grab power, once I realized the other executives were just imbeciles with good hair" (Adams, 1996a, p. 15). These "imbeciles" attempt to cover their tracks by using the rhetoric of phony meritocracy, but their efforts are easily visible from the vistas of Nerdvana. For instance, Dilbert's boss informs him that his new " 'MBWA' or 'management by walking around' " strategy doesn't seem to improve the workplace. "I walked all the way to the park and back," he tells Dilbert, "but I can't say that I see much improvement around here" (Adams, 1996e, p. 20). In another strip Dilbert questions his boss's decision to start "an interdisciplinary task force to study our decision-making process" by asking, "So, you're using a bad decision-making process to decide how to fix our bad decision-making process?" When the boss explains, "I don't know how else we could find the source of our problem," Dilbert suggests, "X-ray your skull?" (Adams, 1996a, p. 183).

The reversal of power in Nerdvana means the power to name now rests in the hands of Dilbert and his colleagues. In the DNRC this power was displayed in the form of a contest among newsletter readers to create "a good derogatory nickname for non-DNRC people. . . . Their name should sound harmless and endearing but have a clever double meaning" (Adams, 1995c, p. 1). The runners-up included, " 'Team Players' because that's a nice way to say 'loser,' " (T. Miller), " 'Sir' and 'Miss' [because] Sir is short for 'servant' and Miss is short for 'mistake' " (D. Schumacher), and " 'Stars' because from our perspective, none of them are very bright and there are more of them than we really need" (G. Guglielmo) (all in Adams, 1995d, p. 7). The winner was "Induhviduals," a term that has remained constant in the newsletters that followed (Heather, in Adams, 1995d, p. 6).

Those newsletters routinely feature examples of induhviduals at work, thanks to contributions from *Dilbert* readers. For example, "A friend . . . thought if he put all his Microsoft Word documents into a tiny font they'd take up less room [on the disk] (Adams, 1996c, p. 3). Another technologically inept person was having problems sending a fax: the recipient kept receiving a cover page then a blank page. The sender explained, "It's a pretty sensitive memo, and I didn't want any-one else to read it by accident, so I folded it so only the recipient would open it and read it" (Adams, 1996d, p. 6). Some induhvidu-als apparently demonstrate their character without technology, as in the case of a rural neighbor who asked authorities to remove a "deer crossing" sign in the area because "many deer were being hit by cars and he no longer wanted them [the deer] to cross there" (Adams, 1997a, p. 7). Adams has even discovered some induhviduals lurking within the DNRC, reporting that he received the following letter: "Your cartoon on 6/9/97 seems to advocate the teaching of criti-cal thinking to children. That's dangerous. Children must be TOLD what is right and wrong, not taught to think! Critical thinking is exactly the sort of thing that caused the Oklahoma City bombing!" (1997b, p. 1). The interview participants also could recall encounters with induhviduals, including one in which Nancy's K-mart coworker "had an argument with a customer about where the front of the store was."[4]

The DNRC newsletter serves as something of a secret clubhouse for members who are dissatisfied with their work experiences but are unable to find a means to voice their discontent. Adams, in fact, re-cently asked DNRC members to serve as "cubicle spies" who would be his lookouts in the work world. Adams promises potential club members that he may call at work at any moment, but "I'll use your secret spy name so you know it's me and not some Induhvidual co-worker playing a prank on you" (Adams, 1997a, p. 9). As noted earlier this language of the secret society is present in urban gangs, too. In both contexts, as Weckman (1987) points out, "a secret society may be an agency for change, rebellion, or reform . . . [and] foster a per-son's sense of identity" (p. 152).

Sharing the inanities they experience serves a number of purposes for *Dilbert* fans/spies such as myself. First, symbolically moving to the "clubhouse" (or promised land of Nerdvana) by reading the news-letter allows us to escape temporarily the material conditions in which we find ourselves; we are released from the constraints of the habitus, and transcend its boundaries, when we imaginatively enter the clubhouse. Getting caught up in the stories and humor of the newsletter provides an immersion into a liminoid discursive realm, even if the newsletter is being read within the material confines of the cubicle. Second, understanding that other people share similar experiences provides the connections communitas affords within the liminoid promised land. DNRC members swap stories through Adams, and he uses their stories as inspiration for the daily *Dilberts*. The symbolic community is generated as the individual fan reads the stories, culling rhetorical fragments from her/his own experiences and imaginatively interacting with other DNRC members. Third, giving literal and/or vicarious voice to their frustrations, while symbolically sharing those frustrations with others, allows fans to return "home" better prepared to cope with their material situation and to enact their hopes for an alternative to that situation. One of the focus group members, for instance, began sharing her collection of her favorite *Dilbert* strips with the rest of the group. After nearly 10 minutes of reading, laughter, and commentary, Beth exclaimed, "This is the most fun I've had all week!"

REDEFINING THE ANTISOCIAL AS PLAYFUL. After people and their abilities are renamed in Nerdvana, a second rhetorical move can occur, one in which the antisocial is defined as playful. Such a move reflects Turner's (1974) belief that communitas "liberates [identities] from conformity to general norms" found in the habitus (p. 274). Again, Conquergood's (1992) Big Red work is illuminating. The tenants of Big Red responded to a new on-site janitor's attempt to make the grounds more respectable (by middle-class standards, Conquergood says)—he declared off-limits public spaces that were used as play areas by the children and social spaces by the adults—by engaging in activities that could be defined as vandalism, trespassing, and arson. Rather than treating these efforts as criminal, however, the janitor halted his plans, and later in the year he hooked up a water sprinkler in the courtyard on a hot summer day so the kids could play in its cooling streams (Conquergood, 1992). He recognized the illegitimate nature of his power in the tenement context, Conquergood claims, and eventually subscribed to the tenants' definitions of the public spaces.

Similarly, actions that could be defined as wasteful, inefficient, and unproductive in Cubeville are redefined as playful in Nerdvana. The workers openly rebel against authority, ignore management's entreaties to work harder, and seek ways to circumvent power surreptitiously—all as part of the game they are able to play with their technological proficiency and knowledge. Dilbert, for instance, realizes, "I get paid the same no matter what I do. I can stand here and flick my fingers and still get paid" (Adams, 1996a, p. 191). In another strip his rebellion intensifies as he sits in his cubicle: "Hey, I haven't done a thing for minutes and yet I still get paid. Hoo-hoo-ha! I'm ripping off the evil corporate empire and there's nothing they can do about it! I have total power!" (Adams, 1995a, p. 209). In perhaps the ultimate form of rebellion, Dilbert stays at home to "telecommute" yet lies around all day in his robe pondering, "Do I owe my employer eight productive hours, or do I only need to match the two productive hours I would have spent in the office?" (2/6/95). Not surprisingly, then, Wally is unfazed by the boss's request that he sign an agreement not to work for the competition for five years should he leave the firm. He thinks, "I haven't done any work *here* for five years, so how hard could it be?" as he sits down to play another game on his computer (5/1/97; emphasis in original).

Prospective members of the DNRC are encouraged to engage in similar playful behavior. For instance, you earn "2 points for every vacation day you've successfully classified as a 'telecommuting' day in the past 12 months," "2 points for convincing your employer that you need Internet access for (hee hee!) 'important business reasons,'" and a whopping "50 points if you've been reprimanded by management for displaying Dilbert cartoons" (Adams, 1994b, p. 2). The display of cartoons is something of a form of office graffiti in Nerdvana, for the strips not only define one's turf, they send a message of resistance to management and other workers. Explains Brian, "'I've been clipping out the cartoons and pasting them on my door in the hopes that our nontechnical management would read them'" (quoted in Garner, 1994, p. 98). E-mail fans offer similar statements. Brooke writes, "I often find myself cutting [the strips] out and putting them on my door because they express my frustrations so well." Affirms Steven, "I cut the strip[s] out and hang them on my door." Practicing "dilberfiti" in one's workplace may prompt managers to think about their behaviors and provides workers with an alternative, resistant form of rhetoric.

Decorating one's territory is part of the process of transforming the confining areas of Cubeville into something imaginatively bigger: promised lands from which to resist illegitimate authority. Dilbert's daydream in one strip echoes the royal rhetoric of the Latin Kings: "I am the king of my cubicle, the absolute ruler of this tiny realm. And these are my loyal subjects: mister computer, mister stapler, and the binder family." When Wally asks, "Who spilled coffee?" Dilbert continues his fantasy: "The barbarian is thwarted at the moat" (Adams, 1996a, p. 153). Other workers also find ways to expand the domain of the confining cubicle. In one strip, for example, Wally stacks company business plans on his chair to elevate his view above the cubicle walls and then encourages others to do the same. The boss, clueless as always, says, "Wow! I've never seen so much interest in our business plan!" as he hands out two more copies to a playful Nerdvanian (Adams, 1996a, p. 185). Dilbert also makes use of company documents, taking them home to burn in order to reduce his heating bills. When the boss says, "I've been noticing how much stuff you take home. You must love your work," Dilbert playfully responds, "It gives me a warm feeling" (1/16/95).

Taking the limited resources available to them in Cubeville, Nerdvanians redefine the use of the materials. DNRC members do the same thing. In a relatively new feature of his newsletter, Adams posts "office pranks" contributed by members. For example, one reader explains how to booby trap a center drawer in a non-DNRC member's desk:

You need: 2 paper clips, one rubber band, a business card and a bunch of "holes" from the hole puncher. Open the drawer and wedge a paper clip on each end, toward the front of the drawer. Stretch the rubber band across the width of the drawer, attaching it at each end by the paper clips. Insert the business card into the center of the rubber band and wind the rubber band many times so that when released the business card will act like a steamboat paddle. Put a pile of paper "holes" under the business card then close the drawer carefully to prevent the rubber band from unwinding. The Induhvidual who opens the drawer will be met with a hail of paper "holes" as a festive tribute to your genius. (Adams, 1995e, p. 2)

Another, more technologically inclined reader, suggests, "Find a screenshot utility (software) and take a nice screen shot of the computer's desktop. Convert it to Windows wallpaper. Now delete all icons off of your desktop. When an Induhvidual tries to use the computer none of the icons will work. Hilarity ensues" (Adams, 1996b, p. 6). Also employing technology as a weapon, an MRI machine operator explains how s/he conned a medical sales person into tossing his wallet through the demagnetizing field of the machine, making his credit cards useless (Adams, 1996c, p. 2).

These pranks allow over 200,000 fans the ability to enact Nerdvanian principles in their workplaces; they can translate the symbolic into the material through actions that at once reflect their meritocratic abilities and their sense of communitas with others. Reading daily *Dilbert*s and sharing in the ideas of other DNRC members can afford fans a new perspective on the workplace that makes it more tolerable, and offers hope for the future. Consequently, the apparent transgressions of established order depicted in *Dilbert* and encouraged in the DNRC are tolerated, even celebrated, within the community because they provide a means of coping with an irrational system disguised in rational rhetoric. They are also a sign that a fan has symbolically journeyed to another place where different rules apply; Nerdvana serves as what Turner calls antistructure, a temporary sacred place that pilgrims visit/create to oppose the existing social structure. There pilgrims have power they do not possess in the habitus. *Dilbert* fans report similar experiences. "Sometimes seeing real life being made fun of is all it takes to make someone feel like they have some form of power," claims Ian via e-mail. Interview participant Beth elaborates: "For me it's a relief that there is another person that recognizes the same absurdities that I see every day, and I think, 'Yes! Yes, you too have experienced it.' . . . To know that others have experienced the same absurdities makes it tolerable, makes it possible for you to deal with it." Nancy, another interview participant echoes that thought: "It's a way for people to really recognize that their situation isn't that unusual. You know, that we all run into bosses who know next to nothing."

Dilbert's antisocial behaviors, then, become a playful reality check, a way of remembering that "we take ourselves, and that's a generic kind of statement, waaay too seriously about how important these things are or how seriously other people take them," as interview participant Gretchen observes. In this respect *Dilbert* encourages its fans to adopt Burke's comic frame in their interactions with the constraints of habitus. As we saw in the previous chapter, "The comic frame should enable people *to be observers of themselves, while acting*" (Burke, 1937, p. 171; emphasis in original). The symbolic pilgrimages *Dilbert* fuels give readers the ability to position themselves together, in a community of like-minded others who see how we take work too seriously. Admits Jeff via e-mail, "I like Dilbert because it takes the seriousness out of corporate America and slaps it in the face!" Leland even appreciates how the strip makes fun of its protagonists: "I like the way Dilbert pokes fun at all the different aspects of business, from managers to co-workers, to engineers themselves." As he continues Leland also illustrates how Nerdvanians enact the modernist elements of the comic frame, acknowledging their perspective as unique, somehow special, compared to other points of view: "I think engineers like to poke fun at themselves more than just about anyone else. It is rare to find an attorney cracking up as he tells a lawyer joke, but engineers seem to take great joy in making fun of their own profession." Reflecting his fans' mindset, Dilbert finds ignoring the entreaties of his boss quite easy. When the boss/warden threatens, "Work harder or I'll have you put in the 'box,'" Dilbert responds, "Really? I thought I was already in the box. Is the box bigger than my cubicle?" (Adams, 1996a, p. 159).

Being part of this irreverent gang is important for *Dilbert* readers because it allows them to imagine themselves as part of a symbolic community whose promised land stretches beyond the habitus. Individual readers envision this territory slightly differently, as each contextualizes the open-to-interpretation promised land of Nerdvana within the fragments of her/his own experiences. Each fan thus is ontologically centering their selves during their epistemologically mobile treks. For example, e-mail participant Leland, an engineering student, recalls, "The whole series about the keyboard missing the letter 'q' was funny to most readers, but it had a lot more meaning to those who knew about the Intel Pentium fiasco." Winona, who works in an office, explains in her e-mail that she uses the communitas of *Dilbert* in another way: "Dilbert is an outlet of humor for my everyday stress at work. It gives me another way to look at things in order for everything not to look so glum and stressful." Beth, who sneaks peeks at *Dilbert*s she receives from a colleague's calendar, contextualizes her enjoyment of the comic within her material experiences of a management position: "It's a real joy. . . . I just get to think about something so absurd and so away from all the other demands on my life. It's sort of a little relief for 15 seconds." Concludes Ian, "Dilbert, in general, is a great vent from the everyday."

The revelation of the irrational, then, offers a double dose of reassurance for Dilbert and his colleagues. First, they realize their status as "losers" is rhetorical rather than material; the discourse of rationality has named them as losers. Exposing the irrationality of the rational reveals that those with the power to name are arbitrarily, rather than naturally, selected. Second, they become aware that a new discourse offers opportunities for renaming. In a true meritocracy the "true losers" are those who are undeserving of success.

Nerdvana and Social Equality

Yet this rhetoric of reversal also threatens to turn the communitas of Nerdvana into simply more social structure. As symbolic pilgrims ritualistically reenact their journeys to and from Nerdvana, they run the risk of petrifying the antistructure of communitas into part of the habitus. As the journeys become routine, the promised land may seem less special and its boundaries more fixed in the imaginations of the fans. Their memories of the promised land of Nerdvana may grow so strong as to preclude other interpretations. At that point the special qualities of communitas break down. As Turner (1973) points out, "Communitas strains toward universalism and openness; it must be distinguished, for example, in principle from Durkheim's notion of 'mechanical solidarity,' which is a bond between individuals who are collectively in opposition to another solidarity group" (p. 216). Communitas, with its romantic and postmodern underpinnings, "puts *all* social structural rules in question and suggests new possibilities . . . [and] differences are accepted or tolerated rather than aggravated into grounds of aggressive opposition" (Turner, 1973, pp. 216 & 222), but mechanical solidarity relies solely on modernist either/or definitions. Thus while Nerdvanians' reversal of definitions represents postmodern playfulness with language, and their establishment of promised land boundaries provides a romantic antidote to meritocratic habitus, their positioning of themselves as intellectually superior to their management superiors also runs the risk of perpetuating the social structure of meritocracy.

Nerdvanians' substitution of a "pure" rationality for an "irrational" rationality relies on modernism's either/or logic, and in this case the excluded middle contains the tradition of social equality, the site most likely to contain Turner's ideal of communitas. Nerdvana, put simply, has no room for evaluations of others based on criteria other than merit, whether defined as intelligence or technological competence. In the annals of *Dilbert* the character of Dogbert best exemplifies this either/or thinking. In fact, e-mail participant Leland opens his message to me by saying, "Hope you don't get too many negative responses, many people let their alter egos show, and in the Dilbert group they tend to try to be more like Dogbert than Dilbert."

Dogbert, whom Adams calls his alter ego, is convinced that people are not as smart as he, just as Adams claims "that we, as a nation, are unable to say to somebody, 'You know, the problem here, Bob, is you're stupid.' And almost all of the problems that I've ever had in any business setting was [*sic*] that somebody's brain wasn't working well" (quoted in Over, 1996, p. 20). The reversal of power in Nerdvana isn't a simple transposing of top and bottom; those who see themselves at the new top, such as Dogbert, find plenty of others at the bottom—not just former managers. For instance, Dogbert's plan to rule the world should be easy to implement, the dog believes. "It shouldn't be too hard," he tells his owner, "given the fact I've probably sneezed more brain cells than the average human uses on election day" (Adams, 1996a, p. 50). To finance his conquest, and to make a few quick bucks, Dogbert is prone to milking the naive, whether it be selling chunks of his sidewalk as pieces from the Berlin Wall (Adams, 1995a, p. 78), creating an evangelical television show called "Healing for Dollars" (Adams, 1995a, p. 178), authoring a book of guesses disguised as future trends (Adams, 1996a, p. 173), or establishing a school of common sense in which he stumps a woman with the following "puzzle": "Who can show me how to get the water out of this boot? If you have trouble, the directions are written on the heel" (Adams, 1995a, p. 182).

Dogbert's dismissive, sometimes manipulative, attitude is also evident in the pages of Adams's electronic newsletter. In his second newsletter, Adams (1994a) concludes his advice for subscribing to the electronic mailing list: "If you still can't figure out how to get on the list, you're probably a 'Family Circus' fan anyway and not destined to mingle with the new ruling class except maybe as domestic help. But hey, clean homes are important, too" (p. 1). Of course, Adams notes in a 1997 newsletter: "There's a big downside to having Induhviduals as servants, especially in the home. For example, they can't always tell the difference between the kids and the house pets. If you don't keep an eye on the nanny, your kids will be eating pellets while your wiener dog is studying romance languages at Harvard. That's not the sort of thing your children will forgive you for later. And your wiener dog will be arrogant" (Adams, 1997a, pp. 1–2). To avoid a lifetime of domestic service, and the stigma of being involved in the "wrong" kind of service work in a postindustrial economy, Adams (1994b) offers in his third newsletter a means of assessing one's status, because "after all, it's not who you are as a person that counts, it's who you're superior to" (p. 1). Consequently, Adams (1997b) suggests induhviduals can be best used as paperweights, taste testers for things you find on the ground, and beta testers for bungee cords. Meanwhile, the votes of 1500 newsletter readers selected as the top annoying business practice "idiots being promoted to management"; in second place was "being forced to work with idiots" (Adams, 1995b, p. 3). No wonder e-mail fan Winona notes, "Everyone who is trying to get ahead wants to be [at the top] because we feel we could do a better job, therefore we think everyone else is stupid. Dilbert is life as we see it and if you don't see it that way you won't laugh."

For Adams and the denizens of the DNRC, displays of wit serve as markers of distinction. They "get" the humor in *Dilbert,* but many of their bosses do not. Workers who post copies of the comic on their office doors and/or walls tell Adams in e-mail messages "that instead of getting the clue, their bosses merely stand outside the cubicle, guffawing about the poor management skills displayed by *other* managers" (Hamilton, 1996, p. 7). Displays of wit, argues Garrett (1993), "build a community for the dispossessed, a world apart in which competitive displays of verbal agility and aplomb provide an alternative way to achieve status" (p. 303). The DNRC, as "a world apart," is thus open only to those who possess the ability to play "the game of wit" (Garrett, 1993, p. 312)—such as playing office pranks on unsuspecting coworkers and identifying those who are unable to "get" the wit. For example, a male DNRC member distances himself from *his spouse* because, he reported to Adams (1997b), she noted that the word " 'individual' is spelled wrong all over [the DNRC newsletter]" (p. 5). Such play may have the purpose of envisioning alternative communities, but it also serves to valorize the self as a superior, transcendent being. "In operating from these values," Garrett (1993) writes, "the game of wit mirrors the operating assumptions of the larger society it springs from. . . . This is especially so if it resorts to obsessive ridicule or simple reversal of the dominant culture" (p. 314).

The power reversal found in Nerdvana, then, perpetuates the same kind of either/or distinctions found in Cubeville; defining oneself in opposition to dehumanizers can lead to more dehumanizing, albeit in a different context. In Nerdvana the dehumanization of the Cubevillians is transposed into the dehumanization of the nonmeritorious. Adams (1997a) explicitly illustrates this dehumanization in the newsletter: "You might be wondering about the fate of thoughtful Induhviduals . . . when Dogbert conquers the planet. I can answer that in one word: skeet" (p. 2).

These comments point to a second, related, danger of the rhetorical redefinitions found in Nerdvana, one that eludes Conquergood (1992, 1994) in his writings about life in an urban Chicago neighborhood: redefining the antisocial as playful can encourage *lateral* exercises of power. Such moves are made possible by an emphasis on a valorization of the individual self as superior to others, even those within the alternative community. For instance, Conquergood (1992) seemingly approves of (or at least withholds judgment on) male Big Red residents' appropriation of a space behind the building for weekend parties, the development of a stolen bicycle ring that brought Big Red children bicycles, and the terrorization of the building's on-site janitor. Each of these acts may contribute to the formation of an alternative symbolic community, but each may *also* encourage the individual engaging in the acts to envision him/herself as "above" the community. For example, did *all* of the building's residents approve of the weekend parties in their social space? Were the bikes shipped in from the 'burbs or were they stolen from other urban residents? Is the destruction of others' property the best means of resolving disagreements about the use of public space?

Just as urban crime can harm its residents more than those who contribute to their material conditions, so the residents of Cubeville/Nerdvana can hurt one another more than their bosses *if* they engage in a process of role distancing or disassociating themselves from their colleagues (Snow & Anderson, 1987). Dilbert and his colleagues may see themselves *individually* ensconced in Nerdvana and believe their peers are "wallpaper," part of the nonmeritorious scene in which they function as active agents (see Solomon, 1985, for a Burkean analysis of dehumanizing rhetoric). Wally, for instance, steals one of Dilbert's cubicle walls to create a roof for his cubicle-turned-office (Adams, 1996e, p. 35). Dilbert returns the favor when he and co-worker Alice hack into the Human Resources computer to send Wally a memo requiring "all short employees to wear [flags on their heads] to improve visibility while in the cubicle aisles." Attempting to one-up themselves, Alice wagers, "I'll bet we can make him wear aluminum foil pants" (6/2/95). These horizontal exercises of power can escalate, just as gang violence may breed more violence. For instance, an unnamed coworker steals office supplies, only to discover that someone stole his desk while he was "out of the house" committing his own crime (Adams, 1995a, p. 160).

Escalation is most apparent in terms of technology, the weapon of choice in Cubeville/Nerdvana. Technology as weaponry is a symbol of the amount of respect due its possessor. In a series of four strips, for instance, Dilbert loads himself with his weapons, "my cellular phone, my pager, palm computer, personal organizer, wireless modem," then confronts Wally: "Wally, I notice that all you have is a pager and a calculator watch. That's pathetic compared to my vast array of personal electronics. Do you yield to my technical superiority?" (Adams, 1996e, p. 13). After Dilbert wins that battle, however, he is reminded of the fact that he, too, is susceptible to technological power. Encountering Techno-Bill reduces Dilbert the strong to Dilbert the groveler. "Please don't hurt me, Techno-Bill!" he exclaims before his antagonist uses his cell phone's autodialing feature to set off Dilbert's technological systems (Adams, 1996e, p. 14).

I found additional evidence of using technology as a meritocratic weapon from, strangely enough, one of my e-mail correspondents in the chapter on *The X-Files.* Bill sent a list, borrowed from *The Wall Street Journal,* of "stupid" technology users, assuring those of us on his list, "Anytime you feel dumb, don't worry. Check out the following excerpts . . . and you'll realize there are lots of people in the world far, far more idiotic than you could possibly be." Included in the message were stories about a new computer owner who thought the mouse was a foot pedal to power the computer, another new owner who used the CD-ROM drive as a cup holder, and a conscientious computer owner who cleaned his keyboard by soaking it in a tub of soapy water for 24 hours. Seeing these types of stories about "inferior others" allows us to locate ourselves in a higher position on the meritocratic ladder, even if we know there are still "superior others" out there. Our identities are thus partially defined by how we see ourselves in relation to others. As Bill points out in his message, "I wish I knew more about computers, but somehow I feel a little more competent after reading this!"

Finally, a third danger lies in the possibility of meritocracy encouraging exploitation of others. Meritocracy allows for individual relative judgments of a person's worth; those less deserving than you deserve what they get. For example, Wally truly believes he deserves a cubicle roof more than Dilbert deserves a cubicle wall, so he takes it. Dilbert believes he is more technologically adept than Wally, so he intimidates him. Conquergood apparently believed the children of Big Red deserved the bikes more than their original owners, so he refused comment on the sudden appearance (and disappearance) of bikes around the building. A cynical interpretation of the Adams-Dogbert relationship would argue that Adams's numerous books of recycled *Dilbert* strips (two each in 1995 and 1996) reflect *his* belief that people are easily fooled into parting with their money, a notion reflected in a parody of the comic strip featured in *This Modern World*. In the parody an intruder to the *Dilbert* strip points out that Adams told an interviewer he supports downsizing, while making wads of money off of "spin-off merchandise" [routinely advertised at the end of Adams's electronic newsletter, as well as at The Dilbert Zone Web site] (Tomorrow, 1996).

To be fair fans of *Dilbert* can elude the meritocratic impulse by reading Adams's daily stories as ironic. That is, his rhetorical reversals may be interpreted as "merely rhetorical," designed to point out the constraints of habitus rather than to be enacted in material life. In such interpretations, what Hutcheon (1994) would call the "ironic edge" of Dogbert's humor is imbibed as therapeutic coping medicine more than as a critical concoction for hoping. Indeed, Adams does attempt to balance the meritocratic impulse in *Dilbert* with periodic reminders of the hope represented in social equality.[5] Dilbert's home, for example, is serviced by the world's smartest garbage man (the character's official name), who routinely repairs Dilbert's flawed inventions. After being corrected by the sanitation engineer, the flipped-tie-wearing engineer remarks, "Gosh. Why are you a garbage man?" an inquiry met with, "I think the question is 'why are *you* an engineer?'" (Adams, 1994c, p. 25; emphasis in original). Early strips, especially, are more likely to comment on the perils of meritocracy and the worship of technology. A 1991 strip finds Dilbert lecturing his dog about technology and knowledge. "Knowledge is power, Dogbert. Someday, the people who know how to use computers will rule over those who don't. And they will have a special name for us," claims Dilbert. Retorts Dogbert, "Secretaries" (Adams, 1995a, p. 98). Unfortunately, these lessons are rarely evident in the daily *Dilbert*s.

Instead the meritocratic perspective prevails, despite its attendant dangers of either/or logic, horizontal exercises of power, and exploitation of others. In this case the temporary experience of communitas runs the very real risk of petrifying an alleged antistructure into the very habitus it opposes.

Conclusion

Dilbert demonstrates the difficulty of holding multiple points of view within a modernist mindset. Although the revelation of the rational/irrational paradox assures us that our potential "loser" status is due to irrational decisions, resolving this paradox in favor of a new allegedly purer form of rationality can prevent alternative points of view from being fully heard. If intelligence and/or technological proficiency become the constructs by which we typically evaluate ourselves and others, we simply substitute one form of universalism (rational/irrational) for another (smart/stupid)—and there's not much difference between the two. We also pass along this flawed logic to future generations. An article in my Sunday newspaper recently illustrated how children have ingested meritocracy. One 11-year-old, studying after school in the public library, told the reporter, " 'I really worry about when I grow up. . . . What will I be? Will I get into a good school and get a good job? Or will I just be an old schmo living by the side of the road?' " (Melvin, 1997, p. 3H).

In the spirit of full disclosure, and to mitigate the sermonesque quality of the preceding paragraph, I have to admit that I take pleasure in the foibles of others as much as the next person. I clipped a short report out of the newspaper, for instance, that reported the "stupid" questions asked of rangers at national parks (e.g., "Was [the Grand Canyon] man-made?" "We had no trouble finding the park entrances, but where are the exits?"). The questions were humorous, but I hope my long-term reaction is similar to a statement Adams—to give him credit—made in a 1995 interview: "My theory is that we are all idiots, including me, only we're idiots about different things at different times" (in Brown, 1995, p. 18).

Hopefully, through the epistemological mobility afforded by symbolic pilgrimages, we become increasingly sensitive to those places/times where we are "idiots." Treating one another as "mistaken," in the spirit of Burke's ideas of the comic frame articulated in the previous chapter, is likely to engender more communitas than mechanical solidarity would produce. In fact, the perpetuation of mechanical solidarity at the expense of communitas is likely to reify the present habitus. To borrow from Gertrude Stein, dehumanization is dehumanization is dehumanization—no matter who engages in the practice.

Notes

A shorter version of this chapter was presented as a paper with the same title as the chapter at the 1998 Western Communication Association conference.

1. I solicited feedback via e-mail from individuals who listed Dilbert as an interest on the World Wide Web sites. Their names were found through the Yahoo and Alta Vista search engines. They, along with the interview participants (see note 5), were promised anonymity in accordance with Ohio University Institutional Review Board protocol. The names used in this chapter are pseudonyms.

2. Most of the *Dilbert* strips used are culled from Adams's book collections. Thus a 1996 citation may well refer to a strip that is several years older. When days and months are used as parenthetical references, the strip is from either a friend's collection or a 1997 desk calendar; those dates refer to original newspaper publication dates.

3. The page numbers listed for the newsletters refer to the printed copies I downloaded from The Dilbert Zone or received as a member of the DNRC. Most copies used 12-point courier font.

4. The names of interview participants have been changed to protect their identities.

5. My espousal of social equality in this chapter should not be read simply as a nostalgic longing for a bygone work environment. I'm well aware that the concept has been part of the nation's habitus, ironically used to *deny* equal treatment by defining some individuals as non- or less-than-human. Compared to meritocracy, however, I believe social equality possesses more capacity to engender harmonious social relations in and out of the workplace. I refer interested readers to Kaus's (1992) treatment of the issue.

5

Transforming the Panopticon Into the Funhouse

Negotiating Disorientation in *The X-Files*

Special Agent Dana Scully: Common sense alone will tell you that these legends, these unverified rumors are ridiculous.
Special Agent Fox Mulder: But nonetheless unverifiable. And therefore true in the sense that they're believed to be true.
Special Agent Dana Scully: Is there anything that you don't believe in, Mulder?

—*The X-Files* (Carter, 1997)

I've been a television fanatic for as long as I can remember. Perhaps I was born to the manner of kicking back in a recliner, for my middle name honors one of my parents' favorite television actors at the time of my birth, Craig Stevens of *Peter Gunn*. (In fact, my parents tell me I was darn close to being named Craig Steven Aden). Television has been an important part of my life ever since. I recall watching *High Chaparral* on our family's black-and-white television when I was only seven years old. A few years later, when my bedtime was extended (and we had a new color TV!), Sunday night was synonymous with *Mannix* and *Mission: Impossible*. During summer vacations from junior high my brother and I spent the mornings watching game shows. In high school I wrote a column for the school paper in which I listed my top ten television programs (including still-syndicated shows *WKRP in Cincinnati* and *Taxi*). Today I look forward to the annual announcements of the networks' new fall lineups. I offer this litany of televisual experiences to my friends and family to explain how I came to be a scholar of popular culture; they tell me that's how I came to be a couch potato (standpoint epistemology at work, I guess).

Despite my background, when *The X-Files* made its debut on Fox in 1993, I resolved not to come near the show with a ten-foot universal remote control. I thought the descriptions of the show, as well as its ad campaign, made it sound like a collection of the kind of wacked-out conspiracy-theory stories that, frankly, have never held the slightest appeal for me. About halfway through that initial season I was talking with a student who shares my interest in television and movies. He told me, with a tinge of guilt, that he thought the show was actually pretty interesting, despite his initial impression that the show "looked really, really lame." After I shared my perceptions of what I thought *The X-Files* was all about, he told me, "Yes and no." He's no conspiracy buff, either, but he said I didn't have to believe the conspiracy stories to enjoy the program; in fact, he continued, I wouldn't see conspiracies mentioned in every episode. Trusting his judgment, I gave the program a chance one Friday evening. I discovered, as did one reviewer, that "*The X-Files* is not another tabloid reality show, but a wry, intelligent, and creepy drama that could be TV's most successful foray into paranormal folklore since *The Night Stalker*" (Davis, 1993, p. 49). Like the folks at *TV Guide*, I found *The X-Files* to be "better than it sounds—a well-produced, suspenseful mystery series that draws you in and keeps you hooked" ("The X-Files," 1993, p. 59).

I've been hooked ever since that first Friday. The main characters, FBI special agents Fox Mulder and Dana Scully, typically find themselves embroiled in one of two kinds of stories: either investigating some sort of unusual or unexplainable phenomenon attached to a crime scene or pursuing cryptic clues related to a murky conspiracy involving the federal government, a shadow government, and the personal lives of each of the agents. No matter what the story, however, a clear solution to the mystery is never completely unveiled. In some episodes the mystery is implied to be the work of the federal government and/or shadowy figures lurking around the edges of government; in other episodes the mystery is partially explained through a combination of medical science (by Scully) and paranormal ponderings (by Mulder). Some episodes take a humorous twist, as when a man who has the ability to adapt his muscular structure to change his identity, takes on Mulder's appearance. In so doing he attempts to woo Scully—an amorous plot twist some fans would like to see—but is interrupted, as their lips part, when the real Mulder bursts into the room.

Perhaps because of people like me, *The X-Files* took some time to build its now-loyal audience. Now, because of people like me, *The X-Files* has a fanatical following. It's the highest-rated program on Fox; it won best actor, best actress, and best drama at the 1997 Golden Globe awards (Weise, 1997); and it's an international phenomenon that is seen in over 60 countries (Lipsky, 1997). In Great Britain the show won the 1996 British Academy People's Award for best television program (Justice, 1996). In Japan *The X-Files* is the only U.S. series on prime-time Japanese television and the nation's top-rated drama program to boot (Fitzpatrick, 1996). In the U.S. "after each episode, hordes of self-described X-philes log on to the Internet and online services to dissect the plot" (Kantrowitz & Rogers, 1994, p. 66). By my count during one random period, just one of *The X-Files*–related bulletin boards indexed 207 messages received between March 15 and March 17, 1997, alone (Fusco, 1997). An archive of fan reviews of every episode was visited over 100,000 times between January 1, 1996, and May 1997 (Episode, 1997). These X-philes are the program's pilgrims, devoted followers who dutifully visit the secondary shrines of Web sites, Usenet groups, and conventions to pay homage. "Like true believers drawn to some sacred UFO site, the X-philes flock to the Meadowlands Exposition Center in northern New Jersey" (Kaplan, 1996, p. 32) to attend one of the 25 conventions held in the U.S. in one year (Justice, 1996).

Just what in the series spawns the pilgrimages of X-philes is difficult to pinpoint. For many the unique tension between Mulder and Scully is compelling. Their playful battles each week are not portrayed as the typical battle between the sexes but as a battle between beliefs, with Mulder as the paramour of the paranormal and Scully the scientific skeptic. Although Scully was initially paired with Mulder to discredit his ideas, the two have grown to share a grudging admiration of each other's points of view, making for what Wild (1995) calls a "very hot platonic chemistry" between the two leads (p. 79). For Pirie (1996), however, the program's chief appeal is its consistent exploration of the relationship among Scully, Mulder, *and* the spectre of big government lurking in the corners of our everyday lives. Big government, he writes, is not just a perpetrator of evil deeds in *The X-Files*; it is "a constant presence between [Scully and Mulder that] frustrates, opposes, threatens, cajoles, insults, attacks and separates them. But, since it is also their employer, its malevolent parental presence happily ensures their relationship can never develop, thereby confirming their essential innocence" (p. 23).

Big government's role in conspiracies and its abuses of power are also mentioned by Davis (1993), who labels the show populist because "all the figures of official authority—local cops, other FBI agents, the NSA, the army—are total bastards, violently dismissive of ordinary citizens and profoundly undemocratic in spirit" (p. 50). The spirit represented in the paranormal phenomena, conversely, is cited as another reason for the devotion of its fans. The program's creator, Chris Carter, explains, " 'I think faith informs almost every episode,'" (Lasswell & Weiner, 1997, p. 32). We turn to *The X-Files*'s spirit-filled stories, Kane (1996) claims, in "the failing hope that our problems can be solved by an appeal to something beyond rational argument and accepted scientific method" (p. 24). The appeal of these stories, Wolcott (1994) points out, is particularly strong for the upper end of the show's 18 to 49 demographic base, especially (as a number of critics have noted) in light of the impending millennium. He writes, "'The X-Files' is the product of yuppie morbidity, a creeping sense of personal mortality. . . . It tries to cheat the big sleep by prying open so many doors into the beyond" (p. 99). In the course of prying open these doors *The X-Files* brings to life a cornucopia of urban legends, rural myths, and tall tales. These "weird, wonderfully weird" stories make *The X-Files* "not just another fill-in-the-blank formula show" (Jarvis, 1994, p. 8)—and strike a responsive chord among a potential viewing audience in which 40 percent believe in the supernatural (Marin, 1996).

My interpretations of *The X-Files* stories, intertwined with the ideas of other fans who shared their thoughts with me via e-mail, through online postings, and in a focus group discussion, suggest there's something to *all* of the views articulated in the previous paragraph. My focus on symbolic pilgrimage, however, led me to a new amalgam of assessments, one that involves the paradox of living in a world that is at once reminiscent of the panopticon prison (more on this in a moment) and the carnival funhouse. Both are disorienting, scary, and controlled by invisible mechanisms, yet the former is unbearable and the latter is enjoyable. The chief difference between the two is perspective; the panopticon provides a stupefyingly steady view for those trapped inside, whereas the funhouse offers a constantly changing outlook for those who are free to move around and exit. *The X-Files*'s stories suggest that we live in a panopticon, but the program's fans can also envision their experiences with these stories—especially in the nonconspiracy episodes—as an adventure in the funhouse.

Each trip to the funhouse is a new yet ritualistic experience for both the agents and their vicarious partners, the fans. In fact, the show's recurring form mirrors the pilgrim's journey as described by Edith Turner: "Pilgrimage has the classic three-stage form of a rite of passage: (1) separation (the start of the journey), (2) the liminal stage (the journey itself, the sojourn at the shrine, and the encounter with the sacred), and (3) reaggregation (the homecoming)" (1987, p. 328). Episodes of *The X-Files* routinely feature Mulder and Scully's separation from their homes and work in the Washington, D.C., area as they journey to locations far away. As part of these liminoid journeys, they typically encounter beings that defy rational explanation. When they return, they must generate a plausible account for their superiors that intertwines Scully's scientific knowledge and Mulder's mysterious experiences. For viewers who accompany the agents on their journeys, *The X-Files* serves as a familiar nexus of the knowable and the otherworldly that they can visit each Sunday evening. In a symbolic sense the world of *The X-Files* is, for fans, a sacred place, which Brereton (1987) defines as a site where "interaction between the divine and human worlds" occurs (p. 528). The "divine" or otherworldly discourses of science and the paranormal found in the program intersect with the very human frailties and fears of the fans and characters to create a paradoxical, postmodern program in which both modernistic medical science and romantic paranormal phenomena recur in discursive form.

In the following pages I hope to illustrate how the seemingly paradoxical nature of *The X-Files* is connected to its espousal of incommensurate beliefs. "The truth is out there" is featured in the opening credits; "I want to believe" is prominently displayed on a poster that adorns Mulder's office wall; and "Trust no one" is the motto of the unofficial shadow government (called the Syndicate) that monitors Scully and Mulder. Interestingly, each belief reflects the essence of the three schools of thought that reappear throughout this book. "The truth is out there" is imbued with the *modernist* quest for absolute, certain answers to perplexing phenomena. "I want to believe" echoes the *romantic* desire for spiritual communion. "Trust no one" perpetuates the *postmodern* tenets of questioning acceptance of "commonsense" beliefs and recognizing the illusory nature of images and symbols.

These beliefs are examined in the remainder of the chapter. I first outline the context from which Scully, Mulder, and fans of *The X-Files* seek escape: the panopticon prison that serves as a metaphor for habitus. In this prison/habitus the agents are constantly observed by both villains and government agents as they attempt to find "the truth out there." Next I illustrate how the panopticon experience can be reenvisioned as carnival funhouse that provides a promised land to which fans journey. Engaging in a symbolic pilgrimage to this promised land provides fulfillment for fans who "want to believe." Finally, I point out how *The X-Files*'s "way of seeing" may promote the anomie its fans ostensibly seek to remedy. The program may induce the adoption of the mantra, "trust no one."

Imprisoned in the Panopticon

The X-Files's world is one in which the spectre of the panopticon looms over the entire cultural landscape. Jeremy Bentham's (1787/

1995) panopticon is a proposed place of punishment in which the prisoners never know when they are under surveillance. According to Bentham, an ideal prison would have all prisoners under continuous observation. "That being impossible," he says, "the next thing to be wished for is, that, at every instant, seeing reason to believe as much, and not being able to satisfy himself to the contrary, he should *conceive* himself to be so" (p. 34; emphasis in original).

Bentham describes the panopticon as a circular institution composed of a central inspection area and cells that stretch toward the outer ring. The cells are partitioned at the sides, preventing the prisoner from seeing, or communicating with, other prisoners. In addition, the prisoner is prevented from seeing out toward the circle's circumference, although a small high window lets light in toward the center of the institution. At the center is the inspection area. The lighting design allows prisoners to see the shape of the inspector, but they are unable to determine if the inspector is actually observing them at any particular moment. The prisoners of the panopticon, then, inhabit an environment in which they cannot see but believe they are always seen. Moreover, Bentham suggests a tin tube run from each cell to the inspector's area so that, if necessary, the inspector can hear the prisoners. Concludes Bentham (1787/1995), "The persons to be inspected should always feel themselves under inspection" (p. 43). Strangely enough, the panopticon's power derives from its *appearance* more so than its *reality*. As Bozovic (1995) explains, if the inspector could be actually seen or heard, the illusion of omniscience would be shattered. "The less the inspector is really present, the more he is apparently omnipresent . . . since a momentary exposure to the eyes of the prisoners is sufficient for him to lose his apparent omnipresence. Here, then, appearance *precludes* reality" (p. 9; emphasis in original).

Michel Foucault (1977/1995) has borrowed Bentham's image to suggest that contemporary postindustrial societies are discursively structured as panopticons. In particular, he argues that the concept of "disciplinarity" in its many forms (punish, divisions, etc.) serves as a symbolic means of invisible surveillance in which those surveilled unknowingly accept their place in hidden power structures:

In each of its applications, it makes it possible to perfect the exercise of power. It does this in several ways: because it can reduce the number of those who exercise it, while increasing the number of those on whom it is exercised. Because it is possible to intervene at any moment and because the constant pressure acts even before the offences, mistakes or crimes have been committed. Because, in these conditions, its strength is that it never intervenes, it is exercised spontaneously and without noise, it constitutes a mechanism whose effects follow from one another. Because, without any physical instrument other than architecture and geometry, it acts directly on individuals; it gives "power of mind over mind." (p. 206)

Although Foucault's image of a panopticon society is more specific and constraining than Bourdieu's vision of habitus, both serve the function of implicitly suggesting what is possible and acceptable. In this case the image presented in *The X-Files* is a postmodern both/and: the panopticon exists within the habitus. And as I pointed out in chapter one, we are increasingly aware of the limitations offered by these images. Appearances and realities may be more confusing, but their complications alert us to appearances that have been traditionally accepted as realities.

Similarly, in *The X-Files* Scully and Mulder are constantly negotiating phenomena that are seemingly unreal yet real. Neither the mutant villains who possess mysterious powers nor the invisible hand of big government (often also represented by the cadre of nebulous figures in the Syndicate who seem to form some sort of conspiratorial shadow government) are what they appear to be, but the ambiguity of both allows them to work in the shadows, nearly invisible, to constrain the actions of Scully and Mulder. As much as the two FBI agents would like to transcend the particulars of their situations, they are unable to transcend their mobile "cell" walls because they are seemingly always under surveillance by one (or both) of the forces housed in the central inspection area. No matter how far they push toward the circumference of the panopticon, they seemingly never escape the power and influence—the "eye"—of the unseen forces that perpetuate history as habitus. After exploring how the villains and government imprison Scully and Mulder, I propose that their incarceration is dehumanizing, or spirit-revoking, just as Dilbert and his colleagues perceived the irrational/invisible logic of their superiors as constraining their spirit. Yet we will see, as the chapter unfolds, how an increased awareness of these unseen constraints affords the agents—and fans—a means of escaping the habitus/panopticon through symbolic redefinition.

The Villains

The X-Files's villains often possess paranormal powers that enable them to act outside of their bodies and/or to become "other" bodies through morphing processes of one kind or another. Scully and Mulder, meanwhile, are imprisoned inside their bodies in these confrontations, leaving the villains in the position of transcendent observers who may be "inside" the two agents' physical/cognitive/emotional cells at any time. Eugene Victor Tooms, for instance, has the ability to stretch and contort his body to inhuman proportions, allowing him to sneak into Scully's residence via the tiny air ducts that empty into every room. Prior to that encounter Tooms's glowing eyes are featured in close-ups from camouflaged locations (sewers, bushes, walls of condemned buildings, etc.) that emphasize his omniscience as he stalks Scully and his other targets (Morgan & Wong,1993a).[1] Tooms's abilities prompt Mulder to wonder whether anyone is safe inside her/his cell/home: "All these people putting bars on the windows, spending good money on high-tech security systems, trying to feel safe. I look at this guy and I think, it ain't enough" (Morgan & Wong, 1993a).

In another episode Mulder has dreams in which a moving red dot leads him to scenes involved in convicted child-killer John Lee Roche's homicidal spree. The dot periodically spells out words and phrases that help Mulder uncover additional, unaccounted for, victims. But as Mulder discovers, the red dot is mysteriously controlled by Roche himself, allowing the serial murderer to escape his cell, imprison Mulder, and threaten the life of another child (Gilligan, 1996b). Says Mulder to Roche, "Somehow you got inside my dreams. I profiled you. I got inside your head. Maybe you got inside mine." Scully also finds herself controlled by a convicted murderer in an earlier episode of the series. Luther Lee Boggs perplexingly accesses Scully's private memories and appears to her as both her deceased father and as a teenage Scully (Morgan & Wong, 1994a). Boggs is inside Scully's head, knowing her as well as she knows herself. "I know what you want," he tells her, "and I know who you want to talk to. Why don't you just go ahead and ask me?" (Morgan & Wong, 1994a). In all these cases the villains generate illusory appearances that are more powerful than reality, leading the agents to believe that others are able to observe their every move and, in some instances, control their thoughts.

Perhaps the most extreme example of thought control surveillance appears in the third season episode called "Pusher" (Gilligan, 1996a). This story features an evil character named Robert Patrick Modell, who possesses the ability to "push" persons into committing acts against their wills through a mysterious telekinetic power. After pushing a police officer, SWAT officer, and police lieutenant to their deaths, Modell looks for a bigger challenge and calls out the Oxford-educated psychologist Mulder to a showdown in a hospital room. Mulder, who goes in unarmed, is "pushed" into picking up Modell's weapon, a revolver loaded with one round. Engaging in a game of Russian roulette with himself, then pointing the weapon at an entering

Scully, Mulder tries to extricate himself from Modell's control, struggling to remain "himself" until Scully pulls a fire alarm to break the "spell" (Gilligan, 1996a). Like a bully cornering his prey, Modell pushes his victims into the corners of their minds, where they finally accede to his wishes. Apparently frustrated by this control, Mulder promptly shoots and kills Modell after Scully hits the alarm.

The Government

Scully and Mulder are also under the apparent omnipresent surveillance of the government. Evidence of government surveillance of the two agents appears early in the pilot episode when Scully introduces herself to her new partner, Mulder, and tells him that she's looking forward to working with him. Mulder replies to Scully's icebreaker, "I was under the impression that you were sent to spy on me" (Carter, 1993a). In a previous scene Scully is told by her boss to do just that. "You will write field reports on your activities along with observations on the validity of the work," he tells her (Carter, 1993a). But Scully the "spy" is also being spied upon; as she is informed of this new assignment, an unnamed, silent onlooker contributes a menacing cloud of smoke to the room. Scully and Mulder discover that this cloud hovers over them at every turn, as the never-named-man—a more sinister version of Dilbert's horns-of-hair boss—diligently works to hamper their investigations and ensure they do not get too close to "seeing the light." In many ways he is the omniscient inspector of the panopticon, appearing in the shadows of Scully's and Mulder's investigations but rarely visible to the two agents. Called the Cigarette Smoking Man by Chris Carter and Cancer Man by the characters and fans, this character is also a "smoking gun," the shadowy inspector of American culture who literally has killed individuals who threaten to shine the light of day on problems or to provide hope to those imprisoned (a 1996 episode reveals that he is the "true" assassin of John F. Kennedy and Martin Luther King [G. Morgan, 1996]). Even the Cigarette Smoking Man is under surveillance, though, as he must answer to the Syndicate.

Scully and Mulder are unable to transcend the presence of the inspector/Cigarette Smoking Man. In the second episode of the series, for instance, Mulder discovers his phone has been tapped, then later is accosted with Scully by dark-suit-and-sunglasses-wearing men in four-door sedans (perhaps not an entirely accidental referencing of the Secret Service) who respond to Mulder's question, "You want to tell me what this is all about?" with a punch and a guttural, "National security" (Carter, 1993b). Near the end of the episode, Mulder is drugged to induce memory loss at the government-run Ellens Air Base. Dazed and confused Mulder encounters another mysterious agent (who has been posing as a reporter while following Mulder and Scully), who warns him, "I just want to say everything you've seen here is equal to the protection we give it. It's you who have acted inappropriately" (Carter, 1993b).

Mulder, then, is the prisoner who has questioned the rules once too often and now must be punished for his transgression. In this respect he bears a resemblance to Randall P. McMurphy of *One Flew Over the Cuckoo's Nest*. Mulder and McMurphy are the only prisoners who attempt to transcend the smothering shadow of the institution/habitus, and their reprimand is a scientific, surgical procedure in which their brains are altered to prevent transcendence (McMurphy received a lobotomy). In *The X-Files* Descartes's modernist equation, "I think, therefore I am," is translated into, "I think, therefore I am *in trouble*."

Dehumanized Agents

Mulder's experience points out how—paradoxically—science, the vanguard of modernist progress, is used to *prevent* progress. Mulder, like McMurphy, attempts to act as an agent of change, but such agents of change (including the apparent victims of the Cigarette Smoking Man's alleged assassinations) are defined as threats to progress by the people in the central inspection area of the panopticon. The subduing of agents of change is reinforced through the naming of the villains in *The X-Files*. Using the full names of Eugene Victor Tooms, Luther Lee Boggs, John Lee Roche, and Robert Patrick Modell activates images of how men such as John Wilkes Booth, Lee Harvey Oswald, and James Earl Ray extinguished the lights of charismatic leaders widely believed to be agents of hope and progress. Even Scully, the scientist who is generally skeptical of Mulder's conspiracy theories, is finally forced to admit their work has been and continues to be hampered by mysterious powerful forces in government. In a fourth-season episode she tells a congressional committee: "What I am saying is that there is a culture of lawlessness that has prevented me from doing my job. That the real target of this committee's investigation should be the men who are beyond prosecution and punishment, the men whose secret policies are behind the crimes that you are investigating" (Spotnitz & Carter, 1996). Scully's use of the anonymous and ominous, "the men," reflects the dichotomous divisions that develop from the use of scientific rhetoric within the habitus. As Montgomery (1996) explains, scientific rhetoric establishes barriers between those who speak it and those who don't, intimidates those who do not understand it, and defamiliarizes the ordinary—all while making scientific language seem naturally superior to conventional language. The panopticon, as a paragon of progress, accomplishes similar results. Its inhabitants are divided from the rest of society, do not understand what is happening around them, and find themselves unable to ascertain the activity that ordinarily occurs in front of and behind them. Confined in a disorienting place, the panopticon's denizens possess unfocused points of view that are constantly blurred by the white noise of captivity.

Although the panopticon is advertised by Bentham as the latest and best in institutional management, its effect is to sap the souls of those it monitors. Just as Dilbert and colleagues find the boss's latest "progressive" dictates drain their desire to achieve, the panopticon displaces its inhabitants through disorientation and downsizes (i.e., makes them feel small) and dehumanizes them. The panopticon's design, and its accompanying scientific discourse, dehumanizes its inhabitants in much the same way as Solomon (1985) indicates the subjects of the Tuskegee syphilis studies were dehumanized by the language of science. Using Kenneth Burke's (1969a) pentad as her means of analysis, Solomon reinforces Montgomery's claim that scientific rhetoric exacerbates division. "The depictions [in the medical reports] deflect attention from the patients by casting them as scene and agency," she writes. "The consequence is dehumanization and a process of division (as opposed to identification) between patients and the scientific community" (pp. 241–242).

In *The X-Files* Scully and Mulder become the equivalents of Dilbert's colleagues wearing tracking collars. Dehumanized, treated like animals in a laboratory experiment, the two FBI agents are cast not as Burkean agents but as part of the scene (the institution of the panopticon/government) and/or as agency (a means of demonstrating the efficacy of the institution). Mulder and Scully are also part of the scene of government conspiracy. Their collected evidence in the pilot episode is destroyed in a suspicious fire; the suspected alien corpse they unearthed is simultaneously stolen. These anything-but-random acts of violence, the agents believe, suggest a higher power at work, one that is manipulating their environment and making their efforts meaningless. Thus Scully could be talking about any number of "unknowables" when she discusses her feelings about the congressional investigators: "It is my natural inclination to believe that they are acting in the best interests of the truth. But I am not inclined to follow my own judgment in this case" (Spotnitz & Carter, 1996).

This feeling certainly parallels the emotions found in *Dilbert*'s Cubeville, as well as in the examples of workforce changes discussed in the first chapter. The postindustrial is an unfathomable, invisible, yet powerful force (e.g., "why are so many people losing their jobs and/or working so hard, yet not experiencing a growth in real wages?") that casts human effort as part of the scene (a company's economic growth and/or the economy's changing nature) and/or as agency (workers are important, but disposable, resources—ranking right behind carbon paper in Cubeville). The postindustrial, for many people, serves as a contemporary panopticon. We may feel trapped, held down, and controlled, but we do not know by whom or why; the invisible forces of the postindustrial habitus keep us under constant surveillance, threatening us with indignity by yanking our work from our lives and our financial security from our families. Yet there must be a rational reason *why* we feel imprisoned and controlled. *Dilbert's* denizens are able to identify their captors, but the panopticon prohibits such easy answers in *The X-Files*. Mulder's and Scully's residence in the panopticon prohibits their adoption of the transcendental personas modernism requires to find "the truth." Scully and Mulder, put simply, cannot get "out there" because they are confined to their cells, unable to break free. As Bentham (1787/1995) predicts, escape attempts are doomed to fail because prisoners require unobserved time and the ability to cooperate with other prisoners. "But what union, or what concert, can there be among persons, no one of whom will have set eyes on any other from the first moment of entrance?" (Bentham, 1787/1995, p. 48).

Rather than redefining the individuals who constrain their actions, like the residents of Cubeville/Nerdvana, X-philes may redefine the experience of disorientation, transforming it from the frightening panopticon to the frightening *and* enjoyable carnival funhouse (particularly in the episodes where the ominous undertones of conspiracy are downplayed). There Scully and Mulder's adventures are envisioned as releases into the liminoid flow of an alternative world where disorientation is pleasurable and community is accessible. The frustration with being confined in the panopticon and not being able to find "the truth out there" is counterbalanced with an inward journey into belief in the unknown. There appearances provide an *alternative* to reality.

Playing in the Funhouse

The adventures of Scully and Mulder serve as a metaphoric reminder of the habitus. Fans of *The X-Files*, whether conspiracy believers or not, certainly can appreciate the effects of living in a panopticon-like culture. As chapter one details, our inability to see a new promised land, a sense of cultural disorientation, and a feeling that forces beyond our control are at work in our everyday lives reflect the central effects Bentham outlines in his explanation of the panopticon. Seeing others—even fictional others like Scully and Mulder—struggle with these feelings of confinement provides the initial impetus for using *The X-Files* as "equipment for living" (Burke, 1941). But as *critical* equipment for living, *The X-Files* must be interpreted in a manner that provides a *response* to life in the panopticon. One response, elaborated upon in the following pages, is to transform the panopticon into a carnival funhouse where a feeling of ritualistic control over the unexplainable can be generated through repeating the disorienting journeys.

Funhouses are a paradox. On the one hand, they are intended to scare the bejeebers out of anyone who dares to enter their confines. On the other hand, they are houses of *fun*, places of entertainment and amusement. I recall my first foray into a funhouse hall of mirrors; even at that young age I experienced both aspects of the paradox. Initially I was fascinated. I was enchanted by the distortions of my body that appeared in front of me, amazed that the "me" I had come to know was not the same "me" that was displayed in front of "me." My ontological centering encouraged me to think of the reflections as "me," but I also felt epistemologically mobile in that I was being afforded a new view of myself. I was also amused by the seemingly infinite openings displayed in the reflections, awed that such a small space could seem so large and open. This fascination may reflect a pervasive theme of *The X-Files*, namely that "there is always a possibility of transcendence of the body through the medium of the body, in near-death or out-of-body experiences as well as in regeneration and mutation" (Badley, 1996, p. 165). The self remains central to our surroundings, but the connection between body and self is fractured in the funhouse and in *The X-Files*. (Interestingly, after developing the metaphor of the funhouse, I was reminded by two fans of an episode called "Humbug," in which Scully and Mulder chase a killer through a funhouse. The operator of the funhouse, Hepcat Helm, claims, "People go through it, they don't have fun. They get the hell scared out of them. It's not a funhouse. It's a Tabernacle of Terror" [D. Morgan, 1995].)

Fascination, then, can also create fear. For instance, my fascination with the funhouse also activated the emotion of fear because initially I could not discover a way out of the reflective maze; the openness had closed in on me. Disoriented, confused, and lacking any sense of direction, the various "me's" I encountered now reminded me that what I saw was deceptive. Upon eventually exiting the hall, however, I couldn't wait to enter again; the disorientation was somehow pleasurable. The experience taught the younger "me" that something could be both fun and frightening—and I wanted more of that unique combination.

The connection between fun and fright has been articulated in another form by scholars of popular story genres who are fond of noting that a fine line distinguishes horror from comedy (this "fine line" was mentioned by both interview participant Palmer and e-mail participant Josie). The notion of a "fine line," however, suggests an either/or rather than the both/and many people find in funhouses. A funhouse disrupts your sense of equilibrium with slides, rolling barrels, and/or halls of mirrors. A funhouse scares you with feelings of being trapped in rooms with no exit, things that go bump in the dark, and/or beings that appear out of nowhere. But a funhouse also entertains you by providing alternative views, extraordinary experiences, and a sense of community with other (temporarily) lost souls. Funhouses leave us wanting more, a sensation similar to e-mail participant Damon's response to *The X-Files:* "I watch the program on a regular basis because the show is so compelling, after one episode I can't wait for the next."[2] Echoes Sandy via e-mail, "It will hook you once you watch it and you will become a fan."

To understand why fans of *The X-Files* such as myself can't wait for the opportunity to engage the show again, I offer an illustration of how ritualistic viewing of the program can be envisioned as a symbolic pilgrimage. First, fans leave their homes to enter the invisible liminoid aura surrounding *The X-Files,* much as carnival goers enter the mysterious darkness of the funhouse. In so doing they engage in an individual flow experience like Nelson's (1989) television viewers. Second, fans work to shape the promised land of the funhouse through the individual gleaning of fragments and the collaborative construction of community, just as funhouse visitors play hit-and-miss with their fragmented options and learn from other visitors along the way. Third, fans return from their journey with a new appreciation for other perspectives as *The X-Files* disrupts a sense of certainty about what is "real," the same way that the funhouse experience provides us with alternative impressions in the mirrors. Finally, fans respond to this increased uncertainty with a desire to travel again, to repeat the playful experience of being disoriented yet part of a community, just as one can ritualistically experience a "new" version of the funhouse with another paid admission.

Entering the Liminoid Funhouse

For fans of *The X-Files* an hour with Dana Scully, Fox Mulder, and the beast of the week is an extended visit to the funhouse, a place where games are played in a dark, disorienting maze. This maze, unlike the panopticon, does have a way out, so every game is at once enjoyable and scary. We may not know what will happen or why, but we know we'll escape—along with Scully and Mulder—unscathed at the end. In nearly every episode of the series, Scully and Mulder engage in a cat-and-mouse game with an invisible force (often manifested in a human being). From the panopticon perspective this game could be seen as dehumanizing the agents, treating them as scene or agency. Mulder, for example, believes Boggs is misleading Scully about his psychic abilities in order to win a stay of execution. Boggs is unwilling to repeat the traumatic experience of being taken to his death so he toys with Scully's emotions by "becoming" her father (singing his favorite song and using her father's nickname for her: "Did you get my message, Starbuck?"), Mulder, and herself at age 14 (Morgan & Wong, 1994a). Mulder, too, is used as part of a game being controlled by another force. Modell, who apparently knows he is dying and is using his power to "push" to entertain himself in the meantime, wants the challenge of trying to best the psychologist Mulder in the ultimate mind game; to Modell Mulder is—like the other law enforcement officers he pushed to their deaths—simply one of the disposable pieces in Modell's "bored" game.

Mulder is also a game piece in Roche's plan to escape. The killer enters Mulder's recurring dream of his sister Samantha's abduction, then uses the details to convince Mulder he is responsible for Samantha's death:

> ROCHE: Watergate was on TV. You and your sister were sitting in front of it, playing a board game with little red and blue plastic pieces. And you wanted to watch a TV show, the one with Bill Bixby—what the heck was the name of that thing?
> MULDER: How could you know what I said?
> ROCHE: I was watching, from the window. (Gilligan, 1996b)

Mulder, to Roche, is as inanimate as the red and blue plastic pieces from the board game; he is agency, a means to the end of escape, abduction, and more murders. Mulder is a part *in* the game as well as a part *of* the game. Invisible forces seem to draw him through the mental maze Roche constructs, but in the end, Roche—as well as Boggs and Modell—lose their games. Mulder wins and gets to play another game the following week, as do the viewers who follow his and Scully's adventures.

Fans of *The X-Files*, like visitors to the funhouse, can be scared to death during the game, but they know the protagonists will safely exit the play palace at the conclusion of the episode. As a result they can take steps to make the game even more frightening, enhancing the distinction between being materially positioned in a living room to being symbolically ensconced in a liminoid flow in the process. For example, Damon and Robert explain via e-mail how they control their material environments to make the move to the symbolic even easier. Damon notes, "I watch the X Files live by myself in a room that is quiet and that has no lights on. I think it gets you more involved in the show and creates a better atmosphere," and Robert explains, "I turn off the lights and turn up the volume. The surroundings can make it creepier. The more I jump, the better."

Damon's and Robert's experiences illustrate how fans of *The X-Files* can experience a period of enjoyment in which they control their play and become thoroughly involved with it, similar to the manner in which individual pilgrims encounter flow experiences that immerse them in the journey. Sandy e-mails: "I watch the X-Files by myself, while my husband works on the computer and listens to it. While I'm watching, I'm only involved with the show and don't do anything else. The X-Files is the only show that I watch that gets my undivided attention." Mary also enjoys the control she feels in watching the program uninterrupted: "There was a time when my mother was calling me during the X-Files. She calls once a week, and I would get so irritated that she picked this one time to call out of all the possible times she could call. A couple of times I didn't answer her call so she had to leave a message. Then I called her after the show. I finally told her that this was the one program I really wanted to watch. She started calling me at a different time." For Mary and other fans *The X-Files* offers a sacred place where "real" time and space are excluded, much the same way in which pilgrims experience the liminoid of communitas "as a timeless condition, an eternal now, as 'a moment in and out of time'" (Turner, 1974, p. 238).

The deep sense of involvement these fans report is also similar to the "flow experiences" reported by pilgrims. These experiences are moments of "ordered existence" that are "relatively lasting and totally absorbing" (Csikszentmihalyi, 1987, p. 362). Not surprisingly, then, most fans of *The X-Files* I visited with indicated that they watch few—if any—television programs in the same absorbed manner that they bring to Sunday night on Fox television. Brian's report of his viewing experience typifies many fans' experiences: "The manner in which I watch the X-Files is singular. I view to the exclusion of all else. I ignore telephones, doorbells, and any other interruptions. I must confess, though, that I might skip the previews of next week's show if the house were on fire." Dan, too, lists the program as one of the few times he encounters a flow experience when watching television. He notes, "My viewing of X-Files is similar to my viewing of

Millennium, Monday Night Football, and championship boxing, namely, that you don't want to interrupt me during these activities." My informal discussions and observations of friends and family over the years lead me to believe fans of *The X-Files* are not the only folks who become enmeshed in flow experiences while consuming popular stories. In fact, as I read the subject of the next chapter, *Sports Illustrated*, each week, I find myself tearing through half the magazine in one sitting, unable/unwilling to halt the flow experience of reading its stories.

Once we are immersed in the liminoid flow of watching *The X-Files* fans such as myself can begin the rhetorical process of constructing a symbolic community that offers an outpost for transcending the habitus. In this case our construction efforts build a community that exists in between the real and unreal, with faith generating the bonds of connection. Such a promised land is not altogether different from a funhouse that distorts the real into unreal dimensions and requires faith that an exit is available.

Shaping the Promised Land

Watching *The X-Files* on a regular basis provides fans with a number of different creepy moments, an experience similar to having someone sneak up behind when you are in the funhouse hall of mirrors. The distorted body image is startling, possibly even unnerving, because our perceptions of what it means to be "human" are abruptly altered by the vision lurking over our shoulder. Many of *The X-Files*'s villains provide the program's fans with a parallel experience and emphasize how the funhouse forays function as pilgrimages, for the villains are liminal beings "who inhabit and cross the edges of social boundaries and codes" (Myerhoff, Camino, & Turner, 1987, p. 382). Because the villains are not clearly one type of "thing" or another, we know we are not in one type of place or another. Leonard Betts, for instance, is decapitated in the opening scene of his eponymous episode, then apparently kicks his headless body out of the morgue locker, regenerating his head in an iodine bath (Gilligan, Shiban, & Spotnitz, 1997). Later in the episode he "gives birth" to another self in an attempt to send Scully and Mulder down a dead-end hallway. Thus Leonard provides two funhouse mirror images: the headless body and the double image. When we see him in one mirror he's headless. When we see him in another there are two of him. Yet neither image is "really him." We're mesmerized by the multiple Leonards but also scared because there should be just one of him.

The scary nature of the villains is reinforced by the partial explanations of their condition; many are victims of science and/or nature gone awry. Leonard Betts's body seems to possess cancer as "the normal state of being," explains Mulder (Gilligan, Shiban, & Spotnitz, 1997); Robert Patrick Modell's psychokinetic abilities result from a gigantic brain tumor (Gilligan, 1996a); the half-man/half-worm creature called "Flukeman" in "The Host" is perhaps the product of Chernobyl-contaminated water (Carter, 1994); the psychotic eight-year-old killers in "Eve" are second-generation results of government-sponsored eugenics experiments (Biller & Brancato, 1993). As we see their conditions unmasked, we are reminded—to borrow from Bentham's explanation of the panopticon—that the strange *appearances* displayed in *The X-Files* are not that far removed from *reality.* As interview participant Don points out in relation to a villain's contraction of a psychosis-inducing infection from ergots in a tattoo dye: "Geez, this could actually happen. A guy could go crazy as a result of this. So I mean, that got me thinking a lot more than a sci-fi one, where 'oh, cool, you know, this'll never happen,' and that's basically the end." Similarly, Joelle notes in her electronic review of the "Squeeze" episode, "I thought to myself, ' . . . I feel sorry for him.' I've grown to like Tooms and even though he is a mutant he is really cool" (Episode, 1.03, 1997). When we see our unreal appearances in the funhouse mirror, we are shocked by the difference in images but also by the incongruity that mirrors are supposed to reflect reality. That's us, but it can't be us, we think. Because we know tumors do strange things to the body, Chernobyl wreaked havoc with the eastern European environment, and the cloning of animals is now routine, *The X-Files's* referencing of these scientific realities imprints the unreal appearances of the villains with the mark of legitimacy—even as we convince ourselves they're not real.

Entering *The X-Files* funhouse, then, means we enter a realm similar to our material surroundings yet one that is terribly different from our material surroundings. Fans find themselves in a world in between the real and the unreal, a place where they can distance themselves from people and things that bother them (recall fans' descriptions of their flow experiences in the previous section) while feeling special. In this respect their personal symbolic pilgrimages reflect the way in which communitas "does not merge identities; it liberates them for conformity to general norms" (Turner, 1974, p. 274). As I pointed out in chapter three, this process involves both a connection with a spiritual community of others and an individual centering process.

A SPIRITUAL COMMUNITY. Interview participant Mary finds the show possesses an easily identifiable spiritual quality: "To me, that's the essence of spirituality ['I want to believe'] because that's what we're seeking, something to believe in." *The X-Files,* in Monica's words, provides "this kind of suggestion that maybe spiritual things . . . maybe they do really exist even though we can't scientifically prove it." Not surprisingly, then, *Newsweek* writer Rick Marin (1996) calls belief in the paranormal "a substitute religion for people who haven't got one and a supplemental one for those who already do" (p. 52).

Being a fan of *The X-Files* places one in a congregation of believers, what Palmer calls "this intricate, like, club and you know all this stuff and you followed this; you have this knowledge that everybody doesn't necessarily have." This kind of club is a secret society of sorts, much like the DNRC of *Dilbert* fans discussed in the preceding chapter, in that you require the possession of esoteric, or "inside," knowledge to call yourself a true believer (see Faivre, 1987). Such a believer, notes Weckman (1987), "undergoes a transforming experience and achieves deeper contact with the meaning of life and the world" (p. 151). Sharing exclusive, special knowledge with other members, fans of *The X-Files* draw distinctions between themselves and others. Lee points out that being a fan of the series means you're aware that you're watching a kind of television that not everyone enjoys. The complexity of the plots hails viewers' attention in a unique way, making the viewers feel special as well. He explains, "So, to follow those arguments [in each episode], one has to actively participate in the progress of the show." As vicarious participants in the stories, partners who join Scully and Mulder's ritual pilgrimages to the shrines of the extraordinary, fans experience communitas. The program itself has overtly encouraged feelings of kinship among its characters and its fans. Creator and executive producer Chris Carter "monitors reactions online and the writers have often included fan references. For example, an airplane-passenger manifest featured names of frequent discussion-group participants (and a crucial clue)" (Kantrowitz, 1994, p. 66).

By participating in this spiritual congregation of believers, X-philes see themselves as unique, special individuals, in other words, as people who possess power. Josie, for example, marvels at the fans' influence on the show's stories. "Personally," she writes: "I sometimes wonder if the writers haven't included more than just 'references' [from fans]. Sometimes it's as if the fans write the show! This especially applies to seasons that end with a cliffhanger to which Carter himself admits he hasn't written an ending. I first read the 'Sophie's Choice' (Mulder's father gave up one of his children) and 'Darth Mulder' (Cancer Man is Mulder's father) themes on the net, and lo and behold, they popped up months later on the show." For Brian watching the show gives him the power to live by his norms instead of those found in the habitus. Viewing *The X-Files* alone, he says, gives him a break from what he calls "loathsome social interactions . . . like talking" (ellipsis in original). Similarly, watching the program gives John a chance to reaffirm his identity as something other than an ordinary college student. He explains, "I try to find others to watch it with me, but they would usually rather party than watch one of the few quality TV shows." John and Brian both appear to use their experiences with *The X-Files* as a means of feeling unique or special; despite watching the show by themselves, they feel attached to the community of nonpresent viewers. In so doing they participate in a very Burkean process of identification and division, defining and reaffirming their identities in terms of what they see as the norm. Mary, too, envisions herself as special, even within the community of fans: "Since I have watched it from the very first episode, something I always point out to others, I have this kind of proprietary feeling toward the show. Sometimes I think I'm sort of a snob about being one of the first viewers—in some way this makes me special? . . . I will never miss a program, and I feel like I've missed out on something important in my life if I do." As the comments of Brian, John, and Mary indicate, part of the appeal of belonging to a special community is feeling special as an individual. Thus the transcendence afforded by belonging to the symbolic community of *The X-Files* funhouse encourages individual fans to center themselves.

INDIVIDUALLY CENTERED. When I asked both interview and e-mail participants how they would describe the program to someone who hasn't viewed an episode, the answers generally fell into three camps: (1) the Mulder/believer–Scully/skeptic pairing (a basic description); (2) a smorgasbord of genres (a unique description); and (3) undescribable. The first answer suggests some fans enjoy the teamwork experience. The second answer implies the viewing experience is one of a kind. The third answer proposes that you just have to experience it. For example, interview participant Nikki, a relative newcomer to *The X-Files*, admits: "I really don't think I could describe it. I would just have to say you just have to sit back and watch one or two shows, then get back to me. There's just too, too much there to try and describe." Veteran fans, too, suggest *The X-Files* must be experienced to be understood. Robert's e-mail explains, "You have [to] watch it to fully know!" Mary, a devotee from the beginning, confesses, "You have to see it to appreciate it."

All of these answers suggest that fans bring a number of interpretive perspectives to bear on the series, depending upon their ontological center. Some like the sci-fi elements, some like the scarier stories, and some like the humorous episodes. Interview participant Palmer lists the latter as his favorite, selecting "Jose Chung's 'From Outer Space,' " in particular, namely because of its combination of fun and fright. He says: "I like the fact that [the episodes are] funny and that sometimes, the story lines seem even more powerful than the other ones. I thought there was this one about, there was one just very sur-real episode about someone writing a book about one of [the two agents'] cases and it was all just about different people's viewpoints and viewing cases from all different perspectives and it was very funny. . . . But at the same time it really seemed, it seemed to have a stronger message than a lot of episodes I've seen." Palmer's appre-ciation of the multiple standpoints in "Jose Chung's 'From Outer Space,' "—even the episode's title is a *play* on words that can be read in two ways—is mirrored by e-mail participant Suzanne, who references a Japanese film that features different points of view on the same event, "Want self-parody, literary allusions, and a host of 'Rashomon' perspectives? Watch the masterful 'Jose Chung's "From Outer Space."' " Interview participant Monica also enjoys the pros-pect of multiple points of view. She says, "I find it very fascinating, all the possibilities that it presents. You know, not that I believe everything obviously, but just the idea of it, is it a possibility?"

Other fans prefer a single point of view. For example, Josie says she has never found *The X-Files* frightening and would tune out if that were the case because, she told me, she does not enjoy being scared: "I remember discussing roller coasters with one friend. The only time I ever rode a roller coaster, I thought I was going to die, and I have never ridden another since. My friend said, 'But that's what's fun about it! That moment when you think, I'm gonna DIE!' I'm not sure I will ever understand this." Similarly, fans who enjoy the platonic chemistry between Scully and Mulder view the program in one way, derogating other fans who would like to see a different kind of spark between the two agents as "relationshippers" or "'shippers." Wooster writes in his electronic review of a 1997 episode, "Finally, for you ''shippers,' the show would just be a cruel and sad ridiculous joke if M & S 'got together.' You ''shippers' can dream, but don't believe or hope it will happen—the show would be dead in the water" (Episode, 4.20, 1997). Other reviewers offer similar comments that distinguish themselves from other viewers in their assessments of the "Paper Hearts" episode. Dana claims, "I knew from the beginning that this episode would not tell us anything important about Samantha Mulder," and Oscar writes, "I could never go for the idea that Roche kidnapped Mulder's sister" (Episode, 4.08, 1997).

That fans of *The X-Files* do not share the same denomination even if they practice the same faith emphasizes the role of ontology in symbolic pilgrimages. We can share the feeling of communitas with other fans, but our personal use of the promised lands provided by popular stories may differ because we are drawing in disparate rhetorical fragments in the sense-making process. For example, three back-to-back-to-back online reviews offer vastly different assessments of the "Paper Hearts" episode. Autumn-Lynn asks, "Are they trying to ruin the show?" Anoyomous [sic] thought the episode was "near perfect" yet castigates the show's creative team for developing "the stupid 'dream nexus' idea. What the hell was that about, anyway?" And Michele opens her review with the statement, "I can't begin to say enough good things about this episode." All three of these fans share the same faith and they are communicating in a shared forum, but their sense of congregation is interpreted differently because of their distinct processes of ontological centering; they share in the kinship of the funhouse experience, but they rate their trips differently.

Perhaps one of the reasons fans of *The X-Files* join different denominations is due to the multilayered texts the series offers. As I noted at the beginning of the chapter, critics have proposed a number of different reasons for the show's success, ranging from the chemistry of the leads to the complex story lines. The abundance of textual fragments within the programs provides fans with a litany of choices as they negotiate their senses of self and community. For example, Scully and Mulder share the belief that the body is a temple that is sometimes desecrated, yet because they disagree about the cause of the desecration, each attempts to test the other's beliefs. Mulder's belief in the paranormal leads him to look for evidence out of the body—discovering unexplainable physical evidence, pointing out instances of incommensurate occurrences, and seeking folk wisdom—that tests Scully's belief in science, just as Scully seeks evidence from the body—conducting physical examinations, reviewing medical records, and performing autopsies to find a rational explanation—that tests Mulder's faith in the paranormal. Ironically, Mulder's belief system relies on a romantic notion of souls that exist inside the body, whereas Scully's Enlightenment-influenced belief system focuses on natural forces external to the body. Their interactions over the years have led them to understand, and appreciate, one another's perspective, despite the tendency of each to believe the other is mistaken. The next two sections develop these parallel realizations.

Returning Home and Appreciating Alternative Perspectives

The distorted images and illusory passages of the funhouse disorient its thrill-seeking patrons perhaps as much as the postindustrial's distortion of past promised lands confuses contemporary workers. At the same time, however, that disorientation may also produce opportunities to appreciate the perspectives of others. When we exit the funhouse and return home, our ways of seeing have changed. What we see is thus interpreted differently. *The X-Files* funhouse experience reminds us that impressions are easily distorted.

As I noted in the discussion of the liminoid, *The X-Files*'s villains are neither fully human nor fully monsters. Their in-between status helps us imagine ourselves in the liminoid, but upon reflection, we can recognize that their status as partially human also points to how individuals are more complex than what we see on the surface. We can often *empathize* with the villains at the same time that we fear them. Just as the funhouse mirrors distort impressions of ourselves, then, the villains of *The X-Files* refract our superficial views of others.

In many instances the villains are depicted as creations of the habitus, just as their victims are. As a result fans have difficulty seeing the villains as *only* nonhuman monsters; they are *also* partially human victims. The Eves, in particular, exemplify this both/and assessment of the villains. They are genetic experiments gone awry, the victims of modernist science run amok. As the Eve "daughters" remark, "We weren't born. We were created" (Biller & Brancato, 1993). They are as confused as we are about their identities in a postindustrial world. For example, one of their genetic mothers, Eve 6, wails about the pain of having multiple versions of herself: "She is me and I am her and we are all together. . . . They made me. But did they suffer? No, no, I suffer. I suffer" (Biller & Brancato, 1993). Similarly, a 1997 episode called "Kaddish" featured a killer seeking vengeance on those who killed him for the "simple" reason that he was Jewish. This killing machine took the form of a human but was soulless because he was literally created by his bereaved fiancée out of mud; he was himself, but he was also dead (Gordon, 1997). Despite fearing the nonhuman form he had become after death, we could feel his sorrow as a victim of a hate crime. Finally, in the 1995 episode, "The Walk," an armed forces quadriplegic possesses the power to transform himself into an invisible "phantom soldier" who mysteriously kills the officers he believes have done him wrong (Shiban, 1995). Although we condemn his vengeful actions, we can also empathize with his plight. As Josie points out, we can even *admire* some of these villains because they are able to elude the forces of the panopticon: "The villains sometimes seem to me as the epitome of resistance: those rogue figures unconstrained by the supposedly omniscient government (sometimes even Scully and Mulder can't catch them)."

In a sense these villains have been disembodied and thus removed from a knowable standpoint because their bodies have been desecrated in some way. Scully and Mulder occasionally experience this possibility themselves. In "Ice," for example, Scully and Mulder are drawn into the investigation because the scientists killed in the opening of the episode left the message, "We are not who we are" (Morgan & Wong, 1993b). Thinking Mulder may be contaminated by the ice-dwelling organism that drove those men mad, Scully ultimately confronts her partner: "Mulder, you may not be who you are" (Morgan & Wong, 1993b). In addition, Mulder is not who he is when put under Modell's spell in "Pusher" (Gilligan, 1996a). First pointing the loaded gun at his own head, then turning on Scully at Modell's psychokinetic request, Mulder doesn't know himself, nor is Scully sure who he is at that precise moment (Gilligan, 1996a). Just as we look in the funhouse mirrors and think, "It's not me," we see the distorted images over our shoulder and admit, "It's not them." The desecration of the villains' bodies, then, diminishes their culpability for their nefarious deeds—and emphasizes that all hell breaks loose when the temple of the body is violated. The Eves murder their adoptive fathers and attempt to kill Mulder and Scully. Flukeman works through the sewer lines to find random victims. Modell engages in deadly mental battles as sport. Betts performs "mercy killings" on persons with cancer. Boggs claims he has visions because his first, aborted trip to the electric chair resulted in the souls of the damned entering his body. The villain/victims are not hated as Others; they are feared and pitied because they are distortions of ourselves. *The X-Files* spins us around, isolates us in rooms with apparently no exits, then confronts us with gnarled images of ourselves/others in the form of the villains—people who could be just like us but for one small difference. As Yeaton (1995) explains in his proposal for an ultimate funhouse in which the real and the unreal would be indistinguishable, "Problems of perception are continually offered, ranging from simple changes in perspective, mazes, and mirrors to more complex identity games" (p. 205). The result, explains Barth's (1968) narrator in "Lost in the Funhouse," is that, "Nothing was what it looked like" (p. 90).

Because we cannot trust superficial impressions, *The X-Files* tells us, we have to acknowledge the possibility of interpretations other than our own. Thus the idea of possibilities, of different points of view, is encouraged by a visit to the funhouse. In the short-term Scully's encounters with Luther Lee Boggs, for example, leave her doubting her beliefs, but in the long-term they open her to "the fantastic as a plausibility" (Carter, 1993a). Yet because Mulder has relied on Scully's scientific knowledge to find proof for his paranormal theories, he is ironically suspicious of Scully's belief in Boggs. Scully, disappointed in Mulder's skepticism, explains, "I thought that you'd be pleased that I'd opened myself to extreme possibilities" (Morgan & Wong, 1994a). Responds Mulder, "Dana, open yourself up to extreme possibilities only when they're the truth" (Morgan & Wong, 1994a).

This "trading places" serves the same function as the role-switching movies I mentioned in chapter three; experiencing the world from a new epistemological standpoint provides additional wisdom and understanding. Scully's visions of her father, and Boggs's ability to channel those visions, render her less skeptical, just as Mulder's appreciation for science makes him more skeptical. By the time he encounters John Lee Roche again Mulder is more than ready to believe that aliens did not abduct his sister. Agents Scully and Mulder, then, can be seen as incomplete when viewed as individual investigators; they require the perspective of the other in order to develop a means of "seeing" and understanding the mysterious phenomenon of the week. Mulder uses the "science" of the polygraph to produce evidence that Tooms may be over 100 years old, sounding like a scientific believer in the process: "He lied on questions 11 and 13. His electrodermal and cardiograph response nearly go off the chart" (Morgan & Wong, 1993a). Scully adopts Mulder's traditional pose when she is faced with the mysterious knowledge of Luther Lee Boggs, asking her skeptical partner, "Mulder, I never thought I'd say this, but what if there's another explanation?" (Morgan & Wong, 1994a).

Together the two agents meld the paranormal and medical sciences to gain a "third" position from which to view the phenomenon. Accused by one of the other scientists in "Ice" of proposing an outlandish hypothesis to account for the worm's effects on the human nervous system, Scully retorts, "The evidence is there" (Morgan & Wong, 1993b). When another scientist responds, "Come on, no thing can survive in subzero temperatures for a quarter of a million years," Mulder reaffirms Scully's assessment: "Unless that's how it lives" (Morgan & Wong, 1993b). Repeatedly reaching similar conclusions from different positions, and/or realizing the validity of the other's position, Scully and Mulder are willing to travel epistemologically. As Scully tells FBI assistant director Skinner in the "Pusher" episode, "I have to agree with Agent Mulder, sir. I can't even begin to explain how, but I think that Modell is responsible for your injuries" (Gilligan, 1996a). And as Mulder tells Scully in "Squeeze," "In our investigations you may not always agree with me, but at least you respect the journey" (Morgan & Wong, 1993a).

Scully and Mulder's respect for one another's beliefs reflects their redefinition of what constitutes "knowledge." In essence they become proponents of what Feyerabend (1978) calls "counterinduction." This way of "knowing" posits that "knowledge . . . is not a gradual approach to the truth. It is rather an ever increasing ocean of mutually incompatible (and perhaps even incommensurable) alternatives, each single theory, each fairy tale, each myth that is part of the collection forcing the others into greater articulation and all of them contributing, via this process of competition, to the development of our consciousness. Nothing is ever settled, no view can ever be omitted from a comprehensive account" (p. 30). Mulder's paranoid perusings are thus respected by Scully, just as her insistence that empirical proof be provided is respected by Mulder. Their journeys together have taught them that "no view can ever be omitted from a comprehensive account."

To some extent, as I noted earlier in the chapter, Mulder and Scully are also pilgrims in the anthropological sense: They are drawn to sacred sites that are home to events of unknown origin. Each week they engage in ritual travel that affords an unusual vista from which to assess the intersection of human behavior and invisible forces. In 1996 and 1997 alone, for instance, they journeyed to Brooklyn, Siberia, Philadelphia, Canada, Martha's Vineyard, and North Dakota among other places. The more they travel, the more they respect one another's opinions and the local knowledges they encounter. Each comes to respect the other's beliefs and, consequently, what counts as knowledge. As Mulder tells Scully in the opening episode of season two, "Seeing is not enough. I should have something to hold on to, some solid evidence. I learned that from you" (Morgan & Wong, 1994c). Through their pilgrimages they discover the only certainty is their own point of view—and, paradoxically, even that foundation shifts. Such a both/and way of knowing suggests a postmodern paradox in which nothing is "just" something, and the interpretations of others must therefore be respected. In teaching this lesson *The X-Files* encourages ritualistic play that uses a comic frame.

Ritualistic Play

Although disorientation can be quite frightening, when we know we can escape the funhouse and visit again, the jarred perspectives can be enjoyable. For instance, I recall spending some of my grade-school summer vacation spinning myself to the point of a dizzy collapse in the office chair my mother used as a secretary at another local elementary school. Upon returning home I would head to the backyard and spin myself in a circle to experience the same disorientation. There was a small bit of fear attached to being in this unusual state, but my repeated journeys to the "state of confusion" were so enjoyable that I made the trip again and again. My experiences there offered me a new way of seeing, a perspective that blurred and blended the images around me, so much so that I wanted to play again.

My quest to repeat the "familiar disorientation" of spinning on office furniture parallels the repeat visits to the funhouse undertaken by X-philes. Entering the funhouse again and again is always a disorienting process, but it is paradoxically orderly in its ritualistic form. The same three-step process of separation, liminality, and reaggregation occurs in each episode, but the return home in the final step merely ensures that another journey is necessary. For viewers of *The X-Files*, then, Scully's and Mulder's pilgrimages are like repeat visits to the funhouse where the game is at once frightening and fun. "The show to me is very entertaining and has a bit of a dark edge to it," writes Sandy in her e-mail message. Mulder's sense of humor, in particular, helps to lighten the dark (in both subject matter and appearance) atmosphere of the program. As Becky e-mails, "Mulder's deadpan humor is great." In the "Leonard Betts" episode, for instance, Mulder takes the frightening situation of a decapitated head opening its mouth and eyes as Scully prepares to autopsy it and turns the event into a fun occasion, pimping Scully on the phone, "Blinked or winked? . . . Scully, you're not saying it's alive are you?" (Gilligan, Shiban, & Spotnitz, 1997). Later in the episode, when Scully and Mulder discover Betts has torn off his thumb to escape from the handcuff attached to his car, Mulder proposes that Betts is a walking evolutionary leap. Asks Scully, "So what you're describing is someone so radically evolved that you would not even call him human?" Mulder's retort transforms this terrifying possibility into fun and games. "On the other hand," he says, glancing at Betts's car, "how evolved can a man be who drives a Dodge Dart?" (Gilligan, Shiban, & Spotnitz, 1997). (Or, as my Sunday newspaper explained in its comparison of cars and the statements they make, a Dodge Dart says, " 'I teach third grade, and I voted for Dwight Eisenhower' " [Garcia, 1997, p. 2H]).

For Mulder and Scully, working the X-files is not altogether different from recess and games of scary monsters. When Mulder proposes a UFO theory to Scully in "Deep Throat," he concludes with, "Tell me I'm crazy," a directive with which Scully is only too happy to comply: "Mulder, you're crazy" (Carter, 1993b). In many ways, Scully and Mulder *are* a couple of crazy kids. In a 1997 episode focusing on Scully, Mulder checks in via cellular phone from his vacation destination, Graceland, where he proceeds to tell Scully fascinating facts about "the king" before slipping on his shades and doing an Elvis impression as he slinks out of the frame (Morgan & Wong, 1997). Later in that same episode Scully is a crazy kid as she drinks too much, then, like a drunken sailor, wakes up the next morning with a tattoo; the "smart girl" sometimes "just wants to have fun," as crazy girl Cyndi Lauper sang in the early 1980s.

The X-Files is careful not to take itself too seriously; the creepy is seasoned with a dash of levity in nearly every episode—a theme e-mail participant John appreciates: "I'm a big fan of [the television series] Doctor Who, and X-files is one of the only other shows I've seen that successfully encompasses both humor and the paranormal." On occasion entire episodes are devoted to paranormal playfulness, such as when mysterious murders occur among a camp of performers from the circus freak show (D. Morgan, 1995) or when campy funnyman Charles Nelson Reilly plays an author named Jose Chung who is writing about paranormal activities (D. Morgan, 1996). "In almost every X-Files episode," writes Suzanne via e-mail, "the wisecracks known as 'Mulderisms' and 'Scullyisms' take the edge off the horror, reminding us that the show is a thrill ride to be enjoyed."

Recess, though, is a peculiar kind of play in that it occurs within the context of a controlled schedule and is repeated at the same times Monday through Friday. Despite its occurrence within the confines of the institutional regimen, the ritualistic repetition of play is nonetheless anticipated as a moment of freedom by children. During recess kids get to make most of the rules; they control the play, just as viewing *The X-Files* feels like part of a controlled, special journey for a number of fans. Explains Mary, "I consider the X-Files hour my special entertainment hour of the week. I really look forward to it, especially the first run episodes, although I also enjoy the reruns." Re-viewing the show is, for some fans, just as pleasurable as the original experience. Brian admits he watches "some episodes several times." When the story of the week pulls through threads from previous episodes, he says, "I watch these repeatedly. I try to note every nuance. Sometimes stepping through vignettes frame by frame." Julie divulges that she even videotapes shows she watches in person "in case I miss something and want to see it again." Watching *The X-Files* thus provides not only the ordered existence of a flow experience; it also allows for the repeat performance of the experience. In these repeat performances the control perceived by the symbolic pilgrims increases dramatically. They not only center themselves ontologically (as beings in control of their surroundings), but in so doing they engage in critical resistance to the postindustrial panopticon through a redefinition of their cultural experiences.

Infused with a feeling of control as they engage in ritual performance, fans of *The X-Files* are not unlike the kids I remember from recess at Lincoln Heights Elementary (I just realized how strange a name this is for a school located in a neighborhood with a terrain that is as perceptibly hilly as the Buchman's kitchen on *Mad About You*) who immediately and routinely gravitated to the tetherball courts (which I believe are now prohibited on elementary school grounds), the gravel-filled football "field" (which built character as it removed skin), or the monkey bars with the oh-so-soft asphalt landing area. As comedian Jack Thomas points out in a bit about the dangers of youth, recess was fun *and* frightening as you ducked from the dodgeball then rose to find another one honing in on your cheekbone, ready to leave its institutional imprint on your visage.

But recess was also a means of coping with the rigors of the institution. Fans of *The X-Files* report a similar coping process. As Lee explains, the series "shows how bureaucracy often prevents people from uncovering answers, and at times it ridicules some of our cultural beliefs and practices. It is these things that offer me some break from the world—perhaps realizing that others share this view and are often frustrated by the current state of things offers me some relief." Similarly, e-mail participant Brian offers, "Watching the X-Files makes me feel more normal," and Suzanne calls the show her "brain-candy" because she's "a Harvard honors grad now trapped in the life of a stay-home mommy." After reading an earlier draft of this chapter, Mary suggested that fans recognize "being in the panopticon and trying to respond to it or defy it" and often rely on the strangeness of the series as an opening to do so.

My description of *The X-Files* promised land as a funhouse suggests that postmodern playfulness is an antidote to the dehumanizing effects of the modernist panopticon. The structures are similar, to be sure, but the funhouse provides safe entertainment as well as *temporary* terror; its visitors usually can't wait to go back again. Joanne, for instance, writes in her e-mail, "All in all, one's appetite is whetted for many things, not the least of which is next week's episode." Similarly, fans of *The X-Files* who can't wait to talk about the program at work or school the next day can log on to a number of cybersites to revisit the show; fans who can't wait for the episodes to be syndicated can rent a number of early episodes at the local video store (my local Kroger grocery store has at least 12 episodes available; the video store I patronize has more than that); fans who can't wait to see a particular story come to life create their own through poaching (including versions, usually featuring a Scully-Mulder "unprofessional interlude," that the authors rate NC-17). The usenet group *alt.tv.x-files.creative*, for example, is replete with a variety of creative offerings called fanfic. There, a four-part short story continues the story line of "Paper Hearts" as Mulder extends his quest to find his sister Samantha; a love poem to Mulder's character begins, "I never fell in love with Mulder. It was never a conscious thought. I just knew"; and a holiday jingle includes the lyrics, "Seven saucers soaring, six deep throats lurking, five floating flukemen." The macabre is made merry by fans of *The X-Files.*

Still, this fun and frightening funhouse possesses the potential to be yet another "f": frustrating. Reflecting on my hall-of-mirrors experience, for example, I kept coming back to the question, "How did they do that?" A simple question—but perhaps not so simple. Initially the query suggests we expect to be able to "figure out" that which is unfamiliar. In addition, I detect a slight aroma of suspicion in such a question, an unstated, "there's got to be a trick" lurking under the surface. Finally, "they" connotes that other people are responsible for things we don't understand. Together these elements of the simple question, "How did they do that?" reveals the influence of modernist thinking in our encounters with the unknown. By golly, we think, we should be able to transcend the confusion and "figure out" what's going on. If we can't, then somebody must be hiding something from us. When the unfamiliar remains unresolved, as is frequently the case in *The X-Files,* skepticism gives way to uncertainty. Suddenly we doubt our ability to *know.* In such circumstances we turn to faith or *belief* as confirmation. We may not know what's behind the curtain, but we're pretty darn certain it's a short guy using a PA system; that we can't prove it, doesn't mean we can't feel confident in our beliefs. We "know" in the spiritual sense rather than the scientific sense.

Such thinking undergirds Bentham's notion of the panopticon— "if we can't see anyone, we'll believe we're being watched"—as well as its metaphoric manifestation in the habitus. In the latter, as the previous chapter illustrated, we seek rational answers for irrational or unresolvable cultural conundrums, such as "why are people being 'downsized' when the economy is thriving?" Unable to come to a logical conclusion, we turn to a belief that the irrational is rhetorically constructed as rational. But beliefs are uncertain themselves. As *The X-Files* points out, neither knowledge nor belief can be trusted as certain. If we assume we can discover certain answers— through knowledge or faith—the program suggests, we are mistaken. Developing an awareness that we are mistaken allows us to use the comic frame to hope for change in the future (the characteristics of the panopticon/postindustrial are not immutable) and to cope with disorientation in the present. Our role models for this lesson are Special Agents Scully and Mulder, both of whom learn to distrust knowledge and belief.

KNOWING IS UNCERTAIN. Engaged in a wide-ranging search for answers because *"The truth is out there,"* Scully and Mulder stubbornly adhere to the modernist belief that a transcendental self can attain objective, certain knowledge. They *know* criminals are not what they appear to be. When the Eve daughters tandemly protest upon capture that "We're just little girls," Mulder's response is quick and confident, "That's the last thing you are" (Biller & Brancato, 1993). Mulder, the paranormal "scientist," is skeptical of their claims to be "just little girls," just as he is skeptical of explanations that ignore unexplainable evidence. Scully, meanwhile, is skeptical of any claims of knowledge that are not supported by hard science. This dialectic is established early in the pilot episode as the two newly partnered agents verbally spar about their beliefs:

> MULDER: Now when convention and science offer us no answers might we not finally turn to the fantastic as a plausibility?
> SCULLY: What I find fantastic is any notion that there are answers beyond the realm of science. The answers are out there. You just have to know where to look. (Carter, 1993a)

When Scully reacts to a Mulder "hypothesis" with, "There is nothing to support that," her partner retorts, "Nothing scientific you mean" (Carter, 1993a).

This clash of ideas routinely recurs in *The X-Files.* After Mulder suggests Eugene Tooms has been killing every 30 years since 1903, Scully cannot provide a scientific explanation and thus believes Tooms's alleged feats to be impossible. When Mulder matches elongated fingerprints from 1903 and 1993, Scully seeks a medical answer, suggesting the 1903 prints might belong to Tooms's great-grandfather. "Genetics might explain the patterns [in the fingerprints]," she says. "It also might explain the sociopathic attitudes and behaviors" (Morgan & Wong, 1993a). When Mulder claims Modell influenced a judge's decision by putting "the whammy" on him, Scully asks, "Please explain to me the scientific nature of the whammy" (Gilligan, 1996a). And when Mulder probes for Scully's reaction to strange lights in the sky, his partner asserts, "Just because I can't explain it, doesn't mean I'm going to believe they were UFOs" (Carter, 1993b).

Yet their repeated failure to discover certain knowledge—episodes are rarely resolved with a sense of closure—is partially due to the inability of medical and paranormal knowledges to answer some of their questions definitively. Scully and Mulder "conclude" that Tooms hibernates for 30 years at a time (paranormal), using the regenerative power of his victims' livers (medical science; as Scully says, "The liver possesses regenerative qualities. It cleanses the blood") to survive without aging (Gilligan, Shiban, & Spotnitz, 1997). The agents, however, are unable to discern exactly *how*

Tooms's body engages in this process. The killer worm in the "Ice" episode is depicted as an invasive organism that will attack another such organism (medical science), and it survives under 6000 feet of ice in a meteor crater for a quarter of a million years (paranormal phenomenon), yet the mystery of its existence is never fully answered because the site where it was discovered is burned to the ground (Morgan & Wong, 1993b). Modell's ability to push his thoughts is linked to his brain tumor (Mulder links the tumor to reports of psychokinesis), but as Scully points out, scientifically speaking, "If Modell did have a brain tumor the effects on his health would be more debilitating" (Gilligan, 1996a).

Faced with such incontrovertibly incomprehensible evidence, Mulder and Scully cannot "know" in the empirical sense. As a result they turn to their belief systems as a way of developing confidence in their assessments of the mysteries they encounter. "Knowing" thus becomes defined as "believing." Faced with insufficient evidence to know, Mulder and Scully nonetheless are typically provided evidence—in the form of dreams, memories, and mysterious phenomena—sufficient to believe. As Kubek (1996) points out, the series "repeatedly throws [Scully and Mulder] (and the viewer) back on alternative epistemologies: faith, memory, even dreams. Although these alternatives do not allow the agents to overcome the system within which they work, Scully and Mulder find in them, and in their faith in each other, the resources with which to continue resisting authority" (p. 170). *The X-Files* thus tells viewers that "knowledge" is anything but certain.

BELIEF IS INSUFFICIENT. But even faith cannot withstand scrutiny in *The X-Files.* As the series has unfolded, both Scully and Mulder have displayed increasing doubts about their own beliefs or ways of knowing. Mulder long believed his sister was abducted by aliens, for example, but Roche's appearance causes him to question that belief in favor of a more mundane explanation. Taunts Roche shortly before Mulder fatally shoots him, "How sure are you [the girl I killed is] not Samantha? Huh? How do you know?" (Gilligan, 1996b). Mulder does not, and cannot, *know* because he has to kill Roche, nor can he *believe* because Roche has cast doubt on his memory of the alien abduction. Faced with two explanations, one otherworldly and the other tragically violent, he tells Scully, "I don't know. I don't know what to believe. I don't know what happened" (Gilligan, 1996b).

Scully, too, has her doubts about what she can believe. Her forays into the world of the paranormal have left her uncertain about the adequacy of even partial scientific explanations. In "Leonard Betts," for example, Scully attempts to explain the movements of the decapitated head by reaching back to scientific scripture: "I mean, I know exactly what it is. It's residual electrical activity stored chemically in the dead cells" (Gilligan, Shiban, & Spotnitz, 1997). But a short time later, when Mulder points out how a controversial photographic process designed to capture the "lifeforce" of objects seems to indicate shoulders attached to the decapitated head, Scully admits, "I don't even know how to explain that part or even what it proves" (Gilligan, Shiban, & Spotnitz, 1997). Though uncertain of what she can know with "certainty," Scully is also afraid to believe in unscientific explanations. In the first season, after witnessing apparitions of her dead father and Luther Lee Boggs's channeling of him, Scully attempts to produce a rational explanation. When Mulder asks, "Dana, after all you've seen, after all the evidence, why can't you believe?" she responds, "I'm afraid. I'm afraid to believe" (Morgan & Wong, 1994a).

The X-Files, then, uses the comic frame to suggest that certainty—in the form of knowledge *and* belief—is illusory. By teaching such a lesson through its lead characters, the program underlines the notion that even the best of us make this mistake. Frustrating as this experience might be, discovering the pervasiveness of uncertainty reminds us to be charitable in our assessments of others, compounding the results of the symbolic pilgrimage. Meanwhile, our modernist tendencies prompt us to want to experience the enjoyable part of the pilgrimage again. Taking yet another journey allows us the opportunity to play with the ironic incongruities The X-Files presents, for the funhouse *is* fun as well as disorienting.

Trusting No One and Our Quest for Closure

Playing with ritual and learning through the comic frame are not the only options available to fans of The X-Files. Although fans may learn from the program's postmodern tendency to resist closure and to test belief, they may also turn to the shelter of modernist certainty and *impose* a sense of closure by envisioning unsolved mysteries as the results of meddling by those in the upper echelons of the social hierarchy, a move The X-Files can encourage in its conspiracy-heavy episodes that feature the secretive Syndicate. This response *reaffirms* the mystery of the social hierarchy rather than challenging the habitus and leads fans back to the surveilled interiors of the panopticon, where they can "trust no one." For example, interview participant Monica implies that the creative forces behind the series function as a mysterious "they" who toy with appearances, reality, and the minds of the viewers: "They don't always reveal everything and so sometimes it's like, 'what's going on?'" Later she elaborates: "One of the biggest complaints—I mean, I sometimes even have it, is that it tends to be very ambiguous, almost deliberately so, where they're not going to give you any real answers and there's very little closure."

Monica's answer is loaded with scientific skepticism. "Real answers," she complains, are not forthcoming; all we're left with—borrowing from an album title of the rock group, Collective Soul—are hints, allegations, and things left unsaid. In addition, the "they" to whom Monica refers are most assuredly the people who create the episodes, but her use of the generic "they" is similar to Scully's reference to the unknown "men" in her congressional testimony excerpted earlier in this chapter; these are the people who could explain the mysterious (because we believe that it *is* explainable) but choose not to provide such an explanation. Interestingly, cyberfans are fond of using the acronym TPTB (the powers that be) in place of "they," yet the acronym sounds even more ominous than the pronoun; TPTB have an apparently omniscient status given their ability to create stories, characters, and conclusions. (TPTB could also be read as a reference to the shadowy figures who make up the Syndicate, the powers who seem to pull the strings that prompt Scully and Mulder's actions.)

All of these rhetorical strategies, I believe, are attempts to construct some kind of symbolic order in an otherwise chaotic cultural space. When perspectives are blurred and/or constantly shifting, when certain answers are unavailable, the modernist quest for knowledge of an ordered universe is placed in jeopardy. Explains interview participant Lee, "We no longer have a clearly defined enemy. . . . [Y]ou have to wonder if perhaps somewhat, you know, we are still searching for the enemy and we feel a lot better off if we have some enemy, even if we're not exactly sure what it is." Assigning control to unknown, invisible forces harkens back to the panopticon, but the prospect of disorder is not sufficiently bearable for many people in a society where concrete visions of promised lands have dominated. Interview participant Palmer, who had researched the appeal of conspiracy theories, was especially helpful in leading me to this conclusion. As he claims, "In a really twisted sort of way, paranoia and conspiracy theories . . . make some kind of order out of everything, instead of saying that some random guy with a gun shot John F. Kennedy and the president can be killed that easily for no real reason. People don't want to believe that. They want to believe that there was something more going on, there was some significance to this event. . . . And as strange as it is, people can find that comforting. There's some kind of order as opposed to this random, messy chaos." Palmer's use of the phrase "*they want to believe*" is nearly a direct quotation of the caption on Mulder's office poster and reflects the spiritual, romantic dimension of conspiracy theories as well as their modernist desire for order. Such theories replace an unfulfilled search for ordered knowledge with a confident faith in the invisible and unknown; faith cannot be disproven, but knowledge can be wrong. Contrary to the lead characters' experiences, then, faith in a way of knowing can seem certain even if the knowledge produced by that epistemology is uncertain.

In this way *The X-Files* illustrates how seemingly irrational or fringe rhetoric may resonate profoundly among audiences who do not see the "common sense" in mainstream answers to social mysteries. The AIDS epidemic can be envisioned as God's curse on a sinful people; the proliferation of crack cocaine in urban areas can be interpreted as an undercover CIA venture designed to enslave African Americans with the shackles of pharmacology; the weakening of the farm economy can be seen as the work of invisible Jewish bankers intent on making a land grab. Although I find each of these conspiracy theories, as I do those found in *The X-Files,* outlandish and devoid of compelling evidence, the difficulty in producing evidence to *deny* these narratives sustains their rhetorical force among those who *believe.* Those charged are presumed guilty, but the charges are of such a nature that they cannot be adequately rebutted *because the villains are unseen.* By remaining hidden from view, they—like the panopticon inspector—appear to be more real than if they really were real. Bozovic's (1995) words from earlier in the chapter are worth repeating here: "The less the inspector is really present, the more he is apparently omnipresent . . . since a momentary exposure to the eyes of the prisoners is sufficient for him to lose his apparent omnipresence. Here, then, appearance *precludes* reality."

The implications of such scapegoating can be summarized by altering the Syndicate's motto from "trust no one" to the double negative version, "do not trust no one," where "no one" can be interpreted as the invisible or the unseen—"no" meaning absent or lacking, as in "no one" is home. The invisible person or organization is not to be trusted because it cannot be held accountable, just as the Syndicate appears to be accountable to no one. A lack of accountability lies at the heart of our fears about social mystery, as the previous chapter also illustrated. When good workers are downsized in an apparently robust economy, the workers want to hold someone accountable for those mysterious or irrational actions. The managers, on the other hand, say they're responding to the dictates of the marketplace, but how does one hold a marketplace accountable? When accountability is absent, when mysteries persist, we rely on rhetoric to help us make the irrational rational, to assign accountability to entities that cannot deny the charges. At that point we have closure; the "reality" fits the appearance.

Fans of *The X-Files* thus face some difficult rhetorical choices. As they watch Mulder and Scully struggle to find closure and begin to doubt their beliefs, fans can (1) appreciate the postmodern lessons of their ritual investigations, (2) grow increasingly frustrated by the inability of the agents to confirm what they want to believe, let alone to find the truth out there, and turn to imposed forms of closure, or (3) embrace both incommensurate perspectives and struggle to make sense of the intersection of contradictory schools of thought. My suspicion is that many of us choose door number three. Opening that door may seemingly provide an escape from the panopticon and an entrance into the funhouse, but each time we exit/enter, our disorientation grows, goading us into embarking on a continuing series of journeys into the mysteries of *The X-Files*.

Conclusion

Earlier in this chapter I noted that a fan named Josie disagreed with my assessment of both funhouses and *The X-Files* as fun and frightening. She claimed to have no desire whatsoever to be frightened while being entertained. Josie's comment reminds us that the funhouse may be more akin to the panopticon, a frightening, joyless institution. For example, in writing this chapter I stumbled onto two references to funhouses that drew from only their frightening elements. In the first an anonymous author in *Progressive* details how the FBI attempted to enlist librarians to report on suspicious people examining government documents and then checked into the librarians who made the reports. "The FBI is coming to resemble one of those back-to-back funhouse mirrors that reflect and re-reflect an image into infinity: If you ask why your neighbor was placed under surveillance, you come under surveillance, too—and on and on until everyone is in the files" ("Funhouse," 1990, p. 10). The second reference was found on the back jacket of Alegria's (1986) novel called *The Funhouse*, and the language there sounds more frightening than fun: "For the Latin American protagonist, newly introduced to American society, the United States functions through amusement-park logic, in which human relationships are doomed to the chamber of horrors which converts love, sex and family into random corruption, violence and inhumanity" (n.p.). These descriptions of a funhouse that resembles a panopticon reaffirm the difficulty in telling the two apart when we attempt to embrace simultaneously beliefs that are modern, romantic, and postmodern. Or as Barth (1968) explains, "In the funhouse mirror-room you can't see yourself go on forever, because no matter how you stand, your head gets in the way" (p. 85).

Recognizing that our head gets in the way, that our images of place and home are bound to be blurry, can make symbolic pilgrimages more enjoyable and less frustrating. To be sure, we cannot avoid the frustration that occurs when new rhetorical fragments enter our personal orbits, but those fragments also present the possibility of a communitas experience. Fans of *The X-Files* may periodically be frustrated by the lack of closure in the series' episodes, but they nonetheless enjoy the sharing of possibilities that occurs within the promised land of the funhouse, so much so that they ritualistically return week after week to watch, visit with one another in cyberspace, and journey again.

Notes

1. I closely examined 10 episodes of *The X-Files*, mostly from the fourth season (when I was writing this chapter) and the first season (many of which are available on videotape). The episodes are listed in the references section (Biller & Brancato, 1993; Carter, 1993a, 1993b; Gilligan, 1996a, 1996b; Gilligan, Shiban, & Spotnitz, 1997; Morgan & Wong, 1993a, 1993b, 1994a; Spotnitz & Carter, 1996). In addition, I relied on my memory and internet-posted episode guides to reference additional characters, events, and plots.

2. The interview participants included undergraduate students, graduate students, and faculty at my campus. The e-mail participants were solicited through stock messages sent to individuals who offered resources regarding *The X-Files* on their home pages as well as those who participated in Usenet groups related to the program. Individuals in both groups are identified by pseudonyms. Interview procedures with both groups followed protocol approved by Ohio University's Institutional Review Board.

6

Playing in a Perfect Place
Sports Illustrated and an American Elysian Field

They say that a picture is worth a thousand words. In this case, the words would have been enough.

—Kathie Toon
Braintree, MA
Sports Illustrated, 12/31/90, "Letters"

Each week more than 3.1 million subscribers read *Sports Illustrated* (*SI*), a whopping five times the number who subscribe to its closest weekly competitor *The Sporting News* (*Ulrich's*, 1996), making it the "kingpin of sports magazines" (Erickson, 1987, p. S20). I'm just one of those people, and although I can't hope to tell you what all of them experience, I do believe my encounters with the magazine over the years—I've been reading *SI* since I was a teenager—can shed some light on its utter dominance of the sports magazine genre.

Being a sports fan, of course, has something to do with fans' interest in the magazine, but that's not the whole story—at least in my case. An anecdote from my first year as a professor represents, in Paul Harvey's words, the rest of the story. One autumn evening in 1989 I was talking with my friend Chris about the magazine. She and I both remarked how we would devour the articles as soon as the weekly issue appeared in our mailboxes. Eventually our talk about the magazine gravitated to an article on fishing. Neither one of us, understand, cares a whit about fishing, yet both of us found the article compelling for some unexplainable reason. We were quite different people, yet we experienced similar reactions to a story on a topic that, had it appeared in any other magazine, we likely would have steered clear of under any circumstances other than an interminable wait in the lobby of a doctor's office. Because both of us teach rhetoric, we began to ponder the magazine's appeal at a symbolic level. Many of the results of that pondering are represented in this chapter.

If you're not a sports fan, this chapter might be tempting to skip. Sports, as a number of scholars have pointed out (e.g., Davis, 1997; Trujillo, 1991), are often portrayed/interpreted as the ultimate valorization of masculinity, the place where "boys will be boys" and the women are "tomboys." Although much can be learned from such analyses, I read *Sports Illustrated* as a magazine that uses sports as a topic to chronicle various exercises of the human spirit. To be sure, *SI* fills you in on the sports news of the week and features exceptional photos of athletes using their bodies in action, but the magazine's reportorial style (most likely due to its status as a weekly, rather than daily publication) is feature- more than news-oriented. Wins and losses are documented each week, but the human struggles that coincide with those wins and losses (on and off the fields of play) provide the narrative drive to the stories verbally and visually illustrated in *SI*.

Its depiction of lessons for living make the magazine more than simply a periodical about sports; in many respects *SI* could just as easily assume the name of one of its corporate brethren: *Life*. When I snag the magazine from the mailbox on Thursday, I can't wait to dive into its "life lessons" of the week. From its character studies of perseverance to its snippet bemoaning the pollution of sports called "This Week's Sign That the Apocalypse Is Upon Us," *SI* is a refreshing reminder not only of how substance triumphs over style (and not just in sport) but of how spirit is the foundation of substance. In this respect reading about the play in *SI* is purposeful. The purposeful play depicted in *SI* and the purposeful play experienced by fans as they read the magazine combine to offer a means of envisioning a place that reminds fans of how ideals can be embodied within the constraints of reality, how the joy of the spirit can be rediscovered, and how communion can be experienced while playing "mere" games. This place, which I call an American Elysian Field, is described in detail following a brief discussion of how the purposeful play of athletes and fans intersect then undergird symbolic pilgrimages involving sports and games.

Purposeful Play

Purposeful play, you may recall from the introduction, reconfigures "escapism" as the use of our imaginations to respond to constraints imposed by living in a habitus. Bourdieu (1980/1990), in fact, reminds us that "only in imaginary experience (in the folk tale, for example), which neutralizes the sense of social realities, does the social world take the form of a universe of possibles equally possible for any possible subject" (p. 64). Although I believe each of the symbolic pilgrimages I illustrate contains a degree of such play, the confluence of the nature of the texts of *SI*—stories about games—and the characteristics of its fans—generally speaking, people who enjoy games—suggest its preeminence in this context. The raw materials used to build this community of purposeful players include not just the texts of *SI* but the cultural memories embedded in the collection of rhetorical fragments that its fans bring to bear in their experiences with the magazine. Before developing these ideas I want to take a moment to discuss how four principles of "play" will underpin the illustration of *SI*'s promised land; each principle corresponds to the four elements of a symbolic pilgrimage: entering the liminoid, building a sacred place/community, gaining respect for others, and returning home to travel ritualistically.

Play Is a Means of Entering the Liminoid

"The play situation," explains Calhoun (1987), "is an island in which the ordinary conditions and pressures of life are suspended and a new set of play rules set up . . . [where] people can overcome the group antagonisms that ordinarily separate them from one another" (pp. 306, 307). In other words, play provides an alternative to the habitus, creating a symbolic site where "a new set of play rules" guides action. Encountering this otherworldly sphere of play through the act of reading enhances the symbolic experience, for we symbolically leave this world when we read for pleasure. "The reality created" by reading, according to Chesebro (1989), "is a social reality or intersubjective reality" (p. 14). And by seeing the pictures corresponding to each story, we can make our personal versions of the promised land more visual, playing with the images to fit our interpretations. The convergence of playful reading and reading about play generates what Brummett (1991) calls a homology, an occurrence in which the subject of the text parallels the experience of reading the text. Homologies, Brummett contends, magnify the interpretive experience. In other words, when the *act* of reading is play and the subject of the reading is play, as in *SI*, the symbolic power of the story is enhanced. Play puts us in a world apart, a place where we seek to build the perfect place.

Play Is About Creating Perfection

When we play games, Csikszentmihalyi (1987) notes, we may enter a flow experience. Such experiences, he (1990) writes, are common to individuals fully immersed in their tasks. These tasks, even if they are work related, provide the individual with a feeling of play because they are uplifting and enjoyable, providing the individual with an "optimal experience." In short, we may feel as if we're in a beer commercial where "it doesn't get any better than this." Play, like the sacred places we visit in symbolic pilgrimages, feels "perfect."

But the play involved in symbolic pilgrimages is about more than the individual flow experience; it is also about making connections with others in an idealized social atmosphere. "The sacred place," writes Brereton (1987), "reveals the ideal order of things, which is associated with the *perfect* realm of divinity, with life and vitality among humans, or with the values to which people should aspire" (p. 529; emphasis added). Brereton's description of sacred places is remarkably consistent with the description of play offered by Huizinga (1938/1970): "Into an imperfect world and into the confusion of life [play] brings a temporary, *a limited perfection*" (p. 29; emphasis added). Not surprisingly, sports—as a particular type of play—fills a "radically religious" impulse in which the play represents "a zest for symbolic meaning, and *a longing for perfection*" (Novak, 1976, p. 19; emphasis added). Play is about perfecting the individual experience at the same time that we enjoy the perfect communal experience.

Reading *SI* as play, and reading about play in *SI*, amplify what Kenneth Burke calls our inherent quest to achieve perfection. We are, Burke (1966) tells us, "goaded by the spirit of hierarchy (or moved by the sense of order) and rotten with perfection" (p. 16). Burke's comment is less an indictment of us than an explanation for our never-ending use of symbols to seek the sense of perfection play seems to promise. According to Burke, who borrows from Aristotle's concept of entelechy, each being strives to perfect itself. In humans, he (1966) claims, "the mere desire to name something by its 'proper' name, or to speak a language in its distinctive ways is intrinsically 'perfectionist'" (p. 16). We are "rotten with perfection" in an ironic sense; we use terms to name concepts and others in order to offer ourselves a sense of security (or a sense of place) in a social hierarchy (Burke, 1966). Play is thus purposeful in that it is used to generate a sense of social perfection. To achieve perfection, of course, requires effort; thus play is participatory and involves others whom we may come to respect for their efforts.

Play Is Participatory

Play, by definition, is active, requiring participation. We must make an effort, however slight, to read (making time, picking up the book, etc.), just as we must make an effort to participate in games or sports. Even watching sporting events as fan, rather than player, necessitates participation. As Novak (1976) notes, "The mode of observation proper to a sports event is *to participate*" (p. 144; emphasis in original). Fans watch intently, cheer, worry, even jump up and down on occasion, as they watch their team play. My friend Chris, for example, would routinely walk out on the front porch to have a cigarette if her beloved Cleveland Browns weren't playing well, somehow "believing" that her participation might help the team. In participating as fans, we implicitly acknowledge the root word of "fan," what Novak (1976) identifies as "the word for temple, *fanum,* the temple of the god of the place: by an exercise of imagination one places oneself under the fate of a particular group, becomes other than oneself, and risks thereby one's security" (p. 144). By risking our security we enhance our appreciation of others. They do not judge our behavior as fans, and we do not judge theirs; we accept and appreciate the myriad ways in which one can participate by being a fan.

Playful participation, then, is also purposeful in that it seeks a sacred—no doubt, perfect—connection with others; it reflects a distant cultural memory equating "fan" with "worship"—imbuing the participatory experience of play with an even more respectful hue. Indeed, for many sports fans, participating in one's favorite team's play is not too far removed from worship. Recall, for instance, the example of Nebraska home football games discussed in chapter three. Like pilgrims drawn to a shrine, the red-clad fans converge in Memorial Stadium on autumn Saturdays to honor the liturgical figures sacrificing on the field. As Novak (1976) explains, sports players do indeed serve as liturgical, albeit secular, figures: "Once an athlete accepts the uniform, he [*sic*] is in effect donning priestly vestments. It is the function of priests to offer sacrifices. . . . Often the sacrifice is literal: smashed knees, torn muscles, injury-abbreviated careers. Always the sacrifice is ritual: the athlete bears the burden of identification. He is no longer living his own life only. Others are living in him, by him, with him. . . . He has given up his private persona and assumed a liturgical persona" (p. 133). Even players are aware of their shift in persona. Former St. Louis Cardinals baseball catcher Joe Garigiola recalls, "When they gave me my own uniform, I mean, I, this may sound sacrilegious but I'm sure it must be like when the pope gives the vestments to make somebody a real cardinal" (quoted in Greenburg, 1992). By participating in the play of sports, in particular, we not only enter a liminoid flow, seek a perfect place, and participate with others, we want to do so over and over again. We are, in short, "rotten with perfection."

Play Is Ritualistic

Play is ritualistic in two senses. First, we can reenact our own rules about *how* we play. As we playfully read about the play in *SI,* we engage in a form of ritual that we have invented as individual fans, for as Stephenson (1967) points out, the act of reading print media is a form of ritualized play. For example, when I'm in an airport I invariably read *USA Today;* my ritual reading order of the sections is red-purple-blue-green. This ritualized play adds another layer to the homology. Second, the ritual allows us to enact an alternative to the habitus through a set of "new" rules, much like the "secret societies" of the DNRC and X-philes serve as shared, symbolic standpoints for opposing elements of the habitus. Explains Huizinga (1938/1970), play "transports the participants to another world. . . . Play is not 'ordinary' or 'real' life. It is rather a stepping out of 'real' life into a temporary sphere of activity with a disposition all of its own" (pp. 37 & 26). The ritual play involved in games—whether athletic endeavors or reading about them—belongs "to the world of imagination. They are pledges of our ultimate liberty or spirit" (Novak, 1976, p. 218). When we play, we are free to make up the rules in concord with the others who play the game.

Together these four characteristics of play enable fans to reinvigorate their spirits within a habitus that has deemphasized spirit. For instance, my initial discussion with my friend Chris led us to believe there was something almost spiritual about our reading experiences with the magazine. We both felt transported to a different, special place as we devoured its stories, yet we certainly didn't go so far as to define reading *SI* as a religious experience. Instead, we saw the articles in the magazine as creating a place where the sacred intermingled with the profane. We decided to call the place an American Elysian Field because it reflects the realities of the American experience as well as the Western ideals of the Roman Elysian Field described by Virgil. As I hope to illustrate, this melding of time and culture—or collective memory—in one symbolic place, or promised land, encourages us to participate in its construction, control our position within the place, and use it to resolve conflicts rooted in sport and culture by observing those conflicts from the symbolically constructed field of sport.[1] These ideas are elaborated in several steps. First, I identify the characteristics of *SI*'s promised land of sport, the liminoid place to which its devoted fans can journey. Next I illustrate how this promised land manifests itself in the pages of *SI* as a perfectly isolated place for play, one that is open to participation and packed with rituals that allow its fans to create an alternative to the dehumanizing habitus. I conclude with an examination of how this "perfect place" can also be envisioned as exclusionary and disrespectful.

America's Elysian Field

The symbolic shrine of sport constructed by the intersection of fan interpretations and *SI*'s reporting and photography produces symbolic clashes revealing ongoing struggles between the real and the ideal within American culture. Those struggles occur primarily through the collision of values reflecting Western ideals emanating from the story of the Elysian Fields and American realities encountered throughout the nation's history.[2] Such a collision produces a liminoid site, a place that is neither a representation of Western ideals, American realities, or the present. Instead, it is a site somewhere in between these cultural memories and contemporary fragments. Fans of the magazine's stories and photos can playfully construct personalized versions of this place as they sort out the conflicts between ideals and realities.

The first struggle occurs over the conceptualization of territory—whether to live in isolation or to engage in intervention. Second, conflict occurs over the type of individuals most valued in the territory—the elite of society or the democratic masses. Third, tension occurs over the kind of action individuals may perform in the territory—play or work. The ideals of the Elysian Fields suggest the former of each option—isolation, elitism, and play; the realities of the United States reflect the need for intervention, democratization, and work. The meshing of the two sets of values generates the image of perfection, the optimal blend of the ideal and the real. The American Elysian Field thus becomes a sacred place. Explains Brereton (1987), "To call a place sacred asserts that a place, its structure and its symbols express fundamental cultural values and principles. By giving these visible form, the sacred place makes tangible the corporate identity of a people and their world" (p. 534).

The Ideal

In Virgil's classic, *The Aeneid*, the title character encounters at the end of his trek a utopia, the "perfect" place reserved as a reward for good people. Three elements constitute the ideal setting of the Elysian Fields: it is isolated, it is home to elites, and it is a place of play. The area comprising the fields is *isolated* to prevent all but the worthy from enjoying its pleasures and to distance its inhabitants from the more mundane concerns of the "real" world. The pastoral character of the fields—full of meadows and valleys—suggests a pristine territory with sufficient space for all its inhabitants to share. As Aeneas is told, " 'It is all our home, the shady groves, and the streaming meadows, and the softness along the river-banks. No fixed abode is ours at all' " (Virgil, 1951, p. 167). The inhabitants of the isolated territory preserve its natural integrity because they are the most deserving persons of the culture, the *elites.* "The band of heroes dwell here, all those whose mortal wounds were suffered in fighting for the fatherland; and poets, the good, the pure, the worthy of Apollo; those who discovered truth and made life nobler; those who served others" (Virgil, 1951, p. 166). These individuals, who exhibited merit in their lifetimes, are portrayed as supernatural. Their admirable deeds earned them immortality and a place in the field. Finally, because the elites reside in an isolated, plentiful territory, they are able to spend their days at *play.* "Some grapple on the grassy wrestling-ground in exercise and sport, and some are dancing, and others singing" (Virgil, 1951, p. 166). Having worked hard for society in their past lives, the inhabitants of the Elysian Fields are rewarded with an infinite amount of play.

The Real

The characteristics of the Elysian Fields represent a universal ideal, a place of spiritual rejuvenation where good people can play unfettered by the concerns of daily living. Conversely, the American experience is packed with values reflecting the need for realism. Individuals must intervene to tame territory, a task that requires work as well as widespread participation. The American experience is symbolically constructed as a series of *interventions* to conquer territory (e.g., the New World, the expanding frontier, international markets, space). Territory, especially the frontier, was designed to be used rather than enjoyed by individuals in this belief system. Slotkin (1985) depicts the taming of the frontier as a series of advances that lead to the establishment of base camps, which, in turn, serve as outposts from which to launch additional expeditions: "As each new Frontier is met and conquered, it in turn becomes a Metropolis, and as such the base for a new and deeper foray into the Wilderness" (p. 41). Whereas the ideal world of the Elysian Fields offers abundant resources, America developed as a nation in search of more resources and thus more territory. This territorial expansion was fueled in part by the economic need to provide opportunities for the citizenry. These opportunities helped promulgate the American political philosophy of *democracy*. Thus the value of democracy was in some ways a realistic response to the needs of an infant society. Strenuous collective participation established the initial American colonies, and collective effort allowed the nation to grow. Collective effort, of course, implies *work*. Intervening to tame territory and participating in the governance of oneself and one's neighbors required an investment of time and labor. Moreover, the Puritans' espousal of a strong work ethic added the power of religious faith to practical necessity. And because the effort to improve the nation continues, work continues.

By framing this "debate" in terms of contrasting positions, I do not mean to suggest we are dealing with dialectical opposites. Because both sets of values are culturally privileged, they coexist in an uneasy both/and relationship. Attempting to provide a definitive resolution to the "conflict," then, is an effort fraught with the potential for folly; no matter which resolution would be selected, it would be inevitably disappointing because of its failure to incorporate fully all of the seemingly contradictory values. *SI* doesn't so much resolve this conflict as it addresses it. By suggesting the unavoidability of definitive solutions, the magazine acknowledges the futility of a modernist answer to the conflict. Yet in attempting to develop a "perfect" place where all of the values are acknowledged, *SI* cannot help *but* offer a potential, romantic answer. In this respect *SI* engages all three schools of thought discussed in chapter one: a postmodern resistance to developing discrete divisions, a modern desire for a particular point of view, and a romantic quest for spiritual fulfillment.

In *SI* the promised land of the American Elysian Field becomes a liminoid place that symbolically exists somewhere in the in-between, not wholly centered in any one particular past (Western or American) and certainly not established in the present. By playing with a number of different rhetorical fragments—and borrowing elements of modernism, romanticism, and postmodernism—fans constructing the American Elysian Field site play with the symbolic resources accessible to them. Moreover, the field's diverse rhetorical influences endow it with the characteristics of a sacred site positioned somewhere above and beyond the habitus. As Brereton (1987) explains, "A sacred place can draw a variety of traditions to itself and thereby become even more powerfully sacred" (p. 527). Compiling fragments of cultural memory, their own experiences, and the stories in *SI*, fans can playfully construct a perfect place that, as the next section demonstrates, transcends material interventions.

Defining the Territory: Intervention/Isolation

Whether to intervene in territory or to leave it isolated is a tension that runs throughout American cultural history. The modernist quest for progress, echoed in the late-18th-century calls of "manifest destiny," suggests we must intervene in new frontiers; or as *Star Trek*'s Captain Kirk narrates, we now explore "space, the final frontier." Intervention reflects the essentialist masculine thinking that territory should be controlled for a society to progress; Father Time is ticking along and we cannot be left behind. On the other hand, the romantic ideal of isolation is reflected in everything from the eschatological story of Adam and Eve to recurring bouts of foreign policy isolationism to current concerns about the environment. Isolation reflects the essentialist feminine thinking that the land should not be pillaged for personal gain; Mother Nature nurtures and protects her children. *SI* addresses these paradoxical values by simultaneously acknowledging the both/and nature of the relationship and privileging a romantic conception of the promised land of sport as an isolated, perfect place that should be ideally sheltered from material intrusions. When such interventions occur, writers and fans are quick to sound an alert.

Isolation

Sport is best, *SI* suggests, when it occurs in isolated, natural territory. Consequently, the magazine routinely features images of "pure" endeavors occurring in isolated territories. The settings of sport usually involve the outdoors or elements designed to mirror those found outdoors (e.g., artificial turf for baseball and football, wood floors for basketball, ice for hockey). Natural efforts and settings remind fans of the purity of nature: it is constant, timeless yet always new, resistant to external efforts to control or manage its dynamics. The "consecrated spots" of play, notes Huizinga (1938/1970), "are temporary worlds within the ordinary world, dedicated to the performance of an act apart" (p. 29).

SI locates these consecrated spots in isolated places, symbolically a world apart from the habitus. For instance, Clive Gammon describes the scene of a fishing expedition in a Latin American jungle, "The tawny water slides fast through the jaguar-haunted rain forest. Yellow orchids trail in the river, similarly colored butterflies dance over it" (8/14/89, p. 82).[3] In Kenya, the road to the home of a promising young distance runner is a wild one: "From Nairobi you head northwest over the Ngong Hills and into the Great Rift Valley. Near Lake Naivasha the roadside impalas shine as if groomed and oiled. Zebras standing out among the green acacias don't look natural. They look published" (2/26/90, p. 73).

Within these isolated venues, *SI* suggests, the best in sport can occur when we interact with nature rather than use it for personal gain. For instance, helicopter skiing in the Canadian Rockies is "powder skiing as few of us had experienced it. The tree-studded slopes were so steep that the overwhelming sensation was of soaring, then compressing" (1/14/91, p. 88). Tug-of-war teams practice within the scenic beauty of America's dairy country: "On most spring and summer evenings, the tidy farming community of Orfordville, Wis., is so peaceful that the main drag (state highway 213) could double as a landscape painting. Except, of course, for the moans, grunts, and whimpers coming from the direction of American Legion Post No. 209" (11/26/90, p. 130). Isolated territory, *SI* suggests, encourages natural—and pure—efforts from us. As a result isolation produces the most ideal experiences of sport: individuals interacting with nature's territory in a relaxed atmosphere. Kansas University basketball coach, Roy Williams, for instance, enjoyed shooting baskets at Biltmore Elementary when he was growing up in Asheville, N.C.: " 'I loved it because I could do it when I was alone,' Williams says. 'Give me a ball and a goal, and I was in heaven. It was my refuge. I could go to Biltmore, and there were no problems in the world' " (3/10/97, p. 58).

This spiritual, uncomplicated world of Williams's reflects the ideal of isolation in an American Elysian Field. Sheltered from intrusions, left alone to reflect and wonder, pilgrims at the field can gain perspective in a manner unimaginable in a more chaotic material world. Fan Stephen reflects this desire for a simple, clear view in his response to a story about high school basketball: "Your story made me realize how much I prefer reading about high school athletics to reading about pro sports. High school teams give us a glimpse of sport in its purest form, that of a child who wants to play the game" (3/17/97, p. 8).[4]

Former University of Tennessee quarterback Peyton Manning apparently preferred playing in that world as well, declining an opportunity to declare early for the NFL draft—despite clear indications he would be the first player selected—because he enjoyed the life of a college student: "I want to walk to class and hear people say, 'Good luck in the game.' I want to see that little orange section in the stands at road games. I really do. I want to tailgate with my parents after the games and then go out to dinner. I don't know if you tailgate in the NFL, but we've been doing it for three years here, and I want to do it for one more" (3/17/97, p. 69). The complicated offenses of the NFL that beckon Manning, the pay-for-play professionalism that could mean failure, the myriad of factors that interrupt his pastoral image of the college game, clearly worry the young man. "'What if I got out there and I just hadn't done it enough times and I was late [in throwing a pass]? I'd be thinking, Damn, I'm not ready. I should have stayed. Maybe I did need one more year" (3/17/97, p. 68). Manning's worries reflect the modernist impulse in U.S. history: the need to intervene in isolation in order to make progress.

Intervention

Manning, as a professional quarterback, would seemingly be playing more for an enhanced standard of living and less for the pure joy of the game. Professional football is simply the next step in a linear progression of improvements in his status, according to this modernist-tinged thinking. The image of playful, front-yard football is replaced with the business of football. Status is measured by moving forward, renegotiating contracts, being rewarded with extravagant signing bonuses. The business of football, like other sports, is winning. And although everyone seems to prefer winning—sports teams that win more frequently tend to draw more fan support—the quest for victories that distinguish us through the either/or of wins and losses carries a steep price tag according to *SI* and its fans.

When territory is envisioned as something to conquer, *SI* claims, the ensuing efforts are tainted and impure. Not content to interact with the territory of sports, we can also see sports as a means to attain territory. For instance, *SI* notes that a failed attempt to insert a football field within the confines of a Hopi reservation allowed the isolated territory to reclaim its own particular beauty: "From goalpost to goalpost, not one blade of green grass shows its crown. The sod has dried up, died and blown away, leaving a spectacular view from the concrete bleachers of desert valley and surrounding mesas" (11/20/89, p. 10). Similar intrusions, such as attempts to conquer the problems of growing real grass indoors and/or in harsh climates by installing artificial turf in stadiums around the country, are always met with disdain by *SI*. The turn of nearly every football and baseball season brings a reminder in *SI*'s pages of the high number of injuries that athletes experience because of the advances in turf technology. The dangers of intervention are reaffirmed in letters to the editor that comment on the death of a helicopter-skiing enthusiast who apparently wanted to conquer more isolated territory. Writes Eric, "Certainly the death of a fellow skier is heartbreaking. However, it should be emphasized that Eric King, the skier who died, was not following the rules" (2/18/91, p. 4). In the next letter printed, Christopher elaborates: "Your article mentions that King routinely veered 100 yards or more to either side of the line established by the guide" (2/18/91, p. 4).

As these letters illustrate, the chief form of intervention is the way in which some individuals approach sport. In particular, *SI* laments sports participants whose foci are attaining wins and dollars. For instance, Colorado's football team damaged its integrity in the eyes of *SI* by accepting a victory obtained through the use of an extra down at the end of the game against Missouri: "Little things like principle and integrity get in the way of the really important stuff, like winning at any cost" (10/15/90, p. 96). This observation prompts fan Carolyn to note that Colorado sacrificed the possibility of spiritual enhancement for material success: "Colorado is throwing away a wonderful opportunity by not giving up the football game it won against Missouri on an illegal fifth down. The school's glory for so doing would far outweigh the loss of the game" (11/12/90, p. 6). Similarly, *SI* reports that college basketball player Marcus LoVett's attention deficit disorder was neglected so he could be used as a cog in the school's winning basketball machine. "The Chiefs' graduation rate since 1988 is 27%, and according to a report by Juli Rhoden of Oklahoma City's KTOK radio, over the same period no more than 10% of the school's black players have earned their diplomas" (2/24/97, p. 66). The urge to win individual awards also intervenes in the isolated territory of sport. For example, Austin Murphy sarcastically sees himself through the eyes of a typical Heisman trophy voter: "How could he be a bona fide candidate if I didn't get a promotional poster of him last July?" (11/27/89, p. 26).

As Murphy suggests, the intrusion of commercial concerns also harms the purity of the metaphorical field. He quantifies the intrusion with a content analysis of an ABC *Monday Night Football* telecast: "Of the telecast's 178 minutes, a quickie by NFL standards, the total action time was 12 minutes. . . . The odd commercial: I counted 99, which gave the telecast an 11 to 9 play to plug ratio" (12/24/90, p. 82). When these intrusions do occur, *SI* is quick to point out how it changes the nature of both sport and sports participants. Remarking on a high school athlete's desire to wear "1" on his jersey in college, *SI* depressingly notes, "On such seeming trifles does recruiting turn. And seasons turn. And coaches get fired. And millions of TV dollars get repositioned" (2/26/90, p. 40).

The NCAA, an organization founded to ensure the integrity of college sports, suffers itself from the pressures of intervention. University of Iowa president Hunter Rawlings III writes in *SI*'s "Point After" feature: "Large universities now play football and basketball primarily for television. TV determines the times and sites of our games, controls our athletic departments' budgets, and dictates conference membership and realignments. Dependence on TV revenue reinforces the need to field winning teams. Hence, the relentless recruiting scandals, abdication of academic responsibility, and, ultimately, in the NCAA's euphemistic phrase, 'loss of institutional control'" (1/21/91, p. 72). As Rawlings points out, winning and money are interrelated factors that encourage intervention in the isolated field of sports.

When combined with a quest for individual glory at the expense of the game, the concoction is a poisonous brew, according to *SI* fans. Louis, for example, excoriates New England Patriots coach Bill Parcells for drawing attention to himself (and his desire to switch teams and make more money) during Super Bowl week: "Bill Parcells' behavior during the week before the Super Bowl was out of line. I am sorry that he took attention away from his team" (3/3/97, p. 21). Similarly, Richard scolds Steve Mariucci for leaving the University of California to coach the San Francisco 49ers for a chance at more glory and more money: "Fourteen months ago Steve Mariucci came to Cal with a lot of noise about how coaching there was the perfect job for him, how happy he was to be back, etc. Now he's gone after one year. You chose not to mention those people to whom he broke a promise—Cal, its fans and alums, and most important, the players he recruited" (2/24/97, p. 8).

The primary culprit in this game of greed, *SI* suggests, is television—a technological intrusion that destroys the isolated nature of the territory by emphasizing the conquering of audiences and opponents. Although money and television reflect the realities of big-time sports, their confluence disrupts what should be the ideal happenings in the field. Thus *SI* contrasts the intrusions of big-time sports with the isolation of less popular sports. Although *SI* cannot completely shelter sport from real, material intrusions such as electronic media, capitalist consumption, efficiency standards such as win-loss records, and human efforts to improve nature, the field is sheltered symbolically from these intrusions because the sacred place of sport is ideal and does not accept material influences. Thus fans jointly involved in creating *SI*'s isolated fields can escape to a promised land where attainment of more "goods" is not a sign of a successful life.

In making this escape these fans engage in liminoid play that seeks perfection. Isolated from habitus-infested forces, fans can enjoy sport in a more "pure" location that exists above and beyond the site of petty squabbles about winning, losing, and who's earning how much in salary and endorsements. In the isolated, idealized American

Elysian Field, the play is about sport and only sport; the "rules" of the habitus—expressed in Rawlings's statement above—are re-formulated as rules that involve only the game. Absent material intrusions, sports are played as they "should be played" in the promised land of the field. Consequently, fans of *SI* will point out "rule violations" when interventions occur in the isolated territory. As the following section demonstrates, defining such a territory makes possible different definitions of individual success and an appreciation for the efforts of all who play the games of sport.

Defining the Individual: Elitism/Democracy

Virgil's Elysian Fields were open only to the elite of society. The American value of democracy, however, suggests that all individuals should enjoy equal opportunities. As chapter four illustrates, we struggle with this tension in a variety of circumstances. We want the best people to make the most important decisions; thus we believe in the latent elitism of meritocracy. But we want all of us to be involved in the decision-making process; thus we simultaneously believe in social equality. The nation's founders struggled with this paradox, as reflected in our American versions of Great Britain's House of Lords (Senate) and House of Commons (House); and as *Dilbert* evidences, we still haven't developed a resolution to this dilemma today. *SI* addresses this tension by admiring the extraordinary *abilities* of elite athletes and the extraordinary *efforts* of all of us who participate in athletics. In playing with this tension between elitism and democracy, fans of *SI* come to appreciate and respect the work of *all* who play sports.

Extraordinary Abilities

Like any amazed sports fan, *SI* marvels at the exploits of "superhuman" athletes. Hockey player Wayne Gretzky, nicknamed the Great One, is described as so gifted that his mortality is questionable: "Rumors that Wayne Gretzky is human have surfaced sporadically throughout his career, but they have always been easily refuted. One merely has to look at the NHL record book" (2/26/90, p. 26). Professional basketball player Shaquille O'Neal was depicted as an athlete with nearly superhuman skills even as an 18-year-old student at Louisiana State University: "Surreal may be a truer description of a kid who, though he will be a teenager for another 14 months, is already the fifth or sixth best center on the planet" (1/21/91, p. 40).

When athletes age, *SI* fans are reminded of their skills. A story looking back at Soviet gymnast Olga Korbut recaptures her ability to defy gravity: "The girl flew across the screens as if she were drawn by a cartoonist's pen. No boundaries existed, no laws of nature. One foot would touch the ground, and she would soar" (11/27/89, p. 35). Fourteen-year-old national figure skating champion Tara Lipinski is also depicted as an "otherworldly" phenomenon: "The littlest came last: a girl so young—14—that only last week she'd lost her final baby molar; a girl as tiny, at 4′8″ and 75 pounds, as the tooth fairy. . . . She spins so fast that she seems to dematerialize, like Tinkerbell, in the midst of her jumps" (2/24/97, pp. 29, 31).

Although some elite athletes are envisioned as simply out-of-this-world, others—to use my nephew's lingo—are "morphs," creatures that are part human, part animal and exist in more than one world. Baseball superstar Ken Griffey Jr.'s skills are described as "breathtaking . . . his great arm, his fluid stride, his viperlike uppercut swing" (5/7/90, p. 39). College basketball player Tim Thomas is similarly portrayed. "A 6′9″ small forward, Thomas plays like a chameleon, able to post up inside on a smaller defender or to drive and stick the three-pointer like a guard" (3/10/97, p. 39). Much like the Greek gods with animal and human characteristics, elite athletes who are seeming "morphs" possess apparently supernatural powers that are worthy of spiritual respect. These beings possess the symbolic capability of transcending the material; they are romantic icons in a modernist environment.

SI's representations of the athletic ideal embodied in superhuman elites is balanced with a focus on the humanity of these gifted individuals; they are also portrayed as humans who have frailties just like the rest of us. This rhetorical representation provides the foundation for *SI*'s valorization of "mere mortal" athletes who give extraordinary effort. The magazine's weekly "They Said It" feature, for instance, offers quotations ranging from stars demonstrating their real ignorance to not-so-stars reveling in their ordinariness. For example:

Charles Barkley, 250-pound Philadelphia 76er forward, on the advantages of playing alongside newly acquired 255-pound Rick Mahorn: "It means people will be able to see I don't have the biggest butt in the league." (11/27/89)

Andy Van Slyke, Pirate outfielder, to Steeler offensive tackle Tunch Ilkin, while they watched the Steelers, who had gone four weeks without a touchdown, working out: "Why do you guys practice kicking off?" (10/15/90)

In an article on famous athletes who committed colossally stupid mistakes or "boners" (such as running the wrong way to score a touchdown for the other team), *SI* reminds us that we share characteristics with the world's best athletes: "Who among us hasn't committed a boner? Is there anyone who hasn't asked himself [*sic*]—sometimes in the middle of the night—'How could I have done that?'" (10/15/90, p. 107). Roberto De Vicenzo's infamous scoring error in the 1968 Masters golf tournament surfaces on the pages of *SI* as one of those inexplicable moments: "Before I cry, because it was the Masters. But after 22 years, I receive so many good things from the game, things maybe if I don't make the mistake, I never receive. . . . I made more money after the Masters mistake than I did after winning the British Open in '67. So many people don't remember I won that tournament. They say this is the guy who made the mistake in the Masters" (10/15/90, p. 110). As De Vicenzo's remarks illustrate, elite athletes may be admired for their extraordinary abilities, but they are sometimes remembered for their human fallibilities. To err is human, *SI* points out, and the human in all of us is worth celebrating, not just bemoaning, when we put forth extraordinary efforts.

Extraordinary Efforts

To emphasize further its commitment to democratic participation in sport, *SI* also typically recognizes the efforts of athletes who are not famous, defining them as worthy of respect in the process. In a weekly feature called "Faces in the Crowd," *SI* briefly outlines the athletic exploits of individuals frequently marginalized in sport and/or society. For example, in three issues I pulled from the stack (11/27/89; 5/14/90; 10/15/90), "Faces" extols the efforts of four white females 13 or younger, three white males in high school, three white females in high school, two black males in high school, two white males over 40, one white female in college, one Asian American female in high school, one Asian American in college, and one 60-year-old white female.

SI's recognition of the nontraditional athlete goes beyond a brief weekly feature. In fact, *SI* routinely highlights the efforts of individuals who are not young, white, middle-class, and/or male. Stories are devoted to Hopi high school football players (11/20/89), Kenyan long-distance runners (2/26/90), senior citizen athletes (8/14/89), a black female professional tennis player (11/27/89), and male and female tug-of-war teams (11/26/90). New York Yankees pitcher Mariano Rivera grew up working on his father's fishing boat in Panama, playing with his "Christmas baseball, all wrapped with tape by midsummer, and a glove made from a cardboard box" (3/24/97, p. 53). Today he is the ace relief pitcher for the most well-known baseball team in the world.

In democratizing sport *SI* recontextualizes the Elysian Fields in an American setting. Whereas Aeneas's journey unveiled a field where only individuals who committed great deeds could play, America's Elysian Field, in *SI*'s pages, is more accessible. This accessibility is actually due to a redefinition of the great deed. *Playing as hard as one can*—a real task available to all—equals a great deed on the pages of *SI.* Thus 8- and 80-year-olds, as well as the able and disabled athletes of the world, are capable of great deeds and deserve time on the field. For whatever reasons, ordinary people can do all kinds of extraordinary deeds on America's Elysian Field of sport—from archery to tug-of-war:

"People think we're a bunch of fellows with a beer in one hand who drag the opposition through a mudhole," says the 64-year-old dairy farmer Rudy Kopp, the group's founder, mentor, and namesake. He has reason to get huffy. Kopp's hearty band of 25- to 45-year-old farmers, factory and construction workers, homemakers and carpenters are masters of an event so grueling that 27-year-old member Ronda Wilson, a receptionist, likens it to the agony of giving birth to her son—only more painful. "Labor ends when the baby's born," she says. "Tug-of-war goes on all season." (11/26/90, p. 130)

The transcendent rejuvenation of sport is a benefit due every person who plays and works hard. Meg Lukens, writing about one-legged Olympic gold medalist skier Diana Golden, pinpoints this redefinition: "And the U.S. Olympic Committee stunned the international sports community when it bypassed all of 1988's two legged competitors and named Golden Female Skier of the Year. Not Disabled Skier. No Asterisk. Just Skier of the Year" (12/31/90, p. 11).

Equal effort deserves equal reward, *SI* suggests. This point is reinforced in a story chronicling the basketball playoff quest of a small Indiana high school in the last year of the state's no division state championship tournament. Following the school's loss in the regional final, one of the team members said he couldn't imagine a playoff system where equality is measured by the number of students enrolled in the school. " 'Do you think class basketball could match the atmosphere here tonight?' " he asked. " 'I guarantee you, when I look back at it, I'll rather have gone out right here, this way. This is what it's all about. And they're killing it' " (3/17/97, p. 33).

The value of social equality is reflected in letters to the editor of *SI*, too. Adam, for instance, commends the magazine for its portrayal of Cleveland Cavaliers point guard Terrell Brandon: "Not many players in the NBA can say that after games they go back to their rooms and think about what they can do to make their kids and parents proud of them. Kudos to Brandon for not letting the money and fame go to his head" (3/10/97, p. 5). In Adam's eyes Brandon is apparently more like an ordinary person who wants to do well by his family rather than an elite athlete concerned with only his personal success. On the other hand, athletes who violate this code by attempting to demonstrate their superior merit are chastised by fans. Fans reacting to the 1997 Super Bowl, for example, were less than pleased with some of the antics of the winning Green Bay Packers. Observes Mike, "You describe the Packers' triumph as a victory over the cocky Patriots, but it was the Packers that I saw duckwalking into the end zone, doing extravagant end zone dances and talking trash" (3/3/97, p. 21).

Finally, to emphasize the notion that the efforts of "regular folks" are as deserving of recognition as are those of the elite, *SI* has recently instituted a short column entitled, "Catching Up With . . . " that chronicles the current efforts of exceptional athletes who have passed their prime. The magazine reflects on the athletic careers of these individuals and salutes their accomplishments outside of sports; the latter, in fact, are frequently described as more noble endeavors. Teenage basketball prodigy Albert King, for instance, "was the focus of a segment on the ABC network evening news" at age 13 "and a retired millionaire at 32. Yet in the fall of 1995, at 35, he was mopping bathrooms, wiping tables and manning the till at a Wendy's in Wayne, Pa." (3/17/97, p. 5). King's story, however, is not a Steinbeckian hard-luck tale. His Wendy's work was simply part of a management training program he was completing before purchasing a franchise in Englewood, N.J. Former national ski champion Jill Kinmont Boothe, who was paralyzed in a skiing accident three days after appearing on *SI*'s January 31, 1955, cover, spent 32 years as a teacher, "the final 21 of which she spent at Bishop Union Elementary School, instructing the handicapped and learning disabled" (2/24/97, p. 5). Then there's Dr. Delano Meriwether, who became one of the world's fastest sprinters at age 27 after seeing U.S. sprinters on television and telling his wife, " 'I could beat those guys' " (3/24/97, p. 4). Meriwether returned to medicine and worked in South Africa for seven years, "ferrying refugees, petitioning aid organizations for supplies, teaching birth control and treating patients. He calls that time 'the most rewarding of my life' " (3/24/97, p. 4).

Whether emphasizing the superhuman abilities of elites, revealing what their lives are like as "real people," or praising the efforts of everyday athletes, *SI* valorizes all individuals who play the games of sport. This move away from spotlighting only the meritorious establishes the promised land of the American Elysian Field as a site of social equality, a place where all individuals who play are worthy of respect. In such a perfect, liminoid community we know that all people—famous or not—can have big butts (see Charles Barkley above), make simple math errors (Roberto De Vicenzo), or wallow in the mud (tug-of-war). What matters most is that we appreciate what these people *do*, whether it be thinking about how to make kids proud of them (Terrell Brandon), helping the underprivileged (Dr. Delano Meriwether), teaching children (Jill Kinmont Boothe), or working in a fast food restaurant (Albert King). Work and play go hand in hand in the American Elysian Field.

Negotiating the Action: Work/Play

Although we frequently view the concepts of work and play as opposites, their relationship is at the least dialectical. As Oriard (1991) notes, "Civilization requires work; culture depends on play as well. In America, the spirit of play has been evoked to defy work but also to revitalize and humanize it" (p. 478). The uncertainty about the *type* of relationship between work and play further complicates the apparent dialectic. " 'Protestant' theories of play tend to make play a *means* to work. Play is a pause that refreshes—for harder work later," notes Novak (1976, p. 219; emphasis in original). But he continues, "The natural activity of human beings *is* play. Play is good in itself. The proper category for play is not moral but natural" (p. 219; emphasis in original). Perhaps the work-play relationship, then, should be conceived as a paradoxical "postmodern both/and" more so than a modernist-tinged dialectic through which we arrive at tentative, changing resolutions over time. As Huizinga (1938/1970) points out, "The contrast between play and seriousness is always fluid. The inferiority of play is continually being offset by the corresponding superiority of its seriousness. Play turns to seriousness and seriousness to play" (p. 27).

This both/and interrelationship is reflected in *SI*'s depiction of sports as activities that are designed to fulfill the ideal of leisure and that require hard work to enjoy and/or master. The traditional purposes of recreating in the Elysian Fields and working in America converge into a paradoxical sport ethic in contemporary America: athletes must work at playing while remembering that playing is more than work. Recognizing that sport has become more than a game, *SI* also shows us that sport *is still a game* and that there are dangers in too much emphasis on sport. In so doing *SI* offers a lesson that transcends sport by advocating a harmonious melding of work and play. Of course, perfectly merging work and play is impossible, leading fans to engage in the rituals of work/play again and again. "Rotten with perfection," we continue to seek the ideal melding of our activities so that they might match the perfect place of the promised land.

In so doing fans of *SI* equip themselves with the rhetorical tools to cope with an emerging postindustrial society, while hoping for the rejuvenation of the work experience in that society. To cope and hope we rely on purposeful play. Initially, ritualistically reading *SI* is a form of play. The *SI* fans with whom I visited followed their own rituals; some routinely begin with the "Scorecard" section near the front of the magazine, some look to the "Point After" column at the end, and some first seek articles on their favorite sports in season. Fan Joshua told me via e-mail, for example, that "often the Scorecard and Letters are among the first [I read] before any actual articles, just to get a vague idea of what's going on. I find the profiles the most interesting, then the articles on the events." But such ritualistic play is also purposeful. By reading about the need to *work at playing, SI* fans can associate the work experience with joy and fun, enabling them to cope with the conditions of the habitus. As Fox's (1994) quote in chapter one reminds us: "The desacralization of work lies at the heart of our alienation" (p. 12). By reading about the need to remember that *play is more than work, SI* fans can envision a site of leisure that transcends the workplace, a place where, as also pointed out in chapter one, we're spending more and more time, reducing the time available for playing away from work. Not only does *SI* address this double bind of playing less at work and having less time to play away from work, it uses the comic frame to notify us of the mistakes others make when they don't work hard enough at playing and/or treat play as the equivalent of work. In so doing *SI* helps us cope.

Working at Playing

Emphasizing the connectedness of all elements of the field, *SI* points out how players of different athletic talents share a determination to work hard while playing. For example, professional bowler (hardly an image that comes to mind when one thinks of a professional *athlete*) Dave Ferraro engages in an exercise routine to make himself a better player: "When he's on the road, he jumps rope 3,500 times in 25 minutes every day. At home, he works out on a Lifecycle and a StairMaster" (5/7/90, p. 64). Meanwhile, professional basketball player Kendall Gill improved his game when "he played basketball in the park with friends for the first time in years. He watched videotapes of his college games, spent three days working on his release . . . and suited up in a summer league with several NBA players" (3/3/97, p. B6). The result: his best season in years. Working at play is more than physical effort; the merger also requires mental effort. Mike Richter, a goalie for the New York Rangers hockey team, realizes, "You're really playing against yourself. You have to learn what you can control and what you can't, and not let what you can't control affect your confidence" (12/3/90, p. 56). As a result players learn to appreciate the interaction between the physical and the mental. Runner Merrill Noden concludes his account of the Fifth Avenue race with a realization: "I limped home that chilly afternoon with a fresh sense of how hard it is to do something so simple so well" (11/27/89, p. 8). Doing something well, *SI* suggests, requires hard work. As a former national coach explains the success of the tennis-playing Maleeva sisters in *SI:* They are " 'just very determined, very consistent and [they] work very, very hard' " (12/3/90, p. 80).

SI's pages are filled with stories of individuals who merge work and play on the job. Baseball player Carlton Fisk can continue to play a young man's position, catcher, at age 42 because he works. The story points out, "Three or four nights a week during the season, even after catching a game, Fisk will go into the clubhouse weight room to pump iron, often until 1 or 2 a.m." (2/26/90, p. 64). This devotion to working at one's game is admired by a fan named Al, who writes in a letter to the editor, "For 20 years Fisk has demonstrated an unrivaled work ethic and zest for baseball" (3/26/90, p. 4). Yet other fans develop different interpretations of this paradoxical pair of values, reflecting their different ontological centering processes—as well as the difficulty of perfectly blending work and play. Explains fan Robert, "There's no question that Fisk is an extraordinary player, but there's also no question that the fact that he's still playing at the age of 42 is attributable more to his $1.75 million salary than to any 'hard-edged New England work ethic' " (3/26/90, p. 4). Al suggests Fisk works hard in an isolated weight room because he loves the game, and Robert implies the intervening variable of money prompts Fisk to continue his quest to be an elite ballplayer. Both fans seem to subscribe to the tenets of the American Elysian Field, yet each interprets the actions of an athlete differently, and each points to the impossibility of perfecting—from all points of view—a harmonious blending of work and play.

Still, *SI* often uses the comic frame to point to seemingly clear instances of individuals and/or teams who do not work hard at playing, encouraging its fans to learn from these mistakes. For instance, the traditionally powerful Boston Celtics basketball team found itself with the worst record in the league in 1996–97 and faced questions of whether it intentionally relaxed on the job in order to have a better chance for the first choice in the draft. "The Celtics' performance in close games has encouraged whispers that Boston has been tanking. Some skeptics point to strange combinations on the floor at crucial moments and puzzling distribution of playing time" (3/17/97, p. 75). Thus even if we cannot attain a perfect merger of work and play, we certainly cannot give up; we must ritualistically repeat our efforts. In so doing we increase our opportunities to engage in play that is more than work.

Playing Is More Than Working

Since sports are games, they occur in a symbolic site that transcends the habitus, a place where different rules apply and where individuals may engage in flow experiences that blot out their material surroundings. As a result *SI* and its fans seem to expect that even professional athletes, who play sports as their work, should remember that they are engaged in an activity that is more than work. For example, a professional baseball player in a senior league, Bill Madlock, knows that he's getting paid for his work, but he's also aware that he's engaged in a form of play that transcends the habitus: "I came down here for therapy, to relax. I was going to have a nervous breakdown swimming with the sharks. The real world—now that's hardball. . . . I just want to have fun. Excuse me while I go do my sprint. That's singular" (11/20/89, p. 32). Football lineman Burt Grossman constantly jabbers while playing a violent game full of the grunts and groans of work. Writes *SI*'s Bruce Newman, "Grossman clearly enjoys being an original, pro football's rebel yell, bodaciously going on and on where no man has gone on and on before. 'All he does all game long is think of what he's going to say after it's over,' says linebacker Gary Plummer" (10/15/90, p. 86).

Fan reactions to the Grossman story illustrate a conundrum introduced in the *Dilbert* chapter: despite our reliance on modernist, denotative definitions of words, we interpret those words through their unstable connotations. In *Dilbert*, for example, the definition of power was used by some characters—as it was in Conquergood's Big Red—to violate principles of social equality. That is, the freedom to redefine can be used to place one's self *above* others. In Grossman's case fan Sean finds the player's—and *SI*'s—definition of "play" perplexing: "Skipping school, taking steroids, shooting people with BB guns and berating opposing players is made to seem quite all right. Both SI and [writer Bruce] Newman should be ashamed for glorifying such a jerk" (11/5/90, p. 6). Sean's ontological centering leads him to define Grossman's actions as antisocial rather than merely playful. As a fan he appears to share in the work/play element of the field defined in *SI*, but his interpretation of the action in that field differs from that of the writer because they are grasping different rhetorical fragments in making sense of the football player's work/play.

As Sean's letter suggests, individuals who do not see play as purposeful, something above the realm of work, suffer. *SI* relies on the comic frame to point to the mistakes of individuals who defined play as hedonist more than spiritual. Former baseball star Steve Garvey, for example, tarnished his character by defining play as indulging the self, going from "a role model's role model" to a person "who had affairs with three women at once, impregnated two and married a fourth." He was unwanted by his children and wanted by his creditors (11/27/89, p. 94). Similarly, fan David chastises young professional basketball player Stephon Marbury for not working to pay for his earlier off-the-court playing: "I was disappointed to learn that Stephon Marbury is being pursued by the mother of his 22-month-old daughter for child support. It's too bad that Marbury the unselfish basketball player can't be more generous with his nearly $2 million salary" (2/24/97, p. 8).

Conversely, when play becomes too much like work, the spirit is removed from the games. For instance, *SI* reports on hockey enforcers, men who once played the game "because they liked playing hockey," who now see their job as work without the joy they experienced as youngsters. They are playing a game, but they have a particular job to complete within the context of that game: to deliver violence. Says "enforcer" Kelly Chase: "It's like when you've had somebody in school organize a fight for you. You know that at 3:30 you've got to go out and have that fight. That's how I feel every game and probably how I've felt since junior hockey. Eventually, that's what chases a lot of guys away from the game" (3/24/97, p. 69). Potential tennis star Mary Pierce has also been driven from "the game," although she continues to participate in the sport. In 1990 Pierce was described as a teenager driven too hard by her father—and not achieving her potential as a result of too much work and not enough play. *SI* quotes part of one session of fatherly advice offered by Mr. Pierce: "'You ain't never gonna be —— if you play like that. You don't have a brain in your head, man, after playing like that. . . . I never saw anybody play so stupid in my life'" (5/7/90, p. 53). Fortunately, Pierce's father is no longer involved in her career.

The comments of Pierce's father reaffirm the importance of enjoying sport in isolation; his intrusion impaired her ability to work and play simultaneously. Notes fan Rick, "She has had to give up her *entire* childhood to come through for her father. What kind of father would deny not only his daughter but also his wife and son the opportunity for a real life?" (6/18/90, p. 6; emphasis in original). For

Mary Pierce tennis becomes an occupation, nothing more. Moreover, her father's apparent insistence that she become an elite limits both her ability to succeed and her capacity to enjoy participating. In meritocratic terms she is positioned as someone who must fulfill her extraordinary potential or be labeled a failure; the fact that extraordinary *effort* is insufficient removes the joy of playing the game.

In many respects, then, the merger of work and play is possible only if the activity occurs in isolated territory and among individuals who privilege effort rather than results. Individuals must exhibit strong character and appreciate and make appropriate use of the opportunities sport provides. To do otherwise threatens one's sense of home, potential for meritocratic advancement, and place in a community of like-minded others. As fan David points out, "Pierce has denied his family a stable home, jeopardized his children's education and alienated many in the tennis community" (6/18/90, p. 6). Pierce's story also illustrates not only how the desire to merge work and play in perfect harmony produces ritual repetition in order to "get it right" but how such rituals provide both coping and hoping mechanisms in an increasingly postindustrial habitus. To cope with the submersion of joy in the work experience (see chapter one), we need to remember to play while working. To hope for an alternative we need to heed the lessons of *SI*'s comic frame and learn from the mistakes of those who worked without playing and/or did not treat playing as purposeful.

Harmonious Opposition

Engaging in this ritual struggle with work and play not only provides *SI* fans with a means of coping with the increasingly postindustrial habitus, it also offers a means of hoping for an alternative. Such hope comes in two forms. First, ritualistically reading *SI* helps fans situate themselves in a community of others who also bemoan technological and commercial intrusions, who appreciate efforts of all kinds, and who understand the paradoxical merger of work and play. This community promotes a harmonious convergence of fans who might be positioned in disparate locations in the habitus but who share residence in the symbolic community of the American Elysian Field. Four fans of *SI* illustrate how this process works as they share their reactions to an article naming former professional football quarterback Joe Montana, "Sportsman of the Year." In letters to the editor males aged 36, 15, and 62 as well as a female of unknown age all find themselves in a similar place, one that is clearly different from their present, material location:

Montana and Montville have successfully permitted this 36-year-old to re-member what it was like to be a kid. (Philip C. Doyle)

I am 15 years old and would love to take over Montana's position one day. (Jarrod Klunk)

I know, because even though I am 62, I still dream of taking the snap from center, running to my right and then throwing the winning touchdown pass to Jerry Rice in the last minute of the game. (George Tansill)

[Montana] stands for more than a "boyhood dream" and unbelievable statis-tics. He represents qualities that are admired by more than just half the popu-lation: poise, dedication, toughness, humility, and many more. Montana is a great guy, which is why his fans include women and men, girls and boys. (Erica Goldman) (1/28/91, p. 4)

These fans share not only the experience of playing in the Ameri-can Elysian Field but in the understanding of what is to be valorized in the field. Each has a different "home" in the habitus, yet all con-verge in the field of play as each imagines what Montana represents from his/her point of view—just as fans Al and Robert shared an in-terpretation of the field but differed in their interpretations of base-ball catcher Carlton Fisk's actions within the field.

Because purposeful play creates an alternative community with a set of rules that may not "make sense" by the naturalized, common-sensical standards of the habitus, *SI* fans position themselves in a place from which they can critique the mystery of the hierarchy in the habitus. As Burke (1966) points out, a social hierarchy is both clouded in mystery (how do people get to the top?) and produces so-cial guilt (not everyone is at the top; therefore we have failed). *SI*'s image of a perfect place, then, can be conceived as a reaction to the mystery and guilt lurking in an impending postindustrial society. As chapter one illustrates, the "rules" for success in U.S. culture are unclear, apparently cloaked in secrecy, in a postindustrial order. Em-ployers, *Dilbert* emphasizes, make irrational decisions within a mod-ernist framework, and employees struggle to determine what course of action they should follow to succeed. Furthermore, the statistical evidence pointing to a declining standard of living adds the spectre of social guilt to the new, mysterious American dream/nightmare. By activating images of Western and American traditions in its con-struction of the perfect place, *SI* pulls through strands of cultural memories to build a foundation from which to react to the mys-tery and guilt of a postindustrial hierarchy. Such a promised land is a haven for us in a postindustrial age in which increasingly efficient and *mysterious* machines (they have few movable parts compared to their industrial counterparts) encourage us both to make the future happen more quickly and to discard allegedly useless information/files when our memory nears the full mark (performance artist Laurie Anderson used a haunting, disembodied voice to make this point in a 1995 concert I attended: "Memory full, please save"). And Middleton and Edwards's (1990) observation, quoted in chapter three, bears repeating here: "Collective remembering is essential to the identity and integrity of a community" (p. 10).

There can be little doubt that we live in a culture in which the characteristics of a mysterious machine are valued, especially now that our primary machine—the computer—has become central to almost all that we do. Daniel Bell (1979) claims that we live in a "techno-economic order" that emphasizes rationality, order, interconnectedness, and efficiency, and Mills (1982) notes that "in the past few decades, machinistic metaphorical vision has received great impetus from the rapid evolution of the computer and of other automated systems" (p. 247). One of the results of living in this mysterious machine is that we aren't sure how we're supposed to make the machine run. On the one hand, we see ourselves as the replaceable parts of the industrial age—the largest private U.S. employer is a provider of temporary employees (Castro, 1993)—subject to being discarded in the same way that Dilbert's boss tossed temps in the dumpster after he had used them. On the other hand, we can't see the parts move, so the logical seems illogical (as *Dilbert* illustrates) and we're left with little to rely on other than beliefs in a mysterious order (as *The X-Files* exemplifies).

SI, however, provides a place from which to resist the postindustrial machine, a place whose power is amplified by the fact that we read it and potentially see ourselves in it; the mystery can be removed in this alternative promised land. First, the field reconnects us with nature, a connection severed by living within the machine. As cities and suburbs (in particular) have grown, we have lost touch with nature, the imagined site of the sacred garden. Since World War II, Hiss (1990) notes, "almost everyone in the Western world has for the first time moved indoors—away from bright sunshine, sealed off from mountains, forests, and streams" (p. 10). In place of these natural areas we have relied on the technological and the commercial to isolate ourselves. Kaus (1992) notes that individuals rely increasingly on artificial environments for leisure activities that used to occur in the few natural places that exist in metropolitan areas: "They join private health clubs instead of using the public pools, parks, and basketball courts. ('[Public] playgrounds are dirty,' the owner of one such franchise explained to *Time* magazine.)" (p. 56).

SI overcomes these displacing elements by situating the field in an isolated territory where technological and commercial intrusions are bemoaned. Although these interventions occur in the real life of sport, they are shunned in the symbolic field of sport created by *SI*. Individuals reading *SI* can escape to a specific promised land that possesses characteristics in direct opposition to the postindustrial machine that typically envelopes them. Also important is that very recent evidence indicates U.S. residents are making a material move that parallels this symbolic move, a shift that reverses a decades-long pattern of growth in cities and suburbs. According to a Census Bureau report covering March 1995–March 1996, metropolitan areas (cities and suburbs) had more people move out than in, despite a definitional change that included more outlying counties in metropolitan areas (Schmid, 1997). The report also noted a decline in our frequency of using Mayflowers with wheels; 16.3 percent of Americans moved during the year studied, compared to a rate of over 20 percent during each year of the 1980s. Although one year does not a trend make, these data suggest we may be making changes in our habitus that reflect the symbolic visions of *SI* (and no doubt other promised lands). One may not cause the other, but the two may well be related.

Playing in the field also provides a sense of purpose and harmony missing from the mysterious machine. The decline of the Protestant ethic in American culture has substantially reduced the "joy" of work (Bell, 1979), and the replacement of full-time jobs with part-time and/or temporary jobs has added an element of fear to working (Castro, 1993). The result is a "sense of *disorientation* and dismay" in American culture (Bell, 1979, p. 55; emphasis added). The purposeful merger of work and play in the fields offers *SI* fans an opportunity to *reorient* themselves in an ideal, symbolic place where work can be spiritually fulfilling and communally connecting, characteristics not typically found in postindustrial jobs (see chapter one). The ambiguous nature of the merger of work and play allows fans with different experiences to converge toward an ideal, even if they disagree about enacting the ideal. A fan who has had little experience with playing while working, for instance, may view a football player's touchdown dance as a long-awaited opportunity for celebration; another fan—one who has had more experience with playing while working—may see the dance as "hot-dogging" or "showboating." Both fans, however, could find themselves neighbors in the same symbolic community, just as *SI* letter writers Al and Robert disagreed about Carlton Fisk's merging of work and play yet implicitly agreed that such a merger was desirable.

Accordingly, the somewhat nebulous boundaries of *SI*'s field allow us to interpret the stories individually; we can escape to our own "special" places yet feel an identification with others. The postindustrial machine, however, prevents such flexibility. Offers Boorstin (1978): "In this Republic of Technology [the United States] the experience of the present actually uproots us and separates us from our own special time and place. For technology aims to insulate and immunize us against the peculiar chances, perils, and opportunities of our natural climate, our raw landscape" (p. 11). Overall, then, *SI*'s American Elysian Field shrine transcends the grasp of the postindustrial machine found in the contemporary American habitus. The field shelters us from the intrusions of the machine-like world and provides a haven where others are respected and appreciated for their efforts. We are still productive—as we must be in the material world—but we enjoy our productivity and resist the routine; we work hard at playing and remember that play is more than work. To be sure, reading *SI* does not allow us to escape physically from the habitus that generates the postindustrial machine, but the very act of reading is a symbolic pilgrimage and thus an empowering move that allows us to rehumanize ourselves in a symbolic setting. That setting can in turn seem more real by virtue of the pictures that correspond to the written text. We can then symbolically escape from and resist both the material conditions of the culture and their manifestation in the image of the mysterious machine.

A Promised Land Not Shared by All

Yet as Burke (1969b) reminds us, any affiliation we generate through symbols produces another division. This paradox explains how we are "rotten with perfection," for perfection through identifications and convergences is simply impossible. As we create one "perfect" place through our symbols, other "imperfect" places are simultaneously created. The place is perfect only for those who are there and, even then, only for a limited time; others are excluded and the culture changes, both of which necessitate the symbolic creation of more perfect places. As Turner (1974) explains, "Communitas . . . is necessarily a transient condition" (p. 274). In other words, our epistemological mobility not only exposes us to additional perfect and imperfect places, it also loses much of its power (though not its allure) as we return home. Both developments ensure that our pilgrimages to promised lands are ongoing and continuous.

In *SI*, for example, the American Elysian Field is shaken from its isolation every February with the annual publication of the magazine's swimsuit issue, a ploy designed to pump up circulation during the winter doldrums. As Daddario (1992) points out, the issue usually doubles *SI*'s weekly circulation. In addition, the magazine is featured in supermarket checkout stands and has been the subject of numerous television specials. Quite clearly this issue is just the sort of commercial intrusion *SI* bemoans—despite its attempt to position the swimsuit models in isolated locales. In fact, Davis (1997) argues that those locales are more problematic than perfect in that they symbolically reproduce images of great white saviors domesticating exotic peoples and lands through colonization, especially in light of the fact that the photographic images of these locales "do 'capture' what are regarded as 'exotic' features of the lands and societies [*SI*] visit[s]" (p. 113). This capturing and gazing is not altogether different from the work performed by Dilbert's boss and the panopticon's inspector. The former confines with cubicles, and the latter constrains with cells, but both watch in order to control. Similarly, the typical male fan of *SI*, Davis explains, "believes that people from (post)colonialized lands are inferior because they are culturally and sexually exotic, uncivilized, and feminized people of color who have a natural inclination for serving other people. Contrarily, the hegemonic masculine subject regards himself as culturally, racially, and sexually superior, and deserving of a superior economic position" (p. 116). *SI*'s penchant for featuring the isolated, unusual locale—not only in its swimsuit issues, but throughout its yearly run—is thus also reminiscent of a colonial brand of thinking that proposes Western ways of acting are perfect, at least compared to those in "underdeveloped" (less-than-perfect) nations. Social *in*equality is the hallmark of the colonizer's thinking. The uncivilized must be controlled in order to make social progress, just as the cubicle workers and panopticon prisoners are confined for the supposed social good (an efficient economy and a safe society, respectively).

Even attempts to achieve a perfect negotiation of work and play in the swimsuit issue are fanciful. Although the television specials, as well as an occasional note from the editor in the magazine, attempt to cast the making of the issue as the consummate example of merged work and play, the attire (or lack thereof) and poses of the swimsuit models certainly suggest only a playful atmosphere, from a heterosexual male point of view. Readers Kimberly, Tamara, and Suzanne pointedly reinforce the imperfection of this issue in their respective questions about the "work clothes" of the swimsuit models:

Why bother including the prices and where to buy the suits if you can't even tell what they look like?

Why do you find it necessary to change your focus and get into the pornography business once a year?

How can you have a swimsuit issue when the models have lost half their suits? (3/24/97, p. 13)

As these readers point out, the swimsuit issue depicts women as literal "boy toys" with whom the imagining heterosexual male fan can play, despite the work of women to be taken seriously.

SI's annual positioning of women as sexual objects actually occurs throughout the year, claims Daddario (1992). Her analysis of the photographs found in one year's worth of magazines discovered that *SI* tends to feature attractive athletes in its photos. *SI*, Daddario argues, "encourages readers to infer an association between the swimsuit model and the female athlete. This association serves to sexualize the athlete and diminish her achievements" (p. 60). For example, in 1997—eight years after Daddario's study—the swimsuit issue displayed women's beach volleyball players and tennis star Steffi Graf in separate swimsuit spreads. The association between female athletes and swimsuit models produces a perfection that is rotten. Writes Daddario, "*SI*'s emphasis on attractive photographic subjects suggests a relationship between physical beauty and athleticism, an ideal which not only is ambiguous but impossible to attain" (p. 62).

Moreover, in emphasizing the role of the body in its depiction of females, *SI* contributes to the traditional assignation of the mind as the province of the male and the body as the realm of the female. "If the mind and rationality are held as 'above' the body, it becomes relatively easy to see the body as a resource for the use of the mind," writes Rothman (1989, p. 61), thus perpetuating inequalities between men (users of the mind, who are rational) and women (users of the body, who are irrational) throughout our culture, not just in sports. Such binary thinking further encourages the use of controlling gazes; the irrational must be harnessed before they get "out of control" with their bodies.

So despite *SI*'s attempts to construct a romantic, spiritual place of perfection that offers modernist transcendence and stability over time, the paradoxes of postmodernism loom. The parade of affiliations and divisions generated by our use of symbols ensures an ever-changing, not universally shared, conception of the promised land. While we continue to strive for perfection, we are reminded of its unattainability. How we see a place is not how others necessarily see a place (if they even see the same place). *SI* fan Julie, for instance, disagrees with the three readers cited above, as well as Daddario, despite suggesting they all share a feminist standpoint: "Cheers to Steffi Graf for appearing in the swimsuit issue. I consider myself a feminist, but I think the whining about the objectification of women has gone too far. There is nothing sinister about human sexuality. It should be celebrated" (3/24/97, p. 13).

Conclusion

Julie's comments above emphasize once more how our different ontological centering processes result in our retrieving of different rhetorical fragments from our personal orbits. At the same time, we must also acknowledge that a shared sense of communitas promotes the exchange of different opinions; knowing that we share understandings of the sacred place encourages relatively free-flowing discussions of the interpretations of actions within the promised land that encompasses the sacred place. As Turner (1974) reminds us, communitas "liberates [pilgrims] from conformity to general norms" (p. 274), meaning that the questioning of another pilgrim's faith may not be necessarily seen as face-threatening as long as the respect for others generated by communitas is enacted—much like Scully and Mulder can simultaneously question and respect each other's beliefs.

SI's fans can engage in such respectful disagreement because their letters seem to indicate a shared knowledge of what constitutes the perfect place of sport/life. Positioned in the American Elysian Field, they have transcended the material conditions of postindustrialism's menacing machines that sever spirit and play from work. From their new perspective they reinvigorate their spirits through play and the apparent attainment of perfection. Returning home from this journey thus allows *SI* fans such as myself to negotiate more adroitly the complex intersection of Western ideals, American realities, and postindustrial constraints. These idealized places are also imbued with a sense of the sacred, for they remind us that the perfect intersection of order and ideals is unattainable. In trying to reach perfection we are reminded of our weaknesses and frailties, as well as our strengths and abilities; the latter combination allows us to glimpse perfection, to envision its possibility, but the former ensures our continued inability to enact perfect possibilities. This lifelong quest to make our world perfect is an extended, generalized, series of symbolic pilgrimages in which the ultimate destination cannot be reached in this lifetime.

Notes

A version of this chapter, to which Christina L. Reynolds substantially contributed as coauthor, was published as "Lost and Found in America: The Function of Place Metaphor in *Sports Illustrated*," *The Southern Communication Journal* 59 (1993): 1–14. The Southern States Communication Association has granted permission to use this article as the basis for this chapter. Dr. Reynolds's contributions to the present version are found in some of the writing in the illustration section of the chapter and, of course, in the discussions that led to the creation of the chapter in article form.

1. The place and its elements described in this essay emanate from an initial, exhaustive two-year textual analysis of every issue of *Sports Illustrated*. The place emerges in each individual issue of the magazine. In the interest of brevity, though, 13 diverse issues from the period of August 1989 through January 1991 were selected. Attempts were made to include regular as well as special issues (e.g., college basketball preview) and issues that covered major as well as unique sporting events. In updating this chapter I examined several issues published in February and March of 1997; the song remains the same.

2. Trujillo and Ekdom (1985) also use a values-in-conflict approach in their analysis of the sportswriting surrounding the 1984 Chicago Cubs. Although a similar approach is used here—I even identify a similar work-play pair—the focus of the chapter and its conclusions differ substantially from the analysis found in the Cubs article.

3. This citation indicates that the quotation can be found in the August 14, 1989, issue of *Sports Illustrated* on page 82. This format will be used throughout the chapter.

4. Fan comments in this chapter are culled from letters to the editor published in the magazine. Some of the letters respond to particular stories I have referenced; others speak to different stories but illustrate the themes highlighted in the textual analysis. The names of the letter writers I use are the names attached to the published letters. A focus group interview was conducted, but mechanical problems prevented its transcription. Thus only one reference is made to fans with whom I personally visited, an e-mail response from a fan named Joshua, who asked that I use his real name.

7

Integrating Self and Community as a Means of Finding Homes

The Shift from Consumerism to Altruistic Producerism in *Field of Dreams*

People will come, Ray. They'll come to Iowa for reasons they can't even fathom. They'll turn up your driveway not knowing for sure why they're doing it. They'll arrive at your door, as innocent as children, longing for the past. . . . Oh, people will come, Ray. People will most definitely come.
—Terence Mann
Field of Dreams

And come they have; in an eerie instance of life imitating art, approximately 350,000 people have visited the original Field of Dreams site since the release of the 1989 movie (Lansing, 1997). Located on a patch of land shared by farmers Al Ameskamp and Don Lansing outside of Dyersville, Iowa (population 3,703), the field has drawn fans from around the world (Worthington, 1990). Ameskamp and Lansing didn't ask for the visitors and don't promote the field as a tourist attraction in national publications. Both, in fact, were puzzled by the initial interest in the field. " 'I sure never thought it would come to this' " Lansing told *People* magazine (Donovan & Nelson, 1989, p. 121). Ameskamp replanted his section of the field with corn, only to replant it with grass after receiving a bushelful of requests from visitors to the field (Worthington, 1990). Apparently, "The power of the images created on the screen has motivated moviegoers to make a journey that the film's creators could not possibly have imagined" (Sanders, 1989, p. 14).

I was initially drawn to the field in 1990, returning to my home in Eau Claire, Wisconsin, after a visit to see friends in Nebraska.

Three of my former students told me of the field's existence in the fall of 1989, so the following summer I decided to take the longer, scenic route home in order to swing by the field. After stopping at a gas station to ask for directions, I was directed to the Chamber of Commerce to pick up a map. What I discovered surprised me. After traveling about three miles north of town, making a few turns, and looking for the landmarks on the map, I first saw the light poles surrounding the field, then the unmistakable farmhouse of the cinematic Kinsella family. As I pulled into the driveway, I discovered I was not alone. Approximately 50 people were milling about the boundaries of the field, peeking into the mysterious cornfield, and/or playing ball on the field itself. I took a quick tour of the place, stood in line with children half my size to take my turn at bat (a clean single!), and played a few positions in the infield in a game that "resembles no game you've ever seen. No strikes, no balls, no outs. Hit the ball and run. Hit the ball and don't run. Swing till you drop. No one seems to care" (Modoono, 1990, p. C1). Men, women, boys, and girls all play by these "rules." As field visitor Garett remarks, "Nobody has to give any direction. Nobody has to say go play this position, or you can pitch or I want to take my turn now" (quoted in Crescenti, 1994). Some of the players enjoy their ability to live by an alternative set of rules so much that they don't want to stop playing. Three twentysomething men spent nearly four hours playing when I revisited the field for three days in 1992.

The lack of rules extends beyond the friendly confines of the field. Fans visiting the site make their own parking spots, create their own "tours" of the site, and spend as much time as they want doing whatever they want, whether it be playing ball, visiting the cornfield, or sitting in the bleachers enjoying the activity. There are no turnstiles to shuffle through, no uniformly attired guides reciting the history of the field, and no "please do not touch" displays from which children must be restrained (other than the Lansing home itself). Observes a field visitor named Terry, "The thing that struck me the most was, do you mean that we can actually walk up there, drive up there, step on this field and there are no restrictive barriers" (quoted in Crescenti, 1994). The only nods to commercialism at the site itself are two souvenir shacks operated by the friends and family of the field's owners.

When I returned to the field in 1992 to play, conduct interviews, and observe the action over an extended period of time, roughly 50–100 people would be exploring the field at any one time during the hazy summer afternoons.[1] Mosher (1991) reports that 257 people from 37 states and 3 nations other than the U.S. signed the register at the field during a four-hour period on the day he visited the field.

Clearly the symbolic place represented by the cinematic field has inspired many individuals to commence a pilgrimage to the literal field in the hope of experiencing some of its shrine-like magic in person. As Edith Turner (1987) points out in regard to tourists, "Like pilgrims, they switch worlds, and they may even experience transcendence in the situation of liminality, in the special state of being freed from social structure" (p. 328). Perhaps that's why "people definitely came" to visit the field by the tens of thousands.

The film, nominated for an Academy Award for Best Picture, features the Kinsella family—Ray, Annie, and their daughter Karin— and their Iowa farm. Hearing a mysterious voice in the cornfield one day, Ray decides to build a baseball field in part of his field. The field is soon inhabited by the legendary ballplayer Shoeless Joe Jackson and some of his teammates from the 1919 Chicago White Sox, nicknamed the Black Sox for conspiring with gamblers to lose the World Series. The loss of income from the plowed-under corn causes Annie's brother Mark to encourage the Kinsellas to sell the farm before the time to foreclose arrives. Meanwhile, the voice directs Ray to meetings with reclusive writer Terence Mann in Boston and, through a bit of mysterious time travel, a doctor and former baseball player named Archibald Graham (who appears as both an old man shortly before his death and as the young ballplayer he was in the 1920s). When all of these characters converge at the field, their individual dreams come true.

The popularity of *Field of Dreams*, I argue in this chapter, is due not only to its intriguing story and happy ending but also to its depiction of the field as a particular kind of place. The cinematic field, now operating as a "real" field, functions in a manner similar to the field discussed in the previous chapter; it is an isolated place, open to all who want to play, as long as they balance work and play. As Ardolino (1990) notes, "Ray Kinsella's creation of the mystical ballfield wipes all memories of a sinful past and replaces them with an Elysian manifestation of baseball, America as pastoral paradise" (p. 45). Yet the Field of Dreams contains a stronger spiritual element than does *Sports Illustrated*'s American Elysian Field. The film's field allows the dead to return, the old to be young, and the confused to be directed by a disembodied voice. All of the major characters, troubled by some event in their past, use the field to atone for their actions and to find a heaven of sorts on earth. From this transcendent shrine they gain perspective on the events, people, and places that surround their lives, and this perspective leads to the establishment of a sense of symbolic home, a personal promised land.

The film's story breaks "the rules" about living and dying, just as the site of the film allows visitors to break "the rules" associated with tourist attractions. Both sets of breaks offer fans an opportunity to imagine alternatives to the habitus, to envision promised lands where what the habitus defines as "common sense" is not common or entirely sensical. The fields offer *hope*. In particular, *Field of Dreams* offers a promised land where altruistic production reenergizes the spirits of individuals tired of functioning within a paradigm of postindustrial consumption. The fields—real and reel—are strongly infused with the romantic spiritual elements of community; their ability to encourage individuals to play with rhetorical fragments scattered throughout time and space is reminiscent of postmodernism; and their suggestion that we each have a "home" reflects the centering processes of the modernist self. By engaging all three schools of thought, the fields make available the possibilities of different but shared "homes" from which the characters and fans attempt to make sense of the de-centering they have undergone in a postmodern culture. In this respect the fields also offer an invitation to rhetorical therapy, an opportunity to *cope*. As Payne (1989) argues in his book, *Coping With Failure: The Therapeutic Uses of Rhetoric*, rhetoric can heal schisms between the self and society, the past and the future, and the spiritual and the material. As the following pages demonstrate, the fields allow visitors and viewers to engage in just such a form of symbolic therapy.

This process is illustrated through (1) a brief examination of the tension between consumerism and altruistic producerism; (2) an analysis of how the fields integrate romanticism, postmodernism, and modernism within a symbolic pilgrimage; (3) an exploration of how self and community are synthesized at the fields; and (4) a discussion of the implications of "home." In exploring these issues I rely on my interpretations of the film, my experiences at the field in Dyersville, over 100 interviews I conducted in which fans to the field discussed their reasons for making the trip to Iowa, and the comments of fans garnered from a documentary video called *Dreamfield* (Crescenti, 1994).

Altruistic Producerism and Postindustrial Consumerism

As chapter one explains, the intrusion of "the machine" into the garden at the end of the 19th century spoiled the sense of America as a place of nature and moved the center of social and economic activity to urban areas (Marx, 1964). In addition, the machine's ability to engage in mass production led to a gradual reassessment of the Protestant-inspired belief in deferred gratification. "If everyone deferred gratification," Coontz (1992) asks, "who would buy the new products?" (p. 170). As the dust from the transformation settled, Lears (1983) claims, America had shifted not only from "a production-oriented society . . . [to] a consumption-oriented society" (p. 3)—an argument I developed in chapter one—but to an increasingly secular society as well.

The end of the 19th century, then, featured the emergence of a new economic paradigm, consumption, and a corresponding change in spiritual beliefs. The meshing of these two developments produced feelings of displacement among many individuals living within that culture, as their promised land was transformed, moved, and despiritualized. This cultural transformation reflects in many ways our current cultural transformation. As we move from the industrial to the postindustrial, the intrusion of the machine into the garden has made us (to resuscitate Kenneth Burke's words from the previous chapter) "rotten with perfection"; the promised land of a technological utopia has not been attained, but in continuing to strive for that unattainable land through faster, more efficient machines, we simply perpetuate the sense of disconnection and despiritualization that the machines are supposed to relieve. Moreover, as we continue to place our faith in these machines (while simultaneously wondering why we do so), we decrease our roles as producers and emphasize our identities as consumers. Put simply, production (in the traditional sense) in a postindustrial age is even less necessary than in an industrial age because, as the first chapter points out, services rather than goods become our chief commodities (recall, for instance, chapter one's notation that Wal-Mart has ascended to the world's largest corporate employer, demoting General Motors to number two on the list). As manufacturing jobs decline steadily (Dentzer, 1991), as the service sector of the economy grows to hold just over three-fourths of all jobs (Plunkert, 1990), and as we work more while feeling downwardly mobile (Newman, 1988, 1993; Schor, 1992), the impact is spiritual as well as economic.

Yet as Coontz (1992) points out, we increasingly depend upon what we consume as a source of our identity. What's more, relying on our status as consumers for at least part of our identity ensures that we will never be satisfied with ourselves; we will never be sufficiently "full" or significantly different. For example, comedian George Carlin has a bit in which he notes how we buy a new house when we run out of space to hold all of our "stuff," but we then find the new house feels empty, leading us to buy more "stuff," and so on. Feagler (1997) calls those of us afflicted with the ill Carlin describes "stuffaholics": "The irony of the stuffaholic is that he [sic] thinks the stuff he accumulates is making his life happier, easier and more manageable. In fact, stuff has made our lives grim, chaotic and less manageable. Once you went to work then you came home and that was that. Now you go to work and when you come home, work follows, pursuing you like a little posse of electronic pages and faxes. There's no place like home used to be" (Feagler, 1997, p. A9). Paradoxically, then, our desire to consume merely feeds the sense of displacement that living in a postindustrial culture generates. The more we consume and accumulate, the more we are likely to continue to consume and accumulate. White (1992) elaborates in her analysis of the Home Shopping Club: "Viewer-shoppers are applauded for acting to fulfill their desires through a process of accumulation that will never be complete because there is always another Capodimonte piece, music box, or household gadget to be purchased" (p. 107). We are, it would seem, "perfectly rotten" shoppers.

Field of Dreams encourages an escape from this never-ending quest for perfection through consumption. It does so by suggesting an alternative form of socioeconomic culture, what I call "altruistic production," in which individuals produce through sacrifice that benefits others. Such actions enhance the quality of life in the community in two ways: first, by improving the situations of others and second, by respiritualizing the community through the common bonds sacrifices produce. These actions also rejuvenate the self, giving individuals a sense of purpose and allowing them to see the products of their efforts in the joy others experience. Altruistic production is not so much an alternative economic structure as it is a way of envisioning, and modeling, our actions as socioeconomic selves.

The character of George Bailey in Frank Capra's film *It's a Wonderful Life* is a "wonderful" example of an individual who moves from consumerism to altruistic production without changing his occupation. For those of you who haven't watched Capra's Christmas-season perennial, George is a small town savings-and-loan president who yearns to be an engineer, a producer of great structures. Seemingly stuck in his job—one that encourages customers to borrow money to consume, although he does not make enough money to consume as much as he would like—George sees little purpose in his life. His role as both a facilitator of consumerism and an incomplete consumer gnaws at his spirit until, faced with financial ruin (it's a long story if you haven't seen the film), George reaches the point that I referenced in the introduction: staring off a bridge, contemplating a suicidal jump into the icy rapids below. At that point George is visited by his guardian angel, Clarence, who takes him through an imaginary-yet-real journey in which George gradually transforms his vision of his role to that of an altruistic producer. Clarence helps George see that he *has* produced through his sacrifices; he has produced happier citizens and a better community. Such a realization spiritually reinvigorates George, allowing him to see, as his brother Harry proclaims, that he's "the richest man in town." Meanwhile, in a reciprocal deed of altruistic production, the citizens George has helped return the favor, bailing him out of his financial predicament. George's job never changed; instead, he reenvisioned his work. His focus shifted from defining himself solely as a distinct individual to recognizing himself as a valued member of the community.

The experience of George Bailey, as well as those of the characters in *Field of Dreams*, suggests we can both cope with the debilitating elements of a postindustrial society and hope for an alternative means of envisioning our contemporary culture. George, and the characters in *Field of Dreams*, do not change the economic structure, but through their imaginations they change their habitus. In short, they change the "rules" by redefining what counts in the game of life. Specifically, *Field of Dreams* tells its fans that they can (1) enjoy a romantic, spiritual connection through sacrifice; (2) experience a postmodern journey through rhetorical fragments of time and space; and (3) receive the reward of finding a modernist "home" in which to center the self. As I outline how these three elements emerge from the movie, I also let fans of the film who visit the field explain how they enact the film's principles. Cumulatively, the stories of the fans and the film illustrate how a symbolic pilgrimage may be envisioned *and* enacted by both watching and "living" the film. As the film's characters embark on a mysterious pilgrimage, fans ritualistically recreate the characters' experiences during their own pilgrimages.

Sacrifice, Playing With Time/Space, and Finding Home

From the Puritans' work ethic (Bell, 1979) to the leaving of the garden for more consumptive pleasures (Lears, 1983; Marx, 1964) to the economic radicalism of liberation theology in contemporary Latin America (McGovern, 1989), matters of the spirit and economic conditions have been connected throughout Western history (Weber, 1958). In the United States politicians have employed themes with religious undertones to promote economic changes: Cries of "manifest destiny" encouraged territorial expansion to find new resources and new markets, and in 1992 presidential candidate Bill Clinton packaged his socioeconomic proposals under the rubric of a "new covenant." The overt religious themes in *Field of Dreams* suggest that the film may also facilitate such connections: the disembodied voice promising that "If you build it *he* will come" then also urging Ray to "Ease *his* pain";[2] Ray as Noah, building his ark/field (Sanders,

1989); the field as a heaven for dead baseball players ("Is this heaven? No, it's Iowa."); and the pilgrimage of vehicles and people to the field in the film's final scene—both in "real" and "reel" life—in which the field serves as a sort of mecca. No wonder fan Tim signs in an electronic guest book, "Every time I watch 'Field of Dreams' it's like a religious experience" (quoted in Left, 1997).

In particular, *Field of Dreams* tells fans that, first, following the Protestant ethic of self-sacrifice connects one to the spiritual voice. Second, the renewed spirituality fostered by self-sacrifice allows transcendence of profane time and space. Third, the perspective gained from transcending time and space allows individuals to find their apparently predestined home on earth. Individuals who complete this pilgrimage to the promised land of the field find a sense of place, harmony with others, a feeling of higher purpose, and economic security. They feel individually centered and communally connected as altruistic producers.

Sacrifice and Spiritual Connection

Each of the major characters in *Field of Dreams* willingly sacrifices for others and in the process emerges with a renewed romantic belief in the spiritual. When Ray hears a voice tell him, "If you build it, he will come," Ray sacrifices the respect of his neighbors and risks his family's future to build a baseball field in part of his cornfield so that Shoeless Joe Jackson can return to play ball. His act is not for his benefit—it imperils his family's financial situation, in fact—but Ray *believes* he must build the field for some mysterious other, the "he" promised by the disembodied voice. Annie, in supporting Ray's decision, shares in this risk. As a result she too loses the respect of her neighbors. For example, she is taunted by another wife at a PTA meeting, who tells Annie, "At least I'm not married to the biggest horse's ass in three counties." Annie's sense of self is quite clearly threatened by such sentiments, yet she has even less to gain by building the field, for she does not hear the voice. She willingly risks the family's economic foundation and her image in the community to support her husband's quest. The reclusive Terence Mann endangers his safety by accompanying Ray, who Mann suspects is crazy, to a Boston Red Sox baseball game. He risks his life and eventually sacrifices his privacy to assist Ray. And Archie Graham twice gives up an opportunity to play professional baseball, clearly a game he loves, in order to practice medicine. These characters make sacrifices only after they choose to *believe* in the possibility of the spiritual. Initial doubts about the existence of the voice surface in each of the characters, yet each is allowed to see what the voice controls after believing in its possibility. Ray is allowed to see an image of Shoeless Joe after he begins to believe that he is not "hearing voices"; Ray then serves as a prophet, persuading the other characters to believe in him and, by extension, the voice.

Once Ray's testimony convinces a character to believe, and he or she demonstrates belief with self-sacrifice, spiritual rejuvenation occurs. Ray sounds like an awestruck teen when he says to himself, "I'm pitching to Shoeless Joe Jackson," and Annie jumps in the air and slides down a school hallway after a PTA meeting. Terence starts a three-person wave with Ray and Annie as they watch the game on the field, and Archie is batting against a major league pitcher only one day after meeting Ray. Additionally, each of these characters experiences a deferred spiritual gratification after fulfilling the terms of his/her sacrifice. The Kinsellas get to meet Ray's father as he appeared in his prime. Terence Mann is allowed to join the players in the cornfield, which presumably will lead to the resumption of his writing career. Archie Graham is able to practice both of his loves in the same location, playing baseball on the field and saving Karin Kinsella's life after she falls from the bleachers.

The types of sacrifices made and the kinds of gratifications received by the film's characters reflect an altruistic spirit, promoting a sense of social harmony within the field. Their apparently selfless denials of immediate gratification, which run counter to the consumerist ethic, bring joy into their lives and the lives of others. After the Kinsellas sacrifice part of their crop and struggle through the winter, Shoeless Joe Jackson and his "deceased" friends from the Chicago White Sox appear, rehabilitated by time, to play on the field. The Kinsellas enjoy the play (Ray even joins in) brought on by their work and sacrifice. Terence Mann's trip to the baseball game with Ray exposes him to the voice and a vision, rejuvenating his writing and reporting instincts. His writing skills influenced, and presumably will again influence, a generation. Graham's decisions to step off the baseball diamond and into healing put a twinkle in his eye and save lives.

After choosing to believe in the possibility of the spiritual and then engaging in self-sacrifice as proof of a commitment to their belief, the characters are granted access to the visions of the voice and permitted to enter the liminoid space surrounding the field. Once there they gain both spiritual rejuvenation and a chance to commune with others who also believe in the possibilities of the spirit; they leave the profane world of the machine and enter the sacred time and place of the liminoid, experiencing a sense of communitas in the process.

Visitors to the Iowa field must also endure some sort of sacrifice to reach their destination. Granted, travel in contemporary America does not involve tremendous sacrifice, but choosing to visit the field involves "going out of your way" and omitting other more consumer-ist tourist destinations from a vacation itinerary. Finding the Field of Dreams site requires a very conscious effort; fans are not likely to stumble on to it. Dyersville is located on U.S. Route 20, about 25 miles west of Dubuque. The highway is fairly well traveled but mostly by Iowans because cross-country travelers use Interstate 80. Even then, travelers on U.S. 20 drive past Dyersville a few miles to the south rather than through the town. Moreover, the Lansing and Ameskamp farms are located about three miles, and several turns, on the north side of Dyersville. Thus the decision to visit the field re-quires forethought and planning, as well as a stop for directions.

That a visit to the field is an excursion requiring a sacrifice of time and money is reflected in the distance many individuals traverse to reach the field. I visited with people from Brooklyn, Indianapolis, Miami, Spokane, and many points in between during my 1992 visit. In 1990, "on a relatively slow Friday, the field's visitors book was signed by people from California, Michigan, Idaho, Florida, Colorado, Missouri, and Massachusetts" (Modoono, 1990, p. C1), and Worth-ington (1990) reports that "a couple from Rochester, NY, drove all the way out just to be married there" (pp. C12–C13).

Perhaps because of the sacrifice in journeying to such an out-of-the-way sacred site, fans treat the field as something special rather than as an ordinary amusement park–type site where consumption is encouraged through adventurous rides that deliver immediate though short-lived gratification. Dennis, for instance, contrasts the field with America's most famous amusement park: "It's not Disney-land. It's not Disneyland." Barb adds, "You know, you can see Disney-land all you want but this is kind of neat, too." What separates the field from traditional amusement parks is not only its structure but the type of amusement people encounter. As Ken points out, "You go to Las Vegas to gamble. You go to Disneyworld to see the little mouse. You come here and you become young again." A visit to the field is an experience quite clearly distinct from that offered by typi-cal, consumer-oriented tourist sites.

The confluence of film and personal performance alters the type of amusement that fans experience. When I enjoyed the short "Back to the Future" ride at Universal Studios, for example, I found myself feeling *as if* I was flying through Hillsdale of the future. But when I was at the Field of Dreams site, I *was* participating in the activity at the literal field, *and* I could play as long as I wanted without be-ing directed by guides who told me when I could have fun and when I was done.

The ability to interact physically with, or perform at, this symbolic shrine is key. A performance, in dramatic terms, is a production for those who put it on. Similarly, playing ball at the field gives fans a chance to produce, to use their bodies in the process of play. In consumer society, as chapter one points out, our bodies are increasingly divorced from economic transactions as technology mediates those experiences. The field, however, encourages fans to touch, feel, and integrate work and play. As Richard observes, "You know, most times you go in and you just look. If you're looking at a museum, you just see things. You don't get to really touch and feel." Jim, too, appreciates the possibilities involved with performing in the field. He explains: "It's a rush just kind of getting out and hearing the sounds and feeling the baseball and bat. Watching how everyone else is kind of like walking around unlike they would be at an amusement park. Even though clearly sport is an amusement, this seems to have a little bit more significance than a regular amusement park." Tracy's comments reaffirm this notion that the field is something special. She says, "You know how everybody likes to be touristy and stuff like that, but I think everybody has some idea in their minds of something that they're searching for and hoping that they'll find it out here."

The performances, or productions, at the field allow fans a means of tapping into the spirit espoused by the film. I brought both my mind and my body, like the characters of the film, to a place where communitas provides "the immediate realization of release from day-to-day structural necessities and obligatoriness" (Turner, 1974, p. 202). I didn't just imaginatively journey to this promised land; I physically entered its boundaries and was caught up in the flow experience of enjoying the activity at the field. Linda had a similar response: "Oh, this is neat! I'm glad they left it this way. It gives us some experience, you know, from the feel of it. To feel like it is to dream." Mark reaffirms this sentiment as he offers his explanation for the "special feel" of the field: "I expect probably getting the feel and actually being here for the dream [Ray] had. The fact that you can dream and that dreams can come true. You kind of feel that when you're out here a little bit." These individuals find themselves in a postmodern both/and place where their personal lives and cinematic experiences intersect. The symbolic place of the field somehow transcends its physical dimensions, leaving fans with an "unreal" perspective also experienced by pilgrims who discover in communitas "a timeless condition, an eternal now" (Turner, 1974, p. 238). This perspective is similar to that experienced by the characters in the film who find the integration of the real and the unreal allows them to play with rhetorical fragments of time and space as a means of transcending the habitus.

Paradoxically, self-sacrifice demands that individuals "leave" their own needs and desires behind, yet in performing self-sacrifice the film's characters are also pursuing their own needs and desires. The difference, of course, is that the former reflect material concerns and the latter primarily spiritual concerns. Thus when the characters sacrifice, they find themselves in an imaginary-yet-real place created by the field's ambience. They spiritually leave their bodies and in so doing find themselves defying the laws of time and space, much like a pilgrimage "removes [a person] from one type of time to another. [Pilgrims are] no longer involved in that combination of historical and structural time which constitute the social process in [their] rural or urban home community" (Turner, 1973, p. 221). As such, the characters enact the modernist, Cartesian dictum—"I think, therefore I am"—that mind and body are separated, with the mind able to transcend the body. *In addition,* however, the characters *embody* a physical transcendence, for their bodies have moved with their minds to this sacred time and place. Afforded a unique view of the profane, the characters experience a postmodern form of movement that is at once romantic/spiritual and modernist/transcendent; *both* mind and body have risen above the material.

Rather than viewing their lives from a point along a modernist, chronological time line, the characters play among points while configuring time. Ricoeur (1981) defines configurational time as an understanding crafted by "'grasping together' . . . significant wholes out of scattered events" (p. 174). In configurational time individuals attempt to surmount temporal constraints. Carr (1986) calls this "the attempt to dominate the flow of events by gathering them together in the forward-backward grasp of the narrative act" (p. 62). As we repeat this process, or continue to reread stories, we can gain an even clearer understanding of the narrative (Ricoeur, 1981). Configurational time recognizes that individual understanding is more likely to occur through a reinterpretation, or synthesis, of selected and scattered events in time. Configurational time thus reflects a process of being in more than one place at once, making the characters postmodern pilgrims who embody elements of romanticism and modernism as well. Eliade's (1957/1959) definition of how sacred time works shares much with the process of configuring time, emphasizing the unique spiritual perspective this type of time travel affords. He writes, "sacred time is indefinitely recoverable, indefinitely repeatable. From one point of view it could be said that it does not 'pass,' that it does not constitute an irreversible duration" (p. 69).

Although configurational time, and the reconfigured space it produces, suggests a rationale for the continued popularity of *Field of Dreams* (i.e., audiences are rereading the movie for increased understanding), it also illustrates how the film's characters come to understand their spirits. The major characters in *Field of Dreams* all possess some degree of regret regarding past events and/or opportunities in their lives. Ray bemoans not knowing his deceased father better. In particular, he laments having stopped playing catch with his dad after reading Terence Mann's *The Boatrocker* and having left home at 17 never to see his father alive again. More important, Ray tells Annie, "I'm 36 years old. I have a wife, a child, and a mortgage, and I'm scared to death I'm turning into my father." Together Annie and Ray seem to regret the passage of time from the 1960s to the 1980s; they miss the spirit of adventure and participation they possessed in their younger years. Terence is clearly an unhappy man, torn by the twin regrets of abandoning his writing and the turmoil his writing produced in the lives of others. He tells Ray, "I don't do causes any more. . . . I want them to stop looking to me for answers, begging me to speak again, write again, be a leader. I want them to start thinking for themselves." Archie seems the most comfortable with the direction his life took, but he still misses the opportunity to bat against a major league pitcher. He confides in Ray about his half inning of major league baseball experience: "It was like having it this close to your dreams and then watching them brush past you like a stranger in a crowd. At the time you don't think much of it. You know, we just don't recognize the most significant moments of our lives while they're happening. Back then I thought, 'Well, there'll be other days.' I didn't realize that that was the only day." Each of these characters, as Archie's statement illustrates, feels disconnected from the past, just as Jameson (1984) suggests that a postmodern culture dehistoricizes the present (see chapter one).

Visiting the field, however, imbues these characters with the ability to reposition history in the present. They do so by configuring episodes from their personal time lines (a.k.a. rhetorical fragments) to make more sense of their current place in time. Like pilgrims experiencing communitas, the characters collectively transcend the constraints of a consumerist habitus and simultaneously become individually invigorated. Annie, for instance, discovers that she can use the spirit of the 1960s in her 1980s farming community. At a local PTA meeting she emerges as a radical yet influential voice in the discussion over whether to remove certain books from the school library. After successfully rallying the crowd, she gleefully exclaims in the hallway outside the auditorium, "Ray, was that great or what! God, it was just like the '60s again!"

Ray, too, seems to recapture the spirit of his youth because of his interaction with the field. He spouts, "This is so bitchin'" and "That is so cool" at various points during his voice-directed quest. More important, he is able to visit his father during the prime of his life. By once again playing catch and visiting with a man he never knew— John Kinsella's brief career as a minor league ballplayer was well over by the time Ray was born—Ray is better able to understand the man he did know. Consequently, Ray can reconcile his present regret about a time in the past because another part of the past has visited his present. He can understand why he told Annie early in the film, "I never forgave [my father] for getting old."

Terence, like Ray and Annie to some degree, has lost his sense of adventure and commitment. He lives above a Boston kosher meats store, holed up in an apartment where he writes computer programs. "I wish I had your passion, Ray," he remarks midway through the quest. His encounter with Ray and the voice, however, inspires him to join Ray's quest and to visit the field. In so doing he meets young Archie and the field's ballplayers, all of whom have been dead for a number of years. Terence rediscovers both his spirit to live and his spirit to write. He moves from a grumpy recluse, greeting visitors with a snarling, "Who the hell are you?" to a chuckling extrovert by film's end. Moreover, he is moved by the spirit to write again, and to write about subjects that will move other people, just as he did 20 years prior to the time of the film. As he prepares to join the players in the cornfield, he tells Ray, "There is something out there, Ray, and if I have the courage to go through with this what a story it'll make." Terence thus reconciles himself with his past, acknowledging that he is at heart a writer whose purpose is to inspire the spirits of others. As he tells Ray, "That's [writing] what I do."

Archie is in some ways the film's most complex character because we see him as an elderly man in 1972, then as a teenager (his age in the 1920s) but in 1989, and finally as the man of 1972 in a 1989 scene. Although he initially indicates to Ray in his 1972 guise that he is happy with the choices he has made, he also indicates a desire to travel back 50 years to fulfill the missing half of his dream of playing professional baseball. "You know, I never got to bat in the major leagues," he explains to Ray. "I'd have liked that chance. Just once, to stare down a big league pitcher." Instead, Archie travels forward 17 years yet regains his appearance from the 1920s. He is able to fulfill his dream, yet he also reaffirms the appropriateness of his choice to become a physician when he steps off the field and into his 1972 age to save Karin Kinsella from choking to death. All of the characters, then, are energized by their pilgrimages to the shrine represented by the field, an experience Turner (1974) says actual pilgrims who travel to physical shrines also report.

Transcending time and space allows the characters to complete their journey to become spiritually whole. Their spirits are rejuvenated, first, through the excitement they experience when encountering the visions of the voice and, second, through finding peace within themselves despite past regrets. Once this spiritual transformation is complete, the characters find their personal promised lands within the space of the field. Their place or home is at once unique to their individual experience yet shared in general terms with the other characters who believe in the power of the place. Transcendence through the configuration of rhetorical fragments thus helps to generate symbolic community.

Similarly, fans visiting the Iowa field experience their own disruptions of time and space. In many cases they responded to my question "How would you describe this place to someone who hasn't seen it?" by struggling to find the right words, a phenomenon I also discovered among fans of *The X-Files*. Tom, for example, explains, "I just, it's a ballfield and there are thousands and thousands of ballfields. . . . Just another ballpark and it's really special, more from—not a visual standpoint—but more from an emotional, psychological standpoint." Similarly, Eric muses: "It's kind of hard to put into words the feelings that you get once you're here, 'cause sitting in Arizona you kind of shrug your shoulders and say, 'Yeah, it's just a baseball field. They've got one down the street.' But it's really different once you're here." Crescenti (1994) encountered similar reactions as he shot his *Dreamfield* documentary. Frank claims, "You feel it as soon as you get here. I'm not so sure you can put your finger on it. It's just a feeling that you get. You walk out here and there's just something different about it" (quoted in Crescenti, 1994). Christine, who made an impulsive journey from Manitoba to the field, explains, "I think it defies logic. I feel like I know why we came. I don't, I can't tell you in words, but I don't want to leave" (quoted in Crescenti, 1994).

Those who had more success offering a description seemed to emphasize the paradoxical feeling that the field was at once real and unreal. Their words appear to parallel those spoken between Ray Kinsella and his "deceased" father, John:

JOHN KINSELLA: Is this heaven?
RAY KINSELLA: It's Iowa.
JOHN: Iowa?
RAY: Yeah.
JOHN: Could have sworn it was heaven.
RAY: Is there a heaven?
JOHN: Oh, yeah. It's the place dreams come true.
RAY: Maybe this is heaven.

This excerpt, from one of the final scenes of the film, reflects the reactions of fans visiting the field: they know they are in a real place, yet they also react as if they have entered an otherworldly time and space.

As fans emerge from the cars and vans, they often exhibit the dazed look film character Terence Mann predicted ("not knowing for sure why they're doing it"). Adults, and even many of the children, step slowly out into the sunlight and gradually absorb their surroundings. There is no rush to see the porch swing, no elbowing into line to hit the ball, and no sprinting to the cornfield (although most fans do all these things at some point). Unlike visitors at a typical tourist attraction, the people visiting the field are initially relaxed, at peace in a way, and reverential. They are more reflective than consumptive. As movie fan and field visitor Garett explains, "People just naturally assume a role of tranquility and serenity" when they arrive at the site (quoted in Crescenti, 1994). Few people move directly toward the cornfield—the spiritual core of the place—suggesting that they hold it in high regard and want to savor the sacred feeling of the entire site. Ralph, for example, says, "I went out and I had to touch the [corn] stalks, to feel, and I stood in there and I got kinda goose bumps" (quoted in Crescenti, 1994). Fans such as Ralph appear to treat the field as a place to pause and ponder in the midst of a materially hectic life. When people reach the edge of the cornfield, they rarely rush in; in fact, many fans *peer* into the cornfield rather than walk into it, as if entering the sacred ground is as forbidden to them as it was to Ray Kinsella in the film; even Ralph, who touched the corn stalks, did not apparently venture far into the corn.

The sense of disbelief is almost palpable. Fans know the place to be real, but they also recognize the field is simultaneously (1) the scene of a fictional movie and (2) stuck in a cornfield. These incongruities prompt fans to recognize the field as a site of congregation—they are at a baseball field and tourist attraction—yet a special place full of communitas not found anywhere in the mundane, consumerist habitus. Jim remarks, "Yeah, it's like a movie set they take down and they put up somewhere else. Obviously this is a piece of real property and only [at] these longitudes, latitudes can just this particular place exist. It's not like pieces of cardboard that they pick up and move to the next town." Similarly, Janet notes: "Well, you know, it looks just like the movie. I mean you're really out in the middle of a bunch of fields. You know, we were here earlier, and I guess someone else from Denver said that it wasn't like a lot of other Hollywood movies that you try to look for what was there before." The incongruity frequently awes fans, as Jeremy indicates: "It's something when you see something on film and then you actually go to the place. You see the scenes in the movie."

By visiting a real place depicted in an "unreal" film, individuals feel as if they are in a different, unique location—a feeling enhanced by the incongruous placement of the field in a cornfield. As fans approach the site, John says, they begin to sense the emergence into the liminoid (my word, not his). He notes, "I tell you, when we came off of the road and we saw this place, I'm sure everyone has to have exactly the same feeling. It just kind of grabs you" (quoted in Crescenti, 1994). Joe seems similarly awed and speechless: "It's kind of a, I don't know, kind of amazing to see a ballfield in the middle of a big cornfield." Lanny clarifies this theme further, adding, "That, I guess, is kind of the mystery or the mystique of it . . . that you walk in the cornfield and you disappeared." The mystique of the field(s) flavors the experiences of the fans with a dash of the unreal, the unexplainable. As Karen explains, "There is something almost magical to the movie when the players come out of the field." Larry, who has spent much of his life in cornfields, reaffirms Karen's thoughts as he points out how the seemingly mundane task of working those fields is anything but routine: "I'm a farmer, and the magic of the corn if you're ever out in it, you know, it's just different. You just get different feelings when you're out there that you can't understand."

The uniqueness of a ballfield in a cornfield certainly seems to jar fans into alternative views, even if they cannot always articulate their new perspective. For these pilgrims the physical site of the Field of Dreams is clearly real ("it's just a baseball field," says Eric, above), but it is also imbued with otherworldly qualities ("it's really special" and "it's really different once you're here"). As fans interact with the field, the alternative understandings are made personal. Keith explains what he likes about the field: "Standing up here and hitting the ball and catching it out on the field and kind of feeling like you're a part of the whole thing." As Keith's words suggest, the field provides fans with a feeling of centeredness, a sense that they are "at home."

Finding Home

The ultimate appeal of the field is its romantic sense of social harmony, the reassurance that we are in the right place with the right people. In essence the promised land of the field offers us the perspective we require to re-center ourselves when we return home from our pilgrimages. This home roots us spiritually in a niche, a modern place of seemingly unchanging comfort from which we can engage the consumerist habitus. This home, however, must allow us to succeed economically, for altruistic production must be economically feasible. The modernist belief in finding the "right" place, then, is also tempered by the postmodern notion that a number of "right" places (or situated knowledges) may exist for others (their homes are not our own) *and* by the seemingly paradoxical equation that altruism produces economic success. In other words, a visit to the field endows fans with the ability to appreciate or respect the homes of others and to engage in a critique of the consumerist habitus by demonstrating how altruistic production may work.

Terence and Archie both discover that their purpose is to give to others; each respects the choices made by the other and the choices made by others in their situations, but they ultimately choose different means of altruistic production. Archie satisfies himself by playing ball, but he never forgets that his calling is to minister to the sick—an activity that is at once self- and other-satisfying. As he explains to Ray, "Son, if I'd only gotten to be a doctor for five minutes, now that would have been a tragedy." Archie leaves home to play ball but "returns" when his medical skills are required because, as he tells Ray in his 1972 doctor's office, "This is my most special place in all the world, Ray." Terence's experience with the field reminds him that his greatest joy is to write for others. He returns to this home knowing of the personal sacrifice involved: people will rely upon his message. Yet he also recognizes that to feel truly rooted he must engage society rather than hide from it. Both Terence and Archie can make a living working out of their homes, too, providing them with the control that pilgrims crave when they critically respond to their material conditions.

Ray and Annie conclude they were in the right material place all along, but they symbolically redefine that site as a place of altruistic production. In the early portions of the movie the Kinsellas are depicted as out-of-place in rural Iowa. Ray, raised in New York and educated in California, feels out of place farming in Iowa. Annie's use of phrases like "far out" and her stand at the PTA meeting suggest that she, too, is out of place on the farm, even though she was raised in Iowa. Their engagement with the field, though, allows them to find the spiritual element missing from their physical surroundings. They may sacrifice living in the more cosmopolitan atmosphere of Berkeley (where they met), but they find physical and spiritual peace in their present surroundings. The wisdom of their choice is confirmed in the film's conclusion as people flock to their material home in hopes of discovering their own symbolic home. And by giving up their peace and quiet, the Kinsellas help others while discovering that people visiting will provide financial support sufficient for them to live comfortably.

The character of Mark provides the comic frame for the film. His interactions with the field suggest he mistakenly views it merely as a commodity, a piece of land with material value. For instance, he asks, "Ray, do you realize how much this land is worth?" Given his preoccupation with only the economic value of the land—he emphasizes its value more than he does his relationship with his relatives— Mark espouses a consumerist ethos of measuring one's self by one's possessions, a philosophy reminiscent of the bumper sticker that claims, "He who has the most toys at the end wins." Ironically, Mark's apparent security in his sense of self—he is the only primary character not to struggle with a feeling of being out of place—is revealed to be the most unstable and spiritually unsatisfying self presented in the movie. He has so consumed the consumerist ethos that he is unable to see his own de-centeredness. Mark's beliefs are shown to be mistaken, however, when he witnesses the ball-playing Archie become Doc Graham to save Karin from choking. Afterward, he testifies, "Do not sell this farm, Ray. You gotta keep this farm."

Mark's testimony is implicitly presented to fans of the film as well. "Don't get caught up in defining yourself through consumerism," his experience suggests. Instead, cope with the consumerist habitus by centering yourself through altruistic production. In so doing you'll find a valuable new perspective upon your return home. Moreover, this perspective will allow you to redefine your socioeconomic role, providing hope for a change in the habitus. At each point in the plot where issues of consumption threaten to drive the Kinsella's from the farm, the voice encourages them to continue their journey toward altruistic production. When they discover that they are "almost breaking even" after using all their savings to build the field, Shoeless Joe Jackson shows up on the field; when they consider, because they are behind on their mortgage payments, whether Ray should travel to Boston to find Terence, Ray and Annie discover that they had the same dream involving Ray and Terence; when Mark and his partners threaten Annie with foreclosure, Ray discovers Archie; and shortly after Mark arrives at the field with foreclosure papers, Archie is magically transformed from ballplayer to doctor in order to help save Karin from choking to death.

The plot structure of *Field of Dreams* and the fate of its individual characters coalesce to suggest that the field's philosophy of altruistic production is superior to contemporary consumerism. The field provides immediate gratification through spiritual rejuvenation and deferred gratification through economic self-sufficiency, whereas consumer-oriented capitalism, according to Ehrenreich (1989), is able to deliver real immediate gratification only to the upper class. Thus the therapeutic ethos of consumerism fails to provide what it promises, and its counterpart in the promised land of the field delivers both spiritual and economic satisfaction. In this respect the promised land provides a place from which symbolic pilgrims can respond to the habitus.

As a supplemental text, the Iowa field provides fans with an opportunity to enact the symbolic transformations modeled on the screen. When visiting the field, fans construct and perform—or produce—personalized versions of the texts that contain aspects of other meaningful, personal symbolic places. The field, then, is the site of the intersection of rhetorical fragments that fans use to produce an alternative to the habitus. By playing and watching baseball, individuals activate the promised land of sport. By reperforming the text of the film, individuals share in *its* lessons for performing within the culture. And by engaging in these activities within the open text of the field, individuals perform personalized texts that reconnect them with a sacred place (symbolic and/or literal) to call home.

Thus as these dense fragments merge within the confines of the field as place, the fans who produce texts derived from the fragments engage in a personalized process of cultural critique. First, they pull in fragments from popular texts and parts of their lives to produce alternative perspectives. As Katriel and Farrell (1991) explain in their exploration of personal scrapbooks, the practice of synthesizing fragments is one "manner of making life 'cohere,' an important link between the individual and the collective" (p. 14). The process of producing and reading a scrapbook is remarkably similar to the process of configuring time enacted by the film's characters. Both feature individuals pulling together fragments of their lives to produce an ordered, coherent "lifestory." This interweaving of life and popular art is another example of what Brummett (1988) calls a "homology," a situation in which a "correspondence between text and experience enables the text to be a response, a rhetorical reply, to problems in experience" (p. 205). Thus as fans reflect on Ray Kinsella's scrapbook experience—*Field of Dreams* even opens with a series of scrapbook-like snapshots—they are performing a similar experience at the field. This particular homology, then, functions much like a lived scrapbook where "the sense of control and mastery attending the creation of this tangible life-account . . . help[s] to turn the world into a home"—the theme of the film (Katriel & Farrell, 1991, p. 15). Fans are modernist creators romantically connecting to the past and others through the postmodern process of pasting fragments into their own symbolic storybooks.

Second, the intersection of metaphorical and physical places allows fans to produce a secure bastion from which to engage in critique. Brummett (1984), for instance, points out that spiritual leaders construct symbolic homes as a base for their struggles within their culture. And as Hamera (1990) explains, individuals engaged in cultural opposition require "spaces for alternative discourses and strategies for self-(re-)presentation" (p. 240). The field is transformed from an abstract concept into a literal place that, given its incongruous characteristics, provides fans with secure, symbolic distance from the more disorienting, material aspects of consumerist culture.

Third, the ability to remake and reperform texts provides fans with a sense of powerful production. Performance itself is an empowering process, as Capo and Hantzis (1990) and Knight (1990) suggest in different contexts. When the performance involves a sense of reperformance with a reconstructed text, however, we possess even more power. For instance, Jenkins (1988) argues that individuals who remake the popular texts of the *Star Trek* series in their own images are empowered over, rather than by, popular culture: "They employ images and concepts drawn from mass culture texts to explore their subordinate status, to envision alternatives, to voice their frustrations and anger, and to share their new understandings with others" (p. 104). Furthermore, the reperformance of reconstructed texts offers individuals a chance to simultaneously reconnect with the culture and restore their sense of power as producers, as Beauvais (1990) discovered when he asked prisoners to reconstruct and perform a speech at the fictional trial of Bigger Thomas in Richard Wright's *Native Son.*

The field as site/movie offers visitors/fans similar opportunities to experience hope. Revisiting the sacred place of the field in its various forms allows fans like me to repeat the symbolic journey, just as pilgrims traveling again to their shrines reenact previous experiences. Because these experiences are infused with the sacred, the repeated quests take on the rhetorical form of ritual. As a ritual the symbolic pilgrimage provides a sense of joy, meaning, and spirit for its participants. Explains Frank, "We got here and it was slightly drizzling and it was overcast and it was really kind of ugly. And we got out of the car and everybody was smiling and happy. And they all act like they'd known you your whole life" (quoted in Crescenti, 1994). Confirms Kent, "I noticed it the first time we had come and I noticed it today. It's only a good experience. I don't hear tears. I don't hear bickering. Only positives, only up. I think the area brings out the best in people" (quoted in Crescenti, 1994). That the field uplifts spirits and generates immense joy prompts Terry, a minister, to call the field "the corn cathedral" (quoted in Crescenti, 1994).

The belief that the field is a site of joy and spirituality that must be visited again is also discursively reflected by fans as they sign in on a Field of Dreams Web site guest book (see Left, 1997). Dan and Renee note, "The field is our favorite vacation getaway! We keep coming back." Kazuhiro says, "I have been visited Field of Dreams movie site twice." Dan proclaims, "Recently made 2nd trip; played ball for an hour in the pouring rain." And Jennifer claims, "I watch the movie all the time, and watched it again last night." Repetition, for these and other fans, is anything but boring; instead, the parallel experiences reflexively build on one another as previous journeys symbolically intersect with and reaffirm the current symbolic pilgrimage and take into account material changes that may have occurred in the pilgrims' lives.

The field's setting within a cornfield encourages individuals to reconstruct performances from their own histories, thus revising and reaffirming their sense of identity or home. Corn, after all, was an emblem of the fertility goddess Demeter, mother of Persephone, whose return from the underworld symbolized not only Nature's rebirth each spring but also the renewal of the human soul in life after death. This soulful rebirth requires a sacred place, as Estes (1992) notes in her discussion of mythic images. For many fans, especially males, a visit to the field allows them to revisit their childhood, a time when they felt living followed the tenets of the place. John asks, "How else do you get to be a little boy? I don't get to be a little boy very often."

The field seems to resonate somewhere deep in its readers' common past; it "brings back childhood memories," according to Donna. Tosha observes, "You feel like a kid again, even though you're pushing 50." Geri reaffirms this feeling based on her observations of the males at the field: "I think it's kind of a nostalgic feeling that you get. I think that's the feeling the men get when they walk on that field. They cross over that line [on the field] and they're kids again" (quoted in Crescenti, 1994). One man donned his former school jersey for the visit, and another told me that he was thinking "what if's" during his visit: "What kept me from baseball [as a possible career] was Vietnam." Bob emphasizes how textual fragments intersect in his interpretation of the field: "A good place to sit back and relive maybe some childhood memories playing ball and you know you come here it's not only what you see here and what you associate with the movie but associate with your background. And I think all of us, especially the guys, played baseball from the time they were little, and it brings you back to your childhood and you start reliving a lot of things besides just baseball itself." Another Bob, interviewed by Crescenti (1994), continues this line of thought: "For myself, and I would imagine a lot of the adults my age and older, this brings back memories of another time, another way of life for us." The sense of reliving/reperforming one's life is mentioned by females as well. Sue explains its appeal as "that feeling of coming home, kind of. We're mothers that watched ball games." Pondering the appeal of the field, Joan continues the theme: "All of a sudden you have a chance to touch home and feel the things that are most important." In short, Ken says, "if you look around, people are in a world of their own. There's nothing really, there isn't anything to it but everybody seems to be a kid right now. . . . You come here and you become young again."

Reperforming one's own life also allows fans to reacquaint themselves with individuals from their pasts. One woman, for example, exclaims that "as we looked at the cornfield it reminds me of maybe our relatives that have gone on and maybe we would stand there on the edge and dream that they might come toward us." Another woman, MaryJo, amplifies this sentiment: "My dad passed away a couple years ago and he was probably the one that I used to watch the games with and everything so it's almost like I can sort of feel that he's here too. Strange." For MaryJo and other fans, visiting the field is a reminder, often nostalgic, of times and places where they felt centered, or at home.

The individuals quoted in the previous paragraphs clearly are using rhetorical fragments of other popular texts, such as baseball and the film's spiritual messages, yet they are employing those fragments for their own unique purposes. As McGee (1990) suggests, they are producing their own texts from the fragments. Moreover, they are also performing those texts to empower themselves to engage the culture in which they live. As a visitor named Mark explains, "Here they're coming to enjoy it as a family, play, live their dreams, and then go home feeling good about themselves." Just as the lessons of the film suggest, then, visitors to the field engage in a meaning-production process that involves sacrifice, transcendence of time and space, and a redefinition of their socioeconomic roles—from consumers to altruistic producers—once they return home.

A Postmodern Place: Homes as Individual Sanctuaries and Communal Gathering Spots

Field of Dreams's symbolic shrine suggests that altruistic producerism offers both economic and spiritual health. When the film's characters sacrifice for others, they are reconnected with their spirit, allowing them to gain perspective on their lives and to find a home that offers spiritual fulfillment and economic plenitude. Our identifications with the characters, combined with a visit to the symbolic field, encourage us to find a "home place" from which we can respond to the cultural conditions of the consumerist habitus.

Moreover, a symbolic pilgrimage to the film's field reminds us that we can reconcile our seemingly contradictory desires to be a unique individual self and to participate in a caring community of others who share our beliefs. This reconciliation constitutes a critical rhetorical move given consumerism's emphasis on creating *difference* both individually and communally. In *Field of Dreams,* and at the field site, individual selves are not distanced from—or even subordinated to—the community but are integrated into a community while remaining unique. Altruistic producerism provides the unique self of consumerism, and *also* develops romantic ties difficult to discover in a consumerist culture that has reduced affect (Jameson, 1984); the self may still be somewhat distant, but it is distant *within* a community. All of the film's characters come to interact within the friendly confines of the communal field. Despite their different ages and backgrounds, they form a community that is open to all, as the film's last scene demonstrates. Yet within that community each individual is free to pursue his/her personal destiny of spiritual fulfillment: Ray meets his father again; Terence rediscovers his muse; Archie reconciles his two callings, etc. Neither individualism nor community dominates; instead, *Field of Dreams* suggests that an individual can freely pursue his or her dream while building community, just as chapter three suggests we produce symbolic communities through a twofold process of individuals' ontologically centering themselves and working with others to denote community boundaries.

Many scholars and cultural observers, however, would have us believe that individualism and community are engaged in a modernist, give-and-take relationship; if we act on our individual whims, we are taking away from the community and vice versa. In general, Taylor (1993a) argues that narratives that emphasize individual characters in conflict lose the ability to articulate a community consciousness. In particular, the Western genre, arguably American culture's most important story form (Nachbar, 1974), is typically described as including the struggle between individual and community (e.g., Cawelti, 1971). Rushing (1983) goes so far as to suggest that the Western would disappear if individualism and community were culturally synthesized. On a larger level Fisher (1973) argues that individual-oriented behaviors converge into a set of beliefs he calls materialism, which conflicts with the set of other-directed behaviors he labels moralism (a pairing only slightly different from the consumerism-producerism pair I have used throughout this chapter). Fisher, like Rushing, suggests that these behaviors are dichotomous.

In part the creation of such a dualism has its roots in our increasingly consumerist culture. Coontz (1992), for example, claims, "Western individualism has always fed daydreams about escaping external constraints and family obligations, but prior to the era of mass consumption, most people . . . knew that the only sure source of self-identity and security lay in relationships with others" (p. 176). In other words, individualism and community lived in peaceful coexistence prior to the acceptance of consumerism as equipment for living. In providing an answer to this alleged conflict between two contradictory impulses, *Field of Dreams* merges the past and present to revalorize the interdependence of individualism and community. The film's agrarian setting—the site of the historical citizen-farmer—contextualizes the message that the two values once were, and still are, intermingled.

By featuring altruistic production as a spiritually healthy and materially satisfying behavior, the film points out that a person can merge the material and the moral, the individual and the communal. Self-sacrifice is intrinsically good, the film demonstrates, but it also produces material and spiritual rewards. Individuals in the film who do not sacrifice, represented by Mark through most of the film, miss these benefits. The individuals who do sacrifice are those individuals who have avoided the consumerist lure in one way or another (Ray and Annie farm; Terence is an urban recluse; Archie is a small town physician).

Field of Dreams drives home the image of a coexisting blend of individualism and community through the symbol of the baseball-playing Shoeless Joe Jackson. The field is Jackson's sanctuary, the place where he can feel at home while atoning for his sin of being associated with the infamous scandal of throwing the 1919 World Series. Jackson's involvement—debated in the film and in other stories—violated the spirit of baseball, yet by accepting the ground rules of the field (only those who "believe" in it can play on it) he is rehabilitated. His individual purpose meshes with the purpose of playing baseball: to reach home safely. "The play advances and runs score through the cyclical actions of the players leaving and returning to home, in the one arena of American life where you can go home again" (Grella, 1975, p. 562). Reaching home is accomplished through individual efforts (hits) and/or self-sacrifice (fly balls, bunts, walks) that allow the community/team to succeed. When individual desires overwhelm team goals, both individuals and the community suffer, as did the individual players of the Chicago "Black" Sox and the community that supported them prior to the discovery of the bribery scandal.

The purpose of many fans, generally speaking, appears to be one of simultaneously reconnecting with oneself and with others, emphasizing one's uniqueness and place in the world. Fans express delight in both the sense of community and the feeling of isolation they encounter at the field. Because they share an appreciation of the film, they often feel as if they are performing with soulmates. Bob reflects, "It's different. I don't know what it is. People come and you don't know anybody and you're still out there playing ball with them. It's just remarkable, isn't it?" Geri continues: "I don't know where else you can get total strangers to go out on a field where you've got 50 or 60 men out there who carry their gloves, and their bats, and their balls from, from Wisconsin and Nebraska and South Dakota and Illinois, from everywhere, to go out and play on this field—just to play catch with their kids" (quoted in Crescenti, 1994). The sense of community extends to the family unit as well, since many fans are families on vacation. Bruce offers his explanation for the presence of so many families: "I guess it's something you can experience all together and, you know, like I say, in my particular case, we can get out and play ball together and just really enjoy the game enough to be here." Similarly, an unnamed male in the *Dreamfield* video observes, "You see all the families here today. They're all smiling. You don't see anybody that is rubbing against each other. They're having a great time. It's just incredible." An Ohio family interviewed by Crescenti (1994) echoed this sentiment when they explained that the field was the only site all members of the family agreed they should visit on vacation.

Sharing extends beyond the family unit, however, as fans reach out to connect with strangers at the field. Just as Ray opened the field to all who wanted to play, fans open the field to all who want to play. Strangers start up conversations, adults give batting tips to other people's children, and everyone is encouraged to play. No organized games occur, but the field is almost always in use. Husbands and wives play catch in the outfield, parents hit fly balls to children in another part of the outfield. In the infield, lines form on busy days to hit the ball, but there is no competition. Pitchers lob easy ones to the plate, children are given as many swings as they like, and infielders share positions and ground balls. All of this activity occurs at a leisurely pace. When one parent notes that his son will "just be a minute" in the batter's box, the pitcher replies, "No, he can take all day. He can take as long as he wants." No one in line or in the field complains. No complaints are heard from the bleachers, either, where other fans soak up sunshine and the play on the field; they share in the purposeful playfulness of those on the field. Furthermore, by mirroring the actions of the cinematic Kinsellas watching the play from the bleachers, these individuals likely feel as if they are sharing in the spirit of the film, too. As one teen girl exclaimed, "I'm sitting where stars sat."

The sharing also occurs away from the action. For instance, a person I had interviewed encouraged me to grab a glove to shag grounders; another interviewee snapped a Polaroid of me from his camera so that I could have a souvenir of my visit; a third person gave me a copy of two newspaper articles about the field when I told him I was researching the subject. Without being asked to pay admission to the field, most fans willingly stuff a dollar or two into the donation boxes discretely posted by Ameskamp and Lansing. Fans of the field, in sharing the field with future fans, seem to follow a National Parks motto, leaving only footprints and taking only photographs; there is no digging up pieces of sod or snagging ears of corn out of the field.

By showing respect for those who created the magic of the field, those who are currently interacting with the field, and those who will use the field in the future, fans establish a sense of both temporal solidarity and transcendence with the field; they pay homage in the present but spiritually link themselves to past and future. In so doing they strengthen their connection with the film's message(s), since the "ghosts" of the cinematic field were from our past but in their future during our present.

At the same time that individuals feel a bond with others, however, they also feel safely isolated within their own thoughts. Many of the adult fans seem to visit the field to reflect. The quiet of the country-side, combined with the pastoral setting of the field, certainly encourages reflection. Adults typically amble around the field, looking at the corn or watching the play. Of course, an observer cannot know if they are reflecting on the movie, thoughts prompted by the movie, or something altogether different. Strikingly, though, the area of the field is rather quiet even when 50 or more people are scattered about. Playing children seem quieter than usual, as if they recognize that they are in a church-like atmosphere where people are engaged in self-talk. In this respect the field resembles a spiritual congregation, a collection of individuals reaffirming their personal missions together. The resultant spiritual rejuvenation is similar to what Terence describes in the film: "It'll be as if they'd dipped themselves in magic waters."

As the fans report in the interviews, they take advantage of the unique opportunity afforded by the field to feel comfortably alone while simultaneously being surrounded by a group of "close strangers"; ontological centering occurs simultaneously with the experience of communitas. Explains Erica: "You don't feel the way hundreds of other people feel about, you have your own feelings. I don't know. You just have your own feelings other than if you're amongst 200 other people—you all do the same thing, you know. It gives you your own individual feeling." Those individual feelings are apparently generated by the sense of picturesque isolation the field affords. Marilyn describes the area as "quiet, and it's just beautiful," and Stan views it as "tranquil and peaceful." The isolation gives rise in turn to a secondary sense of self-connectedness among the fans. Kathy notes the field is "very relaxing, very restful," echoing Dave's description of it as "very serene, very peaceful." Larry goes so far as to suggest the field offers "a different kind of peace—just got to experience stuff to realize what it is." Fans then have the opportunity to enjoy not only a connection with others but also the solitude necessary to mull over and actualize their personal constructions of the site.

Partial Dreams and the Borders Around Homes

According to cultural studies scholar Lawrence Grossberg (1992), fans' reactions to popular stories represent investments in feelings or moods, what he calls affect. "Affect is closely tied to what we often describe as the feeling of life," he writes. "You can understand another person's life: you can share the same meanings and pleasures, but you cannot know how it feels" (p. 56). The fans of the fields of dreams (movie and site), such as myself, can thus share a sense of communal understanding, but we cannot access the individual feelings of our fellow symbolic pilgrims. Conversely, nonfans of the film are unlikely to share our affective investment in the fields. More than one female visitor to the Iowa field, for example, told me she was there because her husband and/or kids wanted to journey to the out-of-the-way farmstead—a sentiment that reflects Nadel's (1997) assessment of the film as a patriarchal homage to invisible "great fathers" (such as the disembodied voice and John Kinsella). In addition, the appeal of the field seems primarily limited to Americans of European ancestry, although a number of Japanese tourists have visited the site, and some have visited one of the Web pages associated with the field (perhaps because of Japan's cultural love of baseball). I noticed only four people of color during my three-day stay in 1992. Although the timing of my visit may have produced an exception to the rule, I suspect the film provides a message mostly to white Americans. Indeed, film critic Harlan Jacobson calls the movie an ode to a "'non-ethnic, vanilla ice cream America'" (quoted in Ingrassia, 1989, p. D14).

Thus the enthusiastic response to the film—it earned over $62 million at the box office (Variety, 1989), racked up another $30 million in rentals in its first year on the shelf (Variety, 1990), and drew hundreds of thousands of people to its Iowa site—and my discussion of it should not be taken as indicators that the lessons of the field are "dreams" shared by all people. Quite clearly the dreams are shared by only a portion of the American citizenry; at the very least, visitors to the Iowa field require the financial flexibility and social mobility that enables them to travel (in some cases) significant distances while taking time off from work. Equally clear, I hope, is the notion that the promised lands described in each of the chapters of this work are not necessarily shared by a particular group of people who "think exactly like me." My solicitations for volunteers at work, for example, did not net a single person who is a fan of *Sports Illustrated, The X-Files,* and *Dilbert.*

Moreover, my reasons for being a fan of these four popular texts are not shared by other fans. Some *SI* readers use the magazine to get caught up on sporting news much more so than I (the focus group, in fact, got into quite a discussion over the worthiness of the magazine's feature articles); some viewers of *The X-Files* enjoy the conspiracy episodes the most (those episodes seem to be the most prevalent options for rental on video); and some fans of *Dilbert* find themselves in working environments—unlike mine—that are mirror images of Dilbert's company (a graduate student with whom I worked says her father is convinced that Dilbert's company *is* his own organization). Clearly the images of shared promised lands I present in these pages should not be interpreted as an argument for the existence of universal promised lands any more than the generalized, historical descriptions of promised lands outlined in chapter one should be understood as universally shared beliefs of sacred places. As Grossberg (1992) elaborates, "This is not to claim that all affective investments are equal or even equivalent; there are, at the least, qualitative and quantitative differences among them" (p. 58).

In the case of *Field of Dreams,* for example, the film's anticonsumerism messages are contradicted by Ray's reliance on consumerism as well as the commercialization—albeit slight—of the field site. First, Ray cannot build the field without the use of credit, the fulcrum of consumerism; the film offers no evidence that the Kinsellas, in debt and with a smaller crop, possess disposable income. In an economy that depends on the purchase of goods, credit is offered as a means of increasing individuals' purchasing power. Using credit is a promise to work "tomorrow" to pay for "today," an economic mode that Bell (1996) calls "the most 'subversive' instrument that undercut the Protestant ethic" (p. 293). Although the field ultimately saves the Kinsellas, Ray's decision to put the family further in debt by building the field relies on one of the central characteristics of a consumer economy. Second, the field site is increasingly commercialized. Although no admission is charged, the souvenir stands are chock-full of merchandise you can purchase to "authenticate" your experience at the field. In addition, at least two Web sites hawk wares related to the field (Left Catalog, 1997; Souvenirs, 1997); in these cases you don't even have to encounter the field personally to "own" a commercialized "affective installment" with the site. After contacting the Web site and inquiring about the *Dreamfield* video, I was put on a mailing list and sent a brochure offering field memorabilia. You can also "rent" some of Doc Graham's spirit by donating to a scholarship fund for an elementary school in Chisholm, Minn. (Graham Scholarship, 1997). Donations are pledged through the purchase of artifacts—baseball cards—representing Graham's real-life history (he was indeed a real person who played professional baseball in 1905, then quit in midseason to become a doctor in his hometown of Chisholm; the editorial praising his good works that was read in the movie was from an actual editorial written by Veda Ponikvar [Graham Scholarship, 1997]).

My own purchase of a T-shirt during my 1990 visit to the field and my temptation to purchase an Archie Graham baseball card make me wonder how much I have affectively invested in the film's message. Did I need to consume (to put inside of myself?) something to validate my spiritual encounter with a sacred place? Am I enhancing the spiritual experience with my consumptive tendencies? If so, doesn't that run counter to the film's lessons? Can I reconcile these differences via a postmodern both/and account? Is a feeling of "home" also a commodity, a spiritual centeredness that one can purchase? These questions remind us that "home" isn't as clearly defined as we might think. Indeed, if we're not even certain how we see our own homes, how certain can we be of our visions of others' homes? Those symbolic borders that we sketch around our, and others', homes are metaphoric fault lines, as unstable as those lines I used to draw on my Etch-a-Sketch; a slight shake, rattle, or roll and they're as gone as Bill Haley. That we continue to configure time, to bring back the cultural memories of bygone days, suggests we're "perfectly rotten" landscape architects, too. Each symbolic pilgrimage tells us we're at home but that our home has changed.

Conclusion

These reflections indicate the cyclical nature of symbolic pilgrimages. As we return home from our journey, we become aware of new rhetorical fragments circling our personal space; home is different, we hope better, but our pilgrimage did not "solve" our disorientation. Accordingly, we desire to commence another symbolic pilgrimage to gain that elusive sense of orientation. *Field of Dreams,* in fact, epitomizes the idea of symbolic pilgrimage. Clearly the *Field*/Field experience involves some type of journey to a special place and back again. For me, watching the movie and reviewing the comments of the fans/tourists/pilgrims activates a renewed desire to find a "home" of my own, both professionally and personally. You would think my inclination to analyze rhetoric would remind me that I'm "rotten with perfection," yet the desire remains the same. The more I read (in all senses of the word), the more I know. But the more I "know," the more I read.

Notes

Portions of this chapter were previously published in three journal articles: Roger C. Aden, Rita L. Rahoi, and Christina S. Beck, " 'Dreams Are Born on Places Like This': The Process of Interpretive Community Formation at the Field of Dreams Site," *Communication Quarterly,* 43 (1995): 368–380; Roger C. Aden, "Iowa's Elysian Fields: Spiritual Rejuvenation at the Field of Dreams," *Elysian Fields Quarterly* 13.2 (1994): 3–10; and Roger C. Aden, "Back to the Garden: Therapeutic Place Metaphor in *Field of Dreams,*" *The Southern Communication Journal* 59 (1993): 307–317. The Southern States Communication Association has granted permission to use this article here. My coauthors' contributions to the first of these articles are largely unreflected in this chapter.

1. The College of Communication of Ohio University provided me with the financial support to travel to the field to conduct the interviews.

2. The citation for the film can be found in the references section under Robinson, Gordon, and Gordon (1989). Because I quote repeatedly from the film, I have opted not to repeat the citation throughout the text. The first names of the fans cited in this chapter are their real names. I did not ask for last names when conducting the interviews and do not list any here. The interview process was approved by Ohio University's Institutional Review Board.

Conclusion

The Return Home

There's no place like home.

—Dorothy
The Wizard of Oz

In some ways the writing of this book has paralleled the imaginary journeys I have called symbolic pilgrimages. First, I have attempted to depart from my theoretical home, the Burkean theories that I learned in graduate school, to enter a liminoid theoretical area that is between those theories and numerous others. In chapters one through three I sought to sketch the nebulous boundaries of this theoretical territory by pointing out that it was neither modernist, postmodernist, nor romantic but a combination of all three philosophies. In addition, I attempted to integrate, though not wholly adopt, theoretical tidbits from humanistic and cultural geography, symbolic interactionism, cultural studies, and feminist scholarship. The theory of symbolic pilgrimages thus is situated in a space that is in between these established theoretical territories. Moreover, this space is in between consumerism and its alternatives, for to embark on a symbolic pilgrimage requires consumption and a desire for difference while simultaneously wishing for responses to the habitus that promulgates these desires.

Second, following an entrance into the liminoid, we traveled to four of my sacred places—*Dilbert*'s Nerdvana, *The X-Files*'s funhouse, *Sports Illustrated*'s American Elysian Field, and the field of *Field of Dreams*—to see how symbolic pilgrimages may occur through the popular stories found in a number of different media. The production of these sacred places, as I indicated in chapter three, involves both an individual fan's situating her/himself in an imagined place and that fan's symbolically interacting with others in a transcendent community. Chapters four through seven began as places that I envisioned in my encounters with the popular stories; as I interacted with others—through focus group interviews, e-mail, and their responses in other media—my vision of that sacred place became clearer to me and, I hope, to you as a visitor to these sacred places. Visiting these sacred places, I believe, allows us to transcend the habitus-inspired notion that being a fan of popular stories is merely an escapist diversion.

Third, my forays into the imaginations of others helped me to generate more respect for the perspectives of others. Like most rhetorical critics, I was educated to believe that I could paradoxically develop a transcendent perspective of a text by immersing myself in that text *and* that such a personal perspective was sufficient evidence to support my claim. In fact, the first draft of this book—which only hinted at the idea of symbolic pilgrimage—repeatedly suggested that fans *could* imagine the sacred places I identified, but I offered little evidence that fans *did* engage in such imaginative odysseys of the mind. Now, having learned a great deal from other fans as I wrote these chapters, I'm convinced that we need to engage the audiences of our texts more frequently. To be sure, critical analyses of texts that point out what fans are *not* seeing has contributed to our increasing awareness of habitus, but we also need to appreciate how individuals—even ourselves—cope and hope with that awareness. If we are resting on our critical laurels, I hope we might also notice that jabbing sensation in our posteriors and recognize the intellectual arrogance that an unyielding "text only" position entails. That is not to say that a critic cannot engage in a "text only" critique but that *as part of a program of research,* a critic of popular culture *also* engages in studies of how individual subjects possess agency or the capacity to change their habitus.

Finally, as the previous paragraph suggests, I have returned "home" from my intellectual sojourn with a new perspective on my own ways of seeing. Not only do I see my critical encounters with popular stories in a different light, I see the sacred places of my favorite stories in a new way. Initially, for example, I was a die-hard fan of *Dilbert*'s DNRC, chuckling along with other members of the "secret society" at the antics of Induhviduals. Now, I'm periodically troubled by the comics and newsletter items that simply reverse power relationships. As I visited with other fans of my favorites, I discovered that most of them were "like me," yet we didn't share entirely the same interests or interpretations. Thus I was reminded upon my return home that my symbolic borders and boundaries include as well as exclude. My self is uniquely centered in a home within a community of fans, *and* that community is distinct from other communities. Completing a symbolic pilgrimage reminds me that (1) I see uniquely; (2) I can similarly, but not exactly, see what others do; and (3) what I see may be different from what others see. Appreciating these distinctions, and learning to understand how others see, are thus critical elements of a symbolic pilgrimage. Without them, we would do little to overcome the postindustrial habitus that encourages difference through consumerism.

We're Home, Now What?

What we do *after* we return home, then, is at least as important as what we do during our imaginative journeys. We have to make sense of how and why home looks different than it did when we left. Yes we can learn from seeing the cultural terrain from the outside (as travelers passing through) and sacred places from the inside (we symbolically live in these places), but as chapter three points out, we should also engage in a third way of seeing: reflection. Reflection informs us of how "homes" are places that are affected by the cultural currents of time and space, that they are both historically based *and* socially constructed. Homes are rhetorical inventions that are as unstable as rhetoric itself. Reflection helps us highlight those instabilities and recognize how our homes, and those of others, are shaped by boundaries affected by history and social relations. In particular, reflection should help us remember three characteristics about our homes, ourselves, and our relations with others.

First, we take our homes with us. Homes are not unchanging abodes, impervious to the workings of time and space. Downs and Stea (1977) remind us of the adage that "you can't go home again": "While it is true that our home serves as an anchor point for many of our beliefs and affections, it is also true that there is no longer a place that is identical to, or sometimes even vaguely resembles, our memories of home" (p. 2). Accordingly, we can't think of "home" as located in one unchanging place. Our homes assume places as we navigate time and space. As hooks (1990) explains, "Home is no longer just one place. It is locations. Home is that place which enables and promotes varied and everchanging perspectives, a place where one discovers new ways of seeing reality, frontiers of difference" (p. 148). Perhaps another way to frame hooks's comments is to say that we live in "mobile homes," homes that move with us, ontological centers with wheels, as it were. Chambers (1990) labels this process of living in mobile homes as " 'being at home' in the world" (p. 104). Or as the eponymous hero of the film *The Adventures of Buckaroo Banzai*

Across the Eighth Dimension counsels, "Always remember: no matter where you go, there you are." The futuristic cowboy called Buckaroo tells us in a very simple phrase that we can find a sense of home that is at once modern, postmodern, and romantic—a place where we are ontologically centered selves, a place that travels with us and that leads us to spiritual connections with others.

Home can function in this way because, second, we live *from* the past rather than *in* the past. We can't—and often don't want to—escape personal and cultural memories, a fact noted by Burke's (1987) detective Robicheaux, who muses near the end of *The Neon Rain*, " 'I don't like the world the way it is, and I miss the past. It's a foolish way to be' " (p. 238). Yet we inevitably draw upon the past—our individual experiences and our cultural memories—to make sense of our place in the present. Even when those memories are unpleasant, they remind us of the path our cultural journeys have followed. The bits of cultural memory we cull from the debris of past promised lands combine with current experiences to provide us with the symbolic resources to construct the "mobile homes" that enable us to move through cultural landscapes. As Chambers (1990) claims, "The past is recomposed in fragments of memories, voices, and languages . . . in the bits and pieces we pick over and put together in the stories we all construct in conferring sense and elaborating a poetics of the possible" (p. 111). Chambers's language implicitly reflects the need to work with multiple discourses. We engage in postmodern play with rhetorical fragments, operate as transcendent modernist sensemakers, and envision a romantic "poetics of the possible."

His language also reminds us, third, that symbolic pilgrims share a politics of "identical differences" in that each of us engages in similar processes of coping and hoping even though how we cope, and what we hope, may be different. This concept incorporates cultural studies theories of identity and difference, ideas that have generally been unable to escape polarizing either/or thinking as they are used to formulate "political" agendas (see Bell, 1996; Bernstein, 1994; Hughes, 1993). "Identity politics," influenced by standpoint epistemology, tends to essentialize identities and concretize differences by suggesting that one's history, loosely defined, dictates a way of knowing that is unknown to others unlike oneself. A popular and familiar manifestation of such thinking is John Gray's (1992) bestseller, *Men Are From Mars, Women Are From Venus*, which suggests men and women are unable to "move" to see the other's point of view. The "movement" theorizing summarized in chapter two offered an alternative to this position, proposing a "politics of difference" in which different standpoints can be visited, appreciated, and respected while groups move together to form temporary coalitions to address issues based upon shared *affinities* rather than shared *identities* (Haraway, 1991). As Larner (1995) explains, "The goal is *not unity based on a common experience, or even experiences,* but rather some form of workable compromise which will enable us to coalesce around specific issues" (p. 188; emphasis added). Although this book has relied heavily on such dynamic theorizing, I believe the experience of a symbolic pilgrimage *is indeed a shared experience,* even if your imaginative travels take you to different promised lands. We share the experience of imaginative travel through rhetorical invention. And we share the desire to escape the habitus by searching for promised lands through popular stories. Our differences, at this general level, are identical—and they are the place to start in envisioning macro-level changes in a habitus.

These characteristics cumulatively offer an alternative means of envisioning ourselves, our homes, and our interactions with others. They may be what Jameson (1984) had in mind when he called for a new "aesthetic of cognitive mapping" in which we seek "to endow the individual subject with some new heightened sense of its place" in a postindustrial/postmodern culture that has seemingly removed depth, affect, and history from our cognitive maps (p. 92). Rather than simply adhering to modernist notions of unchanging homes and selves (a notion reflected in Tuan's [1977] statement that place "is essentially a static concept. If we see the world as process, constantly changing, we should not be able to develop any sense of place" [p. 179]); rather than simply romanticizing home as something unique to our standpoints (a notion reflected in Radhakrishnan's [1996] claim, "It is precisely this obsession with the sacredness of one's origins that leads peoples to disrespect the history of other people and to exalt one's own" [p. 212]); and rather than simply floundering in a postmodern rootlessness (a notion reflected in Buttimer's [1980] observation: "It appears that people's sense of both personal and cultural identity is intimately bound up with place identity. Loss of home or 'losing one's place' may often trigger an identity crisis" [p. 167])—rather than choosing among these three apparently exclusive schools of thought, we can incorporate the "best" of all three in envisioning ourselves and others as living in homes that are historically based and socially constructed.

In so doing we can account for our twin desires, noted at the opening of chapter one, to stay at home and to escape from home. Featherstone (1995) points to the need to develop theories that address this paradox: "The challenge to theorizing today is how to construct theories of communal living in localities which do not merely represent sedentariness as the norm, but seek to consider its various modalities, including displacements into images of imaginary homes/

homelands. Such theories also need to take into account the ways in which those inhabitants who engage in various modes of travel manage to construct and live out their various affiliations and identities" (pp. 144–145). Fans of popular stories "live out their various affiliations and identities" by using their imaginations for purposeful play. As fans we develop feelings of affect or investment that, although made possible by the media technology of the postindustrial, also provide a means of overcoming the waning of affect generated by that technology. Explains Grossberg (1992), "Fandom is, at least potentially, the site of the optimism, invigoration and passion which are necessary conditions for any struggle to change the conditions of one's life" (p. 65).

Accordingly, using one's imagination as a fan makes possible the envisioning of alternatives to the habitus, a way of changing the conditions of our lives. Symbolic pilgrimages remind us, upon reflection, that our homes are mobile yet connected to the past and that others share our experiences. Seeing how the borders and boundaries around our homes are flexible, permeable, and *invented* allows us to imagine new possibilities, to see "the rules" of the habitus as invented rules open to our influence. In short, coming home from symbolic pilgrimages can remind us that "dreaming" provides individuals with "a way to imagine themselves as other than they are, [in] a place made out of possibilities capable of directing their actions, their thoughts, their lives" (Goodall, 1996, p. 142). Manipulating symbols through the purposeful play of imagination enables us to move symbolically, to escape temporarily—and perhaps over time to change permanently—the constraining features of the current habitus. As Feyerabend (1978) urges in his polemic against traditional ways of seeing and knowing, "Now—how can we possibly examine something we are using all the time? . . . The answer is clear: we cannot discover it from the *inside.* We need . . . an entire alternative world, *we need a dream-world in order to discover the features of the real world we think we inhabit*" (pp. 31–32; emphasis in original). Symbolic pilgrimages allow us to see how the "real world" of the habitus is in many ways a "dream world" in which the conventions of history are exposed as merely conventions.

Endowed with new visions, and fortified with the knowledge that others share our beliefs, we can make changes in our material conditions upon our return home. *Dilbert*'s tremendous popularity has prompted managers to reenvision how they work with subordinates. *The X-Files*'s reluctance to offer closure helps fans to redefine the de-centering they encounter in an increasingly postindustrial habitus. *Sports Illustrated* fans openly chastise sports figures who do not merge work and play, informing those and other figures how "the game of life" should be played. *Field of Dreams* prompts fans visiting the site of the field to reflect on their consumerist habits and to appreciate their fellow humans. Individually, and combined with the countless symbolic pilgrimages that are not recounted in this book, these travels help to reveal the contours and constraints of historical habitus—and encourage us to communicate and behave differently upon our return home.

As the habitus changes, however, we must remember that inclusions and exclusions still occur; reflection and critique of the "rules"—even the new ones—must continue (McKerrow, 1989; Ono & Sloop, 1995). That's why *Dilbert*'s Nerdvana must be seen not just as a place where power relationships are reversed but also as a place that generally continues to exclude the idea of social equality; why *The X-Files*'s funhouse must be seen not just as a place to appreciate the unknown but also as a place where conspiracy theories that lack accountability may flourish; why *Sports Illustrated*'s American Elysian Field must be seen not just as a place that is a pastiche of Western ideals and American realities but also as a place that perpetuates the mind-body distinctions that encourage patriarchal ways of seeing; why *Field of Dreams*'s transcendent field must be seen not just as a place where individualism and community coexist in the form of altruistic production but also as a place where a particular kind of consumerism still lingers. Symbolic communities, as Cohen (1985) reminds us, possess borders, and borders—no matter how much they shift—still exist and affect our sightlines.

Seeing Differently

This new way of seeing ourselves and our symbolic communities requires that we break from our modernist either/or habits of describing concepts in dichotomous terms and discarding concepts that appear to be contradictory. Our imaginations do not care about such "rules"; as Feyerabend (1978) emphasizes, alternative "rules" that describe what counts as knowledge can rely on their own counterlogics because they are developed outside of the habitus. The "rules" of symbolic pilgrimages blur distinctions and blend binaries. They suggest that we are simultaneously "centered movers," "individualistic sharers," "purposeful players," and "redefiners who seek perfect definitions."

As *centered movers* we are—as humanistic geographers argue— ontologically centering beings who develop a sense of place through the use of our individual senses and cognitive maps. We center ourselves in relation to people, places, and ideas that surround us; we are "at home" in the world. At the same time, however, we are epistemologically mobile beings who know what we know through our symbolic movements to, through, and between various standpoints. Although we may not be able to experience the material conditions of others, we are able to see and understand different perspectives through our symbolic pilgrimages. Whether these perspectives are accurate or authentic—whether, that is, they reflect "real" life—is not an issue I find worthy of pursuit. *No* fictional depiction will capture the complexity of lived experience, but each fictional depiction tells us something about how people live. For example, Orson Welles's opus, *Citizen Kane*, is ranked by many film critics as the best movie ever made, yet its none-too-disguised portrayal of William Randolph Hearst is terribly incomplete if judged by a standard of lived experience. Similarly, Ed Wood's shoddy *Plan 9 From Outer Space* is ranked by many film critics as the worst movie ever made, yet Tim Burton's touching film biography, *Ed Wood*, illustrated that understanding Wood meant understanding something about how each of us strives to find a purpose in life. We learn about these fictional/real lives through our centered, individual lines of sight, but we do so while paradoxically seeing from their points of view.

Second, we are *individualistic sharers* who perplexingly—in modernist terms—seek a personal center as well as connections with others. As the previous chapter illustrates, we can have our individualism and community, too. Living in an increasingly consumerist habitus encourages us to define ourselves through difference, as unique individuals, but we also seek the romantic affiliations that come with sharing our symbolic space with others. Our imaginings of symbolic communities, then, take two forms: a personalized place in which we are centered, but whose boundaries are stretched sufficiently to allow others to share in a larger yet still meaningful bounded area. This "bounded area" is at once space, distinct from one's individual sense of place, and a concrete place in which an individual is ensconced. Cultural terrain can thus be envisioned as a three-tiered territory of personalized place, meaningful community space/place, and the collection of space/places that exists beyond the community borders. Place and space are more than dichotomous partners; they are embedded in one another as we simultaneously situate ourselves as individuals and as members of a symbolic community.

Third, these imagined territories of self and community reflect our status as *purposeful players*, beings who imagine symbolic communities as alternatives to the constraining features of the habitus. Although I discussed this paradox in the introduction of this book, let me emphasize here that play is serious work. *Dilbert* fans, for example, are not just "blowing off steam" when they enter the liminoid territory of Nerdvana; they are also imagining an alternative to Cubeville that can be "brought back" to their material environments. There, as we have seen, the play of imagination can generate very real changes in the habitus. Reading *Sports Illustrated*, then, isn't just about escaping sociopolitical issues to visit the world of playing games; it's also about seeing positive and negative role models with all the sociopolitical issues those images entail. As Grossberg (1992) urges, "The affective investment in certain places (texts, identities, pleasures) and differences demands a very specific ideological response, for affect can never define, by itself, why things should matter" (p. 60).

Because those changes are inherently incomplete, however, we continue to seek perfect definitions, leading us to redefine continuously. Fourth, then, we are *redefiners who seek perfect definitions.* By compiling fragments of our experiences, our cultural memories, and our contemporary conditions, we can "play" with rhetoric to create new definitions of what the habitus has defined as commonsensical. DNRC members can define logic as illogic, X-philes can treat an encounter with the unknown as playing in the funhouse rather than being surveilled in the panopticon, *SI* readers can see work as spiritually fulfilling play, and fans visiting the Field of Dreams site can envision the destruction of a cash crop as fulfilling a dream. Such play is, of course, purposeful, but it is also never-ending. Each redefinition is imperfect, for the newly envisioned symbolic community contains the same kinds of borders, creating the same kinds of inclusions and exclusions, that the previous boundaries generated. Rotten with perfection, however, we seek to overcome these community differences—while paradoxically enjoying the individual differences—through more rhetorical play. Rhetorical play through redefinition is thus ritualistic.

To summarize, a symbolic pilgrimage is an imaginative, ritual journey to a sacred place that is constructed out of the rhetorical fragments possessed by the fan and the text. This sacred place exists in a liminoid space that is in between the space of the popular story and the material environment of the fan. There the fan extracts symbolic resources for coping with the habitus and for envisioning alternatives to the habitus—alternatives that may gradually move from the imaginative to the material as other members of the symbolic community engage in similar processes of coping and hoping. This symbolic process is thus both therapeutic and critical, encouraging fans to see their constantly changing homes as unstable yet necessary sites of identity and to understand, through the act of crossing symbolic borders, the experiences of others unlike themselves. Paradoxically, this recognition of difference within one's own experience and in comparison to others' experiences *can* remind fans, despite their affiliations with distinct symbolic communities, what they possess in common: a desire to find and create "places that matter."

These promised lands are more than figments of our imagination; in fact, the phrase "figments of our imagination" is far too dismissive. Only through our imagination, as Bourdieu (1980/1990) acknowledges, can we envision alternatives to the constraints of habitus. Only through our imagination can we construct sacred places in a fragmented postmodern culture. Imagination is invention, and in these times invention is undoubtedly the most important of the classical canons of rhetoric. Rhetorical invention leads to the creation of popular stories *and* promised lands. Rhetorical invention is also a capacity we all possess; thus we all have the potential to become symbolic pilgrims. I wish you well on your journeys.

Postscript

My Mobile Home,
or How I Got Here

I've traveled quite a bit in my life, both literally and imaginatively. I've literally been to all 50 of the United States as well as four other nations. Along the way I've joined other pilgrims at Graceland, the USS *Arizona* memorial, Roslyn, Washington (where the exteriors of *Northern Exposure* were filmed). I've joined Cubs fans heading to Wrigley Field on the red line and tourists following Boston's freedom trail. I've imaginatively been to a number of fictional places through my immersion in popular stories. Along the way I've been inside the locker room of the major league baseball team called the Blue Sox (a series of teen-oriented books written by Duane Decker in the 1940s and 1950s), the idyllic worlds of Frank Capra's movies, and various towns all named Springfield. You could easily draw the conclusion that I enjoy escapism in a variety of forms. Yet displayed in my office are three framed photographs of Oregon Trail landmarks near my hometown of Scottsbluff, Nebr. Reprints of those photos also adorn a wall in my home; they keep company with pictures of family and friends with Nebraska roots.

When I left the state in 1989 to begin my career as a professor, I developed a new awareness of my dual position as both insider and outsider. I was materially dissociated from the Cornhusker state, the only "home" I had ever known. Yet symbolically I was still inside that home. As my aunt, a Colorado resident for as long as I've been alive, confided to me at a small family gathering following the 1995 Colorado-Nebraska football game, "There's something about this place that sticks with you." She's right. Her words echo the opening of the Nebraska fight song: "There is no place like Nebraska . . . " In Nebraska the horizon is clearly visible and the streets and roads are laid out in directional grids. No professional sports teams call the state home and only one major university, in Lincoln, fields major college athletic teams. My cognitive maps were thus not terribly complex as I grew up; after all, I only needed to know four directions and that fall Saturdays meant Husker football on the radio, on TV, and/or in person.

Since 1989, however, I have made my "home" in places where hills block views of the horizon, streets bend and turn (sometimes changing names, sometimes not), and loyalties to sports teams are divided. I tell friends that I sometimes feel culturally claustrophobic; those from the great plains nod their head in agreement, those not from that area of the country scratch their heads in confusion.

My symbolic home, then, is bound up with the physical home in which I grew up, the family that raised me, and the social affiliations to which I was, have been, and am connected. It is profoundly influenced by the experience of spending the first 27 years of my life as a resident of the state of Nebraska. I grew up in a physical home at 2023 Avenue E, but I consider Scottsbluff my hometown and Nebraska my home state. Watching a Nebraska football game on television activates many different images of home, and identities, for me—everything from watching the games in person (as a college student), to listening to the Saturday afternoon games on the radio as I bagged groceries at the local Jack & Jill supermarket (as a teen), to gathering around the television with my extended family each Friday after Thanksgiving to watch the game against the rival Oklahoma Sooners (as a child).

My home—both literally and symbolically—has shifted in the years since I have left Nebraska. My parents have changed the look of the house, the family pets are no longer living, the Jack & Jill has closed, the Oklahoma game is no longer traditionally held, the university I attended has undergone cosmetic and personnel changes. I like to think my home (in all senses of the word) possesses a fixed, rooted quality, yet I know it has changed. All of this is another way of saying that my original symbolic home of Nebraska finds itself in some ways in the places I have described in the previous chapters. My interest in writing about symbolic places, in fact, did not arise until after I left the Cornhusker state.

Disoriented both literally and symbolically, I began to reflect on the roots of my cultural confusion. The answer was simple: the place that I called home was, in some ways, no longer the place that I called home. I also knew that I had always loved watching television, going to the movies, and reading good stories. After my discussion with my friend Chris about the fishing story in *SI*, I realized that we can find alternative "places that matter" in a variety of ways. A few years later I grew more familiar with the concept of interpretive communities thanks to my work with Christina Beck. Between those two concepts emerged the belief that we find sacred places, or personal promised lands, in a number of places. So even though we move away from home, we keep coming back to it. As it changes so do we. But throughout our travels we know that the company we keep, and the places we find it, contribute to our sense of who we are. Perhaps that's why I vividly recall another cultural memory, a line in the Nebraska fight song that reminds me of the close-knit community found in the state as well as the harsh climate and flat land that prompted pioneers—as well as contemporary travelers—to make their way through the state as quickly as possible: "We'll all stick together and in all kinds of weather. . . . " There is no place like Nebraska. I'm now aware that I pack that romantic rhetorical fragment in my luggage every time my modernist self embarks on a postmodern symbolic pilgrimage. When I left home in 1989, I began to realize just how often I return home.

Note

An earlier version of this postscript appeared in "Symbolic Pilgrimages in Cultural Space: Reading Maps, Finding Home, and Staying a Spell" (paper presented at the 1996 conference of the Speech Communication Association, San Diego).

References

Adams, J. M. (1996, February 5). The man behind "Dilbert." *Chicago Tribune*, sec. 5, pp. 1, 5.

Adams, S. (1992). *Always postpone meetings with time-wasting morons.* Kansas City, MO: Andrews and McMeel.

Adams, S. (1994a). Newsletter #2. Archived at www.unitedmedia.com/comics/dilbert/

Adams, S. (1994b). Newsletter #3. Archived at www.unitedmedia.com/comics/dilbert/

Adams, S. (1994c). *Shave the whales.* Kansas City, MO: Andrews and McMeel.

Adams, S. (1995a). *It's obvious you won't survive by your wits alone.* Kansas City, MO: Andrews and McMeel.

Adams, S. (1995b). Newsletter #4. Archived at www.unitedmedia.com/comics/dilbert/

Adams, S. (1995c). Newsletter #5. Archived at www.unitedmedia.com/comics/dilbert/

Adams, S. (1995d). Newsletter #6. Archived at www.unitedmedia.com/comics/dilbert/

Adams, S. (1995e). Newsletter #8. Archived at www.unitedmedia.com/comics/dilbert/

Adams, S. (1995f). Newsletter #9. Archived at www.unitedmedia.com/comics/dilbert/

Adams, S. (1996a). *Fugitive from the cubicle police.* Kansas City, MO: Andrews and McMeel.

Adams, S. (1996b). Newsletter #10. Archived at www.unitedmedia.com/comics/dilbert/

Adams, S. (1996c). Newsletter #11. Archived at www.unitedmedia.com/comics/dilbert/

Adams, S. (1996d). Newsletter #13. Archived at www.unitedmedia.com/comics/dilbert/

Adams, S. (1996e). *Still pumped from using the mouse.* Kansas City, MO: Andrews and McMeel.

Adams, S. (1997a). Newsletter #14. Archived at www.unitedmedia.com/comics/dilbert/

Adams, S. (1997b). Newsletter #16. Archived at www.unitedmedia.com/comics/dilbert/

Adler, J. (1995, May 15). Bye-bye, suburban dream. *Newsweek*, 40–45.

Agnew, J., Livingstone, D. N., & Rogers, A. (Eds.). (1996). *Human geography: An essential anthology.* Cambridge, MA: Blackwell.

Ahponen, P. (1996). Cross the border, confront boundaries: Problems of habituality, maginality, and liminality. In F. Geyer (Ed.), *Alienation, ethnicity, and postmodernism* (pp. 171–180). Westport, CT: Greenwood Press.

Alegria, F. (1986). *The funhouse.* Houston: Arte Publico Press, University of Houston.

Anderson, B. (1991). *Imagined communities: Reflections on the origin and spread of nationalism* (Rev. ed.). London: Verso.

Anderson, K., & Gale, F. (1992). Introduction. In K. Anderson & F. Gale (Eds.), *Inventing places: Studies in cultural geography* (pp. 1–12). Melbourne: Longman Cheshire.

Ardolino, F. (1990). Ceremonies of innocence and experience in *Bull Durham, Field of Dreams,* and *Eight Men Out. Journal of Popular Film and Television, 18,* 43–51.

Astor, D. (1996, March 2). The biggest strips in big newspapers. *Editor & Publisher,* 36.

Bachen, C. M., & Illouz, E. (1996). Imagining romance: Young people's cultural models of romance and love. *Critical Studies in Mass Communication, 13,* 279–308.

Bacon-Smith, C. (1992). *Enterprising women: Television fandom and the creation of popular myth.* Philadelphia: University of Pennsylvania Press.

Badley, L. (1996). The rebirth of the clinic: The body as alien in *The X-Files.* In D. Lavery, A. Hague, & M. Cartwright (Eds.), *"Deny all knowledge": Reading* The X-Files (pp. 148–167). Syracuse, NY: Syracuse University Press.

Barber, B. R. (1995). *Jihad vs. McWorld.* New York: Random House.

Barth, J. (1968). Lost in the funhouse. In J. Barth, *Lost in the funhouse: Fiction for print, tape, live voice* (pp. 72–97). Garden City, NY: Doubleday. Story orig. pub. in *The Atlantic Monthly,* 1967.

Baudrillard, J. (1988). The system of objects. In M. Poster (Ed.), *Jean Baudrillard: Selected writings* (pp. 29–56). Stanford, CA: Stanford University Press. (Original work published 1970)

Baudrillard, J. (1988). For a critique of the political economy of the sign. In M. Poster (Ed.), *Jean Baudrillard: Selected writings* (pp. 57–97). Stanford, CA: Stanford University Press. (Original work published 1973)

Beardslee, W. A. (1990). Stories in the postmodern world: Orienting and disorienting. In D. R. Griffin (Ed.), *Sacred interconnections: Postmodern spirituality, political economy, and art.* Albany, NY: SUNY Press.

Beauvais, P. J. (1990). Native Son in prison: Rhetorical performance as restored behavior. *Text and Performance Quarterly, 10,* 306–315.

Beck, C. S. (1997). *Partnership for health: Relational communication issues implicit to quality women's health care.* Hillsdale, NJ: Lawrence Erlbaum Associates. With S. L. Ragan & A. duPre.

Bell, D. (1973). *The coming of post-industrial society: A venture in social forecasting.* New York: Basic Books.

Bell, D. (1979). *The cultural contradictions of capitalism.* London: Heinemann.

Bell, D. (1996). Afterword: 1996. In D. Bell, *The cultural contradictions of capitalism: Twentieth anniversary edition* (pp. 283–339). New York: Basic Books.

Bellah, R. N., Madsen, R., Sullivan, W. M., Swidler, A., & Tipton, S. M. (1985). *Habits of the heart: Individualism and commitment in American life.* New York: Harper & Row.

Belsey, C. (1980). *Critical practice.* New York: Methuen.

Belton, B. (1997, August 29). Downsizing leaves legacy of insecurity. *USA Today,* pp. 1B–2B.

Bennett, L. (1990). *Fragments of cities: The new American downtowns and neighborhoods.* Columbus, OH: Ohio State University Press.

Bennett, T., & Woollacott, J. (1987). *Bond and beyond: The political career of a popular hero.* New York: Methuen.

Bentham, J. (1995). *The panopticon writings.* Ed. & Intro. M. Bozovic. London: Verso. (Original work published 1787)

Berg, L. D. (1993). Between modernism and postmodernism. *Progress in Human Geography, 17,* 490–507.

Berger, J. (1972). *Ways of seeing the world.* Harmondsworth: Penguin.

Bernstein, A. (1995, July 17). The wage squeeze. *Business Week,* 54–62.

Bernstein, R. (1994). *Dictatorship of virtue: Multiculturalism and the battle for America's future.* New York: Knopf.

Berry, P. (1992). Introduction. In P. Berry & A. Wernick (Eds.), *Shadow of spirit: Postmodernism and religion* (pp. 1–8). London: Routledge.

Best, S., & Kellner, D. (1991). *Postmodern theory: Critical interrogations.* New York: Guilford.

Bettelheim, B. (1977). *The uses of enchantment: The meaning and importance of fairy tales.* New York: Vintage.

Biller, K., & Brancato, C. (1993, December 10). Eve (F. Gerber, Director). In C. Carter (Producer), *The X-Files.* Hollywood: Twentieth Century Fox Film Corporation.

Blundo, J. (1994, July 3). In with the old. *The Columbus (OH) Dispatch,* pp. 1J–2J.

Bondi, L. (1993). Locating identity politics. In M. Keith & S. Pile (Eds.), *Place and the politics of identity* (pp. 84–101). London: Routledge.

Bondi, L., & Domosh, M. (1992). Other figures in other places: On feminism, postmodernism and geography. *Environment and Planning D: Society and Space, 10,* 199–213.

Boorstin, D. J. (1978). *The republic of technology: Reflections on our future community.* New York: Harper & Row.

Bormann, E. G. (1985). *The force of fantasy: Restoring the American dream.* Carbondale: Southern Illinois University Press.

Bottomley, G. (1992). *From another place: Migration and the politics of culture.* Cambridge, UK: Cambridge University Press.

Bourdieu, P. (1977). *Outline of a theory of practice.* (R. Nice, Trans.). Cambridge, UK: Cambridge University Press. (Original work published 1972)

Bourdieu, P. (1990). *The logic of practice.* (R. Nice, Trans.). Stanford, CA: Stanford University Press. (Original work published 1980)

Bozovic, M. (1995). Introduction. In J. Bentham, *The panopticon writings* (pp. 1–27). London: Verso.

Bragg, R. (1996, March 5). More than money, they miss the pride a good job brought. *New York Times,* pp. A17–A18.

Braidotti, R. (1994). *Nomadic subjects: Embodiment and sexual difference in contemporary feminist theory.* New York: Columbia University Press.

Brereton, J. P. (1987). Sacred space. In M. Eliade (Ed.), *The encyclopedia of religion* (Vol. 12, pp. 526–535). New York: Macmillan.

Broder, D. S. (1996, February 15). Candidates must address voters' top worry: jobs. *The Columbus (OH) Dispatch,* p. 11A.

Brown, T. (1995, July 3). Decoding the "clueless" manager. *Industry Week,* 14–18.

Brown, T. (1997, March). What does Dilbert mean to HR? *Human Resources Forum,* 3.

Brummett, B. (1984). The representative anecdote as a Burkean method, applied to evangelical rhetoric. *Southern Speech Communication Journal, 50,* 1–23.

Brummett, B. (1988). The homology hypothesis: Pornography on the VCR. *Critical Studies in Mass Communication, 5,* 202–216.

Brummett, B. (1991). *Rhetorical dimensions of popular culture.* Tuscaloosa: University of Alabama Press.

Brummett, B., & Duncan, M. C. (1992). Toward a discursive ontology of media. *Critical Studies in Mass Communication, 9,* 229–249.

Burke, J. L. (1987). *The neon rain.* New York: Pocket Books.

Burke, K. (1937). *Attitudes toward history.* New York: The New Republic Press.

Burke, K. (1941). *The philosophy of literary form: Studies in symbolic action.* Baton Rouge, LA: Louisiana State University Press.

Burke, K. (1965). *Permanence and change.* Indianapolis: Bobbs-Merrill.

Burke, K. (1966). *Language as symbolic action.* Berkeley: University of California Press.

Burke, K. (1969a). *A grammar of motives.* Berkeley: University of California Press.

Burke, K. (1969b). *A rhetoric of motives.* Berkeley: University of California Press.

Buttimer, A. (1980). Home, reach, and the sense of place. In A. Buttimer & D. Seamon (Eds.), *The human experience of space and place* (pp. 166–187). New York: St. Martin's.

Calhoun, C. (1995). *Critical social theory: Culture, history, and the challenge of difference.* Oxford, UK: Blackwell.

Calhoun, D. W. (1987). *Sport, culture, and personality* (2nd ed). Champaign, IL: Human Kinetics Publishers.

Campbell, R. (1987). Securing the middle ground: Reporter formulas in 60 Minutes. *Critical Studies in Mass Communication, 4,* 325–350.

Capo, K. E., & Hantzis, D. M. (1991). (En)gendered (and endangered) subjects: Writing, reading, performing, and theorizing feminist criticism. *Text and Performance Quarterly, 11,* 249–266.

Carey, J. W. (1975). A cultural approach to communication. *Communication, 2,* 1–22.

Carr, D. (1986). *Time, narrative, and history.* Bloomington, IN: Indiana University Press.

Carragee, K. M. (1990). Interpretive media study and interpretive social science. *Critical Studies in Mass Communication, 7,* 81–96.

Carter, C. (1993a, September 10). Pilot (R. Mandel, Director). In C. Carter (Producer), *The X-Files.* Hollywood: Twentieth Century Fox Film Corporation.

Carter, C. (1993b, September 17). Deep throat (D. Sackheim, Director). In C. Carter (Producer), *The X-Files.* Hollywood: Twentieth Century Fox Film Corporation.

Carter, C. (1994, September 23). The host (D. Sackheim, Director). In C. Carter (Producer), *The X-Files.* Hollywood: Twentieth Century Fox Film Corporation.

Carter, C. (1997, November 30). Post-modern Prometheus (J. Ransom, Director). In C. Carter (Producer), *The X-Files.* Hollywood: Twentieth Century Fox Film Corporation.

Castro, J. (1993, March 29). Disposable workers. *Time,* pp. 43–47.

Catch the excitement (1997). http://www.interlace.com/dreamfield/catch.html

Cawelti, J. G. (1971). *The six-gun mystique.* Bowling Green, OH: Bowling Green University Popular Press.

Chambers, I. (1990). *Border dialogues: Journeys in postmodernity.* London: Routledge.

Chambers, I. (1994). *Migrancy, culture, identity.* London: Routledge.

Chesebro, J. W. (1989). Text, narration, and media. *Text and Performance Quarterly, 9,* 1–23.

Clarke, J. (1976). The skinheads and the magical recovery of community. In S. Hall & T. Jefferson (Eds.), *Resistance through rituals: Youth subcultures in post-war Britain* (pp. 99–105). London: Hutchinson & Company.

Clerc, S. J. (1996). DDEB, GATB, MPPB, and Ratboy: *The X-Files'* media fandom, online and off. In D. Lavery, A. Hague, & M. Cartwright (Eds.), *"Deny all knowledge": Reading* The X-Files (pp. 36–51). Syracuse, NY: Syracuse University Press.

Clifford, J. (1992). Traveling cultures. In L. Grossberg, C. Nelson, & P. A. Treichler (Eds.), *Cultural studies* (pp. 96–116). New York: Routledge.

Cohen, A. P. (1985). *The symbolic construction of community.* London: Routledge.

Cohen, S. S., & Zysman, J. (1987). *Manufacturing matters: The myth of the post-industrial economy*. New York: Basic Books.

Conquergood, D. (1992). Life in Big Red: Struggles and accommodations in a Chicago polyethnic tenement. In L. Lamphere (Ed.), *Structuring diversity: Ethnographic perspectives on the new immigration* (pp. 95–144). Chicago: University of Chicago Press.

Conquergood, D. (1994). Homeboys and hoods: Gang communication and cultural space. In L. R. Frey (Ed.), *Group communication in context: Studies of natural groups* (pp. 23–55). Hillsdale, NJ: Lawrence Erlbaum Associates.

Corn, J. J. (1986a). Epilogue. In J. J. Corn (Ed.), *Imagining tomorrow: History, technology, and the American future* (pp. 219–229). Cambridge, MA: MIT Press.

Corn, J. J. (1986b). Introduction. In J. J. Corn (Ed.), *Imagining tomorrow: History, technology, and the American future* (pp. 1–9). Cambridge, MA: MIT Press.

Coontz, S. (1992). *The way we never were: American families and the nostalgia trap*. New York: Basic Books, 1992.

Cranston, M. (1994). *The romantic movement*. Oxford, UK: Blackwell.

Crawford, J. C. (1995, May). Letters. *Movieline*, 6.

Crescenti, T. (Producer). (1994). *Dreamfield* [Film]. (Available from Crescenti Moon Productions, Valencia, CA, or Field of Dreams Movie Site, 28963 Lansing Road, Dyersville, IA 52040)

Csikszentmihalyi, M. (1975). Play and intrinsic rewards. *Journal of Humanistic Psychology, 15*(3), 41–63.

Csikszentmihalyi, M. (1987). Flow experience. In M. Eliade (Ed.), *The encyclopedia of religion* (Vol. 5, pp. 361–363). New York: Macmillan.

Csikszentmihalyi, M. (1990). *Flow: The psychology of optimal experience*. New York: Harper & Row.

Daddario, G. (1992). Swimming against the tide: *Sports Illustrated*'s imagery of female athletes in a swimsuit world. *Women's Studies in Communication, 15*, 49–64.

Daughton, S. M. (1996). The spiritual power of repetitive form: Steps toward transcendence in *Groundhog Day*. *Critical Studies in Mass Communication, 13*, 138–154.

Davis, E. (1993, October 26). Earth's most wanted. *The Village Voice*, 49–50.

Davis, F. (1979). *Yearning for yesterday: A sociology of nostalgia*. New York: Free Press.

Davis, L. R. (1997). *The swimsuit issue and sport: Hegemonic masculinity in Sports Illustrated*. Albany, NY: State University of New York Press.

de Certeau, M. (1984). *The practice of everyday life*. (S. F. Rendall, Trans.). Berkeley: University of California Press.

Deleuze, G., & Guattari, F. (1986). *Nomadology: The war machine*. (B. Massumi, Trans.). New York: Semiotext(e).

Dentzer, S. (1991, April 22). The vanishing dream. *U.S. News and World Report*, 39–43.

Denzin, N. K. (1993). Rain Man in Las Vegas: Where is the action for the postmodern self? *Symbolic Interaction, 16*, 65–77.

Denzin, N. K. (1997). *Interpretive enthnography: Ethnographic practices for the 21st century.* Thousand Oaks, CA: Sage.

Dibbell, J. (1996). A rape in cyberspace: How an evil clown, a Haitian trickster spirit, two wizards, and a cast of dozens turned a database into a society. In M. Stefik (Ed.), *Internet dreams: Archetypes, myths, and metaphors* (pp. 293–313). Cambridge, MA: MIT Press.

Dickinson, G. (1997). Memories for sale: Nostalgia and the construction of identity in Old Pasadena. *Quarterly Journal of Speech, 83,* 1–27.

Donahue, D. (1996a, October 15). Genesis gives seekers a source of spirituality. *USA Today,* pp. 1A–2A.

Donahue, D. (1996b, December 12). Has Oprah saved books? *USA Today,* pp. 1D–2D.

Donovan, M., & Nelson, M. (1989, October 23). For *Field of Dreams* fans who trek to Don Lansing's Iowa farm, the diamond is forever. *People,* 120–121.

Downs, R. M., & Stea, D. (1977). *Maps in mind: Reflections on cognitive mapping.* NY: Harper & Row.

Duncan, J., & Ley, D. (1993). Introduction: Representing the place of culture. In J. Duncan & D. Ley (Eds.), *Place/culture/representation* (pp. 1–21). London: Routledge.

Dvorchak, R. (1994, October 16). Virgin Mary "seen" all around nation. *The Columbus (OH) Dispatch,* p. 3A.

Eberle, G. (1994). *The geography of nowhere: Finding one's self in the postmodern world.* Kansas City, MO: Sheed and Ward.

Edgerton, S. H. (1996). *Translating the curriculum: Multiculturalism into cultural studies.* New York: Routledge.

Ehrenreich, B. (1989). *Fear of falling: The inner life of the middle class.* New York: Harper Perennial.

Eliade, M. (1959). *The sacred and the profane: The nature of religion.* (W. R. Trask, Trans.). New York: Harcourt, Brace and Company. (Original work published 1957)

Eliade, M., & Sullivan, L. E. (1987). Center of the world. In M. Eliade (Ed.), *The encyclopedia of religion* (Vol. 3, pp. 166–171). New York: Macmillan.

Ellicott, S. (1993, November 29). Blue jean dreams. *The New Republic,* 13–14.

Episode ratings, viewer reviews (1997). http://www.amaroq.com/x-files/

Erickson, J. L. (1987, July 13). Foes try hard, but "SI" still laps the field. *Advertising Age,* S20, S22–S23.

Estes, C. P. (1992). *Women who run with the wolves: Myths and stories of the wild woman archetype.* New York: Ballantine.

Faivre, A. (1987). Esotericism. (K. Anderson, Trans.). In M. Eliade (Ed.), *The encyclopedia of religion* (Vol. 5, pp. 156–163). New York: Macmillan.

Feagler, D. (1997, April 27). The stuff of tragedy. *The (Athens, OH) Messenger,* p. A9.

Featherstone, M. (1995). *Undoing culture: Globalization, postmodernism and identity.* London: Sage.

Feyerabend, P. (1978). *Against method: Outline of an anarchistic theory of knowledge.* London: Verso.

Fish, S. (1980). *Is there a text in this class?.* Cambridge, MA: Harvard University Press.

Fisher, W. R. (1973). Reaffirmation and subversion of the American dream. *Quarterly Journal of Speech, 59,* 160–167.

Fiske, J. (1986). Television: Polysemy and popularity. *Critical Studies in Mass Communication, 3,* 391–408.

Fiske, J. (1987). *Television culture.* London: Methuen.

Fiske, J. (1989). *Understanding popular culture.* Boston: Unwin Hyman.

Fitzpatrick, E. (1996, March 23). 20th century Fox finds "X-Files" fans worldwide. *Billboard, 68,* 73.

Flores, L. A. (1996). Creating discursive space through a rhetoric of difference: Chicana feminists craft a homeland. *Quarterly Journal of Speech, 82,* 142–156.

Frankenberg, R. (1996). "When we are capable of stopping, we begin to see." Being white, seeing whiteness. In B. Thompson & S. Tyagi (Eds.), *Names we call home: Autobiography on racial identity* (pp. 3–17). London: Routledge.

Foss, S. K., & Foss, K. A. (1994). The construction of feminine spectatorship in Garrison Keillor's radio monologues. *Quarterly Journal of Speech, 80,* 410–426.

Foucault, M. (1995). *Discipline and punish: The birth of the prison.* (A. Sheridan, Trans.). New York: Vintage Books. (Original work published 1977)

Fox, M. (1994). *The reinvention of work: A new vision of livelihood for our time.* San Francisco: HarperSanFrancisco.

Funhouse mirror. (1990, January 10). *Progressive,* 10.

Fusco, C. (1997, March 17). General discussion index. Found at http://bbs2.iguide.com:80891/x-files/general/msg_index.html

Garcia, J. (1997, March 16). Auto insight. *The Columbus (OH) Dispatch,* p. 2H. (Reprinted from *Ventura County (CA) Star*)

Garner, R. (1994, May 2). Dilbert. *Computerworld,* 98, 101.

Garrett, M. M. (1993). Wit, power, and oppositional groups: A case study of "pure talk." *Quarterly Journal of Speech, 79,* 303–318.

Geertz, C. (1972). Deep play: Notes on the Balinese cockfight. *Daedalus,* 101, 1–37.

Gergen, K. J. (1991). *The saturated self: Dilemmas of identity in contemporary life.* New York: Basic Books.

Gibbs, N. (1993, December 27). Angels among us. *Time,* 56–65.

Gill, S. (1987). *Native American religious action: A performance approach to religion.* Columbia, SC: University of South Carolina Press.

Gilligan, V. (1996a, February 23). Pusher (R. Bowman, Director). In C. Carter (Producer), *The X-Files.* Hollywood: Twentieth Century Fox Film Corporation.

Gilligan, V. (1996b, December 15). Paper hearts (R. Bowman, Director). In C. Carter (Producer), *The X-Files.* Hollywood: Twentieth Century Fox Film Corporation.

Gilligan, V., Shiban, J., & Spotnitz, F. (1997, January 26). Leonard Betts (K. Manners, Director). In C. Carter (Producer), *The X-Files.* Hollywood: Twentieth Century Fox Film Corporation.

Glick, P. C. (1993). The impact of geographic mobility on individuals and families. *Marriage & Family Review, 19*, 31–54.

Gober, P. (1993). Americans on the move. *Population Bulletin, 48*(3), 2–40.

Godkin, M. A. (1980). Identity and place: Clinical applications based on notions of rootedness and uprootedness. In A. Buttimer & D. Seamon (Eds.), *The human experience of space and place* (pp. 73–85). New York: St. Martin's.

Gold, J. R., & Gold, M. M. (1990). "A place of delightful prospects": Promotional imagery and the selling of suburbia. In L. Zonn (Ed.), *Place images in media: Portrayal, experience, and meaning* (pp. 159–182). Savage, MD: Rowman and Littlefield.

Goldscheider, F. K., & Waite, L. J. (1991). *New families, no families? The transformation of the American home.* Berkeley: University of California Press.

Golledge, R. G., & Stimson, R. J. (1997). *Spatial behavior: A geographic perspective.* New York: Guilford.

Goodall, H. L., Jr. (1996). *Divine signs: Connecting spirit to community.* Carbondale: Southern Illinois University Press.

Gordon, H. (1997, February 16). Kaddish (K. Manners, Director). In C. Carter (Producer), *The X-Files.* Hollywood: Twentieth Century Fox Film Corporation.

Gozzi, R., Jr., & Haynes, W. L. (1992). Electric media and electric epistemology: Empathy at a distance. *Critical Studies in Mass Communication, 9*, 217–228.

Graham scholarship fund (1997). http://www.cardmall.com/moonlight-graham/

Gramsci, A. (1971). *Selections from the prison notebooks of Antonio Gramsci.* (Q. Hoare & G. N. Smith, Eds. and Trans.). New York: International Publishers.

Gray, J. (1992). *Men are from Mars, women are from Venus.* New York: HarperCollins.

Greenburg, R. (Executive Producer). (1992). *When it was a game: Part II* [Film]. Los Angeles: Black Canyon Productions.

Gregory, D. (1994). *Geographical imaginations.* Cambridge, MA: Blackwell.

Grella, G. (1975). Baseball and the American dream. *Massachusetts Review, 16*, 550–567.

Griffin, D. R. (1990). Introduction: Sacred interconnections. In D. R. Griffin (Ed.), *Sacred interconnections: Postmodern spirituality, political economy, and art* (pp. 1–13). Albany, NY: SUNY Press.

Griffin, D. R. (1993). Introduction: Constructive postmodern philosophy. In D. R. Griffin, J. B. Cobb, Jr., M. P. Ford, P. A. Y. Gunter, & P. Ochs, *Founders of constructive postmodern philosophy* (pp. 1–42). Albany: State University of New York Press.

Grodin, D. (1991). The interpreting audience: The therapeutics of self-help book reading. *Critical Studies in Mass Communication, 8*, 404–420.

Grossberg, L. (1992). Is there a fan in the house?: The affective sensibility of fandom. In L. A. Lewis (Ed.), *The adoring audience: Fan culture and popular media* (pp. 50–65). London: Routledge.

Grossberg, L. (1993). Cultural studies and/in new worlds. *Critical Studies in Mass Communication, 10,* 1–22.

Gumpert, G., & Drucker, S. J. (1992). From the agora to the electronic shopping mall. *Critical Studies in Mass Communication, 9,* 186–200.

Gumpert, G., & Drucker, S. J. (1995). Place as medium: Exegesis of the cafe—drinking coffee, the art of watching others, civil conversation—with excursions into the effects of architecture and interior design. *The Speech Communication Annual, 9,* 7–32.

Gumpert, G., & Fish, S. L. (1990). Introduction. In G. Gumpert & S. L. Fish (Eds.), *Talking to strangers: Mediated therapeutic communication* (pp. 1–9). Norwood, NJ: Ablex.

Gunkel, D. J., & Gunkel, A. H. (1997). Virtual geographies: The new worlds of cyberspace. *Critical Studies in Mass Communication, 14,* 123–137.

Hage, J., & Powers, C. H. (1992). *Post-industrial lives: Roles and relationships in the 21st century.* Newbury Park, CA: Sage.

Hall, S. (1989). The meaning of new times. In S. Hall & M. Jacques (Eds.), *New times: The changing face of politics in the 1990s* (pp. 116–134). London: Lawrence & Wishart.

Hamera, J. (1990). On reading, writing, and speaking the politics of (self-)representation. *Text and Performance Quarterly, 10,* 235–247.

Hamilton, D. (1996, March 25). Office funnies. *Los Angeles Times,* sec. SS, pp. 7–8.

Handy, C. (1994). *The age of paradox.* Boston: Harvard Business School Press.

Haraway, D. (1988). Situated knowledges: The science question in feminism and the privilege of partial perspective. *Feminist Studies, 14,* 575–599.

Haraway, D. (1991). *Simians, cyborgs, and women: The reinvention of nature.* New York: Routledge.

Harrop, F. (1997, October 26). Sport utility vehicles are abominations. *The Columbus (OH) Dispatch,* p. 3B.

Harrington, C. L., & Bielby, D. D. (1995). *Soap fans: Pursuing pleasure and making meaning in everyday life.* Philadelphia: Temple University Press.

Harvey, D. (1990). Between space and time: Reflections on the geographical imagination. *Annals of the Association of American Geographers, 80,* 418–434.

Hayes-Bautista, D. E., & Rodriguez, G. (1994, April 11). Technobanda. *The New Republic,* 10–11.

Hiss, T. (1990). *The experience of place.* New York: Knopf.

hooks, b. (1990). *Yearning: Race, gender, and cultural politics.* Boston: South End Press.

Hoover, F. (1997, February 1). 20 years later, "Star Wars" still a stellar hit. *The Columbus (OH) Dispatch,* pp. 1A–2A.

Hopper, D. H. (1991). *Technology, theology, and the idea of progress.* Louisville, KY: Westminster/John Knox Press.

Houston, J. M. (1978). The concepts of "place" and "land" in the Judaeo-Christian tradition. In D. Ley & M. S. Samuels (Eds.), *Humanistic geography: Prospects and problems* (pp. 224–237). Chicago: Maaroufa Press.

Hughes, R. (1993). *Culture of complaint: The fraying of America.* New York: Warner Books.

Huizinga, J. (1970). *Homo ludens: A study of the play element in culture.* NY: Harper & Row. (Original work published 1938)

Hulbert, A. (1994, June 6). Animal dreams. *The New Republic,* 42.

Hutcheon, L. (1994). *Irony's edge: The theory and politics of irony.* London: Routledge.

In search of the sacred. (1994, November 28). *Newsweek,* 52–55.

Ingrassia, M. (1989, June 5). Field of dreams or pile of mush?" *Newsday,* [Newsbank 1989 FTV 62:D14–D15].

Isackson, A. (1996, October 10). Got a theory? *USA Today,* p. 11A. The Macarena Files website is located at: http://www.users.why.net/banzai769/macasplash.html

Jackson, M. (1995). *At home in the world.* Durham, NC: Duke University Press.

Jackson, P. (1989). *Maps of meaning: An introduction to cultural geography.* London: Unwin Hyman.

Jameson, F. (1984). Postmodernism, or the cultural logic of late capitalism. *New Left Review, 146,* 53–92.

Jardine, A. (1985). *Gynesis: Configurations of woman and modernity.* Ithaca, NY: Cornell University Press.

Jarvis, J. (1994, February 26). The couch critic. *TV Guide,* 8.

Jeffries, J. (1992). Toward a redefinition of the urban: The collision of culture. In G. Dent (Ed.), *Black popular culture* (pp. 153–163). Seattle: Bay Press.

Jenkins, H., III. (1988). Star Trek rerun, reread, rewritten: Fan writing as textual poaching. *Critical Studies in Mass Communication, 5,* 85–107.

Job loyalty takes a beating. (1996, February 11). *The Columbus (OH) Dispatch,* p. 4B.

Johnson, J. R., Bernhagen, M. J., Miller, V., & Allen, M. (1996). The role of communication in managing reductions in work force. *Journal of Applied Communication Research, 24,* 139–164.

Johnstone, B. (1990). *Stories, community, and place: Narratives from middle America.* Bloomington: Indiana University Press.

Jones, D. (1996, February 19). Managers study up for downsizings. *USA Today,* pp. 1B–2B.

Jones, D. (1997, April 8). Wal-Mart tops GM as largest U.S. employer. *USA Today,* p. 1A.

Jost, K. (1993). Downward mobility. *CQ Researcher, 3,* pp. 627–640+.

Judis, J. B. (1994, February 14). Why your wages keep falling. *The New Republic,* 26–29.

Justice, E. (1996, August 23). We all love X. But why? *New Statesman,* 26.

Kane, P. (1996, August 23). There's method in the magic. *New Statesman,* 24–27.

Kantrowitz, B., & Rogers, A. (1994, December 5). "The truth is X-ed out there." *Newsweek,* 66.

Kaplan, M. (1996, January 20). Invasion of the X-philes. *TV Guide,* 32–34.

Katriel, T., & Farrell, T. (1991). Scrapbooks as cultural texts: An American art of memory. *Text and Performance Quarterly, 11,* 1–17.

Katriel, T., & Philipsen, G. (1990). "What we need is communication": "Communication" as a cultural category in some American speech. In D. Carbaugh (Ed.), *Cultural communication and intercultural contact* (pp. 77–93). Hillsdale, NJ: Lawrence Erlbaum Associates.

Kaufman, J. (1997, March 29). Tuning in to God. *TV Guide*, 33–35.

Kaus, M. (1992). *The end of equality.* New York: Basic Books.

Keith, M., & Pile, S. (1993). Introduction part 1: The politics of place. In M. Keith & S. Pile (Eds.), *Place and the politics of identity* (pp. 1–21). London: Routledge.

Kellner, D. (1982). Television, mythology and ritual. *Praxis, 6,* 133–155.

Kellner, D. (1995). *Media culture: Cultural studies, identity and politics between the modern and the postmodern.* London: Routledge.

Kluback, W., & Wilde, J. T. (1958). Introduction: An ontological consideration of place. In M. Heidegger, *The question of being* (pp. 18–26). (W. Kluback & J. T. Wilde, Trans.). New York: Twayne Publishers.

Knight, J. P. (1990). Literature as equipment for killing: Performance as rhetoric in military training camps. *Text and Performance Quarterly, 10,* 157–168.

Knopp, L. (1997, Fall). The essential geography. *Nebraska Magazine,* 24–29.

Knox, P. L. (1993). Capital, material culture and socio-spatial differentiation. In P. L. Knox (Ed.), *The restless urban landscape* (pp. 1–34). Englewood Cliffs, NJ: Prentice-Hall.

Krippendorff, K. (1995). Undoing power. *Critical Studies in Mass Communication, 12,* 101–132.

Kroeber, K. (1988). *Romantic fantasy and science fiction.* New Haven: Yale University Press.

Krymkowski, D. H., & Krauze, T. K. (1992). Occupational mobility in the year 2000: Projections for American men and women. *Social Forces, 71,* 145–157.

Kubek, E. (1996). "You only expose your father": The imaginary, voyeurism, and the symbolic order in *The X-Files.* In D. Lavery, A. Hague, & M. Cartwright (Eds.), *"Deny all knowledge": Reading* The X-Files (pp. 168–204). Syracuse, NY: Syracuse University Press.

Kunstler, J. H. (1993). *The geography of nowhere: The rise and decline of America's man-made landscape.* New York: Simon & Schuster.

Kunstler, J. H. (1996). *Home from nowhere: Remarking our everyday world for the twenty-first century.* New York: Simon & Schuster.

Lansing, D., & Lansing, B. (fodfod@theonramp.net). (1997, May 11). No subject. E-mail to the author.

Larner, W. (1995). Theorising "difference" in Aotearoa/New Zealand. *Gender, Place and Culture, 2,* 177–190.

Lasswell, M., & Weiner, E. (1997, March 29). Getting religion. *TV Guide,* 28–32.

Lawlor, J. (1994, April 21). More firms offer services for employees. *USA Today,* pp. 1B–2B.

Lears, J. (1998, Dec/Jan). Looking backward: In defense of nostalgia. *Lingua Franca,* 59–66.

Lears, T. J. J. (1983). From salvation to self-realization: Advertising and the therapeutic roots of the consumer culture, 1880–1930. In R. W. Fox & T. J. J. Lears (Eds.), *The culture of consumption: Critical essays in American history, 1880–1980* (pp. 3–38). New York: Pantheon.

Left and center field of dreams (1997). http://www.mebbs.com/cgiwin/viewbook.exe?dreams

Left and center field of dreams catalog (1997). http://www.mebbs.com/dreams/fodcat.html

Leonhardt, D. (1996, May 27). Corporate America's pet gadfly. *Business Week*, 46.

Levy, S. (1996, August 12). Working in Dilbert's world. *Newsweek*, 52–57.

Ley, D. (1989). Modernism, post-modernism and the struggle for place. In J. A. Agnew & J. S. Duncan (Eds.), *The power of place: Bringing together geographical and sociological imaginations* (pp. 44–65). Boston: Unwin Hyman.

Ley, D., & Duncan, J. (1993). Epilogue. In J. Duncan & D. Ley (Eds.), *Place/culture/representation* (pp. 329–334). London: Routledge.

Ley, D., & Samuels, M. S. (1978). Introduction: Contexts of modern humanism in geography. In D. Ley & M. S. Samuels (Eds.), *Humanistic geography: Prospects and problems* (pp. 1–17). Chicago: Maaroufa Press.

Lippard, L. R. (1997). *The lure of the local: Senses of place in a multicentered society*. New York: The New Press.

Lipsitz, G. (1990). *Time passages: Collective memory and American popular culture*. Minneapolis: University of Minnesota Press.

Lipsky, D. (1997, February 20). Chris Carter in the virtue of paranoia: The "Rolling Stone" interview. *Rolling Stone*, 35+.

Living on Dracula time. (1993, July 12). *Newsweek*, 68–69.

Lohr, S. (1996, March 17). Downsizing: How it feels to be fired. *New York Times*, sec. 4, p. 5.

Lois and Clark fanfiction (1997). http://www.win.net/~lcw/fanfic/

Loukides, P., & Fuller, L. K. (1990). *Beyond the stars: Locales in American popular film*. Bowling Green, OH: Bowling Green State University Popular Press.

Lowenthal, D. (1961). Geography, experience, and imagination: Towards a geographical epistemology. *Annals of the Association of American Geographers, 51*, 241–260.

Lowenthal, D. (1975). Past time, present place: Landscape and memory. *The Geographical Review, 55*, 1–36.

Lutwack, L. (1984). *The role of place in literature*. Syracuse: Syracuse University Press.

Lynch, K. (1960). *The image of the city*. Cambridge, MA: MIT Press.

Lyotard, J. F. (1993). *The postmodern explained: Correspondence 1982–1985*. (D. Barry, B. Maher, J. Pefanis, V. Spate, & M. Thomas, Trans.). Minneapolis: University of Minnesota Press. (Original work published 1988)

Manning, A. (1996, December 27). Found: A gene that controls place memory. *USA Today*, p. 1D.

Marin, R. (1996, July 8). Alien invasion. *Newsweek*, 48–54.

Markham, W. T. (1987). Sex, relocation, and occupational advancement: The "real cruncher" for women. *Women and Work, 2*, 207–231.

Marx, K. (1906). *Capital: A critique of political economy.* (S. Moore & E. Aveling, Trans.). New York: The Modern Library. (Original work published 1867)

Marx, L. (1964). *The machine in the garden: Technology and the pastoral ideal in America.* New York: Oxford University Press.

Maryles, D. (1996, September 2). Dilbert rules. *Publisher's Weekly,* 18.

Massey, D. (1994). *Space, place, and gender.* Minneapolis: University of Minnesota Press.

McCormick, P. (1987). Real fictions. *The Journal of Aesthetics and Art Criticism, 46,* 259–270.

McGee, M. C. (1990). Text, context, and the fragmentation of contemporary culture. *Western Journal of Speech Communication, 54,* 274–289.

McGovern, A. F. (1989). *Liberation theology and its critics: Toward an assessment.* Maryknoll, NY: Orbis.

McKerrow, R. (1989). Critical rhetoric: Theory and praxis. *Communication Monographs, 56,* 91–110.

McManus, D. (1995, March). Angels: Their importance in our lives. *Catholic World,* 68–73.

McPhail, M. L. (1996). *Zen in the art of rhetoric: An inquiry into coherence.* Albany: State University of New York Press.

Mead, G. H. (1934). *Mind, self, and society.* Chicago: University of Chicago Press.

Melbin, M. (1984). Issues in using 24 hours of the day. *Research in Social Problems and Public Policy, 3,* 151–168.

Melvin, G. V. (1997, March 16). Younger and younger kids feel pressure for academic success. *The Columbus (OH) Dispatch,* p. 3H.

Meyrowitz, J. (1985). *No sense of place: The impact of electronic media on social behavior.* New York: Oxford University Press.

Middleton, D., & Edwards, D. (1990). Introduction. In D. Middleton & D. Edwards (Eds.), *Collective remembering* (pp. 1–22). London: Sage.

Miles, J. (1997, March 29). Prime time's search for God. *TV Guide,* 25–26.

Mills, C. (1993). Myths and meanings of gentrification. In J. Duncan & D. Ley (Eds.), *Place/culture/representation* (pp. 149–170). London: Routledge.

Mills, W. J. (1982). Metaphorical vision: Changes in western attitudes to the environment. *Annals of the Association of American Geographers, 72,* 237–253.

Mishel, L. (1995, Fall). Rising tides, sinking wages. *The American Prospect,* 60–64.

Modoono, B. (1990, July 29). Heaven on earth. *Pittsburgh Press,* [Newsbank FTV 98:C1–C2].

Momaday, N. S. (1997). *The man made of words: Essays, stories, passages.* New York: St. Martin's.

Montague, B. (1996, February 19). Restructuring, and layoffs, here to stay. *USA Today,* pp. 1A–2A.

Montgomery, S. L. (1996). *The scientific voice.* New York: Guilford.

Morgan, D. (1995, March 31). Humbug (K. Manners, Director). In C. Carter

(Producer), *The X-Files.* Hollywood: Twentieth Century Fox Film Corporation.

Morgan, D. (1996, April 12). Jose Chung's "From Outer Space" (R. Bowman, Director). In C. Carter (Producer), *The X-Files.* Hollywood: Twentieth Century Fox Film Corporation.

Morgan, G. (1996, November 17). Musings of a cigarette smoking man (J. Wong, Director). In C. Carter (Producer), *The X-Files.* Hollywood: Twentieth Century Fox Film Corporation.

Morgan, G., & Wong, J. (1993a, September 24). Squeeze (H. Longstreet, Director). In C. Carter (Producer), *The X-Files.* Hollywood: Twentieth Century Fox Film Corporation.

Morgan, G., & Wong, J. (1993b, November 5). Ice (D. Nutter, Director). In C. Carter (Producer), *The X-Files.* Hollywood: Twentieth Century Fox Film Corporation.

Morgan, G., & Wong, J. (1994a, January 7). Beyond the sea (D. Nutter, Director). In C. Carter (Producer), *The X-Files.* Hollywood: Twentieth Century Fox Film Corporation.

Morgan, G., & Wong, J. (1994b, April 22). Tooms (D. Nutter, Director). In C. Carter (Producer), *The X-Files.* Hollywood: Twentieth Century Fox Film Corporation.

Morgan, G., & Wong, J. (1994c, September 16). Little green men (D. Nutter, Director). In C. Carter (Producer), *The X-Files.* Hollywood: Twentieth Century Fox Film Corporation.

Morgan, G., & Wong, J. (1997, February 2). Never again (R. Bowman, Director). In C. Carter (Producer), *The X-Files.* Hollywood: Twentieth Century Fox Film Corporation.

Morley, D., & Robins, K. (1993). No place like heimat: Images of home(land) in European culture. In E. Carter, J. Donald, & J. Squires (Eds.), *Space and place: Theories of identity and location* (pp. 3–31). London: Lawrence and Wishart.

Morrow, L. (1993, March 29). The temping of America. *Time,* 40–41.

Mosher, S. D. (1991). Fielding our dreams: Rounding third in Dyersville. *Sociology of Sport Journal, 8,* 272–280.

Moyers, B. (1996, October 11–13). America's religious mosaic. *USA Weekend,* pp. 4–5.

Myerhoff, B. G., Camino, L. A., & Turner, E. (1987). Rites of passage. In M. Eliade (Ed.), *The encyclopedia of religion* (Vol. 12, pp. 380–386). New York: Macmillan.

Nachbar, J. (1974). Introduction. In J. Nachbar (Ed.), *Focus on the western* (pp. 1–8). Englewood Cliffs, NJ: Prentice-Hall.

Nadel, A. (1997). *Flatlining on the field of dreams: Cultural narratives in the films of President Reagan's America.* New Brunswick, NJ: Rutgers University Press.

Nakayama, T. K., & Krizek, R. L. (1995). Whiteness: A strategic rhetoric. *Quarterly Journal of Speech, 81,* 291–309.

Nelson, J. (1989). Eyes out of your head: On televisual experience. *Critical Studies in Mass Communication, 6,* 387–403.

Neumann, M. (1993). Living on tortoise time: Alternative travel as the pursuit of lifestyle. *Symbolic Interaction, 16,* 201–235.

Neumann, M. (1996). Collecting ourselves at the end of the century. In C. Ellis & A. P. Bochner (Eds.), *Composing ethnography: Alternative forms of qualitative writing* (pp. 172–198). Walnut Creek, CA: Alta Mira.

Newman, K. S. (1988). *Falling from grace: The experience of downward mobility in the American middle class.* New York: Free Press.

Newman, K. S. (1993). *Declining fortunes: The withering of the American dream.* New York: Basic Books.

Nichols, B. (1994). *Blurred boundaries: Questions of meaning in contemporary culture.* Bloomington: Indiana University Press.

Nothstine, W. L. (1988). "Topics" as ontological metaphor in contemporary rhetorical theory and criticism. *Quarterly Journal of Speech, 74,* 151–163.

Novak, M. (1976). *The joy of sports: End zones, bases, baskets, balls, and the consecration of the American spirit.* New York: Basic Books.

Oldenburg, R. (1989). *The great good place.* New York: Paragon House.

Olsson, G. (1981). On yearning for home: An epistemological view of ontological transformations. In D. C. D. Pocock (Ed.), *Humanistic geography and literature: Essays on the experience of place* (pp. 121–129). London: Croom Helm.

Ono, K. A., & Sloop, J. M. (1995). The critique of vernacular discourse. *Communication Monographs, 62,* 19–46.

Oriard, M. (1991). *Sporting with the gods: The rhetoric of play and game in American culture.* New York: Cambridge University Press.

Ostwalt, C. E., Jr. (1990). *After Eden: The secularization of American space in the fiction of Willa Cather and Theodore Dreiser.* London and Toronto: Associated University Presses.

Over the edge: Virtual humor. (1996, July). *Datamation,* 20–22.

Payne, D. (1989). *Coping with failure: The therapeutic uses of rhetoric.* Columbia, SC: University of South Carolina Press.

Peck, J. (1995). TV talk shows as therapeutic discourse: The ideological labor of the televised talking cure. *Communication Theory, 5,* 58–81.

Peckham, M. (1995). *Romanticism and ideology.* Hanover, NH: Wesleyan University Press.

Peterson, T. R. (1991). Telling the farmers' story: Competing responses to soil conservation rhetoric. *Quarterly Journal of Speech, 77,* 289–308.

Peterson, W. C. (1994). *Silent depression: The fate of the American dream.* New York: W. W. Norton.

Philipsen, G. (1976). Places for speaking in Teamsterville. *Quarterly Journal of Speech, 62,* 15–25.

Philipsen, G. (1992). *Speaking culturally: Explorations in social communication.* Albany, NY: State University of New York Press.

Pile, S. (1994). Masculinism, the use of dualistic epistemologies and third spaces. *Antipode, 26,* 255–277.

Pile, S., & Rose, G. (1992). All or nothing? Politics and critique in the modernism-postmodernism debate. *Environment and Planning D: Society and Space, 10,* 123–136.

Pirie, D. (1996, April). In the cold. *Sight and Sound*, 22–23.

Plunkert, L. M. (1990). The 1980's: A decade of job growth and industry shifts. *Monthly Labor Review, 113*(9), 3–16.

Pocock, D. C. D. (Ed.) (1981). *Humanistic geography and literature: Essays on the experience of place.* London: Croom Helm.

Porteous, J. D. (1990). *Landscapes of the mind: Worlds of sense and metaphor.* Toronto: University of Toronto Press.

Postman, N. (1992). *Technopoly: The surrender of culture to technology.* New York: Vintage.

Price-Chalita, P. (1994). Spatial metaphor and the politics of empowerment: Mapping a place for feminism and postmodernism in geography? *Antipode, 26,* 236–254.

Putnam, R. D. (1996, Winter). The strange disappearance of civic America. *The American Prospect,* 34–48.

Radhakrishnan, R. (1996). *Diasporic mediations: Between home and location.* Minneapolis: University of Minnesota Press.

Radway, J. A. (1984). *Reading the romance: Women, patriarchy, and popular literature.* Chapel Hill: University of North Carolina Press.

Reeves, J. L., Rodgers, M. C., & Epstein, M. (1996). Rewriting popularity: The cult files. In D. Lavery, A. Hague, & M. Cartwright (Eds.), *"Deny all knowledge": Reading* The X-Files (pp. 22–35). Syracuse, NY: Syracuse University Press.

Relph, E. (1976). *Place and placelessness.* London: Pion Limited.

Ricoeur, P. (1981). Narrative time. In W. J. T. Mitchell (Ed.), *On narrative* (pp. 165–186). Chicago: University of Chicago Press.

Rifkin, J. (1995). *The end of work: The decline of the global labor force and the dawn of the post-market era.* New York: Putnam.

Riggs, K. E. (1996). The case of the mysterious ritual: Murder dramas and older women viewers. *Critical Studies in Mass Communication, 13,* 309–323.

Ritter, K. W., & Andrews, J. R. (1978). *The American ideology: Reflections of the revolution in American rhetoric.* Annandale, VA: Speech Communication Association.

Ritzer, G. (1996). *The McDonaldization of society: An investigation into the changing character of contemporary social life* (Rev. ed.). Thousand Oaks, CA: Pine Forge Press.

Ritzer, G. (1997). *Postmodern social theory.* New York: McGraw-Hill.

Robertson, J. O. (1980). *American myth, American reality.* New York: Hill & Wang.

Robins, K. (1993). Prisoners of the city: Whatever could a postmodern city be? In E. Carter, J. Donald, & J. Squires (Eds.), *Space and place: Theories of identity and location* (pp. 303–330). London: Lawrence and Wishart.

Robinson, P. A. (Writer & Director), & Gordon, L., & Gordon, C. (Producers). (1989). *Field of dreams* [Film]. Universal City Studios.

Rodaway, P. (1994). *Sensuous geographies: Body, sense and place.* London: Routledge.

Rorty, R. (1989). *Contingency, irony, and solidarity.* Cambridge: Cambridge University Press.

Rose, G. (1993). *Feminism and geography: The limits of geographical knowledge.* Minneapolis: University of Minnesota Press.

Rose, M. A. (1991). *The post-modern and the post-industrial: A critical analysis.* Cambridge: Cambridge University Press.

Rothman, B. K. (1989). *Recreating motherhood: Ideology and technology in a patriarchal society.* New York: W. W. Norton.

Rubin, A. M. (1993). Audience activity and media use. *Communication Monographs, 60,* 98–105.

Rushing, J. H. (1983). The rhetoric of the American western myth. *Communication Monographs, 50,* 14–32.

Rushing, J. H. (1993). Power, other, and spirit in cultural texts. *Western Journal of Communication, 57,* 159–168.

Ryden, K. C. (1993). *Mapping the invisible landscape: Folklore, writing, and the sense of place.* Iowa City: Iowa University Press.

Sack, R. D. (1992). *Place, modernity, and the consumer's world: A relational framework for geographical analysis.* Baltimore: Johns Hopkins University Press.

Said, E. (1978). *Orientalism.* New York: Vintage.

Samuels, M. S. (1978). Existentialism and human geography. In D. Ley & M. S. Samuels (Eds.), *Humanistic geography: Prospects and problems* (pp. 22–40). Chicago: Maaroufa Press.

Samuelson, R. J. (1995). *The good life and its discontents: The American dream in the age of entitlement, 1945–1995.* New York: Times Books.

Sanders, J. (1989, September). Can of corn. *American Film,* 14–15.

Sauer, C. (1925). The morphology of landscape. *University of California Publications in Geography, 2*(2), 19–53.

Sawicki, J. (1994). Foucault, feminism, and questions of identity. In G. Gutting (Ed.), *The Cambridge companion to Foucault* (pp. 286–313). Cambridge: Cambridge University Press.

Schaefer, R. J., & Avery, R. K. (1993). Audience conceptualizations of *Late Night with David Letterman. Journal of Broadcasting & Electronic Media, 37,* 253–273.

Schlesinger, A. M., Jr. (1992). *The disuniting of America.* New York: W. W. Norton.

Schmid, R. E. (1997, December 3). Cities & suburbs losing population. AP Online. Available: http://web.lexis-nexis.com/universe/

Scholes, R. (1985). *Textual power: Literary theory and the teaching of English.* New Haven: Yale University Press.

Schor, J. B. (1992). *The overworked American: The unexpected decline of leisure.* New York: Basic Books.

Scott, J. C. (1985). *Weapons of the weak: Everyday forms of peasant resistance.* New Haven, CT: Yale University Press.

Segal, H. P. (1985). *Technological utopianism in American culture.* Chicago: University of Chicago Press.

Segal, H. P. (1994). *Future imperfect: The mixed blessings of technology in America.* Boston: University of Massachusetts Press.

Seiter, E., Borchers, H., Kreutzer, G., & Warth, E. (1989). Introduction. In

E. Seiter, H. Borchers, G. Kreutzer, & E. Warth (Eds.), *Remote control: Television, audiences, and cultural power* (pp. 1–15). London: Routledge.

Shiban, J. (1995, November 10). The walk (R. Bowman, Director). In C. Carter (Producer), *The X-Files*. Hollywood: Twentieth Century Fox Film Corporation.

Shields, R. (1992). *Places on the margin: Alternative geographies of modernity*. London: Routledge.

Shotter, J. (1986). A sense of place: Vico and the social production of social identities. *British Journal of Social Psychology, 25,* 199–211.

Silverstone, R. (1994). *Television and everyday life.* London: Routledge.

Sloan, A. (1996, February 26). The hit men. *Newsweek,* 44–48.

Slotkin, R. (1985). *The fatal environment: The myth of the frontier in the age of industrialization.* New York: Atheneum.

Smith, C. R. (1993). Finding the spiritual dimension in rhetoric. *Western Journal of Communication, 57,* 266–271.

Smith, H. N. (1950). *Virgin land: The American west as symbol and myth.* Cambridge: Harvard University Press.

Smith, N., & Katz, C. (1993). Grounding metaphor: Towards a spatialized politics. In M. Keith & S. Pile (Eds.), *Place and the politics of identity* (pp. 67–83). London: Routledge.

Smith, P. K. (1994). Recent patterns in downward income mobility: Sinking boats in a rising tide. *Social Indicators Research, 31,* 277–303.

Snow, D. A., & Anderson, L. (1987). Identity work among the homeless: The verbal construction and avowal of personal identities. *American Journal of Sociology, 92,* 1336–1371.

Soja, E. W. (1989). *Postmodern geographies: The reassertion of space in critical social theory.* London: Verso.

Soja, E. W. (1996). *Thirdspace: Journeys to Los Angeles and other real-and-imagined places.* Cambridge, MA: Blackwell.

Solomon, M. (1985). The rhetoric of dehumanization: An analysis of the medical reports of the Tuskegee syphilis project. *Western Journal of Speech Communication, 49,* 233–247.

Souvenirs (1997). http://www.fieldofdreamsmoviesite.com/product.html

Spivak, G. (1990). *The postcolonial critic: Interviews, strategies, dialogues.* (S. Harasym, Ed.). New York: Routledge.

Spotnitz, F., & Carter, C. (1996, December 1). Terma (R. Bowman, Director). In C. Carter (Producer), *The X-Files*. Hollywood: Twentieth Century Fox Film Corporation.

Stall, S. (1997, December). Escape from the cubicle. *America West,* 56–59.

Steiner, L. (1988). Oppositional decoding as an act of resistance. *Critical Studies in Mass Communication, 5,* 1–15.

Stephenson, W. (1967). *The play theory of mass communication.* Chicago: University of Chicago Press.

Stewart, J., & Philipsen, G. (1984). Communication as situated accomplishment: The cases of hermeneutics and ethnography. In B. Dervin & M. J. Voigt (Eds.), *Progress in communication sciences: Volume V* (pp. 177–216). Norwood, NJ: Ablex.

Stock, B. (1993). Reading, community and a sense of place. In J. Duncan & D. Ley (Eds.), *Place/culture/representation* (pp. 314–328). London: Routledge.

Strobel, F. R. (1993). *Upward dreams, downward mobility: The economic decline of the American middle class.* Lanham, MD: Rowman & Littlefield.

Taylor, B. C. (1993a). *Fat Man and Little Boy:* The cinematic representation of interests in the nuclear weapons organization. *Critical Studies in Mass Communication, 10,* 367–394.

Taylor, B. C. (1993b). Register of the repressed: Women's voice and body in the nuclear weapons organization. *Quarterly Journal of Speech, 79,* 267–285.

Thompson, B., & Tyagi, S. (1996). Storytelling as social conscience: The power of autobiography. In B. Thompson & S. Tyagi (Eds.), *Names we call home: Autobiography on racial identity* (pp. ix–xvii). London: Routledge.

Toffler, A. (1970). *Future shock.* New York: Random House.

Tomorrow, T. (1996, December 12). *This modern world.* [comic strip]

Trujillo, N. (1991). Hegemonic masculinity on the mound: Media representations of Nolan Ryan and American sports culture. *Critical Studies in Mass Communication, 8,* 290–308.

Trujillo, N., & Ekdom, L. R. (1985). Sportswriting and American cultural values: The 1984 Chicago Cubs. *Critical Studies in Mass Communication, 2,* 262–281.

Tuan, Y. F. (1974). *Topophilia: A study of environmental perception, attitudes, and values.* Englewood Cliffs, NJ: Prentice-Hall.

Tuan, Y. F. (1977). *Space and place: The perspective of experience.* Minneapolis: University of Minnesota Press.

Turkle, S. (1995). *Life on the screen: Identity in the age of the internet.* New York: Simon & Schuster.

Turkle, S. (1996, Winter). Virtuality and its discontents. *The American Prospect,* 50–57.

Turner, E. (1987). Pilgrimage. In M. Eliade (Ed.), *The encyclopedia of religion* (Vol. 11, pp. 327–330). New York: Macmillan.

Turner, V. (1973). The center out there: Pilgrim's goal. *History of Religions, 12,* 191–230.

Turner, V. (1974). *Dramas, fields, and metaphors: Symbolic action in human society.* Ithaca: Cornell University Press.

Turner, V. (1983). Liminal to liminoid, in play, flow, and ritual. In J. C. Harris & R. J. Park (Eds.), *Play, games and sports in cultural contexts* (pp. 123–164). Champaign, IL: Human Kinetics Publishers.

Turner, V., & Turner, E. (1978). *Image and pilgrimage in Christian culture.* New York: Columbia University Press.

Turow, J. (1997). *Breaking up America: Advertising and the new media world.* Chicago: University of Chicago Press.

12,000 re-create bloody Antietam (1997, September 14). *The Columbus (OH) Dispatch,* p. 9A.

Uchitelle, L., & Kleinfield, N. R. (1996, March 3). On the battlefields of business, many casualties. *New York Times,* sec. 1, pp. 1, 26.

Ulrich's international periodicals directory: 1997. (1996). Vol. 3. New Providence, NJ: R. R. Bowker.

U.S. Bureau of the Census. (1997). *Statistical abstract of the United States: 1997* (117th ed.). Washington, DC: U.S. Government Printing Office.

Van Biema, D. (1996, March 18). Layoffs for laughs. *Time,* 82.

Vande Berg, L. R. (1995). Living room pilgrimages: Television's cyclical commemoration of the assassination anniversary of John F. Kennedy. *Communication Monographs, 62,* 47–64.

Variety (1989, November 8). p. 6.

Variety (1990, May 2). p. 130.

Virgil (1951). *The aeneid of Virgil.* (R. Humphries, Trans.). New York: Scribner's.

Walton, K. L. (1990). *Mimesis as make-believe: On the foundations of the representational arts.* Cambridge, MA: Harvard University Press.

Warren, S. (1993). "This heaven gives me migraines": The problems and promise of landscapes of leisure. In J. Duncan & D. Ley (Eds.), *Place/culture/representation* (pp. 173–186). London: Routledge.

Weber, M. (1958). *The Protestant ethic and the spirit of capitalism.* (T. Parsons, Trans.). New York: Scribner's.

Weckman, G. (1987). Secret societies. In M. Eliade (Ed.), *The encyclopedia of religion* (Vol. 13, pp. 151–154). New York: Macmillan.

Weise, E. (1997, Oct. 31–Nov. 2). Anti-government theme gave show initial boost. *USA Today,* pp. 1A–2A.

White, M. (1992). *Tele-advising: Therapeutic discourse in American television.* Chapel Hill, NC: University of North Carolina Press.

Wild, D. (1995, November 30). Television "X"-ploitation. *Rolling Stone,* 79.

Williams, R. (1973). *The country and the city.* New York: Oxford University Press.

Wolcott, J. (1994, April 18). "X" factor. *New Yorker,* 98–99.

Wolf, B. D. (1997, May 25). Corner offices remain, but bosses become more open to togetherness. *The Columbus (OH) Dispatch,* pp. 1J–2J.

Wood, J. T. (1992). Gender and moral voice: Moving from woman's nature to standpoint epistemology. *Women's Studies in Communication, 15,* 1–24.

Woodward, K. L. (1993, December 27). Angels. *Newsweek,* 52–57.

Worthington, R. (1990, April 5). They're still going to Iowa, as innocent as children. *San Francisco Examiner,* [Newsbank FTV 53:C12–C13].

Wright, J. K. (1947). Terrae incognitae: The place of the imagination in geography. *Annals of the Association of American Geographers, 37,* 1–15.

The X-Files. (1993, September 18). *TV Guide,* 59.

Yeaton, K. (1995). The great gaming house: A precis. In M. R. Sandford (Ed.), *Happenings and other acts* (pp. 202–205). London: Routledge. (Original work published 1965)

Young, D. (1992, June 19). If you build a ball field, they will come—to Iowa. *Philadelphia Inquirer,* p. B18+.

Zuboff, S. (1988). *In the age of the smart machine: The future of work and power.* New York: Basic Books.

Index

250, 253, 262. *See also* Paradox; Play; Postindustrialism

Power, 11, 65–72, 75–76, 103, 133–135, 137, 141–147, 256. *See also* Panopticon; Rhetoric

Progress, 4, 18–19, 29–31, 33, 39, 40, 77, 121, 122, 158, 195, 197; and panopticon, 159; and postmodernity, 71

Promised land(s), 3, 4, 7–9, 12, 18–19, 100, 129, 137–138, 160, 165–170, 177, 217, 229, 235, 238, 247, 254, 259; alternatives to dominant visions of, 29, 41, 47, 110, 112, 130, 141, 191, 194, 200, 206, 211, 213; dominant cultural visions of, 4, 11, 19–25, 40–41, 65, 79, 83, 112, 171, 182; personal, 41, 79, 221, 233, 262. *See also* American Elysian Field; Communities, imagined or symbolic; Funhouse; Nerdvana

Protestant work ethic, 23, 205, 213, 225, 247; and deferred gratification, 222–223. *See also* Self-sacrifice

Puritanism, 20–21, 23, 194

Radway, Janice, 10, 87, 89

Reflection, as self-critique, 100, 110–111, 252. *See also* Comic frame; Isolation; Seeing, ways of

Resistance, 64, 67, 68–70, 73, 77, 82, 104, 129, 130, 131, 138, 171, 176. *See also* Agency; Movement; Power

Respect, 122, 127–128, 173–174, 201, 217

Reynolds, Christina L., 52, 186, 217 (n.), 262

Rhetoric: and control, 122–127, 215–216; and naming, 126, 133–141, 189; and responses to dominant visions of promised lands, 41–47; critical, 46; symbolic resources of 12; therapeutic functions of, 105, 222

Rhetorical: fragments, 46, 68, 90–93, 95, 102, 137, 141, 170, 185, 188, 192, 194, 209, 217, 222, 229, 231, 233, 238, 240, 249, 253, 258; invention, 92, 111, 252, 254, 259, 262

Ritual, 10, 206, 208, 210; and pilgrimage(s), 84–86, 100–104, 167, 176, 185, 225, 239; communication, 85; reading experiences 116–117, 118, 130. *See also* Play

Ritzer, George, 22, 27–28, 48, 50 (n. 2), 120

Robicheaux, Dave, 90–92, 95, 97, 102, 253

Roche, John Lee, 156, 158, 163, 173, 180

Romanticism, 29, 62, 170, 183, 235, 254, 257; and geography, 53, 56; and modernity, 23, 25, 50 (n. 1); and spirit, 32, 153; defined, 21–22. *See also* Postmodernity; Spirit

Rules, 220; breaking the, 9, 200, 221–222; critiquing, 122, 158, 256; cultural, 2–3; inventing new, 108, 176, 191, 208, 211, 225

Sacred, 87; garden, 4, 18, 20–22, 29, 212. *See also* Place(s)

Scotts Bluff, 59–60

Scottsbluff, 17, 70, 260–261

Scrapbooks, 90, 238

Seeing, ways of, 73–74, 97–99, 153, 171, 173, 174, 251–252, 255–259. *See also* Reflection

Self-sacrifice, 236; and spiritual connection with others, 226–230, 243

Senses, 54, 256; and feminist theory, 73–74. *See also* Bodies; Seeing, ways of

Shrine(s), 84–85, 86, 91–92, 104, 108, 190, 221, 232, 241

Situated accomplishment, 61–62, 95

Situated knowledge(s), 73, 93, 111. *See also* Seeing, ways of

Social equality, 31, 33, 118–119, 123, 127, 132, 142, 146, 148 (n. 5), 200, 203, 205, 215, 256

Space(s), 68, 137, 233, 249; and cultural terrain, 20, 77, 239; and feminist theory, 71; and time, 32, 43, 81, 88, 164, 222, 229, 234, 241, 252. *See also* Place(s)

Spirit, 18, 22–24, 29, 32, 40, 43–45, 77, 151–152, 155, 191, 209, 217, 231–233, 241, 245; and economic conditions, 225–226

Spiritual, 25, 196, 209, 221; fragments of rhetoric, 92; fulfillment, 18, 39, 95, 104, 194, 213, 242; process of purification, 10; rejuvenation, 237; transformation, 233. *See also* Community

Spirituality, 239; postmodern, 48

Sports Illustrated, 12, 112, 165, 186–218, 221, 247, 250, 255–256, 258, 262